FINANCIAL ACCOUNTING
AAT PAPER 9

VNR ACCOUNTANCY PASSBOOKS

Consulting Editor   E. R. Farmer, Financial Management and Training Consultant

Chartered Association of Certified Accountants

Stein   Accounting – CACA Paper 1.1
Hazzard   Cost and Management Accounting 1 – CACA Paper 1.2
Gray and Manson   Auditing – CACA Paper 2.1
Chan   Cost and Management Accounting 2 – CACA Paper 2.4
Robins   Advanced Accounting Practice Book 1 – CACA Paper 2.9

Further titles covering remaining CACA syllabuses will be published in 1989.

Association of Accounting Technicians

Harding   Financial Accounting – AAT Paper 9

VNR ACCOUNTANCY PASSBOOKS

FINANCIAL ACCOUNTING
AAT PAPER 9

Sid Harding
Department of Accountancy and Business Studies
Slough College of Higher Education

VNR
International

First published in 1988 by
Van Nostrand Reinhold (International) Co. Ltd.
Molly Millars Lane, Wokingham, Berkshire, England

Typeset in 10/11pt Palatino by Witwell Ltd, Southport

Printed and bound in Great Britain by
Richard Clay Ltd, Chichester

British Library Cataloguing in Publication Data
Harding, Sid
   Financial accounting: AAT paper 9. —
   (VNR accountancy passbooks).
   1. Accounting
   I. Title
   657   HF5635

ISBN 0-278-00015-0

CONTENTS

Introduction ix
How to use this book x
The AAT Financial Accounting (Paper 9) Syllabus xi
How to pass examinations xii

Part One: Study Chapters
1 SSAPs and Accounting Policies
  Introduction 3
  SSAPs 3
  Accounting concepts and policies 3
  SSAP 2 disclosure requirements 4
  Accounting principles 4
  Summary 5
  Examination hints 5
  Self-assessment questions 5
2 Value Added Tax 6
  Introduction 7
  Accounting entries 7
  SSAP 5 Accounting for Value Added Tax 7
  Summary 9
  Examination hints 10
  Self-assessment questions 10
3 Partnership Accounts: Introduction 10
  Introduction 11
  Partnership 11
  Appropriation accounts 11
  Partners' accounts 11
  Summary 12
4 Partnership Accounts: Changes in Partners 12
  Introduction 14
  Revaluation 14
  Goodwill 14
  Appropriation account 16
  Summary 17
  Examination hints 20
  Self-assessment questions 20
5 Partnership Accounts: Dissolution 21
  Introduction 22
  The realization account 22
  Closing the ledger accounts 22
  Conversion to a limited company 23
  Garner v. *Murray* 26
  Summary 28
  Examination hints 30
  Self-assessment questions 30
6 Partnership Accounts: Joint Ventures 31
  32

	Introduction	32
	Joint venture accounts	32
	Memorandum joint venture account	33
	Summary	35
	Examination hints	35
	Self-assessment questions	36
7	Consignment Accounts	37
	Introduction	37
	The consignor's records	37
	The consignee's records	40
	Unsold stock	40
	Summary	41
	Examination hints	42
	Self-assessment questions	41
8	Goods on Sale or Return	42
	Introduction	42
	Accounting treatment	42
	Summary	43
	Examination hints	43
9	Container Accounts	44
	Introduction	44
	The ledger accounts	44
	Summary	46
	Examination hints	46
	Self-assessment questions	46
10	Royalty Accounts	48
	Introduction	48
	Shortworkings	48
	Royalties payable	49
	Royalties receivable	50
	Summary	51
	Examination hints	51
	Self-assessment questions	51
11	Hire-purchase: Buyer	53
	Introduction	53
	Calculation of interest charge	53
	Accounting entries	55
	SSAP 21	60
	Summary	61
	Examination hints	61
	Self-assessment questions	61
12	Hire-Purchase: Seller	63
	Introduction	63
	Calculation of selling profit and finance charges earned	63
	Accounting entries	64
	Repossessions	68
	Leasing	68
	Summary	68
	Examination hints	68
	Self-assessment questions	69
13	Branch Accounts: Head Office Recording Branch Transactions	70
	Introduction	70
	The accounting records	70
	Branch stock account	72
	The accounting records for branch stock account	72
	Summary	75
	Examination hints	76
	Self-assessment questions	76
14	Branch accounts: Branch Recording Its Own Transactions	78
	Introduction	78

Branch and head office accounts 78
Profit and loss accounts 80
Balance sheets 81
Branch opening trial balance 86
Transfers at cost plus 86
Summary 88
Examination hints 88
Self-assessment questions 88

15 Company Accounts: Share and Loan Transactions 90
Introduction 90
Issue of shares 91
Redemption of shares 94
Issue and redemption of debenture loans 96
Debenture redemption sinking fund 97
Reserves 98
Bonus issues 99
Summary 99
Examination hints 100
Self-assessment questions 100

16 Company Accounts: Taxation 101
Introduction 101
Income Tax 101
Corporation tax 102
Advanced corporation tax 103
Deferred tax 105
SSAP 8 107
Summary 107
Examination hints 108
Self-assessment questions 108

17 Company Accounts: Profit and Loss Accounts 110
Introduction 110
The published profit and loss account 110
Notes to the accounts 115
Earnings per share 115
Extraordinary items 116
Related companies 116
Summary 119
Examination hints 119
Self-assessment questions 119

18 Company Accounts: Balance Sheets 121
Introduction 121
The published balance sheet 121
Notes to the accounts 124
Post balance sheet events 127
Contingent liabilities 127
Small and medium size companies 128
Summary 129
Examination hints 129
Self-assessment questions 130

19 Directors' Report 132
Introduction 132
Contents of the report 132
Summary 133
Examination hints 133

20 Company Accounts: Funds Statements 134
Introduction 134
Preparation of funds statements 134
Interpretation of funds statements 142
Summary 142
Examination hints 143

	Self-assessment questions	143
21	Accounting Ratios and Interpretation	145
	Introduction	145
	Accounting ratios	145
	Reports	150
	The limitations of ratio analysis	151
	Summary	151
	Examination hints	151
	Self-assessment questions	152
22	Historic Cost Convention and Price Level Changes	153
	Introduction	153
	Weaknesses of historic cost accounts	153
	Current cost accounting	154
	Current purchasing power	157
	Summary	158
	Examination hints	158
	Self-assessmentg questions	159
23	Consolidated Accounts: Balance Sheets	160
	Introduction	160
	SSAP 14 Group Accounts	161
	SSAP 1 Associated Companies	161
	Consolidated balance sheets	162
	Adjustments	166
	SSAP 22 Accounting for Goodwill	167
	SSAP 23 Mergers	167
	Summary	169
	Examination hints	169
	Self-assessment questions	169
24	Consolidated Accounts: Profit and Loss Accounts	171
	Introduction	171
	Consolidated profit and loss accounts	171
	Summary	175
	Examination hints	175
	Self-assessment questions	176
25	Stocks and Work in Progress	177
	Introduction	177
	Valuation of stocks	177
	Long-term contract work in progress	178
	Contract accounts	178
	Disclosure requirements	180
	Summary	180
	Examination hints	180
	Self-assessment questions	181
26	Other SSAPs	182
	Introduction	182
	Government grants	182
	Depreciation	182
	Research and development	183
	Investment properties	184
	Summary	184
	Examination hints	184
	Self-assessment questions	184
Part Two: Questions and Answers		
	Examination questions	189
	Sample examination paper	219
	Further examination questions	225
	Answers to examination questions	241
	Answers to questions in sample examination paper	296
	Answers to self-assessment questions	302
Index		308

INTRODUCTION

You are embarking on a course of study of the most relevant of the AAT's examination subjects. The final level financial accounting paper is perhaps the most difficult examination hurdle you have yet faced. This is rightly so as accounting is fundamental to the work of an accounting technician. The task is a difficult one but it is also challenging and rewarding. To have reached this stage of your studies, it is likely that you enjoy accounting and have some aptitude for it. These qualities will stand you in good stead for there is no doubt that the syllabus is large and contains some rather complex topics. However, the main aim of this book is to make the study of these topics as easy as possible within a realistic workload. Aim to enjoy your studies and hopefully you will find the topics interesting and absorbing. You should attempt to master all the topics contained within this book, as each topic could be examined. However, if you work consistently throughout the year you should have enough time for this and the other three subjects. The book has been written with the aim of reducing studying time to a minimum – the author is well aware that many students have demanding jobs and family commitments.

HOW TO USE THIS BOOK

This book has been written specifically for students intending to sit the Level 3 Financial Accounting examination of the AAT.

Each chapter covers a topic area of the syllabus. The chapters have been written assuming that earlier chapters will have been studied, so the best way to approach your task is to work through the chapters in order. You will find that, in general, the smaller topics are covered in the earlier chapters with the larger and more complex topics coming later.

Each chapter specifies at the outset the learning objectives you should attain, with a separate section within the chapter being devoted to each objective. The notes in the margins of each chapter provide additional material that is not essential to mastering the topic. Normally the notes either give additional explanation or provide supplementary information.

At the end of each chapter you will find some self-assessment questions which require you to select one of several answers. These questions are quickly answered and will enable you to check your understanding of the topics studied. The answers for each question, with explanations where necessary, are to be found at the end of the book. One of the purposes of these questions is to help you avoid common errors and misconceptions, so make sure you check your answers.

On completion of each chapter you will be referred to the questions in Part Two which you should answer before proceeding to the next topic. To gain maximum benefit from this book it is very important that you work the questions yourself before you refer to the answers given. Answering these questions is an important part of successful preparation for the examination. Not only will you develop the necessary skills to tackle such questions in examination conditions, but in many cases you may find that the question is even more difficult than it looks! Do not worry if you make mistakes: finding out what went wrong is a useful part of the learning process. However, if you do badly on a particular question you should rework it at a later date to ensure that you have mastered it. Nearly all the questions in Part Two have been selected from past AAT papers, although they have been supplemented where necessary with questions from other sources.

A sample examination paper is also provided for additional practice towards the end of your studies.

The additional questions without answers at the end of the book are for the convenience of lecturers who wish to monitor their students' progress.

THE AAT FINANCIAL ACCOUNTING (PAPER 9) SYLLABUS

The main areas covered by the syllabus are company accounts, special situations (mainly changes in partnerships and the consolidated accounts of a group of companies), special transactions (branch accounts, HP, etc.), and interpretation.

Each main area within the syllabus is given a weighting which indicates its comparative importance within the syllabus as a whole.

The detailed syllabus is as follows:

Final Examination

Paper 9 – Financial Accounting
Aims to develop:
a   an understanding of the principles and practices of financial accounting, and
b   the practical skills and professional competence of an accounting technician.

Syllabus
35% *Company accounts:* the preparation of the accounting statements of companies including source and application of funds statement for publication in accordance with the disclosure requirements of the Companies Act, to include the treatment of taxation in accounts, i.e. the imputation system and VAT, appropriate notes to such accounts, and the directors report. The application of best accounting practice to all accounting entries including an appreciation of the rules contained in statements of standard accounting practice.

25% *Accounting techniques for special situations:* partnership accounts to include change of partners, dissolution, and sale or conversion to a company, and joint ventures. Accounting for share and loan transactions (excluding purchase of own shares). Simple consolidation statements for groups of companies, to include preparation of a consolidated balance sheet and profit and loss account, minority interests, pre- and post-acquisition profits, the reconciliation of current accounts for cash and goods in transit, and the elimination of profit margins on intra-group stocks.

20% *Accounting techniques for special transactions:* branch accounts excluding foreign branches, hire-purchase transactions, consignment accounts, goods on sale or return, royalties, containers.

20% *Analysis and evaluation:* the application of financial ratios and statements of source and application of funds to the interpretation of financial statements of simple business situations. Capital structure and gearing. Working capital requirements and cash flow forecasts. An appreciation of accounting for price level changes in relation to statements prepared under the historic cost convention.

All the above topics are covered within the chapters of this book with the exception of cash flow forecasts which are best studied within the context of the syllabus for cost accounting and budgeting.

A major feature of the syllabus is that an appreciation is required of the rules contained in the Statements of Standard Accounting Practice (SSAPs). These are all covered in the appropriate chapters of this book. By the time you have worked your way through this book you will have come to know them, but it is accepted that you may not come to love them!

HOW TO PASS EXAMINATIONS

The key to passing an accounting examination is thorough preparation. A well planned course of study including plenty of practice working past examination questions and allowing adequate time for revision should enable you to face the examination with some confidence. Inadequate preparation is a common cause of examination nerves.

You should check the examination hall location and travelling arrangements well in advance and allow yourself plenty of time for the journey so that you will arrive early. Make sure that you take everything that you may need, including spare calculator batteries.

At the start of the examination read the examination paper instructions very carefully and make absolutely sure that you have properly understood them. Read through the whole paper before choosing which optional questions you will tackle and work out the time allowance for each question based on the number of marks allocated. Don't panic if all the questions seem impossibly hard; you will be surprised how easy it is to obtain a pass mark on a hard question. Most questions will contain a lot of marks for comparatively easy tasks as well as the marks that are more difficult to earn. Your aim must be at least to score the easy marks and do as well as you can on the rest. When making your choice of questions consider your ability to undertake the tasks required and the time it will take you in relation to the marks available. Some questions may be recognizably time consuming, others less so. Your aim should be to score a mark at least every 2½ minutes (allowing 15 minutes to read the paper you will have 2 hours 45 minutes for your answers) this will give a score of 66 which will do very nicely thank you.

Answer the question that you think is the easiest first and save the hardest to last; this will minimize the damage if you get carried away and overrun the time allowed for an earlier question. When answering the questions read and reread the question requirements and make absolutely sure that what you will be doing is precisely what is required. If the question requires a written answer plan your answer first. This is desirable in any case but will also stop you drifting away from the question requirements in the heat of the moment. Try to work in your normal way as you would at home. Work at the same speed throughout the examination and stick to the time allowed for each question, leave it rather than overrun time. If a question is going well but time is running out, complete the entries for the figures you are working on, quickly carry out any tasks that you think may carry easy marks and move on. If you can save time on later questions you may be able to return to the question left. The reason for giving this advice is that in most questions the marks allocated to the really difficult bits do not necessarily have to be scored to obtain a pass mark on that question and can be disproportionately time consuming.

Make sure that your handwriting is legible; do not get carried away by time pressure and produce a scrawl that is difficult to decipher. Neat layout and presentation are well worth the effort: your script should look competent and professional—try not to hand in a script that looks a mess to start with. Working past questions will help you to build up the skill to lay out accounts with plenty of spacing, produce separately headed workings and make neat alterations to your answers. Any additions should be your last task in answering a question.

ACKNOWLEDGEMENTS

Acknowledgement is given for the permission to use past examination questions granted by The Association of Accounting Technicians, The Chartered Association of Certified Accountants and The Chartered Institute of Management Accountants.

PART ONE
STUDY CHAPTERS

In this part of the book there are twenty-six chapters which provide a complete course of study designed to prepare you for the AAT Financial Accounting Paper 9 Examination. Each chapter contains the following common ingredients:

☐ **Chapter contents**. A simple reference tool which should help you to find your way about the book.

☐ **Learning objectives**. These will help you to concentrate your mind on the main purpose of each chapter.

☐ **Marginal notes**. Brief explanatory comments which have been devised to carry information or advice which is *not* essential to your understanding of the subject or your mastery of the syllabus. They carry information, warnings, hints, advice and, sometimes, recommendations for further reading which should *enhance* your understanding of the subject and your ability to pass the examination.

☐ **Self-assessment questions**. These have been designed to *test* your understanding of the main points in each chapter, so you should attempt them when you are advised to do so. Answers are provided towards the end of the book (starting on page 302). If you answer any of the questions *incorrectly*, make sure you check back in the text to find out why.

☐ **Summary/Examination hints.** Both sections are included at the end of each chapter as an additional reminder of the main points which you should have mastered. Use them as a convenient way of revising when you return to the book after a break in your study, or before tackling the sample examination paper, or before the *real* examination.

Follow all instructions carefully. The questions which appear in Part Two should not be attempted until you have studied the appropriate chapter or chapters in Part One. Each chapter ends with a recommendation of what you should do next.

CHAPTER 1

SSAPs AND ACCOUNTING POLICIES

Chapter contents

Introduction 3   SSAPs 3   Accounting concepts and policies 4   SSAP 2 disclosure requirements 4   Accounting principles 5   Summary 5   Examination hints 5

Learning objectives

After studying this chapter you should be able to:

☐ describe the role of Statements of Standard Accounting Practice;

☐ explain the four fundamental accounting concepts identified by SSAP 2 and the terms 'accounting base' and 'accounting policy';

☐ state the disclosure requirements of SSAP 2 Disclosure of Accounting Policies;
☐ state the accounting principles that should be applied to meet the requirements of the Companies Act 1985.

Introduction

Accounts should be prepared in accordance with generally accepted accounting principles. The book-keeping part of accounting is a fairly straightforward exercise, but the preparation of profit and loss accounts and balance sheets requires judgement in deciding how to treat certain items, for example the value to be placed on stock. Previous generations of accountants have dealt with these items in ways that were acknowledged to be acceptable practice; however, a comprehensive list of 'generally accepted accounting principles' had not been published by the accountancy bodies.

The Accounting Standards Committee (ASC) was formed in 1970 to bring uniformity into accounting practice. A 'Statement of Standard Accounting Practice' (SSAP) published by the ASC is an authoritative statement that describes the best practice that should be followed in the accounting treatment of the topic covered, for example SSAP 9 covers the valuation of stock.

The syllabus requires you to have 'an appreciation of the rules contained in SSAPs', and you will find every SSAP (other than those that have been withdrawn) covered in the appropriate chapters of this book.

The ASC is a joint committee of the main UK accounting bodies.

Prior to issuing a SSAP the ASC publish an Exposure Draft (ED) of the proposed standard for comment. In addition to SSAPs the ASC have begun to publish Statements of Recommended Practice (SORPs) which are of specialized application in particular sections of commerce or deal with matters that are of less importance.

SSAPs

SSAPs describe methods of accounting approved by the UK accounting bodies. The members of the accounting bodies must use their best endeavours to ensure that the SSAPs are observed in the preparation of accounts with which they are concerned and, if not observed, ensure that the non-compliance is disclosed and explained in the accounts.

SSAPs have no statutory backing. Their authority is given to them by the accountancy bodies and the Stock Exchange.

The SSAPs are authoritative statements on best accounting practice and aim to narrow the differences and variety in accounting practice. They are not, however, a code of rigid rules as it would not be practicable to cater for all business situations and circumstances.

One of the main aims of SSAPs is to narrow the choice of accounting treatment so that financial statements are reasonably comparable.

Accounting concepts and policies

SSAP 2 is the standard that deals with the general principles to be used in accounting. It does not list all the principles but instead requires accounts to be prepared in accordance with four fundamental concepts. These fundamental accounting concepts are the broad basic assumptions used in preparing accounts. SSAP 2 identifies the four main fundamental concepts as:

The going concern concept is justification for carrying forward costs that will be recovered against related income arising from future operations.

1 *The going concern concept* that the company will continue to operate for the foreseeable future. The significance of this is that the profit and loss account and balance sheet are prepared on the assumption that the company will not stop operations or be liquidated. If liquidation is foreseen it would have a material affect on the accounts:

   a fixed assets would be valued at their net realizable values. These may be considerably lower than their net book values representing costs not yet depreciated which will be recovered in future years against income arising from using the assets;

   b stocks would need to be written down to their net realizable value on a liquidation. This would be considerably less than if they could be sold in the normal course of business;

   c debtors would need to be reviewed to provide for additional bad debts that would arise if the company ceased to operate.

The alternative to the accruals concept would be to prepare accounts on a cash basis, i.e. a receipts and payments basis.

2 *The accruals concept* that income and costs are reported in the period that they are earned and incurred. It is the basis for the accounting treatment of prepayments and accruals. Costs are matched to the same period as the income to which they relate. This *matching concept* is the justification for carrying forward part of the cost of fixed assets to be depreciated when they are used in the future to earn profits.

The consistency concept stops 'creative' accounting such as providing additional depreciation in a year when profits are high and less in a year when profits are low.

3 *The consistency concept* requires consistent treatment of like items within each period and from one year to the next. The preparation of accounts on the same basis from one year to the next enables the results to be validly compared. A change in accounting policy should only be made if it is justifiable and necessary, and the effect on profits for the year of the change should be disclosed.

Because prudence avoids overstating profits and assets, accountants have the reputation in some circles of being pessimists. Prudence is not pessimism, but rather the realistic assessment of transactions, avoiding undue optimism.

4 *The prudence concept* that income is only included in the profit and loss account if it is realized in the form of cash or other assets which it is reasonably certain will ultimately realize cash. Provision is to be made for all known expenses and losses. This concept is sometimes called *conservatism*. Prudence is exercised in such matters as:

   a estimating the useful life of a fixed asset for depreciation purposes;

   b estimating the net realizable value of stocks;

   c providing for doubtful debts.

Different accounting bases exist for many other items, for example development costs, stocks and work in progress, deferred taxation and hire purchase.

SSAP 2 defines *accounting bases* as the methods developed for applying fundamental accounting concepts to financial transactions and items in the accounts, particularly in deciding in which years income and costs should be taken to the profit and loss account and in determining the amounts at which items are stated in balance sheets. For example, the common accounting bases for depreciation are the straight line and reducing balance methods, but there are other less common bases such as the 'sum of the digits', depletion unit and machine hour methods.

SSAPs are obviously of great importance to a company in determining its accounting policies.

The *accounting policies* of a company are the specific accounting bases used by the company, as being best for its own circumstances.

SSAP 2 Disclosure requirements

The disclosure requirements of SSAP 2 are:

1 If the accounts are prepared on the basis of assumptions that differ from any of the four fundamental accounting concepts, the accounts should contain a clear statement to that effect and explain the facts.

2 The accounting policies should be disclosed by way of a note to the accounts. The explanations should be clear, fair and as brief as possible.

Knowledge of the accounting policies applied is necessary to assess the position disclosed by the accounts.

Accounting Principles

The requirements of the Companies Act 1985 are very similar to SSAP 2. The actual requirements are:

1 The company shall be presumed to be carrying on business as a going concern.

2 Accounting policies shall be applied consistently from one financial year to the next.

3 The amount of any item shall be determined on a prudent basis, and in particular:
   a only profits realized at the balance sheet date shall be included in the profit and loss account; and
   b all liabilities and losses which have arisen or are likely to arise in respect of the financial year to which the accounts relate or a previous financial year shall be taken into account.

4 All income and charges relating to the financial year to which the accounts relate shall be taken into account, without regard to the date of receipt or payment.

5 If it appears to the directors of a company that there are special reasons for departing from any of the principles stated above in preparing the company's accounts in respect of any financial year they may do so, but particulars of the departure, the reasons for it and its effect shall be given in a note to the accounts.

A 'realized' profit does not necessarily mean that it must have been realized in cash. For example, a profit on a sale is normally treated as realized when the goods are delivered, even though the customer may pay at a later date.

A fifth principle in the Act is that each individual asset or liability should be determined separately in arriving at the aggregate amount to be shown for the item in the accounts.

Note that the overriding requirement of the Companies Act 1985 is that the accounts should disclose a true and fair view.

Summary

1 SSAPs are statements of best accounting practice.

2 SSAP 2 Disclosure of Accounting Policies requires a note to the accounts disclosing the policies used.

3 Accounting policies are the accounting bases used by a company as being those most appropriate to its circumstances.

4 The four fundamental accounting concepts are going concern, accruals, consistency and prudence.

Examination Hints

A question on the rules of SSAP 2 is likely to require a written answer. Read the question carefully to determine precisely what is required and spend a little time in planning your answer prior to starting to write. It is helpful in planning the answer to jot down, as workings, a key word for each point that you wish to make or an area that should be covered.

If the question is divided into sections, apportion your time to each section according to the weighting of the marks. Do not repeat any points you make; stating the same point in different words will not gain extra marks. Length of answer is not important, a point made briefly and clearly is preferable to a long rambling statement.

Try to answer the following questions before reading on.

Self-Assessment Questions

In each question, choose the correct answer from the five alternatives given.

See page 302 for answers.

1.1   Which of the following is not a fundamental accounting concept:
    a   conservatism
    b   consistency
    c   going concern
    (d)   historic cost
    e   matching.

1.2   Which of the following is not an accounting base for depreciation:
    a   machine hour
    (b)   net realizable value
    c   reducing balance
    d   straight line
    e   sum of the digits.

1.3   Which of the following does not require to be noted as an accounting policy:
    a   providing for depreciation
    (b)   accruing expenses
    c   valuing stock
    d   providing for deferred tax
    e   treatment of development costs.

If you have answered the above questions correctly, and are sure you understand the key points in this chapter, then turn to Part Two and try to answer question 1 on page 189 before moving on to Chapter 2.

CHAPTER 2

VALUE ADDED TAX

Chapter contents

Introduction **7**   Accounting entries **7**   SSAP 5 Accounting for Value Added Tax **9**
Summary **10**   Examination hints **10**

Learning objectives

After studying this chapter you should be able to:

☐ make the necessary entries for VAT within the accounting records;

☐ comply with SSAP 5 Accounting for Value Added Tax in preparing a profit and
loss account and balance sheet.

Introduction

The syllabus includes the treatment of VAT in the preparation of the accounting
statements of companies. We are only concerned with the accounting treatment, VAT
itself is included in the syllabus for Paper 12: Auditing and Taxation. You may already be
familiar with the accounting entries required, particularly as the entries for VAT are
included in the syllabus of the intermediate accounting paper.

VAT is a tax on the final consumer. It is collected and paid over to the Customs and
Excise at each stage of the production and distribution chain by businesses that are
registered for VAT purposes. However, VAT is not normally an expense to these
registered traders. They have to pay over to the Customs and Excise VAT charged to
their customers, but may deduct from this, with just a few exceptions, the VAT charged
to them by their own suppliers. Items included in the profit and loss account of a
registered trader will not normally include any VAT.

The balance of VAT collected but not yet paid over is a liability in the balance sheet. If a
business is in the position of reclaiming VAT, because the VAT charged by its suppliers
exceeds the VAT charged to its customers, the balance due will be included as a debtor in
its balance sheet.

Non-registered traders will not charge VAT to their customers, but will not be able to
recover the VAT on their purchases and expenses. In these circumstances the VAT is an
expense and will be included as part of the normal cost of purchases, expenses and fixed
assets in the non-registered trader's accounts.

Accounting entries

Where a business is required to charge VAT on the goods or services it supplies to its
customers the accounting entry will be:

Debit   The customer   –   with the invoice total.

Registration for VAT is required
if taxable supplies exceed
quarterly or annual limits. A
company registered for VAT
will charge VAT on the supply
of goods and services unless
they are exempt supplies or
zero rated.

Credit Sales   – with the charge for goods or services.
Credit VAT   – with the VAT.

When a remittance for the total invoice amount is received from the customer the entry will be:

Debit   Bank   } with the amount received.
Credit The customer

The VAT account will be kept in the nominal ledger. Normally the entry in the sales and VAT accounts will be made monthly, the sales day book total being analysed between goods and VAT.

Where a company may reclaim all the VAT included in its purchases the entry will be:

A company that also supplies goods and services that are exempt, as well as standard rated and zero rated supplies, may only recover a proportion of the VAT on its purchases.

Debit   Purchases   – with the goods and services.
Debit   VAT   – with the VAT.
Credit The supplier – with the invoice total.

The entries in the purchases and VAT accounts are normally monthly totals from the purchases day book.

If a business does not keep ledger accounts for its suppliers of expenses, but merely records the transaction only when the expense is paid, the VAT has to be analysed out from these payments. The entry will be:

If a company records its expenses by entering the invoices into the purchases day book and suppliers' accounts the VAT will be debited from the day book in the same way as for purchases. In this case the total payment made to the supplier will be debited to the supplier's account.

Debit   Expense   – with the goods and services.
Debit   VAT   – with the VAT.
Credit Bank or Cash – with the total paid.

The balance on the VAT account will normally be a credit balance representing the amount due to the Customs and Excise. When a payment is made the entry will be:

A return of VAT has to be made to the Customs and Excise.

Debit   VAT   } with the amount paid to the Customs and Excise.
Credit Bank

(A debit balance in the VAT account will be recoverable from the Customs and Excise. The entry when the refund is received will be the reverse of the above.)

Example

The following transactions were undertaken by a company:

1.1.X7   Purchases from Black Ltd £10,000 + VAT £1,500
10.1.X7   Sales to Brown Ltd £15,000 + VAT £2,250
18.1.X7   Purchases from Black Ltd £5,000 + VAT £750
23.1.X7   Sales to Brown Ltd £20,000 + VAT £3,000
30.1.X7   Paid telephone bill £500 + VAT £75
31.1.X7   Paid Black Ltd £17,250

Purchases ledger

Black Ltd

		£			£
			1.1.X7	Goods	11,500
31.1.X7	Bank	17,250	18.1.X7	Goods	5,750
		£17,250			£17,250

Sales ledger

Brown Ltd

		£		£
10.1.X7	Sales	17,250		
23.1.X7	Sales	23,000		
		£40,250		

Nominal ledger

Telephone

		£			£
30.1.X7	Bank	500			

VAT

		£			£
1.1.X7	Purchases – Black Ltd	1,500	10.1.X7	Sales Brown Ltd	2,250
18.1.X7	Purchases – Black Ltd	750	23.1.X7	Sales Brown Ltd	3,000
30.1.X7	Bank – Telephone	75			
31.3.X7	Balance c/d	2,925			
		£5,250			£5,250

Purchases

		£			£
1.1.X7	Black Ltd	10,000			
18.1.X7	Black Ltd	5,000			
		£15,000			

Sales

	£			£
		10.1.X7	Brown Ltd	15,000
		23.1.X7	Brown Ltd	20,000
				£35,000

Bank (Cash Book)

	£			£
		30.1.X7	Telephone	575
		31.1.X7	Black Ltd	17,250
				£17,825

Miscellaneous points to note are:

1 Cash discounts offered to customers may be deducted from the invoiced amount in calculating the amount of VAT to be added to an invoice, even though the cash discount may not be taken by the customer.
2 Not all of the VAT on purchases and expenses can be claimed. The exceptions are:
   a motor cars (unless bought for re-sale) – the total of the invoice, including VAT, must be debited to the fixed asset account;
   b entertainment expenses (other than of staff and customers from overseas) – the total expense, including VAT, will be debited to entertainment expenses.
3 Any VAT included in bad debts written off due to the insolvency of a customer may be recovered. The double entry will be:

Debit	Bad debts	–	with the irrecoverable amount of goods and services.
Debit	VAT	–	with the irrecoverable VAT.
Credit	Customer	–	with the bad debt written off.

VAT on commercial vehicles purchased is recoverable.

SSAP 5 Accounting for Value Added Tax

This is a short standard that requires:

If it is desired to show the gross turnover, the VAT should be shown as a deduction to arrive at the turnover exclusive of VAT.

1 *Turnover* shown in the profit and loss account should not include the VAT charged to customers.

2 *Irrecoverable VAT* on motor cars and entertainment should be included in these items (and not shown separately).

3 *The net amount of VAT payable* (or *recoverable*) to the Customs and Excise should be included in the balance sheet figure for creditors (or debtors) and need not be disclosed separately.

Note that in the accounts of non-registered traders VAT will be included as part of the normal cost of purchases, expenses and fixed assets.

Summary

1 The VAT account will record the VAT charged to customers and recoverable with regard to purchases and expenses. Payments to or from the Customs and Excise will also be recorded.

2 SSAP 5 requires any irrecoverable VAT on purchases, expenses and fixed assets to be included as part of the cost of the item to which it relates.

3 The balance on the VAT account should be included in the balance sheet as a debtor or creditor.

Examination Hints

VAT is not an important examination topic in its own right. A question requiring ledger account entries may more reasonably be expected at the intermediate level. However, VAT may arise in questions dealing with other topics, for example published accounts (Chapters 17 and 18) and the accounting treatment of taxation (Chapter 19).

Try to answer the following questions before reading on.

Self-Assessment Questions

See page 302 for answers.

In each question, choose the correct answer from the five alternatives given.

2.1   Sales included in a profit and loss account will include VAT in the accounts of:
  a   a non-registered trader
  b   a registered trader selling zero rated supplies only
  c   a registered trader selling standard rated supplies
  d   a sole trader
  e   none of the above.

2.2   The following expense appearing in the profit and loss account of a registered trader may include VAT:
  a   wages
  b   purchases
  c   audit fee
  d   depreciation of motor cars
  e   depreciation of motor lorries.

2.3   The following item will not appear as a debit on the VAT account:
  a   VAT on purchases
  b   VAT on expenses
  c   VAT on sales returns
  d   VAT on purchase returns
  e   payment to Customs and Excise.

If you have answered all of the above questions correctly, and are sure you understand the key points in this chapter, then try to answer question 2 on page 189 before moving on to Chapter 3.

PARTNERSHIP ACCOUNTS: INTRODUCTION

Chapter contents

Introduction 11   Partnership 11   Appropriation accounts 11   Partners' accounts 12   Summary 13

Learning objectives

After studying this chapter you should be able to:

☐ define a partnership;

☐ prepare a profit and loss appropriation account showing the division of profits between partners;

☐ write up the partners' capital and current accounts.

Introduction

This chapter introduces the accounts required for the partners themselves in the accounting records of a partnership. The preparation of basic profit and loss accounts and balance sheets is examined at the intermediate level and you will probably be familiar with the contents of this chapter already.

Examination questions are frequently set involving changes of partners or dissolution of a partnership. These topics will be covered in the next two chapters.

Partnership

The Partnership Act 1890 (yes, you read it correctly, 1890) defines a partnership as 'the relationship which subsists between persons carrying on a business in common with a view of profit'.

Where two or more persons are in business together as a partnership the following apply:

1 They will share profits and losses between themselves. Often a partnership deed is drawn up specifying the agreement between them; for example with regard to the capital to be provided and how profits should be shared.
2 Each partner has personal liability for all the firm's debts.

Most partnerships in this country are formed by members of the professions who are not allowed by their professional bodies to practise under the protection given by a limited liability company, for example accountants and doctors.

Appropriation accounts

The manufacturing, trading and profit and loss accounts of a partnership are prepared in the same way as for a sole trader. In the accounts of a sole trader the net profit is transferred to the proprietor's capital account. In the accounts of a partnership the net profit is carried down in the profit and loss account to an appropriation section where it is divided between the partners.

There are no rules relating to the division of profit. It will be divided as the partners agree between themselves. Sometimes one or more partners will be given a prior share of the profit before the remainder is divided. These prior shares may take the form of a 'salary' or 'interest on capital', etc., and are given to make the division fair, for example one partner may spend more time working in the partnership or the partners may have different amounts of capital invested. The remainder of the profit will be divided between the partners in the agreed profit sharing ratios.

The Partnership Act 1890 states that in the absence of agreement profits should be shared equally.

A partner's 'salary', 'bonus', 'commission' or 'interest on capital' are not expenses but appropriations of the net profit. These items must not be included in the profit and loss account otherwise net profits will be understated. They must be included in the profit and loss appropriation account.

Example

Alfred, Bertram and Charles are in partnership with capital accounts of:

	£
Alfred	100,000
Bertram	80,000
Charles	60,000

Their agreement provides for each partner to be given interest on his capital of 10% per annum, and for Charles to receive a salary of £10,000 per annum. Otherwise profits and losses are to be shared in the proportions of 4:3:2.

The net profit for the year ended 31 December 19X9 was £70,000. This will be divided as follows:

Profits shared in the proportions 4:3:2 indicates that Alfred will receive 4 out of a total of (4+3+2) 9 shares, i.e. four-ninths. Bertram will receive three-ninths and Charles two-ninths.

Profit and loss appropriation account for the year ended 31 December 19X9

	£	£
Net profit (b/d from the profit and loss section)		£70,000
Divided:		
Salary – Charles	10,000	
Interest on capital:		
– Alfred	10,000	
– Bertram	8,000	
– Charles	6,000	
Residual profit:		
– Alfred ($\frac{4}{9}$)	16,000	
– Bertram ($\frac{3}{9}$)	12,000	
– Charles ($\frac{2}{9}$)	8,000	£70,000

Although the last item in the appropriation account is described as residue of profit it is not a partner's total share of profits. Any salary and interest on capital are also shares of the profit even though they are not so described.

All the above items will be credited to the partners' current accounts (the entries above being debits in the profit and loss appropriation account).

This example is continued in the next section of this chapter.

Partners' Accounts

A capital account is maintained for each partner. Each account records the long-term investment of an individual partner. The amount of capital provided by each partner is normally fixed by the partnership agreement.

A current account will also be kept for each partner. These accounts record each partner's amount of the net profit as divided in the profit and loss appropriation account. Each partner is normally free to withdraw the balance on his current account without reference to the other partners for their agreement. Any withdrawals of cash or goods from the firm will be charged to the partner's current account, as will any private expenses and tax bills paid on his behalf by the firm.

Some partnerships will open separate accounts for drawings. In this case the total drawings for the year are transferred to the current accounts at the end of the year.

Example (continued)

At 1 January 19X9 the balances in the partners' current accounts were:

	£
Alfred	4,800
Bertram	6,100
Charles	300

The balances represent profits of earlier years that were not withdrawn by the partners.

During 19X9 the partner's drawings were:

		£
Alfred	– cash	20,000
	– private expenses paid by the firm	500
Bertram	– cash	15,000
	– goods withdrawn	1,200
Charles	– cash re salary	10,000
	– other cash drawings	9,000

The double-entry for drawings is:

Debit   The partner's current account.
Credit   Bank or cash (if goods are withdrawn credit purchases with their cost).

The partners' current accounts will appear as follows:

	Alfred	Bertram	Charles		Alfred	Bertram	Charles
	£	£	£		£	£	£
Drawings:				Balance b/d	4,800	6,100	300
– cash	20,000	15,000	9,000	Profit and loss			
– cash (expenses)	500			appropriation:			
– cash (salary)			10,000	– salary			10,000
– goods		1,200		– interest on			
				capital	10,000	8,000	6,000
Balance c/d	10,300	9,900	5,300	– residue of profit	16,000	12,000	8,000
	£30,800	£26,100	£24,300		£30,800	£26,100	£24,300

This layout incorporates the current accounts for all the partners within one account. The layout is called 'in columnar form'.

When preparing a balance sheet the capital and current account balances for each partner should be disclosed. A suitable layout would be:

Balance sheet extract at 31 December 19X9

Partners' Accounts:	Alfred	Bertram	Charles	Total
	£	£	£	£
Capital accounts	100,000	80,000	60,000	240,000
Current accounts	10,300	9,900	5,300	25,500
	£110,300	£89,900	£65,300	£265,500

The layout discloses the total capital employed provided by the partners (£265,500) and how this is split between fixed capital (£240,000) and the current accounts (£25,500). It also discloses the position of each partner.

Summary

1   Separate capital and current accounts are normally kept for each partner.
2   The division of profit between the partners, in accordance with the partnership agreement, is disclosed in the profit and loss appropriation account.
3   Each partner's current account will be credited with their share of net profit (salary, interest on capital and share of residue).
4   Drawings (cash, goods and private expenses) will be debited to the partner's current account.

If you are sure you understand the key points in this chapter, then move on to Chapter 4.

CHAPTER 4

PARTNERSHIP ACCOUNTS: CHANGES IN PARTNERS

Chapter contents

Introduction **14** Revaluation **14** Goodwill **16** Appropriation account **17** Summary **20** Examination hints **20**

Learning objectives

After studying this chapter you should be able to:

☐ make the necessary entries for revaluation of assets prior to a change in partners;
☐ calculate and make the necessary entries for adjustments arising from goodwill;
☐ prepare a profit and loss appropriation account for a year during which there has been a change in partners.

Introduction

The repayment of an amount due to a leaving partner poses a considerable problem for many firms. Sometimes an assurance policy will have been taken out by the other partners to provide the funds necessary. Sometimes a retiring partner will leave part of the amount due to him as a loan, to be repaid by instalments in the future. In this case the loan is included on the balance sheet as a liability, and not as part of the partners' accounts.

Strictly any revaluation surpluses or losses on current assets, such as stock or debtors, should be taken to the profit and loss account. However, it is normal practice to take these to the revaluation account to arrive at the total adjustment required on revaluation.

When a partner leaves a firm, or a new partner joins, the legal position is that the old partnership is terminated and a new partnership formed. Accounting practice, however, is not to close the books of the old partnership and open a set of accounting records for the new partnership. Normally the books are continued and the changes in the partners are recorded on the partners' accounts within the nominal ledger.

Revaluation

If a partner leaves a firm he will be repaid the amount due to him. This is represented by the balances on his capital and current accounts. In other words, he will be repaid the capital he introduced into the firm together with any share of profits, while he was a partner, that he did not withdraw.

To be sure that he received his fair entitlement the assets of the firm may be revalued. The classic example of why this is necessary is that property may have increased in value while he was a partner, but the gain may not have been recorded in the books. The opportunity is normally taken to revalue all fixed assets and to review current assets and liabilities to ensure that the amounts at which they are recorded are reasonable.

A revaluation account may be opened to which all surpluses and losses on revaluation are taken. The net surplus (or loss) is then divided between the old partners in their profit sharing ratios.

On a revaluation of a fixed asset the double entry is:

Debit	Provision for depreciation	} with accumulated depreciation to date.
Credit	The fixed asset account	

Debit	The fixed asset account	} with the surplus of the valuation over
Credit	Revaluation	the net book value.

This entry will, of course, be reversed for any loss arising on revaluation.

The double entry relating to current assets is:

Debit	Revaluation	} with any write-down of old or
Credit	Stock	damaged stock.

and

Debit	Revaluation	} with any write-down of debtors that
Credit	Provision for doubtful debts	is necessary.

Any expenses relating to the revaluation, e.g. valuer's fees, will be entered

Debit	Revaluation	} with expenses paid.
Credit	Bank	

The balance on the revaluation account is then transferred to the partners' capital accounts in the *profit sharing ratio*, the entry being:

Debit	Revaluation	} with the net surplus on revaluations.
Credit	Capital accounts	

This entry will be reversed if there is a net loss on revaluations.

Transferring the accumulated depreciation to the fixed asset account reduces the cost to net book value. This is then compared with the revaluation amount (which takes account of the age and condition of the asset).

The surplus on revaluation is an unrealized profit that should be credited to the partners' capital accounts, and not to their current accounts, as it would not normally be regarded as withdrawable by the partners.

Example 1

A firm has three partners sharing profits equally. The trial balance at 31 December 19X6, after preparation of the profit and loss account, is:

	£	£
Capital accounts:		
Edward		20,000
Frederick		20,000
George		20,000
Current accounts:		
Edward		900
Frederick		1,500
George		1,100
Premises – cost and depreciation	10,000	2,000
Vehicles – cost and depreciation	14,000	4,000
Stocks	15,000	
Debtors and creditors	12,000	16,000
Bank	34,500	
	£85,500	£85,500

At 1 January 19X7 Edward retires. Premises are to be revalued to £50,000 and stocks are valued at £12,000. Edward is repaid the amount due to him.

The entries on the revaluation account will be:

Revaluation

	£		£
Stocks	3,000	Premises	42,000
Surplus on revaluation			
Edward (⅓)	13,000		
Frederick (⅓)	13,000		
George (⅓)	13,000		
	£42,000		£42,000

The partners' capital accounts will be:

Capital accounts

	Edward	Frederick	George		Edward	Frederick	George
	£	£	£		£	£	£
Bank	33,000			Bal. b/d	20,000	20,000	20,000
Bal. c/d		33,000	33,000	Revaluation			
				surplus	13,000	13,000	13,000
	£33,000	£33,000	£33,000		£33,000	£33,000	£33,000

The payment to Edward will be £33,900 (Capital £33,000 + Current account £900). This will reduce the bank balance to (£34,500 – £33,900) £600.

The revised balance sheet will be:

Frederick and George
Balance sheet at 1 January 19X7

	£	£
Fixed assets:		
Premises – at valuation		50,000
Vehicles – at cost	14,000	
Less Accumulated depreciation	4,000	
		10,000
		60,000
Current assets:		
Stock	12,000	
Debtors	12,000	
Bank	600	
	24,600	
Less Current liabilities:		
Creditors	16,000	
		8,600
		£68,600
Financed by:		
Partners' accounts:		

	Frederick	George	Total
	£	£	£
Capital	33,000	33,000	66,000
Current	1,500	1,100	2,600
	£34,500	£34,100	£68,600

Goodwill

Goodwill is an intangible asset; it is the value placed upon a business's ability to earn greater profits than is normal. To understand this consider the following position.

The tangible assets of a business are £18,000. The business earns profits of £10,000 per annum. A businessman considering purchasing the business may be prepared to value the business at £50,000 if he requires a return on his investment of 20% per annum. (The profits of £10,000 will equal a return of £10,000/£50,000 × 100 = 20% on his investment of £50,000.) As the tangible net assets are only valued at £18,000 the difference between these and the total value of the business of £50,000 must be the value placed upon the goodwill, £32,000.

It is exceptionally difficult to value goodwill. The valuation is based on future profit levels which are difficult to forecast. However, when a partner retires the valuation to be placed on goodwill may be agreed between the partners. It would be unfair not to

The existance of goodwill may be due to many factors, for example first-class employees, convenient location of premises, reputation of the firm and its products, possession of trade marks and patents, and good customer loyalty.

recognize this asset in the case of a partner who has worked hard to build up, for example, efficient staff and good customer connections.

SSAP 22 Accounting for Goodwill does not allow companies to include goodwill on a balance sheet at an increased valuation. Goodwill is only allowed to be recorded as an asset if it has been purchased. Consequently, if a partnership wishes to credit a retiring partner with his share of the surplus on the revaluation of goodwill, it would be best practice if the revaluation surplus is immediately written off by the new partners. This can be achieved by the following entries in the partners' capital accounts for any surplus arising on the revaluation of goodwill:

SSAP 22 is considered further in Chapter 23 dealing with consolidated accounts.

Debit   Goodwill.
Credit   Capital accounts of partners of old firm in *old* profit sharing ratio.

and then eliminate goodwill by:

Debit   Capital accounts of partners of new firm in *new* profit sharing ratio.
Credit   Goodwill.

Often the debit and credit entries to the goodwill account are omitted, only the entries on the capital accounts being made for the surplus on revaluation of goodwill, as follows:

These entries may also be made if the partners of a firm decide to change the ratio in which they share profits.

Debit   Partners of new firm in new profit sharing ratio.
Credit   Partners of old firm in old profit sharing ratio.

Appropriation Account

On a change of partners during an accounting year, a profit and loss account will be prepared to the date of change and the net profit divided between the old partners in the appropriation account. A separate profit and loss and appropriation account is then prepared for the remainder of the year for the new partnership. If this is not done it will be necessary to apportion the profit for the year between the period of the old partnership and the period of the new partnership, and prepare separate appropriation accounts for the two periods.

The appropriation accounts be may prepared in columnar form.

Example 2

Green and Brown have carried on business for a number of years sharing profits in the ratio of 4:3 after charging interest on capital at 10% per annum. Gray was admitted into partnership on 1 October 19X2 and the terms of the partnership from then were agreed as follows:

Annual salaries to be: Green £12,000; Brown £9,600; Gray £9,600.
Interest on capital to be charged at 10% per annum.
Profits to be shared; Green four-ninths; Brown three-ninths, Gray two-ninths.

On 1 October 19X2 Gray paid £7,000 into the partnership bank account and of this amount £2,100 was in respect of the share of goodwill acquired by him. Since the partnership has never created, and does not intend to create, a goodwill account, the full amount of £7,000 was credited for the time being to Gray's capital account.
The trial balance of the partnership at 30 June 19X3 was as follows:

		£	£
Cash at bank		1,784	
Stock at 1 July 19X2		11,320	
Purchases		202,630	
Sales			305,810
Wages		26,200	
Other expenses		40,800	
Capital accounts:	Green		22,000
	Brown		11,000
	Gray		7,000

		£	£
Current accounts:	Green	12,200	
	Brown	10,100	
	Gray	6,740	
Debtors and Creditors		27,480	23,744
Fixed assets at 1 July 19X2 at book value		30,300	
		£369,554	£369,554

Note that on the 30 June 19X3:

1 Stock was   £20,000
2 Expenses owing   £3,600
3 Expenses prepaid   £800
4 Depreciation of fixed assets is to be provided at 20% per annum of book value.

Apportionment of net profit is required to be made on a time basis.

Required:

After taking into account the above information and the adjustment required for goodwill, prepare a trading and profit and loss account for the year ended 30 June 19X3 and profit and loss appropriation accounts for each of the periods 1 July 19X2 to 30 September 19X2 and 1 October 19X2 to 30 June 19X3, and a balance sheet at 30 June 19X3. Partners' capital and current accounts in columnar form are also required.

Solution

The valuation placed on goodwill can be calculated from the information given that Gray's share of $\frac{2}{9}$ is valued at £2,100. The total value of goodwill is therefore (£2,100 × $\frac{9}{2}$) £9,450.

Goodwill is apportioned in the following profit sharing ratios:

					£
Old firm:					
Green	$\frac{4}{7}$	×	£9,450	=	5,400
Brown	$\frac{3}{7}$	×	£9,450	=	4,050
					£9,450
New firm:					
Green	$\frac{4}{9}$	×	£9,450	=	4,200
Brown	$\frac{3}{9}$	×	£9,450	=	3,150
Gray	$\frac{2}{9}$	×	£9,450	=	2,100
					£9,450

The first stage is to prepare the capital accounts as follows:

Capital accounts

	Green	Brown	Gray		Green	Brown	Gray
	£	£	£		£	£	£
Goodwill –							
contra	4,200	3,150	2,100	Balance b/d	22,000	11,000	
				Cash			7,000
				Goodwill –			
				contra	5,400	4,050	
Balance c/d	23,200	11,900	4,900				
	£27,400	£15,050	£7,000		£27,400	£15,050	£7,000

The entry for goodwill reduces Gray's capital from £7,000 to £4,900. Remember, however, that Gray will be credited with £2,100 on the next occasion that goodwill is revalued.

The interest on the capital can now be calculated:

							£
1/7/X2 to 30/9/X2 = 3 months:							
Green	$\frac{3}{12}$	×	$\frac{10}{100}$	×	£22,000	=	550
Brown	$\frac{3}{12}$	×	$\frac{10}{100}$	×	£11,000	=	275
1/10/X2 to 30/9/X3 = 9 months:							
Green	$\frac{9}{12}$	×	$\frac{10}{100}$	×	£23,200	=	1,740
Brown	$\frac{9}{12}$	×	$\frac{10}{100}$	×	£11,900	=	892
Gray	$\frac{9}{12}$	×	$\frac{10}{100}$	×	£ 4,900	=	367

The next stage is to prepare the profit and loss account:

Trading and profit and loss account for the year ended 30 June 19X3

	£	£
Sales		305,810
Less Opening stock	11,320	
Purchases	202,630	
	213,950	
Closing stock	20,000	193,950
Gross profit		111,860
Less Wages	26,200	
Expenses (£40,800 + £3,600 − £800)	43,600	
Depreciation	6,060	75,860
Net profit		£36,000

The net profit is then apportioned between the old firm (3 months) and the new firm (9 months):

Profit and loss appropriation accounts

	1/7/X2 to 30/9/X2			1/10/X2 to 30/6/X3	
	£	£		£	£
Net profit b/d:					
($\frac{3}{12}$ × £36,000)		£9,000	($\frac{9}{12}$ × £36,000)		£27,000
Salaries:					
Green ($\frac{9}{12}$ × £12,000)				9,000	
Brown ($\frac{9}{12}$ × £9,600)				7,200	
Gray ($\frac{9}{12}$ × £9,600)				7,200	23,400
Interest on capital:					
Green	550			1,740	
Brown	275			892	
Gray	—	825		367	2,999
Residue of profit:					
Green ($\frac{4}{7}$)	4,671		($\frac{4}{9}$)	267	
Brown ($\frac{3}{7}$)	3,504		($\frac{3}{9}$)	200	
Gray	—	8,175	($\frac{2}{9}$)	134	601
		£9,000			£27,000

Finally the current accounts and balance sheet can be prepared:

Current accounts

	Green	Brown	Gray		Green	Brown	Gray
	£	£	£		£	£	£
Balances b/d	12,200	10,100	6,740	Salaries	9,000	7,200	7,200
				Interest on			
				capital:			
				to 30/9/X2	550	275	—
				to 30/6/X3	1,740	892	367
				Residue of profit:			
				to 30/9/X2	4,671	3,504	—
Balances c/d	4,028	1,971	961	to 30/6/X3	267	200	134
	£16,228	£12,071	£7,701		£16,228	£12,071	£7,701

Balance sheet at 30 June 19X3

	£	£	£	£
Fixed assets				24,240
Current assets:				
Stocks			20,000	
Debtors			27,480	
Prepayments			800	
Cash			1,784	
			50,064	
Less Current liabilities:				
Creditors		23,744		
Accruals		3,600		
			27,344	
				22,720
				£46,960
Financed by:				
Partners' accounts:				

	Green	Brown	Gray	Total
	£	£	£	£
Capital accounts	23,200	11,900	4,900	40,000
Current accounts	4,028	1,971	961	6,960
	£27,228	£13,871	£5,861	£46,960

Summary

1   Any surpluses and deficits on revaluation will be transferred to a revaluation account. The balance on this account will be shared between the partners in their profit sharing ratio.
2   Any value placed upon unrecorded goodwill can be adjusted for by a contra on the partners' capital accounts.
3   If there is a partnership change part-way through an accounting period, the profit up to the date of change will be shared between the old partners in accordance with the old agreement.

Examination Hints

The crucial item in a question relating to a change in partners is the date on which the partner left or joined. If a partner joins or leaves during the year it will be necessary to apportion the profit before dividing the profit of the earlier period between the old partners in accordance with the old agreement and the later period between the new partners according to the new agreement. In this situation remember that a salary will only be for the relevant number of months and not for a whole year.

In many questions the change in partners takes place at a year end in which case all the net profit for the year should be divided between the old partners, if this has not already been done.

It is normally advisable to open up a revaluation account and also to show the partners' capital and current accounts in columnar form. Any surplus on revaluation should be divided between the old partners in the profit sharing ratio. Do not forget to make the contra entries for goodwill, where necessary, on the partners' capital accounts.

Try to answer the following questions before reading on.

Self-Assessment Questions

In each question, choose the correct answer from the five alternatives given.

See page 302 for answers.

4.1   The following item relating to a partner will not appear in a profit and loss appropriation account:
   a   commission on sales
   b   bonus calculated on gross profit
   c   drawings
   d   salary
   e   share of profit.

4.2   A, B and C are partners with capitals of £20,000 each. They share profits in the ratio 2:1:1. Premises that are recorded at cost of £100,000 less accumulated depreciation of £10,000 are revalued at £150,000. After the revaluation, the capital of B will be:
   a   £32,500
   b   £35,000
   c   £36,667
   d   £40,000
   e   £70,000.

4.3   A, B and C are in partnership sharing profits 2:1:1 with capitals of £20,000 each. D joins as a new partner introducing £20,000 of capital. The profit shares will be 3:2:1:1. An adjustment is made for goodwill on the partners' accounts. If the goodwill is valued at £28,000 the balance on D's capital account after the goodwill adjustment will be:
   a   (£8,000)
   b   £8,000
   c   £16,000
   d   £20,000
   e   £24,000.

4.4   The following item may appear on the assets side of a partnership balance sheet:
   a   motor car owned by the firm but used by a partner
   b   capital introduced by partners
   c   partner's current account debit balance
   d   partner's private expenses paid in advance
   e   loan from partner.

If you have answered all of the above questions correctly, and are sure you understand the key points in this chapter, then try to answer questions 3 and 4 on pages 189–190 before moving on to Chapter 5.

CHAPTER 5

PARTNERSHIP ACCOUNTS: DISSOLUTION

Chapter contents

Introduction **22** The realization account **22** Closing the ledger accounts **23** Conversion to a limited company **26** *Gardner v. Murray* **28** Summary **30** Examination hints **30**

Learning objectives

After studying this chapter you should be able to:

☐ make the necessary entries in a realization account;
☐ close the ledger accounts of the partnership;
☐ make the opening entries in the books of the company on conversion of a partnership into a limited company;
☐ apply the 'Garner v. Murray' rule where necessary.

Introduction

Dissolution of a partnership will arise if the partners decide to cease trading, sell off the business assets and pay off the liabilities. The business may be sold as a going concern, the purchaser acquiring most or all of the assets and sometimes taking over the liabilities as well. A partnership is also dissolved in the situation where the partners decide to trade as a limited liability company, the assets and liabilities being sold to the new company in return for shares in the company.

On a dissolution the profit or loss arising from selling the assets is determined in the realization account and is divided between the partners. Any final cash balance is used to repay the amounts due to the partners. After all the entries have been made there should be no balances left on the ledger accounts.

The Realization Account

The double entry for writing up the realization account is as follows:

Debit	Realization	}	with the *net book value* of assets to
Credit	Asset accounts	}	be realized.
Debit	Liability accounts	}	with any liabilities taken over by a
Credit	Realization	}	purchaser.
Debit	Bank	}	with proceeds received on the sale of
Credit	Realization	}	any assets for cash and from debtors.
Debit	Realization	}	with any dissolution expenses paid.
Credit	Bank	}	

Cash at bank and in hand should be transferred to the realization account only if it is being acquired by another party, for example if the purchaser of the business is taking over the cash in addition to other assets.

If separate accounts are maintained for the cost and accumulated depreciation of fixed assets the entry will be:

Debit Realisation — with the net book value.
Debit Provision for depreciation — with the accumulated depreciation.
Credit Fixed asset account — with the cost of the fixed asset.

Debit   Purchaser   } with the total *purchase price* of assets
Credit Realization account } and liabilities taken over.

Debit   Partners' capital   } with the *value* placed upon any assets
Credit Realization account } taken over by them.

The balance in the realization account will now represent the total profit or loss on realization and is divided between the partners according to the profit sharing ratio, the entries being:

Debit   Realization account } with the profit on realization (entries
Credit Partners' capitals   } reversed for a loss).

The realization account is debited with the book value of the assets being disposed of and credited with the proceeds. A profit on realization arises if the proceeds on sale of the assets exceeds their book value.

Closing the Ledger Accounts

Any liabilities not taken over will be paid off by the partnership. The double entry is:

Debit   Creditors, loans, etc. } with amounts paid.
Credit Bank   }

If an account has been opened for a purchaser of the business it will be closed when the consideration is received by the partnership, as follows:

If any discounts are received they should be transferred to the realization account.

Debit   Bank   } with amount received.
Credit Purchaser }

The consideration may be received in assets other than cash. The partners will agree between themselves who will take the assets received from the purchaser, the double entry being:

Debit   Partners' capitals } with the value placed on assets (received
Credit Purchaser   } from the purchaser of the business) taken
                             over by the partners.

At this stage the only accounts remaining with balances upon them will be the partners' accounts and cash. Any partner's loan account should be repaid by the partnership first, and then the remaining balance due to each partner. To ascertain this, the current account balances may be transferred to the capital accounts. After the entries for repayment of the partners have been made all the ledger accounts will be closed, i.e. will have nil balances.

Example 1

Peter and Rodney share profits in the ratio 2:1. The balance sheet of the partnership is:

Balance sheet at 31 December			
	Cost	Depreciation	Net
Fixed assets:	£	£	£
Premises	100,000	20,000	80,000
Equipment	50,000	15,000	35,000
Vehicles	20,000	8,000	12,000
	£170,000	£43,000	£127,000
Current assets:			
Stock		32,000	
Debtors		21,000	
Bank		3,000	
		56,000	
Less Current liabilities:			
Creditors		25,000	31,000
			£158,000

Financed by:			
Partners' accounts:			
	Peter	Rodney	Total
	£	£	£
Capital accounts	70,000	70,000	140,000
Current accounts	6,000	12,000	18,000
	£76,000	£82,000	£158,000

The partnership is dissolved on 1 January. The premises, equipment, stock and debtors are taken over by Smith Ltd at a purchase price of £200,000 settled in cash. One vehicle is to be kept by Peter, the value placed upon this being £5,000. The other vehicles are sold for £5,500. The creditors are settled by payment of £24,750, and there is a final cash distribution to the partners.

The ledger accounts will be closed as follows:

Realization

The individual accounts for the assets realized have not been shown as they will merely be closed by transfer to the realization account.

	£		£
Premises	80,000	Smith Ltd – purchase price	200,000
Equipment	35,000	Peter – vehicle at valuation	5,000
Vehicles	12,000	Bank – vehicles	5,500
Stock	32,000	Creditors – discount	250
Debtors	21,000		
	180,000		210,750
Profit on realization			
– Peter ($\frac{2}{3}$)	20,500		
– Rodney ($\frac{1}{3}$)	10,250		
	£210,750		£210,750

Creditors

Creditors have not been transferred to the realization account as they are not taken over by the purchaser of the business.

	£		£
Bank	24,750	Balance b/d	25,000
Realization – discount received	250		
	£25,000		£25,000

Smith Ltd

	£		£
Realization – purchase price	£200,000	Bank	£200,000

Bank

	£		£
Balance b/d	3,000	Creditor	24,750
Smith Ltd	200,000		
Realization – vehicles	5,500	Balance c/d	183,750
	£208,500		£208,500
Balance b/d	183,750	Peter	91,500
		Rodney	92,250
	£183,750		£183,750

Partners' accounts

	Peter	Rodney		Peter	Rodney
	£	£		£	£
Realization – vehicle	5,000		Capital accounts	70,000	70,000
Balances c/d	91,500	92,250	Current accounts	6,000	12,000
			Realization – profit	20,500	10,250
	£96,500	£92,250		£96,500	£92,250
Bank	£91,500	£92,250	Balances b/d	£91,500	£92,250

Immediately prior to the cash distribution to the partners the balance on the bank account equals the total of the balances on the partners' accounts. Each partner is then paid the amount due to him.

In the above example Smith Ltd has acquired the business for cash. Instead of cash the purchase consideration may take the form of other assets, normally shares and debentures in the purchasing company.

Example 2

The data is the same as in the previous example, except that instead of settling the purchase price totally by cash, the consideration given by Smith Ltd is:

	£
10% debentures in Smith Ltd	30,000
£1 ordinary shares in Smith Ltd	90,000
Cash	80,000
	£200,000

Peter and Rodney decide to share the debentures between them in proportion to their capital accounts, and the ordinary shares in their profit sharing ratio.

The realization account and creditors account will remain unchanged. The other accounts will be:

Smith Ltd

	£		£
Realization	200,000	10% debentures:	
		– Peter $(^{70}/_{140})$	15,000
		– Rodney $(^{70}/_{140})$	15,000
		£1 ordinary shares:	
		– Peter $(^2/_3)$	60,000
		– Rodney $(^1/_3)$	30,000
		Bank	80,000
	£200,000		£200,000

The ordinary shares in Smith Ltd have been allocated to the partners in the proportions that they have agreed to take. Peter has received 60,000 £1 ordinary shares valued at £1 each and Rodney has received 30,000. The entry should be based on the value of the shares. For example, if the shares had been 45,000 £1 ordinary shares valued at £2 each, the entry would still be for the total value of £90,000. Peter would have received 30,000 shares valued at £60,000 and Rodney would have received 15,000 shares valued at £30,000.

Bank

	£		£
Balance b/d	3,000	Creditors	24,750
Smith Ltd	80,000		
Realization – Vehicles	5,500	Balance c/d	63,750
	£88,500		£88,500
Balance b/d	63,750	Peter	16,500
		Rodney	47,250
	£63,750		£63,750

Partners' accounts

	Peter	Rodney		Peter	Rodney
	£	£		£	£
Realization – vehicle	5,000		Capital accounts	70,000	70,000
Smith Ltd:			Current accounts	6,000	12,000
– 10% debentures	15,000	15,000	Realization profit	20,500	10,250
– £1 ordinary shares	60,000	30,000			
Balance c/d	16,500	47,250			
	£96,500	£92,250		£96,500	£92,250
Bank	£16,500	£47,250	Balance b/d	£16,500	£47,250

Note that the position is still arrived at where the balance on the bank account will equal the total of the partners' accounts prior to the remaining cash being distributed to them.

Conversion to a Limited Company

The above entries would be the same if Smith Ltd had been formed by Peter and Rodney as a new company to acquire the business. In this situation Peter and Rodney would in effect have converted their partnership into a limited company.

In the books of the new limited company the assets taken over would be recorded at valuation, which may be different from their book values in the partnership. If the purchase price exceeds the valuation placed on the net assets the difference will be recorded as purchased goodwill; if the net assets exceed the purchase price the difference (negative goodwill) will be recorded as a capital reserve.

Example 3

Matthew and Jonathan are in partnership sharing profits and losses equally. The following is their balance sheet at 31 December:

	£	£
Fixed assets:		
Premises		100,000
Equipment		20,000
Motor vehicles		25,000
		145,000
Current assets:		
Stock	60,000	
Debtors	40,000	
Bank	20,000	
	120,000	
Less Creditors	70,000	50,000
		£195,000
Financed by:		
Partners' accounts:		

	Matthew	Jonathan	Total
	£	£	£
Capital accounts	80,000	80,000	160,000
Current accounts	20,000	15,000	35,000
	£100,000	£95,000	£195,000

On 1 January they convert the partnership into a limited company named Paul Andrews Ltd. Premises are valued at £120,000, the remaining assets and liabilities being taken over at book value. The purchase consideration is £230,000 which is satisfied by the issue of 100,000 £1 ordinary shares at par and £130,000 10% loan stock. Matthew and

Jonathan agree to divide the ordinary shares equally between themselves and take 10% loan stock in satisfaction of the remaining balances due to them.

Required:

The closing entries in the books of the partnership and the balance sheet of Paul Andrews Ltd immediately after the conversion.

Solution

Books of Matthew and Jonathan

Realization

	£		£
Premises	100,000		
Equipment	20,000		
Motor vehicles	25,000		
Stock	60,000		
Debtors	40,000		
Bank	20,000	Creditors	70,000
Profit on realization:			
Matthew (½)	17,500	Paul Andrews Ltd –	
Jonathan (½)	17,500	purchase price	230,000
	£300,000		£300,000

Partners' accounts

	Matthew	Jonathan		Matthew	Jonathan
	£	£		£	£
Paul Andrews Ltd:					
– £1 ordinary Shares	50,000	50,000	Capital accounts	80,000	80,000
– 10% loan stock			Current accounts	20,000	15,000
(balancing figure)	67,500	62,500	Profit on realization	17,500	17,500
	£117,500	£112,500		£117,500	£112,500

Paul Andrews

	£		£
Realization – purchase price	230,000	£1 ordinary shares	
		– Matthew	50,000
		– Jonathan	50,000
		10% Loan Stock	
		– Matthew	67,500
		– Jonathan	62,500
	£230,000		£230,000

Paul Andrews Ltd
Balance Sheet at 1 January

	£	£
Fixed assets:		
Intangible – goodwill (balancing figure)		15,000
Tangible – premises	120,000	
– equipment	20,000	
– motor vehicle	25,000	
		165,000
		180,000

	£	£
Current assets:		
Stocks	60,000	
Debtors	40,000	
Bank	20,000	
	120,000	
Less Creditors	70,000	50,000
		£230,000
Financed by:		
£1 ordinary shares		100,000
10% loan stock		130,000
		£230,000

Note that the goodwill of £15,000 would arise as a balancing figure on the opening journal entry in the books of Paul Andrews Ltd which would have been:

Journal

	Debit	Credit
	£	£
Premises – at valuation	120,000	
Equipment	20,000	
Motor vehicles	25,000	
Stocks	60,000	
Debtors	40,000	
Bank	20,000	
Creditors		70,000
Matthew and Jonathan –		
purchase price		230,000
Goodwill (balancing figure)	15,000	
	£300,000	£300,000
Matthew and Jonathan	230,000	
£1 ordinary shares		100,000
10% loan stock		130,000
	£230,000	£230,000

Garner v. Murray

In the preceding examples each partner has had a credit balance on his account prior to the cash distribution to the partners, and has been paid the amount due to him. If a partner has a debit balance on his account at this stage, he will be required to pay this to the partnership prior to the cash distribution to the other partners.

Example 4

Mark, Luke and John dissolve their partnership. After realization of the assets and payment of the liabilities the following balances appear in the books:

	Debit	Credit
	£	£
Bank	50,000	
Mark		40,000
Luke	10,000	
John		20,000
	£60,000	£60,000

Luke will be required to pay £10,000 into the business.

The ledger accounts will be closed as follows:

Bank

	£		£
Balance b/d	50,000	Mark	40,000
Luke	10,000	John	20,000
	£60,000		£60,000

Partners' accounts

	Mark	Luke	John		Mark	Luke	John
	£	£	£		£	£	£
				Balance b/d	40,000	(10,000)	20,000
Bank	40,000	—	20,000	Bank	—	10,000	—
	£40,000	—	£20,000		£40,000	—	£20,000

Problems arise if a partner has a debit balance on his account, but he is insolvent and cannot pay the amount due to the partnership. In these circumstances the debit balance on his account is transferred to the other partners prior to the final cash settlement. The proportion of this loss borne by each partner may be specified by the partnership agreement. In the absence of any agreement the rule laid down in *Garner* v. *Murray* (1903) applies.

The *Garner* v. *Murray* rule is that the deficiency of an insolvent partner, in the absence of agreement, should be borne by the other partners in the *ratio of their last agreed capital balances*.

Example 5

Faith, Hope and Charity share profits and losses equally.

Balance Sheet at 31 December

	£
Assets	200,000
Bank	10,000
	£210,000

Financed by:				
Partners accounts:	Faith	Hope	Charity	Total
	£	£	£	£
Capital accounts	100,000	30,000	50,000	180,000
Current accounts	20,000	(2,000)	12,000	30,000
	£120,000	£28,000	£62,000	£210,000

The partnership is dissolved, and assets realize only £80,000. Hope is insolvent and cannot contribute any deficiency. The *Garner* v. *Murray* rule applies, as there is no agreement on the sharing of any such deficiency.

The ledger accounts will be closed as follows:

Realization

	£		£
Assets	200,000	Bank	80,000
		Loss on realization:	
		– Faith ($\frac{1}{3}$)	40,000
		– Hope ($\frac{1}{3}$)	40,000
		– Charity ($\frac{1}{3}$)	40,000
	£200,000		£200,000

Garner v. Murray is an old case that only applies in circumstances that are not very common. It is more logical that any deficiency of an insolvent partner should be borne by the other partners in their profit sharing proportions and this could be specified in the partnership agreement.

Bank

	£		£
Balance b/d	10,000		
Realization of assets	80,000	Balance c/d	90,000
	£90,000		£90,000
Balance b/d	90,000	Faith	72,000
		Charity	18,000
	£90,000		£90,000

Partners' accounts

	Faith £	Hope £	Charity £		Faith £	Hope £	Charity £
Realization				Capital			
loss	40,000	40,000	40,000	accounts	100,000	30,000	50,000
Balances c/d	80,000	(12,000)	22,000	Current			
				accounts	20,000	(2,000)	12,000
	£120,000	£28,000	£62,000		£120,000	£28,000	£62,000
				Balances b/d	80,000	(12,000)	22,000
				Contra re			
				Garner v.			
Balances c/d	72,000	—	18,000	Murray	(8,000)	12,000	(4,000)
	£72,000	—	£18,000		£72,000	—	£18,000
Bank	£72,000		£18,000	Balances b/d	£72,000		£18,000

Hope's deficiency of £12,000 is borne by the other partners in proportion to their last agreed capital balances of Faith £100,000 and Charity £50,000 as follows:

Faith   (100,000/150,000 × 12,000)   £8,000

Charity   (50,000/150,000 × £12,000)   £4,000

£12,000

Note that in examination conditions there is no need to carry balances down on the partners' accounts at each stage. This has only been done in the above example for the sake of clarity.

Summary

1   A realization account will record the book values of assets disposed of and the proceeds realized. The profit or loss on realization will be shared between the partners in their profit sharing ratio.

2   The partners' capital accounts will be debited with the value placed upon assets they receive from the firm and with the final cash settlement.

3   In the books of the purchaser of a business the assets acquired will be recorded at the valuation placed upon them by the purchaser. Any difference between the total value placed upon the net assets acquired and the purchase price will represent goodwill.

4   Conversion to a limited company consists of the dissolution of the partnership and the purchase of the business by the new company, the consideration normally taking the form of shares in the new company.

5   The *Garner* v. *Murray* rule may apply if an insolvent partner owes money to the partnership.

Examination Hints

Read the question carefully to determine precisely the form that the answer should take. Normally the ledger accounts will be required. Open up ledger accounts for every item on the balance sheet. This can be short-cut by entering the balance sheet values of the assets to be realized directly onto the debit side of the realization account, but separate accounts will normally be required for creditors, loans, bank and the partners' accounts. Both the capital and current account balances should be entered onto the partners' accounts.

The transactions recording the selling of the assets and payment of liabilities may then be entered. Open up an account for any purchaser of the business, debiting it with the purchase price, which is credited to the realization account.

The balance on the realization account (the profit or loss on realization) should be transferred to the partners' accounts in their profit sharing ratio.

The purchaser's account is then credited with the proceeds received, bank account being debited with cash received and the partners' accounts being debited with any shares divided between them. After these entries the only accounts showing balances should be the bank and partners' accounts; it is advisable to carry down the balances on these accounts at this stage. The total of the partners' balances should equal the bank balance. (If this is not the case there is an error. The error may be in your double entry or a balance sheet item may have been omitted. Do not waste time looking for this error unless you are within the time you have allocated to the question; instead finalize by paying the partners the balances shown on their accounts, leaving a bank balance.)

If one of the partner's balances is a deficiency (a debit balance) this must be shared between the other partners in the proportions given in the question. If the question only gives the profit sharing ratio and does not mention the proportion applying to the deficiency, the rule in *Garner* v. *Murray* should be applied.

The final entries will be for the payment to the partners of the credit balances on their accounts.

Try to answer the following questions before reading on.

Self-Assessment Questions

In each question, choose the correct answer from the five alternatives given.

5.1   The profit on realization is divided between the partners in the proportions of: See page 303 for answers.
    a   profit sharing ratio
    b   capital accounts
    c   current accounts
    d   capital and current accounts
    e   equally.

5.2   In the absence of an agreement an insolvent partner's deficiency should be divided between the other partners in the proportions of:
    a   profit sharing ratio
    b   capital accounts
    c   current accounts
    d   capital and current accounts
    e   equally.

5.3   The balance sheet of a partnership shows assets of £150,000 and liabilities of £20,000. At that date the business is acquired by a company which takes over all the assets and liabilities. The consideration received is 100,000 £1 ordinary shares valued at £2 per share. The profit on realization is:
    a   (£30,000)
    b   (£50,000)
    c   £30,000
    d   £50,000
    e   £70,000.

5.4   A, B and C have capitals of £10,000 each and share profits in the ratio 2:2:1. Part of the proceeds of selling their business is 60,000 ordinary shares of £1 (valued at £1.50 each) in a limited company which they agree to share in proportion to their capital accounts. The number of shares that B will receive is:
    a   10,000
    b   12,000
    c   18,000
    d   20,000
    e   30,000

If you have answered the above questions correctly, and are sure you understand the key points in this chapter, then try to answer questions 5 and 6 on pages 191–2 before moving on to Chapter 6.

CHAPTER 6

PARTNERSHIP ACCOUNTS: JOINT VENTURES

Chapter contents

Introduction **32**   Joint venture accounts **32**   Memorandum joint venture account **33**   Summary **35**   Examination hints **35**

Learning objectives

After studying this chapter you should be able to:

☐ write up the joint venture account in the books of each party;

☐ prepare a memorandum joint venture account.

Introduction

For example, a joint venture may exist when two businesses combine together to purchase and sell some bankrupt stock. It may be that one party can acquire the stock and has the funds available to do so, and the other party has the contacts that will enable the stock to be sold.

A joint venture is a temporary partnership that is undertaken by two or more individuals or businesses. The joint venture will be undertaken for a limited period of time to carry out a particular project; there is no intention to form a long-term partnership. Each party to the joint venture will continue their normal businesses. It is often a feature of joint ventures that each party can provide some resources or expertise not available to the other. They therefore join forces to carry out the venture, sharing any profits or losses between themselves in agreed proportions.

The memorandum joint venture account is not a ledger account in any set of books. It is a purely memorandum summary of all the transactions undertaken by all parties.

Because a joint venture is a temporary exercise, no separate set of books need be maintained for it. Instead each party will record the transactions they undertake for the joint venture in their own accounting records. At the end of the venture all the transactions undertaken by the parties are summarized in a memorandum joint venture account to determine the amount of profit and its division. There will then be a final cash settlement between the parties of the amounts due to and from each other.

Joint Venture Accounts

Each party to the venture will open a joint venture account in their own books in which will be recorded the sales, purchases and expenses that they have undertaken on behalf of the venture. The double entry is:

If the purchases are not made on credit, but for cash, the entry will be:

Debit   Joint venture
Credit Bank

Similarly the entries for any cash sales will be:

Debit Bank
Credit Joint venture

Debit	Joint venture	}	with purchases on credit.
Credit	Supplier		
Debit	Supplier	}	with payment made.
Credit	Bank		
Debit	Joint venture	}	with expenses paid.
Credit	Bank		

Debit	Customer	} with sales on credit.
Credit	Joint venture	

Debit	Bank	} with remittances received.
Credit	Customer	

Debit	Joint venture	} with any bad debts.
Credit	Customer	

After the memorandum joint venture account has been prepared (see the next section) the share of profit is recorded as follows:

Debit	Joint venture	} with own share of profit.
Credit	Profit and loss	

The balance on the account is then settled:

If a debit balance:

Debit	Bank	} with remittance received from the other party.
Credit	Joint venture	

If a credit balance:

Debit	Joint venture	} with payment made to the other party.
Credit	Bank	

If there is a balance on the joint venture account at the date of preparing a balance sheet, the balance will be included in debtors or creditors.

Memorandum Joint Venture Account

This will be a memorandum statement prepared in the same format as a profit and loss account. It is prepared by summarizing the entries in the individual joint venture accounts of each of the parties. It is only by amalgamating all the transactions that the total profit or loss can be determined. The memorandum joint venture account does not form part of double entry.

Example

Jack and Jill undertake a joint venture to buy and sell 10,000 leather buckets which are surplus to the requirements of a contact of Jack. Jack will sell the buckets to firms he knows in the interior design field. Jill will sell to chandlers and saddlers. Both parties are to receive a commission of 5% on sales, any profits or losses being shared equally.

On 1 July Jill sent Jack a cheque for £10,000. Thereafter the transactions were:

Jack:		£
Jul. 10	Purchase on credit from Leather Ltd	30,000
11	Paid advertising	500
18	Cash sales	5,000
25	Cash sales	8,000
Aug. 6	Paid Leather Ltd after deduction of 1% cash discount	29,700
12	Cash sales	2,000

Jill:		£
Jul. 12	Paid advertising	2,000
12	Paid insurance	200
31	Cash sales for month	12,000
Aug. 31	Cash sales for month	20,000
31	Paid carriage	1,000

The joint venture ceased on 31 August, all the buckets having been sold.

The ledger accounts with regard to the joint venture will initially appear as follows:

In Jack's Books

Joint venture with Jill

		£				£
Jul. 10	Leather Ltd – purchases	30,000	Jul.	1	Bank – Jill	10,000
11	Bank – advertising	500		18	Bank – cash sales	5,000
				25	Bank – cash sales	8,000
			Aug.	6	Leather Ltd – discount	
					received	300
				12	Bank – cash sales	2,000
				31	Balance b/d	5,200
		£30,500				£30,500

Leather Ltd

		£			£
Aug. 6	Bank	29,700	Jul. 10	Joint venture	30,000
6	Joint venture – cash discount	300			
		£30,000			£30,000

In Jill's Books

Joint venture with Jack

		£			£
Jul. 1	Bank – Jack	10,000	Jul. 31	Bank – cash sales	12,000
12	Bank – advertising	2,000	Aug. 31	Bank – cash sales	20,000
12	Bank – insurance	200			
Aug. 31	Bank – carriage	1,000			
31	Balance c/d	18,800			
		£32,000			£32,000

Each party will send the other a statement of the transactions they have effected on behalf of the joint venture and the memorandum statement will be drawn up.

Jack and Jill

Memorandum joint venture account re leather buckets
For the period 1 July to August 31

	£	£
Sales (£15,000 + £32,000)		47,000
Less Purchases		30,000
Gross profit		17,000
Add Discount received		300
		17,300
Less Advertising (£500 + £2,000)	2,500	
Insurance	200	
Carriage	1,000	
		3,700
Net profit		£13,600
Divided:		
5% Commission on sales:		
– Jack (5% × £15,000)	750	
– Jill (5% × £32,000)	1,600	
Residue of profit:		
– Jack (½)	5,625	
– Jill (½)	5,625	
		£13,600

Note that only profit and loss items will appear in the memorandum joint venture account, remittances between the parties will be omitted.

If any of the parties takes over any unsold stock the entry in their books will be:

Debit   Purchases account
Credit Joint venture account

with the value placed upon the stock.

The stock taken over should appear as an item in the memorandum joint venture account.

Jack and Jill will enter their commissions and share of profits in their books. A final cash settlement of the balances on their accounts will then be made between them.

Jack's Books
Joint venture with Jill

	£		£
Aug. 31 Balance b/d	5,200		
31 Profit and loss:			
– commission	750		
– Profit on joint venture	5,625	Aug. 31 Bank – Jill	11,575
	£11,575		£11,575

The cash settlement would normally be effected at a later date after the memorandum joint venture account has been agreed by all the parties.

Jill's books
Joint venture with Jack

	£		£
Aug. 31 Profit and loss:		Aug. 31 Balance b/d	18,800
– commission	1,600		
– profit on joint venture	5,625		
	7,225		
31 Bank – Jack	11,575		
	£18,800		£18,800

Note that immediately prior to the cash settlement the balances on the joint venture accounts were:

In Jack's books – Debit balance of £11,575
In Jill's books – Credit balance of £11,575

Jill was therefore in the position of owing Jack this amount. The final balances on the joint venture accounts should always be equal but opposite.

Summary

1 Each party will maintain a joint venture account in their own books in which will be entered the transactions they undertake in respect of the venture.
2 A memorandum joint venture account is prepared by summarizing the joint venture accounts in the books of the parties to the venture to disclose the profit. The profit will be shared by the parties to the venture in accordance with their agreement.
3 Each party will record their share of the profit in their own books. There will then be a final cash settlement between the parties to clear the balances remaining on the joint venture accounts in their books.

Examination Hints

Joint venture questions have not been popular with the examiners in the past. A feature of joint venture questions is that they test basic double-entry accounting skills and as such are perhaps more appropriate to lower level examinations.

A joint venture account will be kept by each party in their own books. The account will only record their own transactions in respect of the venture.

The memorandum joint venture account must be prepared before entries relating to the division of the profit can be made in the books of the parties.

If a question does not mention a final cash settlement the balance on the joint venture account should be left as a balance. However, in these circumstances a note to the examiner stating which party will pay the other can do no harm.

Try to answer the following questions before reading on.

Self-Assessment Questions

In each question, choose the correct answer from the five alternatives given.

See page 303 for answers.

6.1   The following statement with regard to a joint venture is untrue:
   a   it is a temporary venture
   b   it is subject to the Partnership Act 1890
   c   there may not be only one party
   d   each party may record their own transactions
   e   profits must be divided equally.

6.2   The following item will appear on the credit side of a joint venture account:
   a   commissions paid
   b   purchases
   c   discounts allowed
   d   stock taken over by one party
   e   storage costs.

6.3   The following item will appear on the debit side of a joint venture account:
   a   discounts received
   b   stock taken over by one party
   c   sales
   d   cash received from the other party
   e   share of profit on the venture.

If you have answered the above questions correctly, and are sure you understand the key points in this chapter, then try to answer question 7 on page 193 before moving to Chapter 7.

CHAPTER 7

CONSIGNMENT ACCOUNTS

Chapter contents

Introduction **37**   The consignor's records **37**   The consignee's records **40**   Unsold stock **40**   Summary **41**   Examination hints **41**

Learning objectives

After studying this chapter you should be able to:

☐ write up the consignment account and the agent's account in the books of the consignor;

☐ write up the consignor's account in the books of the agent;

☐ determine the value to be placed upon any unsold stock to be carried down as a balance on the consignment account.

Introduction

Goods may be sent by a principal (the consignor) to an agent (the consignee) to be sold by the agent on the principal's behalf. The goods will remain the property of the consignor until they are sold by the agent. The agent will normally be entitled to a commission on the sales he effects. The agent will normally collect the sale proceeds from the customers and remit these, less his commission and any expenses he may have incurred, to the consignor.

Consignments of this nature normally relate to goods sent to an agent abroad.

The Consignor's Records

Goods sent out on consignment should be recorded at their cost in a consignment account. All expenses incurred by the consignor in respect of the shipment will be charged to this account. At agreed intervals the agent will send the consignor a statement of the sales made, commission earned and expenses incurred in respect of the consignment. These transactions will also be recorded in the consignment account which is, in effect, a profit and loss account for the consignment.

The statement prepared by the agent may be called an 'Account sales'.

The double entry to record these transactions is:

Debit   Consignment
Credit   Goods sent on consignment   } with the cost of stock sent.

Debit   Consignment
Credit   Bank (or supplier)   } with expenses paid with regard to the consignment (or incurred on credit).

A separate consignment account should be opened for each consignment.

When a statement is received from the agent:

Debit   Agent
Credit Consignment   } with sales made by the agent.

Debit   Consignment   } with commission earned and expenses
Credit Agent   } incurred by the agent.

When all the goods have been sold and the above entries made, the balance on the consignment account will be the profit or loss on the consignment. It is transferred as follows:

Debit   Consignment   } with the profit on the consignment
Credit Profits and losses on   } (entry is reversed for a loss).
          consignments

The latter account is closed to the profit and loss account as follows:

Debit   Profits and losses on
          consignments   } with the total profit on all
Credit Profit and loss   } consignments for the year.

The goods sent on consignment account is closed to the trading account at the end of the accounting year as follows:

Debit   Goods sent on consignment }
Credit Trading account   } with the total cost of all goods sent.

The cost of these goods will of course already be included in the trading account, either as opening stock or as purchases. The above entry eliminates their cost from the trading account, which will then show the gross profit on ordinary sales. We have already seen that the profit earned on consignments is included as a separate item in the profit and loss account.

At any time the balance on the agent's account will be the amount due from him. Monies received from the agent will be recorded as follows:

Debit   Bank   } with remittance received.
Credit Agent

If the agent sells the goods on credit some bad debts may be incurred. If the agent is paid an additional commission – called a 'del credere' commission – the bad debts will be borne by the agent and no entry will be made for them in the consignor's books. If a del credere commission is not paid any bad debts will be an expense borne by the consignor, the double entry being:

Debit Consignment account
Credit Agent's account

The agent will of course have been debited with the sales effected. The above credit entry reduces the amount due from him.

Example 1

Green prepares his accounts to 31 December each year. On 1 January he sent a consignment of 20 microcomputers, cost £15,000, to his agent Grey. Green paid insurance and freight charges of £500 on 3 January.

In due course Green received the following statement from Grey:

Account sales for consignment S5 sold by order of and
for the account of Green
Period 1 January to 15 June

	Singaland	Singaland
	$	$
Cash sales (20 microcomputers)		60,000
Less Handling and carriage charges	600	
Commission – 10% of sales	6,000	
		6,600
Balance due – remittance enclosed		$53,400

This is a statement of the transactions effected by Grey in Singaland dollars. Before these transactions can be recorded in Green's books they must be translated into sterling. If the exchange rate for the period was 3 dollars to £1 the translated statement will be:

	£	£
Sales ($60,000/3)		20,000
Less Handling and carriage charges		
($600/3)	200	
Commission ($6,000/3)	2,000	
		2,200
Balance due – remittance enclosed		£17,800

These transactions will be recorded in the ledger accounts of Green as follows:

Goods sent on consignment

	£		£
Dec. 31 Trading account	15,000	Jan. 1 Consignment S5 to Grey	15,000

The goods sent on consignment account will record the cost of all goods sent out on all the consignments during the year.

Consignment S5 to Grey

	£		£
Jan. 1 Goods	15,000	Jun. 15 Grey – sales	20,000
3 Bank – insurance and			
freight	500		
Jun. 15 Grey:			
– Handling and carriage	200		
– Commission	2,000		
15 Profit on consignment	2,300		
	£20,000		£20,000

Profits and losses on consignments

	£		£
Dec. 31 Profit and loss	2,300	Jun. 15 Consignment S5 to Grey	2,300

Grey re consignment S5

	$	£		$	£
Jun. 15 Sales	60,000	20,000	Jun. 15 Handling and		
			carriage	600	200
			15 Commission	6,000	2,000
			20 Bank	53,400	17,800
	$60,000	£20,000		$60,000	£20,000

The account for the consignee (Grey) records his indebtedness to the consignor. Any balance on this account at an accounting date will be included in the balance sheet as a debtor.

(The $ columns are purely memoranda.)

If the remittance from Grey was received at a date when a different exchange rate applied, a difference will arise on Grey's account. This difference will be due to the movement in the exchange rate and is transferred to the profit and loss account as a gain or loss on exchange.

Example 2

The remittance of $53,400 from Grey was received on 20 June when the exchange rate was $3.10 to £1. The account for Grey will show:

Grey re consignment S5

	$	£			$	£
Jun. 15 Sales	60,000	20,000	Jun. 15 Handling and			
			carriage	600	200
			15 Commission	6,000	2,000
			20 Bank		
			($53,400/3.10)	53,400	17,226
			Dec. 31 Profit and loss		
			– exchange loss	—	574
	$60,000	£20,000			$60,000	£20,000

The Consignee's Records

The goods received on consignment by the agent belong to the consignor and no entries are required to be made in respect of these, although memorandum stock records would normally be kept. The double entry for the entries in the agent's books is as follows:

Debit   Bank
Credit   Consignor   } with cash sales.

Debit   Customers
Credit   Consignor   } with credit sales.

Debit   Bank
Credit   Customers   } with remittances from credit customers.

Debit   Consignor
Credit   Bank or cash   } with expenses paid with regard to the consignment.

Debit   Consignor
Credit   Commissions receivable   } with commission on sales.

Debit   Consignor
Credit   Bank   } with payments made.

If the agent receives a del credere commission and thus bears any bad debts himself the entry in his books will be:

Debit   Bad debts
Credit   Customer

If the bad debts are borne by the consignor the entry will be:

Debit   Consignor
Credit   Customer

Example 3

The transactions undertaken by Grey with regard to consignment S5 from Green will be recorded as follows:

Green re consignment S5

	$			$
Jan. 1		Jan. 1	
to		to	
Jun. 15 Bank – expenses	600	Jun. 15 Bank – sales	60,000
Jun. 15 Commission receivable	6,000		
15 Bank	53,400		
	$60,000		$60,000

It will be seen that this account is a mirror of Grey's account in the books of the consignor.

Unsold stock

The consignor will request his agents to send account sales for transactions up to his accounting date in order that he can prepare his own profit and loss account and balance sheet.

No entries for stock are required in the consignee's books; the problem of unsold stock only arises in the books of the consignor. Such a problem arises if some stock out on consignment remains unsold at the accounting date when a profit and loss account and a balance sheet are to be prepared.

When preparing annual accounts the consignor will value the unsold stock at cost plus a proportion of the costs incurred in getting the stock to its present location and condition.

These costs will include any relevant expenses incurred by the agent as well as the consignor, but they should not include any selling expenses such as the agent's commission. When the stock valuation is ascertained it is carried down as a debit balance on the consignment account. The balancing figure on the consignment account will then be the profit earned on sales to date.

This method of stock valuation is in accordance with SSAP 9. The valuation of stocks is covered more fully in Chapter 25.

Summary

1   A consignment account will record the cost of goods sent, expenses, sales and any stock remaining unsold. The balance on the consignment account will be the profit or loss that has been made.
2   Unsold stock will be valued at cost plus a proportion of the expenses incurred in getting the stock to its present location and condition.
3   An account will be opened to record the amounts due from the agent.

Examination Hints

Consignment accounts are not a common examination topic. If you are faced with a question take care to identify whether the question requires the accounts in the books of the consignor or consignee, although sometimes both may be required.

When writing up the consignor's books it may be helpful to remember that the consignment account is effectively a profit and loss account for the consignment and that the consignee's account is a debtor's account that records the amounts receivable from the agent.

If any stock remains unsold at a balance sheet date a proportion of the appropriate expenses should be included in its valuation.

Try to answer the following questions before reading on.

Self-Assessment Questions

In each question, choose the correct answer from the five alternatives given.

See page 303 for answers.

7.1   The following item will not appear on the debit side of a consignment account:
    a   cost of goods sent
    b   carriage charges
    c   advertising costs
    d   commission earned by the agent
    e   loss on the consignment.

7.2   In the books of the consignor the following item will not appear in both the consignment and agent's accounts:
    a   goods sent by the consignor
    b   sales made by the consignee
    c   advertising paid by the consignee
    d   bad debts borne by the consignor
    e   commission earned by the consignee.

7.3   Goods that had cost £100,000 were sent on consignment, transportation costs of £8,000 were paid by the consignor and £2,000 by the consignee. By the accounting date 70% of the goods had been sold. The stock valuation will be:
    a   £30,000
    b   £32,400
    c   £33,000
    d   £38,000
    e   £40,000

If you have answered the above questions correctly, and are sure you understand the key points in this chapter, then try to answer question 8 on page 194 before moving on to Chapter 8.

GOODS ON SALE OR RETURN

Chapter contents

Introduction **42**   Accounting treatment **42**   Summary **43**   Examination hints **43**

Learning objective

After studying this chapter you should be able to:

☐ apply the correct accounting treatment to any goods sent out on sale or return.

Introduction

A business may send goods to a customer on approval, a sale not being effected if the customer returns the goods within a specified period. Sometimes a business will send goods to a customer under an agreement whereby the transaction is not treated as a sale until the customer in turn sells the goods to one of his own customers. In both these situations the reality is that the goods are still owned by the 'seller' until such time as a sale is effected.

Accounting Treatment

Goods sent are normally accompanied by a 'pro forma' invoice stating the terms of the transaction and the prospective selling value.

Goods sent out on sale or return must not be recorded as sales. Ownership of the goods is retained. The goods are treated as stock, even though they are on the premises of third parties, until such time as they are sold. On a sale materializing, a sales invoice will be entered in the accounting records in the normal way.

On preparation of a profit and loss account any goods out on sale or return are included in stock at the lower of cost and net realizable value.

The valuation of stocks is covered in Chapter 25 of this book.

A memorandum record is normally kept of goods sent, returned and sold. This memorandum record will enable the cost of the stock out on sale or return to be ascertained.

Sometimes goods sent on sales or return are treated as sales, even though this is not the legal situation, a sales credit note being issued if the goods are returned. In this situation any goods out on sale or return but not sold at the balance sheet date must be eliminated from sales and debtors and included in stock at the lower of cost and net realizable value.

Example

The following data relates to the year ended 31 December 19X9:

	£
Net sales	100,000
Opening stock	20,000

Purchases	70,000
Closing stock	30,000
Debtors at 31.12.19X9	15,000

At 31.12.19X9 goods still out on sale or return of £10,000 have been included in both sales and debtors. The cost of these goods was £6,000.

The appropriate figures to be included in the year-end accounts are:

Trading account for year ended 31 December 19X9

	£	£
Sales (£100,000 – £10,000)		90,000
Less Cost of sales:		
Opening stock	20,000	
Purchases	70,000	
	90,000	
Less Closing stock (£30,000 + £6,000)	36,000	54,000
Gross profit		£36,000

Balance sheet extract

	£
Current Assets:	
Stocks	36,000
Debtors (£15,000 – £10,000)	5,000

Summary

1   Goods out on sale or return at a balance sheet date should be included in the balance sheet as stock. The normal valuation principle of at the lower of cost and net realizable value applies.

Examination Hints

Goods on sale or return is a topic which has rarely appeared in examination questions in the past.

If you are sure you have understood the key points in this chapter, then move on to Chapter 9.

CHAPTER 9

CONTAINER ACCOUNTS

Chapter contents

Introduction **44**   The ledger accounts **44**   Summary **46**   Examination hints **46**

Learning objective

After studying this chapter you should be able to:

☐ write up the containers stock and containers suspense accounts.

Introduction

If a company charges its customers for returnable cases, which are credited on return, the accounting treatment for the cases will be the same as for containers.

Some businesses sell products that require special containers, for example gas cylinders. To encourage the customers to return the containers they will sometimes make a charge for the containers on delivery and issue a credit note when the containers are returned. In some instances the customers may be charged more than the credit given on return, the difference being a hire charge for the use of the containers.

The Ledger Accounts

Compare this with the consignment account studied in Chapter 7 which is also a specialized profit and loss account.

A containers stock account will be kept that will record the stock of containers owned (both on the premises and out with customers), expenses incurred, hire charges to the customers and any other sundry income. The balancing figure on this account will be the profit or loss on containers. In effect the containers stock account is a separate profit and loss account for containers.

If customers retain the containers they will forego the credit note that would have been issued on return. Practically this has the same effect as if the retained containers had been sold to the customers at a price equal to their returnable value.

Containers sent to customers are not credited to the sales account; instead the credit for these is to a containers suspense account. When the containers are returned the credit notes issued will be debited to this account, the balance on the account representing returnable containers out with customers. If customers fail to return any containers within the time allowed the credit note value that they forego is transferred from the suspense account, as income, to the containers stock account.

The double entry is:

A business may make an insurance claim for lost or damaged containers. The double entry to raise a debtor for a claim is:

Debit   Insurance company
Credit Containers stock

Debit Containers stock	}	with containers purchased.
Credit Supplier (or bank)		
Debit Containers stock	}	with expenses, e.g. repairs
Credit Supplier account (or bank)		and insurance.
Debit Bank	}	with proceeds on sale of scrapped
Credit Containers stock		containers.
Debit Customers' accounts	}	with invoice value of containers
Credit Containers suspense		delivered.

Debit Containers suspense Credit Containers stock	} with any hire charge included in the invoice value.
Debit Containers suspense Credit Customers'	} with credit note value of containers returned by the customers.
Debit Containers suspense Credit Containers stock	} with containers retained by customers.

Containers retained by customers are entered at the value at which credit notes would have been issued had the containers been returned.

At the accounting date the stock of containers owned will be carried down as a balance on the containers stock account and included in the balance sheet with the other stocks. Normally two balances will be carried down, the stock of containers on the premises and the stock of containers in the hands of customers that are still returnable.

The balancing figure on the containers stock account will then represent the profit or loss on containers and is transferred to the profit and loss account, the entry being:

Debit Containers stock Credit Profit and loss	} with profit on containers (entries reversed if it is a loss).

The balancing figure on the containers suspense account is carried down as a liability and deducted from debtors in preparing the balance sheet. It represents credit notes that may be issued in the future when the containers are returned by the customers.

Deduction of the containers suspense account from the debtors in the balance sheet will contra out the amounts included in the debtors for containers out with customers.

Control may be kept on the number of containers owned and with customers by maintaining memorandum quantity columns in the containers stock and containers suspense accounts.

Example

At 1 January 19X7 a business owned 10,000 containers of which 3,000 were in stock and 7,000 were out with customers. During 19X7 30,000 containers were sent out to customers and 28,000 returned. At 31 December 19X7 there were 8,000 containers out with customers that were still returnable and 3,200 in the depot. 2,500 containers were purchased on 1 July 19X7 for £35,000. On 30 September 19X7 300 damaged containers were sold for a scrap value of £150.

The same containers will be sent out and returned several times a year. The quantities delivered to customers during the year will therefore normally be a much greater quantity than the number of containers owned.

Containers are charged to customers at £25 each, the customers being credited with £20 if the container is returned in good condition within three months of delivery. Containers are valued at £7 each for stock purposes.

The ledger accounts to record the above follow. The quantity columns are purely memoranda and the price columns are shown as workings.

Containers stock

		Quantity	Price	£			Quantity	Price	£
1.1.X7	Balance b/d:				30.9.X7	Bank – scrapped	300	—	150
	Stock:				31.12.X7	Containers			
	– in hand	3,000	£7	21,000		suspense – hire			
	– with					charges	—	—	150,000
	customers	7,000	£7	49,000		– retentions	1,000	£20	20,000
1.7.X7	Bank –				31.12.X7	Balance c/d			
	purchases	2,500	£14	35,000		Stock – in hand	3,200	£7	22,400
31.12.X7	Profit and loss					– with			
	(balancing					customers	8,000	£7	56,000
	figure)			143,550					
		12,500		£248,550			12,500		£248,550

Sometimes in examination questions one of the quantity figures is not given in the question and has to be arrived at as a balancing figure in the quantity columns. If in the above example the closing stock at the depot had not been given, the quantity of 3,200 would have been the balancing figure. If all the information is given and the quantity columns do not balance, the difference will be the stock loss or gain for the period. This may be included to balance the quantity columns but no entry in the £ column is required.

Containers suspense

		Quantity	Price	£			Quantity	Price	£
19X7	Containers				1.1.X7	Balance b/d	7,000	£20	140,000
	stock:								
	– hire charges				19X7	Debtors	30,000	£25	750,000
	(30,000 × £5)	—	—	150,000					
19X7	Debtors –								
	returns	28,000	£20	560,000					
31.12.X7	Balance c/d	8,000	£20	160,000					
31.12.X7	Containers								
	stock:								
	– retentions								
	(balancing								
	figure)	1,000	£20	20,000					
		37,000		£890,000			37,000		£890,000

The figure required to balance the quantity columns is the number of containers that have not been returned by the customers within the time allowed.

Note that the quantity columns record the movements of containers. No entry is made in the quantity column for hire charges as these are purely a value adjustment.

Summary

1   The containers stock account will record the containers owned by the company (both in stock and out with customers), expenses, hire charges and sundry income. The balancing figure on this account will be the profit or loss on containers.
2   The containers suspense account will record the charges to customers with regard to containers sent out. The balance, representing future refunds on the return of the containers still out with customers, is deducted from debtors in preparing the balance sheet.
3   Both the containers stock and the containers suspense accounts will contain memorandum quantity columns.

Examination Hints

A container accounts question will normally contain a lot of data. Enter the quantities and prices into your answer, crossing out the relevant section of the question as you go. When all the data in the question has been entered the ledger accounts can be balanced to ascertain any missing figures as balancing items.

To avoid common errors make sure that you:

1   include containers both in hand and out with customers in the stock balances on the containers stock account (both at the beginning and the end of the year!);
2   do not make any entry in the quantity columns for hire charges.

Try to answer the following questions before reading on.

Self-Assessment Questions

In each question, choose the correct answer from the five alternatives given.

See page 303 for answers.

9.1   Which of the following will not appear on the debit side of the containers stock account:
a   stocks of containers c/d
b   purchases of containers
c   insurance of containers

d   cost of overhauling containers

e   profit on containers.

9.2   Which of the following statements is false:

   a   stocks of containers in hand are an asset

   b   returnable containers out with customers are an asset

   c   containers retained by customers are an expense

   d   the balance on the containers suspense account is a liability

   e   hire charges are income.

9.3   A business purchased 10,000 containers. Containers sent to customers totalled 50,000. Of these 43,000 were returned but customers failed to return 2,000 within the time allowed. The business has 3,000 containers on its premises. The total quantity of containers to be included in stock is:

   a   3,000

   b   5,000

   c   7,000

   d   8,000

   e   10,000.

If you have answered the above questions correctly, and are sure you understand the key points in this chapter, then try to answer question 9 on page 194 before moving on to Chapter 10.

CHAPTER 10

ROYALTY ACCOUNTS

Chapter contents

Introduction **48**   Shortworkings **48**   Royalties payable **49**   Royalties receivable **50**
Summary **51**   Examination hints **51**

Learning objectives

After studying this chapter you should be able to:

☐ calculate the amount of any shortworkings;

☐ write up the ledger accounts in the books of the payer;

☐ write up the ledger accounts in the books of the receiver.

Introduction

Royalties arise when:

1   a tenant (the lessee) has the right to extract minerals from land and is required to pay the landlord (the lessor) a rental based on the amount extracted each year;
2   a manufacturer has the right to make products protected by patent, paying the patent holder a sum for every item made (or perhaps sold);
3   payments relating to copyright are made to authors, etc.

   Royalties payable are an expense for the period in which they are incurred. Similarly royalties receivable are treated as income for the period in which they are earned.
   The entries are straightforward but become more complicated if there is a *shortworkings clause* in the contract under which the royalties are paid. A shortworkings clause normally requires a minimum amount to be paid each year. It will often give the right to recover any excess (of the minimum amount over what would otherwise have been paid) by reduction of future payments.

Shortworkings recoverable should not be carried forward when there is no reasonable expectancy of recovery in the future. The concept of prudence (see Chapter 1, SSAP 2) should be applied. Questions normally ignore this point and examiners expect shortworkings recoverable to be carried forward until they become time-expired unless the question clearly indicates otherwise.

Shortworkings

The surplus of any minimum payment made over the royalties for the period may be carried forward as an asset and recovered in future years, providing this is allowed by the contract. A time limit for recovery may be in force; in this case any shortworkings that have not been recovered must be written off when they become time-expired.

Example 1

Licensee Ltd manufacture ribbon cassettes under a licence granted by the patent holder.

The terms of the agreement are that a royalty of 10 pence per cassette manufactured is payable on 31 December each year, subject to a minimum payment of £10,000 per annum. Any shortworkings are recoverable in the two years following that in which they arise.

Production by Licensee Ltd was:

Year	19X1	19X2	19X3	19X4
Quantity produced	60,000	110,000	120,000	130,000

Required: Calculate the royalties payable.

Solution

	19X1	19X2	19X3	19X4
Quantity manufactured	60,000	110,000	120,000	130,000
× pence per unit	10	10	10	10
	£	£	£	£
= Royalties incurred	6,000	11,000	12,000	13,000
+ Shortworkings arising	4,000			
− Shortworkings recovered		1,000	2,000	
= Payment (at least £10,000)	10,000	10,000	10,000	13,000

Under the terms of the contract the 19X1 shortworkings not recovered by the end of 19X3 are time-expired and cannot be recovered in 19X4.

Royalties Payable

An expense account will be opened to record the royalties incurred. An account is opened for any recoverable shortworkings carried forward as an asset. The amounts payable and their settlement are shown in the creditor's account.

The double entry is

Debit	Royalties payable	} with royalties incurred.
Credit	Creditor's	
Debit	Manufacturing	} with royalties incurred for the
Credit	Royalties payable	} year.
Debit	Shortworkings recoverable	} with any shortworkings arising.
Credit	Creditor's	
Debit	Creditor's	} with any shortworkings recovered.
Credit	Shortworkings recoverable	
Debit	Creditor's	} with payment made (this must not
Credit	Bank	} be less than the minimum).
Debit	Profit and loss	} with shortworkings written off
Credit	Shortworkings	} due to time expiry.

Royalties payable on production will be charged to the manufacturing account. Royalties payable on sales are a selling expense and should be included in the profit and loss account.

Irrecoverable shortworkings are not a production expense of the year in which they are written off. Because of this they are not charged to the manufacturing account but to the profit and loss account.

Example 2

The royalty details given in the earlier example will be recorded in the books of Licensee Ltd as follows:

Royalties payable

19X1	Patent holder	£6,000	19X1	Manufacturing a/c	£6,000
19X2	Patent holder	£11,000	19X2	Manufacturing a/c	£11,000
19X3	Patent holder	£12,000	19X3	Manufacturing a/c	£12,000
19X4	Patent holder	£13,000	19X4	Manufacturing a/c	£13,000

Patent holder

		£			£
19X1	Bank	10,000	19X1	Royalties payable	6,000
				Shortworkings recoverable	4,000
		£10,000			£10,000
19X2	Bank	10,000	19X2	Royalties payable	11,000
	Shortworkings recoverable	1,000			
		£11,000			£11,000
19X3	Bank	10,000	19X3	Royalties payable	12,000
	Shortworkings recoverable	2,000			
		£12,000			£12,000
19X4	Bank	£13,000	19X4	Royalties payable	£13,000

Shortworkings recoverable

		£			£
19X1	Patent holder	£4,000	19X1	Balance c/d	£4,000
19X2	Balance b/d	4,000	19X2	Patent holder – recovery	1,000
				Balance c/d	3,000
		£4,000			£4,000
19X3	Balance b/d	3,000	19X3	Patent holder – recovery	2,000
				Profit and loss –	
				irrecoverable	1,000
		£3,000			£3,000

Royalties receivable

The entries in the books of the recipient are fundamentally a mirror of those in the books of the payer. The shortworkings are recorded in a shortworkings allowable account which is carried forward as a liability in the balance sheet.

Example 3

The entries in the books of Patent Holder will be:

Royalties receivable

		£			£
19X1	Profit and loss	£6,000	19X1	Licensee Ltd	£6,000
19X2	Profit and loss	£11,000	19X2	Licensee Ltd	£11,000
19X3	Profit and loss	£12,000	19X3	Licensee Ltd	£12,000
19X4	Profit and loss	£13,000	19X4	Licensee Ltd	£13,000

Licensee Ltd

		£			£
19X1	Royalties receivable	6,000	19X1	Bank	10,000
	Shortworkings allowable	4,000			
		£10,000			£10,000
19X2	Royalties receivable	11,000	19X2	Bank	10,000
				Shortworkings allowable	1,000
		£11,000			£11,000
19X3	Royalties receivable	12,000	19X3	Bank	10,000
				Shortworkings allowable	2,000
		£12,000			£12,000
19X4	Royalties receivable	£13,000	19X4	Bank	£13,000

Shortworkings allowable

		£			£
19X1	Balance c/d	£4,000	19X1	Licensee Ltd	£4,000
19X2	Licensee Ltd	1,000	19X2	Balance b/d	4,000
	Balance c/d	3,000			
		£4,000			£4,000
19X3	Licensee Ltd	2,000	19X3	Balance b/d	3,000
	Profit and loss –				
	irrecoverable	1,000			
		£3,000			£3,000

A complicated situation arises if a tenant, paying a royalty on minerals extracted, sublets to a subtenant on similar terms. In this situation both royalties payable and royalties receivable will be recorded in the books of the tenant in the way outlined in this chapter. However, a point to note is that the royalties payable by the tenant will be based on the total extraction of the tenant and the subtenant.

Summary

1 Royalties will be treated as an expense or income of the period in which they are incurred or earned.
2 Payments made must not be less than any agreed minimum sum.
3 Any shortworkings that are recoverable may be carried forward to be set off against future payments. Irrecoverable shortworkings should be written off as soon as they become time-expired.

Examination Hints

An examination question on royalties is not likely to be very difficult and the book-keeping is reasonably straightforward, the only problem being to remember what it is!

The usual pitfalls can be avoided by reading the question very carefully to determine:

1 which set of books: royalties receivable or royalties payable;
2 if a minimum rent is payable;
3 the period over which any shortworkings may be recovered.

Most students find it helpful to calculate the royalties and any shortworkings arising and recovered prior to making the book-keeping entries. When carrying down a balance on the shortworkings account double check to make sure that no time-expired shortworkings are included in the balance.

Try to answer the following questions before reading on.

Self-Assessment Questions

In each question, choose the correct answer from the five alternatives given.

10.1 A rent of £40 per tonne is payable, merging into a minimum annual rent of £400,000, for extraction of tin under an agreement starting 1.1.X1. Shortworkings may be recovered in the following year. Production for the first three years was 19X1 8,000 tonnes; 19X2 9,000 tonnes; and 19X3 12,000 tonnes. The payment to the landlord for 19X3 will be:

See page 303 for answer.

a £320,000
b £360,000
c £400,000
d £440,000
e £480,000

10.2 Shortworkings recoverable will be included in the balance sheet as a
  a fixed asset
  b deferred asset
  c current asset
  d current liability
  e reserve.

If you have answered the above questions correctly, and are sure you understand the key points in this chapter, then try to answer question 10 on page 195 before moving on to Chapter 11.

CHAPTER 11

HIRE-PURCHASE: BUYER

Chapter contents

Introduction **53**   Calculation of interest charge **53**   Accounting entries **55**
SSAP 21 **60**   Summary **61**   Examination **61**

Learning objectives

After studying this chapter you should be able to:

☐ calculate the amount of interest to be charged to the profit and loss account for each period in accordance with the methods given in SSAP 21;

☐ make the accounting entries relating to the purchase of fixed assets under hire-purchase contracts.

Introduction

This chapter is concerned with recording the entries necessary in the accounting records when a business acquires a fixed asset under a hire-purchase contract. The fundamental situation is that the business acquires the use of a fixed asset, but the payment for the asset is spread over a period of time and interest charges are incurred. In this situation the asset is recorded as if it is owned by the business, even though the legal title to the asset may not be obtained until the last payment under the hire-purchase contract, when often a nominal payment transfers the title.

The contents of SSAP 21 Accounting for Leases and Hire-purchase Contracts are mainly concerned with leasing.

The accounting treatment follows the principle of recording a transaction in accordance with the economic substance of the situation rather than the strict legal position. Assets acquired under these agreements are depreciated in the normal way over their useful working lives. The interest charges incurred are charged to the profit and loss account as an expense each year.

Calculation of Interest Charge

'A hire-purchase contract is a contract for the hire of an asset which contains a provision giving the hirer an option to acquire legal title to the asset upon the fulfilment of certain conditions stated in the contract.' Normally the conditions are fulfilled on the payment of the last instalment, when the asset is purchased for a nominal sum.

This definition of hire-purchase is given in SSAP 21.

The *cash price* is the normal selling price of the asset in a cash sale transaction. The *hire purchase price* is the cash price plus the total interest payable under the contract. The *total interest* is the hire-purchase price less the cash price.

Example 1

A machine is purchased on 1 January 19X5 under a hire-purchase agreement. The normal selling price of the asset is £2,986. Under the agreement a deposit of £500 is to be paid, followed by three annual instalments of £1,000 payable on 31 December each year.

	£
The cash price is	2,986
Less Deposit	500
Balance of cash price	2,486
Add Total interest over the period	
of the agreement	514
Balance of the hire-purchase price	£3,000

The balance of the hire-purchase price is the sum of the instalments payable, in this example three annual instalments of £3,000.

The hire-purchase price is the depost of £500 plus three instalments of £1,000 each, totalling payments of £3,500. The total interest charge over the three year period is £514, being the hire purchase price of £3,500 less the cash price of £2,986. The rate of interest may be expressed as a nominal rate per annum based on the amount borrowed (the balance of the cash price). If the interest of £514 is merely divided by three the annual interest would be £171, which on the balance of the cash price of £2,486 gives a *nominal interest rate* of 6.9%.

If the same amount of interest is charged to each period, despite the fact that the balance owing is reduced by each instalment, the treatment is known as the *straight line* method, otherwise known as *level spread*. Under this method, if each instalment was to be analysed between repayment of the cash price (repayment of principal) and payment of interest, it would be as follows:

	Total	Interest	Principal
	£	£	£
1st instalment	1,000	171	829
2nd instalment	1,000	171	829
3rd instalment	1,000	172	828
	£3,000	£514	£2,486

However, the nominal interest rate ignores the fact that part of the cash price is being repaid with each instalment. If the interest is calculated on the balance of the cash price remaining owing after each instalment is repaid, the *actuarial rate of interest* is 10%. This can be demonstrated as follows:

	£
1.01.X5 Cash price	2,986
Less Deposit	500
1.01.X5 Balance of cash price	2,486
31.12.X5 *Add* Interest for 19X5 (10% × £2,486)	249
	2,735
31.12.X5 *Less* Instalment	1,000
	1,735
31.12.X6 *Add* Interest for 19X6 (10% × £1,735)	174
	1,909
31.12.X6 *Less* Instalment	1,000
	909
31.12.X7 *Add* Interest for 19X7 (10% × £909)	91
	1,000
31.12.X7 *Less* Instalment	1,000
	—

In this example the repayments are made annually and therefore the actuarial rate of interest has been calculated on the balance of cash price outstanding at the beginning of each year. If the instalments were payable monthly the calculation would be based on monthly steps. Normally the actuarial rate of interest will be very much higher than the nominal rate.

Each instalment would then be analysed as follows:

	Total	Interest	Principal
	£	£	£
1st instalment	1,000	249	751
2nd instalment	1,000	174	826
3rd instalment	1,000	91	909
	£3,000	£514	£2,486

An alternative way of calculating the interest allocation to each period is the *sum of the digits* method, otherwise known as the *rule of 78*. Where instalments are paid the sum of the digits is calculated by adding together the number of instalments not yet due at the beginning of each period. In the example there are three annual instalments paid at the end of each year. The sum of the digits for the instalments is (3 + 2 + 1) = 6. The interest would be apportioned on this basis, i.e.:

	Total	Interest	Principal
	£	£	£
1st instalment	1,000 (³⁄₆ × £514)	257	743
2nd instalment	1,000 (²⁄₆ × £514)	171	829
3rd instalment	1,000 (¹⁄₆ × £514)	86	914
	£3,000		£514	£2,486

The sum of the digits method gives an interest charge for each period which approximates to that arrived at using the more precise actuarial method. The calculations, however, are more straightforward. The method is sometimes referred to as the rule of 78 because the sum of the digits for twelve monthly instalments is (12 + 11 + 10 + 9 + 8 + 7 + 6 + 5 + 4 + 3 + 2 + 1) = 78. In this situation the first month would bear $^{12}/_{78}$ths of the total interest, the second month $^{11}/_{78}$ths and so on for each of the twelve months.

In this example we have calculated the interest chargeable to each period using three different methods as follows:

	Straight line	Actuarial	Sum of the digits
	£	£	£
1st instalment	171	249	257
2nd instalment	171	174	171
3rd instalment	172	91	86
Total interest	£514	£514	£514

The sum of the digits can be calculated using the formula:

$$\frac{x(x+1)}{2}$$

where **x** is the number of instalments e.g. the sum of the digits for three instalments:

$$\frac{3(3+1)}{2} = 6$$

and the sum of the digits for 12 instalments:

$$\frac{12(12+1)}{2} = 78$$

The three different methods are significant in that one of these methods has to be used to determine the amount of interest to be charged to the profit and loss account for each period.

SSAP 21 Accounting for Leases and Hire Purchase Contracts indicates that the interest should be allocated to accounting periods to produce a constant periodic rate of charge on the remaining balance of the cash price during each accounting period, or a reasonable approximation. The acturial method gives the most accurate result and the sum of the digits method gives an acceptable approximation. The straight line method may be used if the total interest is not material in size or significance in the circumstances of the company.

An examination question on this topic would normally indicate the method to be used.

Accounting Entries

A fixed asset acquired under a hire-purchase agreement is recorded in the appropriate fixed asset account at the cash price (the fair value) and is depreciated over its useful working life in the normal way. The hire-purchase price is recorded as a liability and is reduced by the payment of the deposit and the instalments. The total interest is recorded on a suspense account and the interest charge for the year is transferred to the profit and loss account year by year over the life of the agreement.

The initial double entry is:

Debit	A fixed asset account	– with the *cash price*.
Debit	HP interest suspense	– with the *total interest*.
Credit	HP loan	– with the *total HP price*.

A separate HP interest suspense account and HP loan account should be opened for each agreement.

Any payments made are:

Debit	HP loan	} with the *deposit* and *instalments paid*.
Credit	Bank	

On preparing a profit and loss account:

Debit	HP interest	} with the *interest charge for the period*.
Credit	HP interest suspense	

and then

Debit	Profit and loss	} with the total interest charge for the
Credit	HP interest	period for all agreements.

If the company is only buying one asset it would only have one HP interest suspense account, and in these circumstances the interest could be charged straight to the profit and loss account. The HP interest account is only necessary where there are two or more agreements, in order to arrive at the total interest that would appear, as only one amount, in the profit and loss account.

Example 2: Basic principles

Using the data for Example 1, the ledger accounts would be:

Machinery – at cost

		£			£
1.1.X5	Cost	2,986			

HP Loan re Machine

	£			£
1.1.X5 Bank – deposit	500		1.1.X5 HP Price	3,500
31.12.X5 bank – 1st instal.	1,000			
31.12.X5 Balance c/d	2,000			
	£3,500			£3,500
31.12.X6 Bank – 2nd instal.	1,000		1.1.X6 Balance b/d	2,000
31.12.X6 Balance c/d	1,000			
	£2,000			£2,000
31.12.X7 Bank – 3rd instal.	1,000		1.1.X7 Balance b/d	1,000

HP Interest suspense re Machine

	£			£
1.1.X5 Total interest	514		31.12.X5 P&L a/c	257
			31.12.X5 Balance c/d	257
	£514			£514
1.1.X6 Balance b/d	257		31.12.X6 P&L a/c	171
			31.12.X6 Balance c/d	86
	£257			£257
1.1.X7 Balance b/d	£86		31.12.X7 P&L a/c	£86

The sum of the digits method has been used in this example. Interest charge for the year has been transferred directly to the profit and loss account on the assumption that there are no other hire-purchase agreements. It should be noted that the machine would be depreciated each year, but the entries for this have not been shown above.

When preparing a balance sheet assets being purchased under hire-purchase agreements are not separately identified on the balance sheet, but are included under fixed assets together with the other assets owned by the company. A note to the accounts should be given of the net book value of assets held under hire-purchase contracts.

The balance on the hire-purchase interest suspense account is deducted from the balance on the hire-purchase loan account and the net amount, which represents the balance of the cash price outstanding, is included on the balance sheet as a creditor and described as 'Obligations under hire-purchase contracts'. They should be analysed between current liabilities or long-term liabilities, as appropriate, depending on when the instalments are payable. For example:

Balance sheet extract

	As at	
	31.12.X5	31.12.X6
	£	£
Long-term liabilities:		
Obligations under hire-purchase contracts (£1,000–£86)	914	—
Current liabilities:		
Obligations under hire-purchase contracts (£1,000–£171)	829	914
	£1,743	£914

Note: These amounts are represented by the balances on the following accounts and can be reconciled as follows:

	31.12.X5	31.12.X6
	£	£
HP company – credit balance	2,000	1,000
Less HP interest suspense – debit balance	257	86
	£1,743	£914

Example 3: Quarterly instalments and disposal of asset

On 1 April 19X0 Trader purchased a machine under a hire-purchase agreement. The cash price of this machine was £20,000 and £4,000 was paid as a deposit, the balance payable by twelve quarterly instalments of £1,750. The first instalment was payable on 30 June 19X0, and thereafter on the last day of each quarter.

Trader paid the instalments as they became due until he sold the machine on 1 July 19X2 for £8,600. The hire-purchase company accepted £4,100 in settlement of the balance of the hire-purchase commitment.

Trader provided depreciation in respect of the machine at the rate of 20% per annum on the straight line basis providing depreciation for each month of use. Hire-purchase interest was deemed to accrue evenly over the period of the agreement.

The financial year of Trader ends on 31 December.

Required:
Show the ledger accounts in the books of Trader recording the above transactions for the years 19X0, 19X1 and 19X2.

Solution
The first step is to calculate the hire-purchase price and total interest as follows:

	£
Deposit	4,000
Instalments (12 × £1,750)	21,000

	£
HP price	25,000
Less Cash price	20,000
Total interest	£5,000

The initial entry will be:

Debit	Machinery	– £20,000 cash price.
Debit	HP interest suspense	– £5,000 total interest.
Credit	HP loan	– £25,000 HP price.

The second step is to calculate the apportionment of interest. The interest charge for each accounting period is to be accrued evenly over the period of the agreement; this is the straight line method. Note that only nine months interest will be chargeable to the first accounting period as the machine was purchased on 1st April 19X0, three months through the year.

Total interest would normally be apportioned over the 36 months of the agreement as follows:

		£
Year ending 31 December 19X0	($9/36 \times$ £5,000)	1,250
Year ending 31 December 19X1	($12/36 \times$ £5,000)	1,667
Year ending 31 December 19X2	($12/36 \times$ £5,000)	1,667
Year ending 31 December 19X3	($3/36 \times$ £5,000)	416
		£5,000

But as the machine is sold on the 1 July 19X2, and the hire purchase interest is settled at that date, the actual interest will be restricted to:

		£
Year ending 31 December 19X0		1,250
Year ending 31 December 19X1		1,667
Year ending 31 December 19X2	($6/36 \times$ £5,000)	833
		£3,750

The balance of total interest (£5,000 – £3,750) = £1,250 will not be incurred and is transferred to the HP loan, reducing the balance outstanding on that account.

The ledger accounts will be written up as follows:

Machinery

	£		£
1.4.X0 Addition	20,000	1.7.X2 Disposal	20,000

In this example no opening balances are given for the machinery and provision for depreciation of machinery accounts in relation to assets already owned in order that the effect of the entries for the machine purchased can be clearly seen.

Provision for depreciation of machine

	£		£
		31.12.X0 P&L (£20,000 $\times 20/100 \times 9/12$)	3,000
		31.12.X1 P&L	4,000
			7,000
1.7.X2 Disposal	9,000	31.12.X2 P&L (£20,000 $\times 20/100 \times 6/12$)	2,000
	£9,000		£9,000

HP loan

	£		£
1.4.X0 Bank deposit	4,000	1.4.X0 Machinery HP (£4,000 +	
31.12.X0 Bank (3 × £1,750)	5,250	12 × £1,750)	25,000
Balance c/d	15,750		
	£25,000		£25,000
To			
31.12.X1 Bank (4 × £1,750)	7,000	1.1.X1 Balance b/d	15,750
Balance c/d	8,750		
	£15,750		£15,750
To			
30.6.X2 Bank (2 × £1,750)	3,500	1.1.X2 Balance b/d	8,750
HP interest	1,250	1.7.X2 Disposal	100
Bank	4,100		
	£8,850		£8,850

HP interest suspense

	£		£
1.4.X0 Machinery	5,000	31.12.X0 P&L ($\frac{9}{36}$ × £5,000)	1,250
		Balance c/d	3,750
	£5,000		£5,000
1.1.X1 Balance b/d	3,750	31.12.X1 P&L	1,667
		Balance c/d	2,083
	£3,750		£3,750
1.1.X2 Balance b/d	2,083	1.7.X2 HP Co.	1,250
		31.12.X2 P&L	833
	£2,083		£2,083

Disposal of machinery

	£		£
1.7.X2 Machine	20,000	1.7.x2 Depreciation	9,000
HP Co.	100	Bank	8,600
		31.12.X2 P&L	2,500
	£20,100		£20,100

On the disposal of the machine the cost and accumulated depreciation are transferred to a disposal account and any proceeds of sale are credited to the disposal account. Any balance remaining on the HP loan account is also transferred to the disposal account; in this example the HP company appears to have made a charge of £100 for earlier termination of the contract. The balance on the disposal account represents depreciation under- or over-provided during the asset's working life and is transferred to the profit and loss account; in this example depreciation under-provided amounts to £2,500.

Note that the example specified that interest was to be apportioned using the straight line method. If the example had specified that the sum of the digits method was to be used the calculations would have been as follows:

Quarter commencing	No. of instalments not yet due	Interest £	Apportioned £
1.4.X0	12	769	
1.7.X0	11	705	
1.10.X0	10	641	
19X0			2,115
1.1.X1	9	577	
1.4.X1	8	513	
1.7.X1	7	449	
1.10.X1	6 ÷ 78 × £5,000	385	
19X1			1,924
1.1.X2	5	321	
1.4.X2	4	256	
1.7.X2	3	192	
1.10.X2	2	128	
19X2			897
1.1.X3	1	64	
19X3			64
Sum of the digits	78	Total interest	£5,000

Where instalments are paid monthly the interest would have to be calculated for each month, rather than for each quarter as in this example.

Using this method the HP interest suspense account would have shown the following entries:

HP interest suspense

	£		£
1.4.X0 Machinery	5,000	31.12.X0 P&L	2,115
		Balance c/d	2,885
	£5,000		£5,000
1.1.X1 Balance b/d	2,885	31.12.X1 P&L	1,924
		Balance c/d	961
	£2,885		£2,885
1.1.X2 Balance b/d	961	1.7.X2 HP Co. (£192 + £128 + £64)	384
		31.12.X2 P&L (£321 + £256)	577
	£961		£961

SSAP 21

A company (the lessee) may lease an asset rather than purchase it outright or buy it on hire-purchase. Under a lease the company will pay rentals rather than hire-purchase instalments. Hire-purchase is within the examination syllabus but leasing is not mentioned. SSAP 21, however, covers both hire-purchase and leasing.

SSAP 21 defines a *lease* as a contract between a lessor and a lessee for the hire of a specific asset. The lessor retains ownership of the asset but conveys the right to the use of the asset to the lessee for an agreed period of time in return for the payment of rentals.

Under a finance lease the legal title to the asset normally never passes to the user.

A *finance lease* is one that transfers substantially all the risks and rewards of ownership of the asset to the lessee. An *operating lease* is a lease other than a finance lease.

The accounting entries for a finance lease are very similar to the entries required for hire-purchase agreements. The difference between the total rentals payable and the cash price is the total interest (called 'finance charge'). The finance charge is apportioned to each accounting period using the actuarial, sum of the digits or straight line method as appropriate. On the balance sheet the asset is included at the cash purchase price and is depreciated in the usual manner, except that it should be depreciated over the length of the lease if this is shorter than the asset's working life. The liability included on the balance sheet is the future rentals payable less the finance charges included therein.

The initial accounting entries are

Debit A fixed asset account with the *cash price*.
Debit Lease finance charges suspense account with the *total interest*.
Credit Lessee's account with the total *rentals*.

The accounting treatment for an operating lease is entirely different. The lease will be for a short period and it is not recorded as an asset because the lessee will not have the use of the asset for most of its working life. The rentals payable are treated as an expense and are debited to the profit and loss account of the period to which they relate. No liability to pay rentals for future periods is included, although, of course, rentals that have accrued due but have not been paid will be provided for as an expense owing.

SSAP 21 requires a *note to the accounts* to be made analysing the balance sheet liability with regard to finance leases and hire-purchase agreements falling due after more than one year, between the amounts due in the second to fifth years, and thereafter. A note is also required stating the total of future rentals to be paid under existing operating leases, similarly analysed between one year, two to five years, and thereafter.

The ASC guidance notes on SSAP 21 state that the straight line method may be appropriate in connection with a relatively small lease as it may produce figures which in any year are not significantly different from those which would be produced by one of the other methods.

The user is called the *lessee*; the owner is called the *lessor*.

Summary

1   A fixed asset acquired under a hire-purchase agreement will be recorded at cash price and depreciated in accordance with the company's normal policy.
2   The hire-purchase price will be recorded as a liability in a hire-purchase loan account; payments made in respect of the agreement will be debited to this account.
3   The total interest (the excess of the hire-purchase price over the cash price) will be debited to a hire-purchase interest suspense account. Interest incurred may be charged to the profit and loss account each year using the actuarial or the sum of the digits methods. The straight line method may be used if the interest is not material.
4   When preparing the balance sheet the balance on the hire-purchase interest suspense account will be deducted from the balance on the hire-purchase loan account.

Examination Hints

The question must be read carefully to determine the period for which the ledger accounts should be written up. Often a question will require ledger accounts for only one or two years and not for all the years of any particular agreement. Do not omit to bring down any opening balances on the fixed asset and provision for depreciation accounts. Carry down the balances on all accounts at each accounting year end.

The cash price and the hire-purchase price (or total finance lease rentals) must be ascertained to determine the total finance charges. These must be written off to the profit and loss account in accordance with the method specified by the question. Calculate the finance charge prior to writing up the ledger accounts. Be careful to charge interest for only the appropriate number of months in the first year of the contract.

If payments are made monthly it will be acceptable to enter the total for each accounting period.

Do not omit to provide for depreciation each year, if this is required by the question.

Try to answer the following questions before reading on.

Self-Assessment Questions

In each question, choose the correct answer from the five alternatives given.

See page 303 for answers.

11.1   Fixed asset accounts record all:
    a   assets owned
    b   assets owned and purchased under hire-purchase contracts
    c   assets owned, leased and purchased under hire-purchase contracts
    d   assets owned, used under finance leases and purchased under hire-purchase contracts.
    e   assets in use.

11.2 The balance on the account for the HP loan is the balance of the:

a HP price
b cash price
c total interest
d hire-purchase price less total interest
e hire-purchase price plus total interest.

11.3 The total hire-purchase interest may be apportioned to each year of the agreement by the following number of methods:

a one
b two
c three
d four
e five.

11.4 One of the differences between a finance lease and an operating lease is:
a the asset is not owned under an operating lease
b the asset is recorded as owned under an operating lease
c the rental under an operating lease is apportioned between finance charges and repayment of fair value
d payments under a finance lease represent substantially the whole of the fair value of the asset
e rentals under a finance lease are treated as an expense.

If you have answered the above questions correctly, and are sure you understand the key points in this chapter, then try to answer question 11 on page 195 before moving on to Chapter 12.

CHAPTER 12

HIRE-PURCHASE: SELLER

Chapter contents

Introduction **63** Calculation of selling profit and finance charges earned **63** Accounting entries **64** Repossessions **68** Leasing **68** Summary **68** Examination hints **68**

Learning objectives

After studying this chapter you should be able to:

☐ calculate the profit to be taken in the year of sale with regard to hire-purchase sales;

☐ calculate the amount of finance charges earned to be credited to the profit and loss account for each year in accordance with SSAP 21

☐ make the accounting entries for the sale of goods under hire-purchase contracts;

☐ make the necessary entries for goods repossessed.

Introduction

Hire-purchase sales in the books of the seller should not present too many problems if the entries in the books of the buyer are understood. Additional material to be studied relates to the recognition of profit and to the repossession of goods on default of a customer.

The excess of the hire-purchase price over cost is the gross earnings on the hire-purchase contract. This may be analysed into:

1 the *selling profit*: the difference between cash sale price and cost represents profit on sale, which may be recognized in the year of sale;

2 the *finance charge*: the interest charged, which is credited to the profit and loss account over the life of the contract.

A finance company's earnings on a contract will be their finance charges to the customer.

Most businesses selling goods on both hire-purchase and cash (or credit) terms will use the services of a finance company for the hire-purchase sales, in effect selling the goods to the finance company. This chapter deals with the situation of a manufacturer or dealer undertaking both types of sales.

Calculation of Selling Profit and Finance Charges Earned

The selling profit under a hire-purchase contract is the excess of the cash selling price of the goods over the cost to the seller. This profit may be taken to the profit and loss account in the year of sale.

In cases where the cash selling price is not known, the fair value of goods is used. The fair value is the price at which an asset could be exchanged in an arm's length transaction.

Hire-purchase contracts frequently calculate the total interest as a fixed percentage for the life of the contract on the balance of the hire-purchase price after deduction of any deposit. This fixed percentage is only a nominal rate; the actuarial rate will be higher, as the nominal rate does not take account of the amount of the loan being repaid in each instalment. The sum of the digits method approximates to the actuarial rate of interest.

Similar entries are required for sales under finance leases.

The excess of the hire-purchase price over the normal selling price represents the total finance charge (the interest) over the period of the agreement and is apportioned to the profit and loss account over the life of the contract. The interest should be apportioned by using an actuarial method that will give a constant periodic rate of return. The calculation of such methods is complex and is more appropriately examined at advanced professional levels. The sum of the digits method is an acceptable approximation. The calculations for this method are the same as in Chapter 11.

Accounting Entries

The total amounts receivable under a hire-purchase contract should be analysed by the seller between cash price and finance charges. The initial entry is:

Debit	HP debtor	—	with the *total HP Price*.
Credit	Sales	—	with the *cash price*.
Credit	HP interest suspense	—	with the *total interest*.

Note that, unlike in the books of a purchaser, a separate account would not be opened for the finance charge for each agreement. A separate account in the sales ledger would of course be opened for each customer.

Any payments received are:

Debit   Bank
Credit HP debtor
} with the *deposit and instalments received*.

On preparing a profit and loss account:

Debit   HP interest suspense
Credit Profit and loss
} with the *interest earned for the period*.

Example

A trading company sells one standard product, either for cash or through a finance company. During the year it has started to make some sales under its own hire-purchase scheme.

The trial balance at 31 December 19X7 is:

	£	£
Share capital		50,000
Profit and loss account		100,000
Fixed assets	130,000	
Amount due from finance company	60,000	
HP instalments receivable	23,400	
Bank	4,600	
Stock – 1 January 19X7	84,000	
Creditors		114,000
Sales – cash		44,000
– finance company		682,000
– hire-purchase		26,000
Purchases	635,000	
Expenses	79,000	
	£1,016,000	£1,016,000

Stocks at 31 December 19X7 were £90,000.
Hire-purchase sales were on the following terms:

	£
Cash price	2,200
Less Deposit	200
	2,000
Add Interest	400
Balance	£2,400

The balance is payable by 24 monthly instalments of £100.
Hire-purchase instalments receivable consist of

	Oct.	Nov.	Dec.	Total
	£	£	£	£
Sales – HP price	2,600	10,400	13,000	26,000
Less Cash received				
Deposits	(200)	(800)	(1,000)	(2,000)
Instalments	(200)	(400)	—	(600)
Balance due	£2,200	£9,200	£12,000	£23,400

Required:
Profit and loss account for the year ended 31 December 19X7 and a balance sheet at that date.

Solution
The first problem is to calculate the total hire-purchase interest. The HP price of each item sold is:

	£
Cash price	2,200
Total interest	400
HP price	£2,600

The HP sales have been credited with 10 items sold at the HP price of £2,600 = £26,000. Only the cash price of £2,200 per item should be credited to sales, the interest of £400 per item should be credited to a HP interest suspense account. The sales should therefore be reduced by (10 × £400) £4,000 interest which should be taken to the HP interest suspense account.

The next problem is to determine how much of the interest has been earned during the year and can be transferred to the profit and loss account from the HP interest suspense account. Using the sum of the digits method it is helpful first to determine the number of instalments received and outstanding for each contract. These are:

Month of sale:	Oct.	Nov.	Dec.	Total
Number of items sold:	1	4	5	10
HP sales	£2,600	£10,400	£13,000	
HP price	£2,600	£2,600	£2,600	
No. of instalments received:	2	4	—	6
Cash received	£200	£400		
Instalment	£100	£100		
No. of instalments not yet due:	22	92	120	234
Total instalments	(1 × 24) 24	(4 × 24) 96	(5 × 24) 120	240

It is now necessary to apportion the interest to the instalments received. For each item the total interest is £400. Interest earned will be calculated for each month as:

$$\frac{\text{Number of instalments not yet due}}{\text{Sum of the digits of total number of instalments}} \times £400$$

Assuming that all sales were effected on the last day of the month, October sales would earn interest for November and December only.

The sum of the digits of 24 is

$$\frac{(24 / 25)}{2} = 300.$$

Interest Earned

			£
Re Oct. sales:			
1st instalment:	$\frac{24 \times £400}{300}$	$= £32 \times 1$ item	32
2nd instalment:	$\frac{23 \times £400}{300}$	$= £31 \times 1$ item	31
Re Nov. sales:			
1st instalment:	$\frac{24 \times £400}{300}$	$= £32 \times 4$ items	128
			£191

Interest to be carried forward at 31 December 19X7 will be (Total interest £4,000 – Interest earned £191) £3,809.

The balance to be carried forward on the HP interest suspense account for interest not yet earned can be proved using the formula:

$$\frac{\text{Sum of the digits of no. of instalments not yet due}}{\text{Sum of the digits of total instalments}}$$

	No. of instalments not yet due	Sum of the digits			Provision for unearned interest
Oct. sales:	22	253	$\frac{253 \times £400}{300}$	$= £337 \times 1$ item	337
Nov. sales:	23	276	$\frac{276 \times £400}{300}$	$= £368 \times 4$ items	1,472
Dec. sales:					
Sold on 31 December (no interest earned)				$£400 \times 5$ items	2,000
					£3,809

The year end accounts will be:

In this example the selling price is £2,200 therefore the number of items sold was:

Cash	$\frac{£44,000}{£2,200} = 20$
Finance company	$\frac{£682,000}{£2,200} = 310$
Hire-purchase	$\frac{£22,000}{£2,200} = 10$
	340

The cost of each unit sold was $\left(\frac{£629,000}{340}\right)$ £1,850

The gross profit of £119,000 represents 340 items sold at a selling profit of (£2,200 – £1,850) £350 per item.

Trading and profit and loss account for year ended 31 December 19X7

	£	£
Sales – cash	44,000	
– finance company	682,000	
– hire-purchase (£26,000 – £4,000)	22,000	
		748,000
Less Cost of sales:		
Opening stock	84,000	
Purchases	635,000	
	719,000	
Less: Closing stock	90,000	
		629,000
Gross profit		119,000
Add Income:		
Interest from hire-purchase contracts		191
		119,191

	£	£
Less Expenses		79,000
Net profit for year		40,191
Balance brought forward		100,000
Balance carried forward		£140,191

Balance sheet as at 31 December 19X1

	£	£
Fixed assets		130,000
Current Assets:		
Stock	90,000	
Debtors – finance company	60,000	
– hire purchase customers		
(23,400 – £3,809)	19,591	
Bank	4,600	
	174,191	
Less Creditors	114,000	
		60,191
		£190,191
Financed by:		
Share capital		50,000
Profit and loss account		140,191
		£190,191

Note that the hire-purchase debtors represent the balance of the cash price not received (calculated by deducting interest not yet earned from the total amount due from the hire-purchase customers). A provision for doubtful debts should be created to cover any likelihood that customers will default on paying instalments.

A very much more prudent method of recognizing profits is sometimes adopted by spreading the selling profit on hire-purchase sales over the life of the agreement, normally in proportion to the cash received from the customers. If this method was applied to this question an additional item would appear in the profit and loss account as a deduction from gross profit:

	£
Provision for unrealized profit on hire-purchase sales	3,117

Calculated as follows:

$$\frac{\text{Balance not due}}{\text{HP sales}} \times \text{Selling profit}$$

$$= \frac{£19,591}{£22,000} \times 10 \text{ items} \times £350$$

$$= \frac{£19,591}{£22,000} \times £3,500$$

$$= £3,117$$

This provision would also be deducted from the hire-purchase debtors on the balance sheet. In subsequent years it would only be necessary to debit or credit the profit or loss account to increase or reduce the balance brought forward on this account to the amount required at the end of the year.

Repossessions

In some cases of default, by non-payment of the instalments, the seller will repossess the goods. The accounting entries necessary will be:

Debit Repossessed goods
Credit Customer
} with the outstanding instalments.

Debit HP interest suspense
Credit Repossessed goods
} with the interest on the contract that has not been earned at the date of repossession.

Debit Repossessed goods
Credit Bank (or creditor)
} with any expenses incurred with regard to repossessed goods.

If the goods are then re-sold the entry will be:

Debit Customer
Credit Repossessed goods
} with the selling price.

If the goods remain unsold at the balance sheet date, carry down the goods at the valuation placed upon them for stock purposes as a debit balance on repossessed goods account and include in stock on the balance sheet.

Any remaining difference on the repossessed goods account should be transferred to the profit and loss account as the profit or loss on repossessed goods.

Leasing

An asset held to be let under an operating lease will be treated as a fixed asset and be depreciated over its useful life. Such an asset may be leased to several customers during the course of its life. Rentals receivable from operating leases are credited to the profit and loss account as income earned for the year to which the rental relates.

The gross earnings from finance leases will be apportioned to each year of the lease in accordance with one of the specialized actuarial methods outlined in SSAP 21. These are outside the scope of your syllabus.

Summary

1 The cash selling price will be credited to the sales account.
2 Total interest will be credited to a hire-purchase interest suspense account, from where it will be credited to the profit and loss account over the life of the agreement using either the actuarial or the sum of the digits methods.
3 The customer's account will be debited with the hire-purchase price and credited with payments received.
4 When preparing a balance sheet the balance on the hire-purchase interest suspense account will be deducted from debtors.

Examination Hints

The accounting records for HP sales are a complex and specialist area. However, if faced with a question in an examination remember that the principles are the same as for the more straightforward records of a buyer. It will be important to apportion the interest earned in precisely the method asked for by the question; this could reasonably be expected, at this level of examination, to be the sum of the digits method, although past questions have required gross earnings to be apportioned on the basis of cash received.

Try to answer the following questions before reading on.

Self-Assessment Questions

In each question, choose the correct answer from the five alternatives given. See page 304 for answers.

12.1   Profit taken in the year of a hire purchase sale is:
    a   gross profit on the sale
    b   gross profit plus a proportion of total interest
    c   gross profit less a proportion of total interest
    d   a proportion of gross profit less a proportion of total interest
    e   gross profit plus total interest less a proportion of both.

12.2   The sum of the digits of 10 is:
    a   50
    b   55
    c   78
    d   110
    e   220.

12.3   HP debtors on a balance sheet represent:
    a   future instalments receivable from customers
    b   arrears of instalments which have become due but have not been paid by customers
    c   arrears of instalments plus future instalments not yet due
    d   arrears of instalments plus future instalments not yet due less interest included in future instalments
    e   arrears of instalments plus future instalments not yet due plus interest included in future instalments.

12.4   Repossessed goods taken back into stock are credited to repossessed goods account at:
    a   cost
    b   selling price
    c   lower of cost and selling price
    d   lower of cost and net realizable value
    e   deposit and instalments received.

If you have answered the above questions correctly, and are sure you understand the key points in this chapter, then try to answer questions 12, 13 and 14 on pages 196–7 before moving on to Chapter 13.

CHAPTER 13

BRANCH ACCOUNTS: HEAD OFFICE RECORDING BRANCH TRANSACTIONS

Chapter contents

Introduction **70**   The accounting records **70**   Branch stock account **72**   The accounting records for branch stock account **72**   Summary **75**   Examination hints **76**

Learning objectives

After studying this chapter you should be able to:

☐ write up the accounts in the books of the head office necessary to record the transactions of the branch;

☐ state the advantages of charging a branch at selling price for goods sent to it;

☐ write up the branch stock account where goods are charged at selling price.

Introduction

A business will often operate from many locations, for example from a factory, office and distribution depots. Its ledger accounts would normally be organized so that it can determine the expenses incurred in respect of each location by having separate expense accounts. If a business sells goods or provides services from another location, this is normally called a branch and is the administrative responsibility of a branch manager. This chapter deals with the organization of the head office accounting records to determine the profit and loss made by the branch.

Larger branches may be self-accounting, keeping their own independent set of accounting records. This situation will be covered in the following chapter. This chapter covers the recording in the head office books of the transactions undertaken by the branch where the branch does not keep its own set of books.

The Accounting Records

Branch accounting, where all the accounting records are kept by head office, is essentially a matter of analysing transactions by branch.

Most introductory costing and data processing textbooks discuss the design of coding structures.

A head office will normally wish to keep separate accounts in the nominal ledger for sales made by the branch, any purchases made by the branch, its various expenses, assets and liabilities and the cost of any goods that have been sent to the branch by the head office. Effectively this means that the head office will have a section of its nominal ledger devoted to the branch. If it adopts this method it will be able to prepare a separate profit and loss account for the branch.

The preparation of the profit and loss account and balance sheet for the whole business will require the addition of the accounts for the head office and the branch for each item. To facilitate this a business will often use the same code numbers for each nominal ledger account, with a prefix identifying the head office and branch. For example:

	Head Office	East Ham Branch	Slough Branch	Watford Branch
Share capital	A0001			
Profit and loss account	A0101			
Stocks	A0201	E0201	S0201	W0201
Sales	A0301	E0301	S0301	W0301
Purchases	A0401	E0401	S0401	W0401
Rent receivable	A0501	E0501	S0501	W0501
Rent payable	A0601	E0601	S0601	W0601
Rates payable	A0602	E0602	S0602	W0602
Motor vehicles	A1001	E1001	S1001	W1001
Provision for depn. of motor vehicles	A1101	E1101	S1101	W1101
Loan payable	A1201			
Cash	A2001	E2001	S2001	W2001
Bank	A2101			

This is just a small selection of the accounts to give an indication of a coding structure that could be used. In the case of the above business it is:

Account numbers	Type of account
1 – 100	Share capital accounts
101 – 200	Reserve accounts
201 – 300	Stock accounts
301 – 400	Sales accounts
401 – 500	Purchases accounts
501 – 600	Income accounts
601 – 1000	Expense accounts
1001 – 1100	Fixed asset accounts
1101 – 1200	Provision for depreciation of fixed asset accounts
1201 – 1300	Liabilities accounts
2001 – 2100	Cash accounts
2101 – 2200	Bank account

There would be separate sections of the nominal ledger for each branch; often nominal ledger controls are maintained for each section. Most introductory financial accounting textbooks have a chapter devoted to control accounts.

The branches will not have their own share capital and reserves and therefore accounts are not required for these. In this example, although it is not always the case, the branches do not have their own bank accounts, all receipts being paid into the one bank account and all payments by cheque being made by head office, where the accounting staff and records are located. The branches will normally have a petty cash float each, reimbursed under the imprest system.

Internal control is greatly increased by requiring all branches to bank receipts intact each day, and by having separate systems for petty cash and cheque payments.

Where branches bank cash sales the double entry will be:

Debit   Bank
Credit   Branch cash sales

Where branches effect credit sales the double entry will be:

Debit   Customer
Credit   Branch credit sales

The head office will normally sectionalize the sales ledger, each section containing the customer accounts for one branch.

Purchases made by the branch will be entered:

Debit   Branch purchases
Credit   Supplier

Often the purchases ledger is not sectionalized, purchases made by the head office and the branches from the same supplier will all be credited to the one supplier's account. This facilitates payment to the supplier.

A head office may send goods out of its own stock to a branch. The double entry will be:

Debit   Branch goods received from head office
Credit   Head office goods sent to branch

Departmental accounts will have been studied at an earlier stage and may be revised by reference to an introductory financial accounting textbook such as Frank Wood's *Business Accounting 1* (Longman 1984).

In preparing profit and loss accounts the accounts relating to the transfer of goods will be entered in the trading accounts; otherwise preparation of the final accounts is a very similar exercise to that of departmental accounts.

Branch Stock Account

In some organizations branches will make no purchases themselves but receive all their supplies via head office. Typically this will apply where the branches are retail outlets and are numerous, as in the case of a chain store.

The selling price of the goods may be fixed by the head office rather than left to the discretion of individual managers. If this is so, it is possible to maintain control over the branch stocks by recording the goods sent to the branch at selling rather than cost price. The opening stock at the branch valued at selling price plus the selling value of goods sent to the branch during a period less the sales actually accounted for during the period should represent the remaining unsold stock at sales value. Any discrepancy between the stock so calculated and actual stocks valued at selling price may be due to:

The system depends on the branch making regular stock counts and returning these to head office. Most organizations will have internal audit checks on the actual branch stocks.

The detailed stock records for the branch may be kept at head office. Some businesses may not keep branch stock records for economy reasons, relying on the control in total provided by the branch stock account.

1 Stock wastage;
2 Stock losses arising from shoplifting and theft;
3 Cash sales not banked or misappropriated;
4 Credit sale invoices not raised;
5 Charging incorrect selling prices to customers;
6 Accounting errors at head office, particularly in pricing goods sent to branch;
7 Errors in stock count and valuation.

These factors are all of importance to management and the early detection of such situations existing above a normal acceptable level is highly desirable so that the causes for the discrepancy can be investigated and corrected.

The advantages of charging branches at selling price are:

Branch managers may be given the authority to reduce selling prices, particularly in selling off discontinued lines and damaged stocks. In such instances the manager would make a return to head office of the price reductions he has authorized.

1 Early identification of abnormal stock losses, so that they can be investigated.
2 Control over accounting for sales made by the branch, particularly identification of cash sales not banked.
3 The system automatically notifies the branch manager the price at which goods are to be sold, thus enabling head office to determine selling prices at a national level with local variations where necessary.
4 More readily available management information, particularly the total value of stock held at each branch.

Examples of where the system may be used are supermarkets, chemists and shoe retailers.

The disadvantages of the system are few and relate to the additional administration costs of pricing the deliveries to the branches.

The Accounting Records for Branch Stock Account

A branch stock account would be kept for each branch in which the goods sent to the branch and sales would be recorded, the balance on the account being the stock. The excess of the selling price over cost (the mark-up) would be recorded on a branch stock adjustment account.

Double entry to record the transactions will be:

Goods returned to head office by the branch would be a reversal of this entry.

Goods sent to branch:
  Debit   Branch stock   – with the selling price.
  Credit   Branch stock adjustment   – with the mark-up.
  Credit   Goods sent to branch   – with the cost.

Cash sales banked by branch:
  Debit   Bank
  Credit   Branch stock

Reductions in selling price:
  Debit   Branch stock adjustment
  Credit   Branch stock

Credit sales by branch:
    Debit   Customer
    Credit   Branch stock

Normal wastage:
    Debit   Branch stock adjustment
    Credit   Branch stock

In some businesses an allowance for normal wastage is required.

The actual stock valued at selling price will be carried down as a balance on the branch stock account, any stock losses will then be a balancing figure on the branch stock account. The double entry for this is:

Stock losses:
    Debit   Branch stock losses   – with the cost.
    Debit   Branch stock adjustment   – with the mark-up.
    Credit   Branch stock   – with the stock loss at selling price.

Note that the branch stock losses account is an expense account that will appear in the branch profit and loss account.

When preparing a profit and loss account for the branch, *provision must be made for the unrealized profit included in the closing stock*. This is done by carrying a provision down as a credit balance on the branch stock adjustment account. The balancing figure on the branch stock adjustment account will then be the gross profit made on the sales for the period, and is transferred to the branch profit and loss account.

The cost of the closing stock is ascertained for the balance sheet by deducting the credit balance for the provision from the debit balance for the stock.

Example

Broadfit operate a chain of retail shoe shops. The following transactions relate to the East Ham branch for the year ended 31 March 19X5.

	£
Branch stocks, at cost 1 April 19X4	9,000
Goods sent to branch, at cost	94,000
Cash sales banked	135,600
Authorized reductions in selling price	1,500
Branch stocks, at cost, at 31 March 19X5	11,100

Broadfit maintain all accounting records at their head office. All purchases are made centrally and goods sent to the branches are charged to the branches at selling price, which is cost plus 50%.

Required:
Write up the goods sent to branch account, branch stock account (maintained at selling price) and branch stock adjustment account for the year ended 31 March 19X5 as they would appear in the books of the head office.

Solution
Note that the mark-up on cost is 50%. The goods sent to the branch at cost £94,000 will therefore have a selling value of (150/100 × £94,000) £141,000.

The stocks at the beginning of the year will be brought down as a debit balance on the branch stock account valued at selling price (150/100 × £9,000) £13,500. The provision for unrealized profit at the beginning of the year will be (50/150 × £13,500) £4,500.

The accounts will be written up as follows:

Goods sent to Branch			
	£		£
31.3.X5 Head office trading	94,000	31.3.X5 Branch stock-cost	
		of goods sent	94,000
	£94,000		£94,000

All goods purchased by head office will be included on the head office trading account, consequently goods sent to the branch are credited to that account:

Branch stock

1.4.X5 Balance b/d – stock	13,500	31.3.X5 Bank – cash		
31.3.X5 Goods sent at selling		Sales	135,600	
price	141,000	31.3.X5 Branch stock		
		adjustment –		
		reductions in selling		
		price	1,500	
		31.3.X5 Stock losses		
		(balancing fig.)	750	
		31.3.X6 Balance c/d – stock		
		(150/100 × £11,100)	16,650	
	£154,500		£154,500	

All entries on the branch stock account are at selling price.

Branch stock adjustment

	£		£
31.3.X5 Branch stock –		1.4.X4 Balance b/d –	
reductions in		provision for	
selling price	1,500	unrealized profit	4,500
Branch stock – profit		31.3.X5 Branch stock –	
not realized re stock		mark-up on goods	
losses	250	sent (50/150 ×	
Branch P&L – gross		£141,000)	47,000
profit (bal. fig.)	44,200		
Balance c/d –			
provision for			
unrealized profit			
(50/150 × £16,650)	5,550		
	£51,500		£51,500

The branch stock adjustment account records the gross profit that will be made on selling the goods; the balancing figure on this account, after provision for the profit included in the unsold stock, represents the gross profit actually made on goods sold and is transferred to the branch profit and loss account.

Note that the stock losses (£750) disclosed by the difference on the branch stock account are at selling price. The mark-up that is included in this (£250) represents profit that has not been made on selling the goods and is debited to the branch stock adjustment account, the cost of the goods (£500) being debited to branch stock losses account.

Branch stock losses

	£		£
31.3.X5 Branch stock – cost		31.3.X5 Branch P&L	500
of stock losses			
(100/150 × £750)	500		
	£500		£500

Note that stock losses are included as an expense, at cost, in the branch profit and loss account. If any insurance claim is made in respect of these losses, the double entry would be:

    Debit   Insurance company
    Credit   Branch stock losses

with the amount of the claim, thus raising a debtor and reducing the loss.

On the balance sheet at 31 March 19X5 the branch stock will be included at cost, determined as follows:

	£
Stock at selling price per branch stock account	16,650
Less Provision for unrealized profit per branch stock adjustment account	5,550
Stock at cost	£11,100

Alternative Solution

The above method of recording the accounting entries using a branch stock adjustment account is common in examination questions. A perhaps simpler method is to not maintain this account, but to keep a memorandum record of the selling value on the branch stock account as follows:

Branch Stock

			Memorandum selling price				Memorandum selling price
		£	£			£	£
1.4.X4	Balance b/d – stock	13,500	9,000	31.3.X5	Bank – cash sales	135,600	135,600
31.3.X5	Goods sent	141,000	94,000	31.3.X5	Reductions in selling price	1,500	—
				31.3.X5	Stock losses	750	500
31.3.X5	Branch profit and loss– gross			31.3.X5	Balance c/d –		
	profit (bal. fig.)	—	44,200		stock	16,650	11,100
		£154,500	£147,200			£154,500	£147,200

Goods sent to branch

		£			£
31.3.X5	Head office trading	94,000	31.3.X5	Branch stock – goods sent	94,000

Branch stock losses

		£			£
31.3.X5	Branch stock	500	31.3.X5	Branch profit and loss	500

As can be seen, all entries relating to the goods sent are made at cost. The branch stock account is in reality a trading account, the balancing figure being the gross profit on the goods sold.

The selling price columns do not form part of double entry but are merely a memorandum record of the selling value of the stock at the branch. The stock loss at selling price (£750) is the figure required to balance the selling price columns. After this amount has been ascertained, the cost of the stock loss (£500) is entered in the double entry column:

Debit   Branch stock losses
Credit   Branch stock

Note that the reductions in selling price are purely an entry in the memorandum column.

Summary

1   A business may adopt a coding structure that will enable it to record its branch's transactions, assets and liabilities in separate accounts.

2 If control is exercised by charging goods to the branch at selling price;
a all entries on the branch stock account will be at selling price;
b the profit loading will be recorded in the branch stock adjustment account;
c provision must be made for the unrealized profit included in the branch stocks valued at selling price. Stocks will then be included in the balance sheet at cost (or lower net realizable value).

Examination Hints

Questions may be set on the situation where a head office maintains all the accounting records and transfers goods to the branch at cost. Questions in which goods are sent to the branch at selling price are more common. It is important to check and recheck the percentages that you will be using, e.g. a mark up of 25% on cost is a gross profit of $((25/100 + 25) \times 100)$ 20% on selling price. Pay particular attention to identifying whether the figures in the question are stated at cost or at selling price.

Questions do not always specify whether the branch stock account should incorporate memorandum selling price columns or should be maintained at selling price. The latter method is more universally applicable. To avoid common errors remember:

1 to bring down on the branch stock adjustment account the provision for unrealized profits on *opening* stocks, as well as carrying down the provision on closing stocks;
2 any stock losses will arise as the balancing figure on the branch stock account. The gross profit will arise as the balancing figure on the branch stock adjustment account. Check that you have made all the other entries required before calculating these balancing figures.

Try to answer the following questions before reading on.

Self-Assessment Questions

See page 304 for answer.

In each question, choose the correct answer from the five alternatives given.

13.1 If gross profit as a percentage of sales is 20%, the mark-up on cost will be:
a 16.67%
b 20%
c 25%
d 31.25%
e 50%.

13.2 Goods costing £1,000 were sent to a branch at a mark up of 50%. The branch manager was later authorized to reduce the selling price by 10%. The entry for reduction of selling price will be for:
a £33
b £50
c £100
d £150
e £200.

13.3 The provision carried down on the branch stock adjustment account represents gross profit:
a earned for the period
b not earned on sales during the period
c for the next period
d on stock losses
e not earned on closing stock.

13.4 If actual stocks at selling price are less than stocks disclosed by the branch stock account the deficiency may be due to:
a goods sent to branch not recorded by head office
b overcharging customers

   c   duplicated stock sheet entries
   d   credit notes not entered for goods returned to the branch by customers
   e   cash sales not recorded.

If you have answered the above questions correctly, and are sure you understand the key points in this chapter, then try to answer questions 15 and 16 on page 198 before moving on to Chapter 14.

CHAPTER 14

BRANCH ACCOUNTS: BRANCH RECORDING ITS OWN TRANSACTIONS

Chapter contents

Introduction **78**   Branch and head office accounts **78**   Profit and loss accounts **80**
Balance sheets **81**   Branch opening trial balance **86**   Transfers at cost plus **86**
Summary **88**   Examination hints **88**

Learning objectives

After studying this chapter you should be able to:

☐ write up the branch account in the head office books and the head office account in the branch's books and reconcile the balances;

☐ prepare profit and loss accounts for the head office, branch and whole business;

☐ prepare the balance sheet for the whole business;

☐ produce opening trial balances for the head office and branch;

☐ make a provision for unrealized profits if any goods are included in stock at a transfer value that is higher than cost.

Introduction

This chapter deals with the accounts of branches that are self-accounting entitites. Typically these are branches large enough to maintain their own records and controls and are managed independently of head office. The branch will keep its own set of double-entry accounting records up to the trial balance stage, including the preparation of a separate profit and loss account.

Branch and Head Office Accounts

These accounts are often referred to as the interbranch accounts. Some organizations will maintain two accounts, the branch capital account recording the initial investment in the branch and the branch current account recording day-to-day transactions.

Transactions between the head office and the branch will be recorded in each set of books as both will be keeping their own accounting records. In the books of the head office double entry will be completed by making an entry in the branch account. In the books of the branch double entry will be completed by making an entry in the head office account. The transactions between the two will be recorded from opposite points of view, e.g. head office will receive cash paid to it by the branch. Because of this the two accounts will be recording the same transactions but on opposite sides. A transaction that has been debited to the branch account in the head office's books will be credited in the head office account in the branch's books.

It is important to recognize that transactions between the two are recorded as a debit and a credit in the head office books and also as a debit and a credit in the branch's books. Remember that both entities are maintaining a balancing set of accounts. Merely to debit the branch account in one set of books and credit the head office account in the other set of books would cause a difference to arise on both trial balances.

Double entry for typical transactions is

Note		Head office books Debit	Credit	Branch books Debit	Credit
1	Fixed assets purchased by HO for delivery to branch	Branch	Bank	Fixed asset	HO
2	Goods sent by HO and received by branch	Branch	Goods sent to branch	Goods from HO	HO
3	Cash paid by branch and received by HO	Bank	Branch	HO	Bank
4	HO expenses charged to branch	Branch	Expenses	Expenses	HO
5	Drawings of cash from branch by a partner	Drawings	Branch	HO	Bank
6	Net profit of branch	Branch	P&L appropriation	P&L	HO

Notes

1 A branch is set up by head office. When it does so it will have to arrange the premises and equipment and transfer or appoint staff. The balance on the branch account in the head office books is normally a debit balance, representing the investment in the branch made by head office and profits made by the branch which have not been remitted to HO.

2 If a branch is trading in the same goods as its head office it will normally be more economic for head office to purchase in bulk and transfer goods to branches as required. Branches may well purchase goods independently in addition to receiving goods from HO.

3 If a head office is paying for purchases, branches will normally have a surplus of cash arising from their sales less expenses. This cash is remitted to head office.

4 A head office will often provide services to its branches, for example property maintainance. Any expenses incurred by the head office on behalf of the branch will be recharged. Often a head office will make a lump sum administration charge to a branch each year to recover expenses apportionable to its branches.

5 The head office books will contain the accounts relating to the proprietor's or partners' capital and current accounts (or the share capital and reserve accounts of a limited company) and the profit and loss appropriation account.

6 The net profit of branches is transferred to the profit & loss appropriation account maintained in the head office books.

At the accounting year end the balances on the branch and head office accounts will have to be agreed in the same amount. Typically there will be transactions which will have been entered in one set of books but not yet entered in the other. These are:

1 *Goods in transit from head office to branch*. These are items that have left head office but have not yet arrived at the branch and been recorded. They may be on a vehicle or with British Rail.

2 *Cash in transit from branch to head office*. A cheque may be in the post that has been recorded in the branch books as being paid but not yet recorded as being received by the head office.

Entries for goods returned by a branch to head office will be the reverse of the entries for goods sent.

Where there are two or more branches goods are sometimes transferred between them. In this case each branch would have to open an account for the other to record these transfers.

The branch prepares its own profit and loss account and maintains its own accounting controls, including those relating to stock.

Adjustments for goods and cash in transit are made in the head office books by carrying these items down as separate balances on the branch account and showing them as assets on the balance sheet.

Example 1

On 1 January, London Ltd appointed a manager to open an autonomous branch in Watford. £100,000 was transferred into a bank account for the branch, and equipment costing £30,000 was purchased on credit by the head office for delivery to the Watford branch.

During the year goods that had been purchased by the head office and cost £350,000 were sent to the branch, although of these £10,000 of goods were not received at Watford until after the end of the year.

During the year Watford remitted £370,000 to head office, which had received £365,000 by the year end, £5,000 being in transit.

Watford maintained its own double-entry accounting records and prepared a profit and loss account showing a net profit of £40,000 for the year.

The current accounts recording the interbranch transactions will appear as follows:

Head office books

Branch current account

	£		£
Jan. 1 Bank	100,000	Dec. 31 Bank	365,000
Suppliers	30,000	Balance c/d –	
Dec. 31 Goods sent to branch	350,000	goods in transit	10,000
P&L appropriation –		Balance c/d –	
net profit	40,000	cash in transit	5,000
			380,000
		Balance c/d	140,000
	£520,000		£520,000

Branch books

Head office current account

	£		£
Dec. 31 Bank	370,000	Jan. 1 Bank	100,000
		Equipment	30,000
		Dec. 31 Goods received from HO	340,000
Balance c/d	140,000	Profit and loss –	
		net profit	40,000
	£510,000		£510,000

As can be seen the two final balances are equal but opposite and contra each other out.

Profit and Loss Accounts

The branch will prepare its own profit and loss account and the net profit will be transferred to the head office account.

The head office will prepare its own profit and loss account. The net profit made by the head office and each branch is transferred to the profit and loss appropriation account kept in the head office books. This account summarizes the net profit made by the business as a whole and records the division of the profit in a partnership, or the taxation and appropriation of profits in the case of a limited company.

Often a detailed profit and loss account is prepared for the business as a whole disclosing the total sales and expenses for the year. This will be a memorandum statement prepared from the double-entry profit and loss accounts of the head office and the

branches. Transactions between the head office and a branch will not appear as they will
contra out.

Balance Sheets

The assets and liabilities of the head office and branches are added together to prepare a
balance sheet for the whole business. Balances due to and from the head office and a
branch contra out and will not appear on the balance sheet.

Example 2

The trial balances of a head office and branch at 31 December 19X6 were:

	Head office		Branch	
	£	£	£	£
Sales		100,000		50,000
Opening stocks	16,000		12,000	
Purchases	95,000		—	
Goods transferred		36,000	35,000	
Expenses	15,000		8,000	
Branch account	11,500			
Head office account				10,000
Bank balance	3,000		1,000	
Other assets and liabilities	20,500		4,000	
Share capital		20,000		
Profit and loss balance		5,000		
	£161,000	£161,000	£60,000	£60,000

Notes
1 Closing stocks are head office £17,000; branch £13,000.
2 Cash in transit from branch to head office £500.
3 Goods in transit from head office to branch £1,000.

Required:
Trading and profit and loss accounts for the head office and the branch for the year ended
31 December 19X6 and a balance sheet for the whole business at that date.

Solution
The first step is to identify the reasons for any difference between the branch account and
the head office account. The difference is (£11,500 – £10,000) £1,500 which is attributable
to cash and goods in transit. The items in transit will be included in bank and stock in the
balance sheet. The remaining balance on the branch account in the head office books will
be contra'd by the balance on the head office account in the branch's books and will not
appear in the balance sheet for the whole business.
    The final accounts can now be prepared.

Trading and profit and loss account
for the year ended 31 December 19X6

	Head office		Branch	
	£	£	£	£
Sales		100,000		50,000
Less Cost of sales:				
Opening stock	16,000		12,000	
Purchases	95,000			
Transfers	(36,000)		35,000	
	75,000		47,000	
Less Closing stock	17,000		13,000	

	Head office		Branch	
	£	£	£	£
		58,000		34,000
Gross profit		42,000		16,000
Less Expenses		15,000		8,000
Net profit		£27,000		£8,000

Profit and loss appropriation account
for the year ended 31 December 19X6

	£
Net profit – Head office	27,000
– Branch	8,000
	35,000
Add Balance brought forward from previous year	5,000
Balance carried forward	£40,000

Balance sheet at 31 December 19X6

	£
Stocks (£17,000 + £13,000 + £1,000)	31,000
Bank (£3,000 + £1,000 + £500)	4,500
Other assets and liabilities (£20,500 + £4,000)	24,500
	£60,000
Financed by:	
Share capital	20,000
Profit and loss account	40,000
	£60,000

A more comprehensive example giving full workings follows.

Example 3

Black and Berry are in partnership carrying on a business as wholesalers. The head office and main warehouse are in Wisbech with a branch warehouse at Lynn. All goods are purchased by Wisbech and goods sent to Lynn are charged at cost.

Berry is entitled to a 10% commission on the net profit of Lynn, otherwise profits and losses are shared equally.

The trial balances at 31 March 19X2 were as follows:

	Wisbech		Lynn	
	Debit	Credit	Debit	Credit
	£	£	£	£
Equipment:				
– at cost	155,800		145,000	
– depreciation to 31.3.X1		92,000		43,000
Motor vehicles:				
– at cost	225,000		135,800	
– depreciation to 31.3.X1		100,000		65,000
Bank balance	12,100		7,900	
Stock at 31.3.X1	320,000		112,000	
Debtors	170,600		196,600	
Creditors		442,000		12,300
Sales		2,298,000		1,389,000
Purchases	2,550,000		120,000	
Goods sent to branch		892,000		
Goods received from head office			882,000	

	Wisbech Debit £	Wisbech Credit £	Lynn Debit £	Lynn Credit £
Wages and salaries	250,000		140,000	
Expenses	303,000		180,000	
Drawings – Black	25,000			
– Berry	20,000			
Head office current account				410,000
Branch current account	425,000			
Loan		200,000		
Capital accounts – Black		200,000		
– Berry		200,000		
Current accounts – Black		22,000		
– Berry		10,500		
	£4,456,500	£4,456,500	£1,919,300	£1,919,300

The following additional information is available:

1 Stocks at 31 March 19X2 valued at cost were –
   Wisbech £340,000
   Lynn £130,000
2 Depreciation is to be provided on cost –
   Equipment 10%
   Motor vehicles 20%
3 Goods charged out at £10,000 on 31 March 19X2 had been recorded in the head office books but were not received by the branch until after that date. On the same date the branch had sent cash of £5,000 which was not received by head office until after the year end.

Required:
a   Trading and profit and loss accounts for the head office, branch and whole business; also the appropriation account for the year ended 31 March 19X2.
b   Balance sheet at 31 March 19X2.

Solution
In preparing the final accounts required by this example no adjustments are required to be made to the items appearing on the trial balance that relate to the profit and loss account. These items can be entered straight into the answer. Notes (1) and (2) require the inclusion of additional items. Note (3) does not affect the trading and profit and loss accounts, the note identifies that the difference between the head office and branch current accounts of (£425,000 – £410,000) £15,000 is attributable to goods and cash in transit to be included in the balance sheet.
    The accounts will appear as follows:

Trading and profit and loss accounts for the year ended 31 March 19X2

	Wisbech £	Wisbech £	Lynn £	Lynn £	Whole business £	Whole business £
Sales		2,298,000		1,389,000		3,687,000
Less Cost of sales						
Opening stocks	320,000		112,000		432,000	
Purchases	2,550,000		120,000		2,670,000	
Transfers	(892,000)		882,000		—	
	1,978,000		1,114,000		3,102,000	
Less Closing stocks	340,000		130,000		480,000	
		1,638,000		984,000		2,622,000
Gross profit		660,000		405,000		1,065,000

	Wisbech		Lynn		Whole business	
	£	£	£	£	£	£
Less:						
Wages and salaries	250,000		140,000		390,000	
Expenses	303,000		180,000		483,000	
Depreciation:						
– Equipment	15,580		14,500		30,080	.
– Motor vehicles	45,000		27,160		72,160	
		613,580		361,660		975,240
Net profit		£46,420		£43,340		£89,760

Profit and loss appropriation account
for the year ended 31 March 19X2

	£	£
Net profit – Wisbech		46,420
– Lynn		43,340
		£89,760
Division:		
Commission – Berry (10%)	4,334	
Share of profits – Black (½)	42,713	
– Berry (½)	42,713	
		£89,760

Lynn obtain the majority of their supplies from Wisbech but also make some direct purchases themselves. Note that in preparing the trading accounts the transfers entered into the head office and branch columns differ by £10,000, the goods in transit. However, goods in transit are included in total stocks appearing in the balance sheet and in the whole business trading account as follows:

	£
Stocks:	
– Wisbech	340,000
– Lynn	130,000
– Goods in transit	10,000
	£480,000

Bank balances entered onto the balance sheet are:

	£
Wisbech	12,100
Lynn	7,900
Cash in transit	5,000
	25,000

The branch and head office current accounts will appear as follows:

Wisbech books
Lynn branch

	£		£
Balance per trial balance	425,000	Balance c/d	
Net profit	43,340	– Goods in transit	10,000
		Balance c/d	
		– Cash in transit	5,000
			15,000
		Balance c/d	453,340
	£468,340		£468,340

Lynn books
Wisbech head office

	£		£
		Balance per trial balance	410,000
Balance c/d	453,340	Net profit	43,340
	£453,340		£435,340

The two balances are offset and do not appear on the balance sheet.

In preparing the rest of the balance sheet the head office and branch items for each asset and liability are added together. Accumulated depreciation will be:

	At 31.3.X1	Profit and loss	At 31.3.X2
	£	£	£
Equipment:			
– Head office	92,000	15,580	107,580
– Branch	43,000	14,500	57,500
			£165,080
Motor vehicles:			
– Head office	100,000	45,000	145,000
– Branch	65,000	27,160	92,160
			£237,160

The partners' current accounts will be:

	Black	Berry		Black	Berry
	£	£		£	£
Drawings	25,000	20,000	Balance per trial balance	22,000	10,500
			Commission		4,334
Balance c/d	39,713	37,547	Share of profits	42,713	42,713
	£64,713	£57,547		£64,713	£57,547

The term 'current account' is common in three instances:
— a bank current account, as opposed to a bank deposit account;
— a partner's current account, as opposed to a partner's capital account;
— a branch current account, as opposed to a branch capital account.

Balance sheet at 31 March 19X2

	£	£	£
Fixed assets:	Cost	Acc. deprec.	
Equipment	300,800	165,080	135,720
Motor vehicles	360,800	237,160	123,640
	£661,600	£402,240	259,360
Current assets:			
Stocks		480,000	
Debtors		367,200	
Bank		25,000	
		872,200	
Less Creditors		454,300	
			417,900
			677,260
Less Loan			200,000
			£477,260
Financed by:			
Partners' accounts:			

	Black	Berry	
	£	£	
Capital accounts	200,000	200,000	400,000
Current accounts	39,713	37,547	77,260
	£239,713	£237,547	£477,260

Branch opening trial balance

When a branch keeps its own double entry accounting records the trial balance prepared from the balances left in its books, after the preparation of the year-end accounts, must agree. This also applies of course to the head office books.

The balances left in the branch's books will relate to assets and liabilities only, the profit and loss account having been closed off by transferring the net profit to the head office account.

The trial balance of the Lynn branch at 1 April 19X2 will be:

This trial balance is at the start of business on 1 April 19X2. Included in the transactions to be recorded in the first few days of the new period will be the receipt of the £10,000 of goods in transit.

	Debit	Credit
	£	£
Equipment:		
– at cost	145,000	
– depreciation to 31.3.X2		57,500
Motor vehicles:		
– at cost	135,800	
– depreciation to 31.3.X2		92,160
Bank balance	7,900	
Stock at 31.3.X2	130,000	
Debtors	196,600	
Creditors		12,300
Head office current account		453,340
	£615,300	£615,300

This trial balance demonstrates clearly that the assets and liabilities of the branch are financed by head office.

The head office opening trial balance at the same date will be;

	Debit	Credit
	£	£
Equipment:		
– at cost	155,800	
– depreciation to 31.3.X2		107,580
Motor vehicles:		
– at cost	225,000	
– depreciation to 31.3.X2		145,000
Bank balance	12,100	
Stock at 31.3.X2	340,000	
Debtors	170,600	
Creditors		442,000
Loan		200,000
Capital accounts – Black		200,000
– Berry		200,000
Current accounts – Black		39,713
– Berry		37,547
Branch current account	453,340	
Goods in transit	10,000	
Cash in transit	5,000	
	£1,371,840	£1,371,840

Transfers at cost plus

Sometimes a head office will charge goods to a branch at cost plus a percentage in addition to cover its expenses and perhaps provide some profit to head office. In this situation the trading accounts are prepared in the normal way but an additional item is required in the head office profit and loss account to eliminate the percentage addition that the head office has taken on goods which remain unsold. This is necessary in order to include stock in the balance sheet at cost, not at an inflated value.

A *provision for unrealized profits included in stock* is created. Any increase or decrease in the provision is entered in the profit and loss account each year. The balance on the provision account is deducted in arriving at the stock figure to be included in the balance sheet.

The provision has to be made in respect of all stocks held that are valued at the cost plus transfer price. These will be goods in transit as well as stocks at the branch.

When preparing the whole business column of a profit and loss account the stocks are included at the balance sheet figure which is after deduction of the provision. The amount in the head office column for the increase or decrease in the provision is not entered in the whole business column.

> The provision is operated in a similar way to a provision for doubtful debts, where the increase or decrease in the provision is taken to the profit and loss account and the balance on the provision account is deducted from debtors on the balance sheet.

Example 4

The data given in Example 3 for Black and Berry will be used, except that as from 1.4.X1 goods transferred to Lynn were charged at cost plus 10%. During the year goods with a transfer value of £892,000 were sent. Lynn's stocks at 31.3.X2 of £130,000 include £122,000 at transfer value, the remaining £8,000 having been purchased directly by Lynn and valued at cost.

In this case the profit and loss account for the year will be as follows:

	Wisbech		Lynn		Whole business	
	£	£	£	£	£	£
Sales		2,298,000		1,389,000		3,687,000
Less Cost of sales:						
Opening stocks	320,000		112,000		432,000	
Purchases	2,550,000		120,000		2,670,000	
Transfers	(892,000)		882,000		—	
	1,978,000		1,114,000		3,102,000	
Less Closing stocks	340,000		130,000		468,000	
		1,638,000		984,000		2,634,000
Gross profit		660,000		405,000		1,053,000
Less:						
Wages and salaries	250,000		140,000		390,000	
Expenses	303,000		180,000		483,000	
Depreciation						
– Equipment	15,580		14,500		30,080	
– Motor vehicles	45,000		27,160		72,160	
Stock provision	12,000		—		—	
		625,580		361,660		975,240
Net profit		£34,420		£43,340		£77,760

The stock provision for unrealized profits is calculated:

	£
Stocks at branch ex head office	122,000
Goods in transit to the branch	10,000
Stocks valued at transfer price	£132,000
Profit included (10/110 × £132,000)	£12,000

> Goods are transferred at cost plus 10%. The transfer value is therefore (100% + 10%) 110% of cost. The provision required is in the proportion 10/110 of the transfer value.

Balance sheet stocks will be:

	£
Wisbech	340,000
Lynn	130,000
Goods in transit	10,000
Stock provision	(12,000)
	£468,000

Note that this is the first year in which a provision is required. In later years the opening whole business stocks will be reduced by the provision at the beginning of the year and only the increase or decrease in the provision will be taken to the profit and loss account.

Summary

1 Where a branch is a self-accounting entity transactions between the head office and the branch will be recorded in both sets of books.
2 At the accounting date:
 a goods in transit and cash in transit should be carried down as debit balances on the branch account in the head office books;
 b entries should be made to transfer the net profit of the branch to the head office;
 c the debit balance of the branch account in the head office books will offset the credit balance on the head office account in the branch's books and neither will appear on the balance sheet of the whole business;
 d transactions between the head office and the branch will not appear in the profit and loss account for the whole business;
 e if goods are transferred to the branch at cost plus a provision should be made for the unrealized profit included in branch stocks at the year end.

Examination Hints

Read the question requirements carefully. Normally a columnar trading and profit and loss account is required for the head office and the branch, but some questions will also require an additional column for the whole business. Remember that the profit and loss appropriation account is maintained in the books of the head office. Normally a balance sheet is only required for the whole business.

If the question requires the branch and head office accounts to be given, enter the balances shown in the trial balances. Carry down as balances on the branch account in the head office books any cash and goods in transit. Any items that appear in the branch trial balance in respect of accounts maintained in the head office books only (e.g. drawings) should be transferred through the head office and branch accounts. Remember that any recharge of expenses, and also the net profit of the branch, are transferred through these accounts. The final balance on the two accounts should contra each other and only the balances for cash and goods in transit will be included in the balance sheet.

Try to answer the following questions before reading on.

Self-Assessment Questions

See page 304 for answers.

In each question, choose the correct answer from the five alternatives given.

14.1 Cash in transit to head office is recorded as:
 a an asset in the books of the head office
 b a liability in the books of the head office
 c an asset in the books of the branch
 d a liability in the books of the branch
 e a memorandum item in the reconciliation of the interbranch accounts.

14.2 The balance on the branch account in the head office books represents:
  a the net assets of the branch
  b the original investment in the branch by the head office
  c goods that have been sent to the branch but not paid for
  d profits of the branch that have not been remitted to the head office
  e administration charges made by the head office but not paid for.

14.3 In the books of the branch, goods returned to head office will be:
  a debited to goods received from head office and credited to head office
  b debited to head office and credited to sales
  c debited to purchases and credited to head office
  d debited to head office and credited to purchases
  e debited to head office and credited to goods received from head office.

14.4 In the books of the head office the net profit of the branch is:
  a debited to branch profit and loss and credited to the profit and loss appropriation
  b debited to the profit and loss appropriation and credited to branch profit and loss
  c debited to branch profit and loss and credited to head office
  d debited to branch and credited to the profit and loss appropriation
  e debited to branch and credited to head office.

If you have answered the above questions correctly, and are sure you understand the key points in this chapter, then try to answer questions 17 and 18 on pages 199–200 before moving on to Chapter 15.

CHAPTER 15

COMPANY ACCOUNTS: SHARE AND LOAN TRANSACTIONS

Chapter contents

Introduction **90** Issue of shares **91** Redemption of shares **94** Issue and redemption of debenture loans **96** Debenture redemption sinking fund **97** Reserves **98** Bonus issues **99** Summary **99** Examination hints **100**

Learning objective

After studying this chapter you should be able to:

☐ make the entries relating to:
 – the issue of shares
 – the redemption of shares
 – the issue and redemption of debenture loans
 – a debenture redemption sinking fund
 – reserves
 – bonus issues.

Introduction

Ordinary shares are the most common form of share capital. Many companies will only issue ordinary shares, each share carrying the right to one vote. The ordinary shares are the 'equity' share capital, the 'equity interest' being the ordinary shares plus the reserves.

Some companies may also issue preference shares. The rights of preference shareholders are prescribed by an individual company's memorandum and articles; typically they will have a preferential right to payment of a fixed dividend before any ordinary dividend may be paid. Usually preference shares also have a preferential right to repayment on a liquidation before the ordinary shares. Cumulative preference shares carry forward the right to receive any dividend not declared, due to insufficient profit for the year, as arrears to be paid in later years. No accounting entry is made for any such arrears until they are eventually proposed to be paid, but any arrears should be disclosed in a note to the accounts.

A few companies will have more than one class of ordinary shares, and perhaps other types of share as well.

Each class of share capital is divided into a number of shares of a given nominal value. When a company is formed the shares are normally issued at their nominal value and the holders of the shares are recorded in the shares register. If a shareholder transfers his shares to a third party the transfer is merely recorded in the share register. It is only when a company issues shares or redeems shares that an accounting entry is required.

The price at which shares are bought and sold by shareholders will typically be different to the nominal value, the market value being determined by supply and demand and anticipation of the likely level of future profits and dividends. If a company issues additional shares it will issue them at a value approximating to the market value of the existing shares, not at nominal value. The excess of the issue price over the nominal value is called the premium. Note that a company may not issue shares at a discount, i.e. at a price lower than nominal value.

A company may issue shares up to the maximum amount authorized by its memorandum. The authorized share capital is disclosed in a note to the accounts. Only the share capital that has been issued and called up for payment of the issue price to the company by the shareholders is shown in the balance sheet.

Disclosure requirements are given in Chapter 17.

Issue of Shares

When shares are issued for cash the proceeds are debited to the bank account and the nominal value credited to the appropriate share capital account, any surplus being credited to the share premium account.

A company making an additional issue of shares may offer them to the existing shareholders on a pro rata basis according to the number of shares they already hold; this is called a rights issue. Alternatively the public at large may be invited to apply for the shares. If in the latter case the number of shares applied for exceeds the number available the directors may refuse some applications and refund any monies received. Alternatively they may only allot a proportion of the shares applied for, setting any excess application monies received against the amounts due when the shares are allotted. Sometimes the amount receivable on application and allotment is not the full amount of the issue price, the balance being called for by the directors at a later date or dates.

The double entry required in this situation is:

Debit	Bank	} with application monies
Credit	Application and allotment	received.

Debit	Application and allotment	} with any refunds of
Credit	Bank	application monies.

A separate account will be kept for each class of share capital. The account will record the called-up capital, i.e. the nominal value received or currently due to be received from the shareholders.

Debit   Application and allotment   – with total amount due on both application and allotment.
Credit   Share premium   – with any premium included.
Credit   Share capital   – with the balance.

Debit	Bank	} with allotment monies received.
Credit	Application and allotment	

If at a later date any balance is called for:

Debit	Call	} with amount due on the call.
Credit	Share capital	

Debit	Bank	} with call monies received.
Credit	Call	

Any debit balances on the application and allotment and call accounts will represent amounts due from the shareholders.

Example 1

Balance sheet at 31 January

	£		£
£1 'A' ordinary shares	100,000	Net assets	202,000
Share premium account	20,000		
Profit and loss account	82,000		
	£202,000		£202,000

The company issued 50,000 £1 'B' ordinary shares at £2 per share payable as follows:

14	February	On application	£0.50 per share
28	February	On allotment	£0.80 per share
30	June	First and final call	£0.70 per share

By 14 February applications had been received for 85,000 shares. The directors rejected the application for 10,000 shares and refunded the application monies. The 50,000 shares were allocated pro rata to the remaining applicants for 75,000 shares on the basis of 2 shares for every 3 applied for. The excess monies received on application were retained by the company, the amount payable on allotment being reduced accordingly. The amounts due on the call were received in due course.

The journal entries for the above transactions are:

		Debit	Credit
		£	£
Feb. 14	Bank	42,500	
	Application and allotment		42,500
	Application monies received (85,000 × £0.50).		
Feb. 14	Application and allotment	5,000	
	Bank		5,000
	Application monies refunded (10,000 × £0.50).		
Feb. 28	Application and allotment	65,000	
	Share premium		50,000
	£1 'B' ordinary shares		15,000
	Amount due on application and allotment		
	(50,000 × (£0.50 + £0.80)) including premium		
	of £1 per share.		
Feb. 28	Bank	27,500	
	Application and allotment		27,500
	Allotment monies received		
	(£65,000 – (£42,500 – £5,000)).		
Jun. 30	Call	35,000	
	£1 'B' ordinary shares		35,000
	Call of £0.70 per share.		
Jun. 30	Bank	35,000	
	Call		35,000
	Call monies received.		

This clears the balance on the application and allotment account. It represents:

	£	£
Amount due on application and allotment (50,000 × (£0.50 + £0.80))		65,000
Less Received on application (85,000 × £0.50)	42,500	
Less Refunded	5,000	
		37,500
		£27,500

The ledger accounts affected by these entries will appear as follows:

Application and allotment

	£		£
Feb. 14 Bank – refunds	5,000	Feb. 14 Bank – applications	42,500
Feb. 28 Share premium	50,000	Feb. 28 Bank – allotment	27,500
Feb. 28 £1 'B' ordinary	15,000		
	£70,000		£70,000

Call

	£		£
Jun. 30 £1 'B' ordinary	35,000	Jun. 30 Bank	35,000

£1 'B' Ordinary shares

	£		£
		Feb. 14 Application and allotment	15,000
		Jun. 30 Call	35,000
			50,000

Share premium

	£		£
		Feb. 1 Balance b/d	20,000
		Feb. 14 Application and	
		allotment	50,000
			70,000

Bank

	£		£
Feb. 14 Applications	42,500	Feb. 14 Refunds	5,000
Feb. 28 Allotment	27,500		
Jun. 30 Call	35,000		
	105,000		

The overall effect of these entries in total has been to debit the bank with £100,000 and credit share capital with £50,000 and share premium with £50,000.

If a shareholder fails to pay any amounts due on the shares the directors may declare the shares to be forfeited and perhaps issue them to another shareholder. The double entry required would be:

Debit   Forfeited shares
Credit Application and allotment   }   with any arrears.
Credit Call

Debit   Share capital   }   with the called–up
Credit Forfeited shares   }   nominal value of
                                    the shares.

and on re-issue:

Debit   Forfeited shares   }   with the called-up nominal
Credit Share capital   }   value of the shares.

Debit   Bank   }   with proceeds received on
Credit Forfeited shares   }   re-issue.

Debit   Forfeited shares   }   with the balance on the forfeited
Credit Share premium   }   shares account.

Example 2

The details of the share issue are the same as given in the previous example except that the holder of 100 shares failed to pay the call and the shares were forfeited on 31 July. They were re-issued on 30 September at a price of £1.90 per share.

The application and allotment account would remain unchanged as all monies due at that stage were received. The other ledger accounts would appear as follows:

Call

	£		£
Jun. 30 Nominal value	35,000	Jun. 30 Bank (49,900 × 70p)	34,930
		Jul. 31 Forfeited shares	
		(100 × 70p)	70
	£35,000		£35,000

£1 'B' ordinary shares

	£		£
Jul. 31 Forfeited shares	100	Feb. 14 Application and allotment	15,000
		Jun. 30 Call	35,000
Sept. 30 Balance c/d	50,000	Sept. 30 Forfeited share re-issued	100
	£50,100		£50,100

Forfeited shares

Jul. 31	Call – arrears	70	Jul. 31	£1 'B' ordinary shares	100
Sept. 30	£1 'B' ordinary shares		Sept. 30	Bank (100 × £1.90)	190
	re-issued	100			
Sept. 30	Share premium	120			
		£290			£290

The additional premium of £120 on re-issue represents

	£
Cash received on application and allotment	130
Less Premium included	100
Cash received re-nominal value	30
Cash received on re-issue	190
	220
Less Nominal value	100
Additional premium	£120

Share premium

	£			£
		Feb. 1	Balance b/d	20,000
		Feb. 14	Application and allotment	50,000
		Sept. 30	Forfeited shares	120
				£70,120

Redemption of Shares

A company may issue redeemable shares, providing that it also has ordinary non-redeemable shares in issue. The redeemable share capital will be repaid to the shareholders by the company in accordance with the terms laid down on the issue.

One of the underlying principles of the Companies Acts has been that the share capital of the company has to be preserved intact to protect the interests of the company's creditors. The share capital acts as a buffer to absorb losses so that the assets in theory will still be sufficient to pay the creditors in full providing the losses do not exceed the share capital and reserves. The creditors cannot rely on revenue reserves, such as the profit and loss account balance, because these may be distributed to the shareholders by way of a dividend. The capital reserves are, however, subject to Company Act restrictions preventing them from being distributed as a cash dividend.

In addition to redemption of shares in this way, companies may purchase some of their own shares from their shareholders for cancellation. This, however, is excluded from the syllabus.

The restrictions are detailed in the section of this chapter dealing with reserves.

If redeemable shares are repaid the Companies Act 1985 requires the capital of the company to be maintained by *either*:

1 the issue of new shares, *or*
2 transferring an amount equal to the nominal value of the shares redeemed from distributable reserves to a non-distributable *capital redemption reserve*.

If the proceeds of a new issue of shares, including any premium, are less than the nominal value of the shares redeemed a transfer to the capital redemption reserve has to be made for the balance.

If shares are redeemed at a premium the premium is charged to the profit and loss account, except where the Companies Act 1985 allows it to be charged to the share premium account. The amount of the premium on redemption which may be charged to the share premium account is the lower of:

1 the premium received on the original issue of the shares, and
2 the existing balance on the share premium account (including any premium received on the issue of any replacement shares).

The double entry is:

For any new issue:

Debit	Bank	– with proceeds of any new issue.
Credit	Share capital	– with nominal value.
Credit	Share premium	– with the premium.

For the redemption:

Debit	Redeemable shares	– with their nominal value.
Debit	Share premium (or, if not allowed, debit profit and loss)	– with any premium on redemption.
Credit	Bank	– with amount paid.

For the transfer (if required):

Debit   Profit and loss
Credit   Capital redemption reserve   } with the excess of the nominal value of the shares redeemed over the proceeds of the new issue.

Example 3

Balance sheet at 30 June

	£		£
£1 ordinary shares	100,000	Bank	60,000
10% redeemable preference			
shares of £1	50,000	Other assets	200,000
Share premium	40,000		
Profit and loss	70,000		
	£260,000		£260,000

On 1 July the redeemable preference shares, which had originally been issued at par, were redeemed at a premium of 5 pence per share. The journal entries will be:

	Debit	Credit
	£	£
10% redeemable preference shares of £1	50,000	
Profit and loss – premium on redemption	2,500	
Bank		52,500
Redemption of shares		
Profit and loss	50,000	
Capital redemption reserve		50,000
Transfer required by the Companies Act 1985.		

The balance sheet at 1 July, after the redemption, will be:

	£		£
£1 ordinary shares	100,000	Bank (£60,000 – £52,000)	7,500
Capital redemption reserve	50,000	Other assets	200,000
Share premium	40,000		
Profit and loss			
(£70,000 – £2,500 – £50,000)	17,500		
	£207,500		£207,500

Note that the share capital has been maintained intact. The called-up share capital and capital reserves at 30 June were (£100,000 + £50,000 + £40,000) £190,000 and at 1 July are (£100,000 + £50,000 + £40,000) £190,000. The capital redemption reserve has replaced the redeemed shares.

Example 4

Balance sheet at 30 June

	£		£
£1 ordinary shares	100,000	Bank	10,000
10% redeemable preference			
shares of £1	50,000	Other assets	250,000
Share premium	40,000		
Profit and loss	70,000		
	£260,000		£260,000

On 1 July 30,000 £1 ordinary shares were issued at £1.50 per share and the preference shares, which had originally been issued at par, were redeemed at a premium of 5 pence.
    The journal entries will be:

	Debit	Credit
	£	£
Bank	45,000	
£1 ordinary shares		30,000
Share premium		15,000
Issue of shares		
10% redeemable preference shares of £1	50,000	
Profit and loss – premium on redemption	2,500	
Bank		52,500
Redemption of shares		
Profit and loss	5,000	
Capital redemption reserve		5,000
Transfer required by the Companies Act 1985.		

Calculated as follows:

	£
Nominal value of shares redeemed	50,000
Less Proceeds of new issue	45,000
Transfer required	£5,000

The balance sheet at 1 July after redemption will be:

	£		£
£1 ordinary shares		Bank (£10,000 + £45,000 – £52,500)	2,500
(£100,000 + £30,000)	130,000		
Capital redemption reserve	5,000	Other assets	250,000
Share premium (£40,000 + £15,000)	55,000		
Profit and loss			
(£70,000 – £2,500 – £5,000)	62,500		
	£252,500		£252,500

Issue and Redemption of Debenture Loans

Loan stocks and debentures that have been issued by a company are liabilities. The holders of the loan stocks or debentures are creditors of the company until such time as they are repaid. They are not shareholders and do not have any voting rights. The loan stocks and debentures are normally transferrable and can be sold by their holders to third parties in much the same way as shares. Debentures are typically divided into units of £100 and have their rights and security protected by a trust deed. Stocks may be held and transferred in any quantity and may be secured or unsecured. Both of these types of loans carry a fixed rate of interest.

As an incentive to prospective investors issues may be made at a discount and may be redeemed at a premium. Any discount or premium may be charged to the share premium account if one exists, otherwise the charge should be to the profit and loss account.

The double entry is:

On issue

Debit	Bank	– with the proceeds.
Debit	Share premium (or profit and loss)	– with the discount.
Credit	Debenture loans	– with the nominal value.

On redemption

Debit	Debenture loans	– with the nominal value.
Debit	Share premium (or profit and loss)	– with the premium.
Credit	Bank	– with payment.

No transfer to a capital redemption reserve is required, but a company may make a transfer to a debenture redemption reserve if it so wishes.

The terms of a debenture trust deed may require debentures to be redeemed over a period of years, lots being drawn each year to determine which units are repaid. The entries for the repayment of these parcels of units are the same as when all the debentures are redeemed at the same time. Some deeds will allow the company to

The market value is dependent on such factors as interest rates generally, the security given by any trust deed and the length of time to maturity.

Debentures are normally secured by a fixed charge on fixed assets and possibly a floating charge on the current assets that crystallizes on default by the company (e.g. non-payment of interest) to become a charge on the stock and debtors, etc. that exist at that date.

Interest on debentures is an expense and is thus charged to the profit and loss account. Note that dividends are an appropriation of profit and thus are entered in the profit and loss appropriation account.

If debentures are purchased for cancellation at a price below their nominal value the entry will be:

Debit Debentures – with the nominal value.
Credit Bank – with the payment.
Credit Profit and loss – with profit on redemption.

purchase its own debentures on the Stock Exchange and cancel them; again the entries are the same.

Debenture Redemption Sinking Fund

A company will be faced with the problem of ensuring sufficient cash to redeem loan stocks and debentures when they mature. This is often met by making a new issue to raise the funds. However, a company may decide to invest some cash each year over the life of the debenture loans to provide the funds to meet the repayment without fresh borrowings, the investments being sold to provide the cash required.

A very formal way of doing this is to set up a sinking fund. Contributions are appropriated from profit each year and sunk into a fund which is invested outside the business. The contribution is smaller than would otherwise be required because interest earned on the investments is also taken to the fund and invested. The balance on the sinking fund account will be represented by sinking fund investments of the same amount. When the investments are eventually sold any profit or loss on the realization is taken to the sinking fund, the balance of which is then transferred to a general reserve.

The double entry is:

Sinking funds contravene the principle of SSAP 6 that all profits and losses should be reported in the profit and loss account. Strictly the investment income should be credited to the profit and loss account and then transferred out to the sinking fund.

Debit Profit and loss appropriation
Credit Sinking fund   } with the annual contribution.

Debit Bank
Credit Sinking fund   } with the interest received.

Debit Sinking fund investments
Credit Bank   } with the investment of annual contributions and interest.

Debit Bank
Credit Sinking fund investments   } with the proceeds of sale.

Debit Sinking fund investments
Credit Sinking fund   } with any profit on sale of the investment. (Reverse entry if a loss.)

Debit Sinking fund
Credit General reserve   } to close the sinking fund.

Example 5

A company issues £100,000 12% debentures at par on 1 January 19X1 repayable on 31 December 19X5. A sinking fund is set up with an annual contribution of £16,380 to be invested on the 31 December each year in local authority bonds earning interest of 10% per annum.

The ledger accounts will appear as follows:

The short period of five years has been chosen for this example to avoid repetition of entries each year. Debentures are often issued for longer periods.

12% Debentures 19X5

	£		£
31.12.X5 Bank	100,000	1.1.X1 Bank	100,000

Debenture redemption sinking fund

	£		£
		31.12.X1 Profit and loss appropriation	16,380
		31.12.X2 Bank – interest at 10%	1,638
		Profit and loss appropriation	16,380
			34,398

	£		£
		31.12.X3 Bank – interest	3,439
		Profit and loss	
		appropriation	16,380
			54,217
		31.12.X4 Bank – interest	5,421
		Profit and loss	
		appropriation	16,380
			76,018
		31.12.X5 Bank – interest	7,602
		Profit and loss	
		appropriation	16,380
31.12.X5 Transfer to general			
reserve	100,000		
	£100,000		£100,000

Debenture redemption sinking fund investments

	£		£
31.12.X1 Bank	16,380		
31.12.X2 Bank (£1,638 + £16,380)	18,018		
	34,398		
31.12.X3 Bank (£3,439 + £16,380)	19,819		
	54,217		
31.12.X4 Bank (£5,421 + £16,380)	21,801		
	76,018		
		31.12.X5 Bank – sale proceeds	76,018
	£76,018		£76,018

The last year's interest and contribution is not invested as it is needed to repay the debentures. The funds to meet the repayment come from:

	£
Last contribution not invested	16,380
Interest received not re-invested	7,602
Proceeds from sale of investments	76,018
	£100,000

Reserves

The Companies Act 1985 restricts the amounts which may be charged to the two statutory reserve accounts as follows:

1 The *capital redemption reserve* is a capital reserve that may only be used for the issue of fully paid bonus shares.
2 The *share premium account* is a capital reserve that may only be used for:
   a the issue of fully paid bonus shares;
   b writing off the preliminary expenses on a company's formation;
   c writing off expenses on the issue of shares and debentures (including any discount on debentures);
   d any premium on the redemption of debentures;
   e any premium on the redemption of shares (but this is subject to restriction).

The capital redemption reserve, share premium account and revaluation reserve are capital reserves that may not be distributed as cash dividends.

When land and buildings are revalued the double entry is:

Debit   Provision for depreciation   } with the accumulated
Credit   Fixed asset cost account   } depreciation to date.

Debit   Fixed asset cost account   } with the surplus of the market
Credit   Revaluation reserve   } valuation over the net book value.

The fixed asset account now records the asset at the revaluation and, except in the case of freehold land, this revalued amount should be depreciated over the remaining useful life.

The *revaluation reserve* may not be distributed as a cash dividend to the shareholders as it represents an unrealized profit. It may be used for the issue of fully paid bonus shares.

The balance on the profit and loss account may be described on the balance sheet as 'Retained earnings' or 'Unappropriated profits'.

The balance on the *profit and loss account* is a revenue reserve that *is* distributable to the shareholders. Other revenue reserves are those which are not required by the Companies Act but have been set up by the directors by transfer from the profit and loss appropriation account, for example:

1 *General reserve* which it is intended to retain permanently in the business;
2 *Dividend equalization reserve* which is to be used to maintain dividends at a normal level in years of low profitability.

Note that *provisions* are not reserves. They are amounts that are set aside for known liabilities the amount of which cannot be determined precisely.

Bonus Issues

A company may permanently capitalize some of its reserves by converting them into additional shares. No cash is received by the company on a bonus issue; fully paid share certificates are sent to the existing shareholders and a book-keeping entry is made for the transfer from reserves to share capital.

A bonus issue is sometimes called a 'scrip' issue. A rights issue is different; it is the issue of shares for cash to existing shareholders, each shareholder being given the right to apply for more shares on a pro rata basis according to the number of shares held.

Example 6

Balance sheet at 30 June

	£		£
£1 ordinary shares	100,000	Net assets	350,000
Capital redemption reserve	20,000		
Share premium	30,000		
Profit and loss	200,000		
	£350,000		£350,000

The directors make a 1 for 1 fully paid bonus issue on 1 July. The journal entry will be:

	Debit	Credit
	£	£
Capital redemption reserve	20,000	
Share premium	30,000	
Profit and loss	50,000	
£1 ordinary shares		100,000
1 for 1 bonus issue		

Note that the capital reserves are normally capitalized first on a bonus issue, the balance coming from revenue reserves.
The balance sheet after the bonus issue will be:

	£		£
£1 ordinary shares	200,000	Net assets	350,000
Profit and loss (£200,000 – £50,000)	150,000		
	£350,000		£350,000

The shareholders will not receive any material benefit from the bonus issue. Prior to the bonus issue the holder of 1,000 shares will own (1,000/100,000) 1%; after the bonus issue the holding will still be (2,000/200,000) 1%. If the market value of the shares had been, say, £4 prior to the issue his holding would be worth £4,000 in total. The price per share is likely to fall to about £2 per share after the bonus issue, when his holding will still be worth £4,000 in total.

Bonus issues are made to rationalize the capital structure of the company where there are large permanent reserves. They also reduce the market price per share; this may encourage more trading in the shares if the price before the issue was so large as to discourage investors.

Summary

1 Share capital accounts will be credited with the called-up nominal value of the shares. Any premium will be credited to the share premium account. An application and allotment account and call accounts may be necessary if the proceeds of a share issue are receivable in instalments.
2 If shares are redeemed the capital of the company must be kept intact by either the

issue of new shares or a transfer to the capital redemption reserve.

3   Loan stocks and debentures are not share capital, they are liabilities. A sinking fund may be set up to meet their repayment.

4   The Companies Act restricts the items that may be debited to the capital redemption reserve, share premium and revaluation reserve.

5   A company may capitalize part of its reserves by making a bonus issue of fully paid shares.

Examination Hints

Questions dealing with the issue and redemption of shares and debentures may require an answer in the form of journal entries or ledger accounts or both. Read the question requirements carefully. When preparing journal entries many students find it helpful to draw up ledger accounts in their workings.

When shares are redeemed remember to consider if a transfer to the capital redemption reserve is required. This is a very important entry that is easily overlooked.

If a revised balance sheet is required showing the position after the transactions have been completed the balances will be the final balances on the ledger accounts. If journal entries only have been prepared, each item on the opening balance sheet should be adjusted by the journal entries relating to it. These may be shown as bracketed workings on the balance sheet. Tick each journal entry item as you do this to ensure that no items are overlooked.

Try to answer the following questions before reading on.

Self-Assessment Questions

See page 305 for answers.

In each question, choose the correct answer from the five alternatives given.

15.1   Share capital is included in the balance sheet at:
    a   market value
    b   issue price
    c   nominal value
    d   called-up nominal value
    e   nominal value received to date.

15.2   Which of the following is not a liability:
    a   redeemable preference shares
    b   unsecured loan stock
    c   secured loan stock
    d   debentures
    e   bank loan.

15.3   Which of the following is not a reserve:
    a   share premium account
    b   dividend equalization account
    c   debenture redemption sinking fund
    d   debentures
    e   retained earnings.

15.4   A company has an issued and fully paid share capital of 600,000 10 pence ordinary shares and a balance on its capital redemption reserve of £10,000. It makes a bonus issue of 1 for 3. The amount of retained earnings capitalized will be:
    a   £10,000
    b   £20,000
    c   £170,000
    d   £190,000
    e   £200,000.

If you have answered the above questions correctly, and are sure you understand the key points in this chapter, then try to answer questions 19 and 20 on pages 201–2 before moving on to Chapter 16.

CHAPTER 16

COMPANY ACCOUNTS: TAXATION

Chapter contents

Introduction **101**   Income tax **101**   Corporation tax **102**   Advanced corporation tax **103**   Deferred tax **105**   SSAP 8 **107**   Summary **107**   Examination hints **108**

Learning objectives

After studying this chapter you should be able to:

☐ make the necessary entries in the ledger accounts for income tax, corporation tax, advanced corporation tax and deferred tax;

☐ calculate the amount of advanced corporation tax payable on dividends;

☐ present taxation in the profit and loss account and balance sheet in accordance with SSAP 8 and SSAP 15.

Introduction

Limited companies are bodies corporate and as such are liable to corporation tax. In the profit and loss account corporation tax will be shown as a deduction from profits. On payment of a dividend a company is liable to pay advanced corporation tax (ACT) to the Inland Revenue. ACT is not an additional expense as it is normally merely a payment of part of the corporation tax liability at an earlier date than it would otherwise be due.

Income tax is not an expense of the company; any income tax that is deducted from receipts or payments is reclaimed from, or paid over to, the Inland Revenue.

Deferred tax is purely an accounting exercise designed to equalize the effect of corporation tax on the profit and loss account from year to year. A company is not assessed to deferred tax; it represents *future* corporation tax liabilities.

Income Tax

Annual payments such as loan interest, royalties and covenants are made under deduction of income tax. Only the net amount after deduction of income tax is paid to the recipient, the income tax deducted is paid to the Inland Revenue. Deduction of income tax at source in this manner has administrative advantages for the Inland Revenue. As far as the paying company is concerned the gross amount may be allowed as a deduction in computing its profits assessable to corporation tax and it is the gross amount that is entered in the profit and loss account as an expense.

Similarly if any income is received net, after deduction of income tax, the income tax may be recovered from the Inland Revenue. The gross income is taken to the profit and loss account and corporation tax may be payable on the gross amount.

Income tax deducted from receipts may be set off against income tax deducted from payments and only the difference is payable to, or recoverable from, the Inland Revenue.

Payment to the Inland Revenue is required on the 14th of the month following the end of each quarter.

Any amounts payable or recoverable at the balance sheet date will be included in creditors or debtors.

The accounting entries are

Debit   The expense account (e.g. loan interest payable)
Credit Bank
} with net amount paid.

Debit   The expense account (e.g. loan interest payable)
Credit Income tax
} with income tax deducted.

Debit   Bank
Credit The income account (e.g. loan interest receivable)
} with net amount received.

Debit   Income tax
Credit The Income account (e.g. loan interest receivable)
} with income tax deducted.

Debit   Income tax
Credit Bank
} with payment to the Inland Revenue. (Entries reversed for refund.)

Example 1

A company receives and pays the following items under deduction of income tax during the year ended 30 June 19X7. The rate of income tax is 29%.

30.6.X7   Interest received on £100,000 10% debentures   £7,100
          Interest paid on £200,000 12% loan stock   £17,040

The ledger accounts will record:

Investment income – interest receivable

	£		£
30.6.X7 Profit and loss	10,000	30.6.7 Bank	7,100
		Income tax	2,900
	£10,000		£10,000

The income tax deducted from interest received is 29% of the gross interest of £10,000. When only the net amount received is known, the tax can be calculated as $^{29}/_{71}$ × the net amount, e.g. $^{29}/_{71}$ × £7,100 = £2,900.

Interest payable – 12% loan stock

	£		£
30.6.X7 Bank	17,040	30.6.X7 Profit and loss	24,000
Income tax	6,960		
	£24,000		£24,000

Income tax

	£		£
30.6.X7 Interest rec'd	2,900	30.6.X7 Interest paid	6,960
Balance c/d	4,060		
	£6,960		£6,960

Balance sheet extract at 30.6.X7

	£
Creditors: amounts falling due within one year	
Other creditors	4,060

This chapter introduces the layout for the balance sheet required by the Companies Act 1985.

Corporation Tax

A 'small companies' rate will apply to companies with profits below a certain level.

Any company resident in the UK is liable to corporation tax on its assessable profits for each chargeable accounting period. The corporation tax is normally payable 9 months after the end of the accounting period.

However, companies which were trading before April 1965 will pay corporation tax on dates which previously applied under income tax rules, which may be up to 21 months after the end of the accounting period. These companies will therefore have two years' corporation tax liabilities unpaid at any balance sheet data.

At the end of each accounting period companies will prepare their tax computations and provide for the estimated liability for the year. The provision is charged to the profit and loss account and credited to the corporation tax account. Later on the actual liability will be agreed with the Inland Revenue and paid. Any over- or under-provision will be adjusted in the following year's profit and loss account.

The accounting entries are:

Debit   Profit and loss   } with the provision for the estimated
Credit Corporation tax   } liability for the year.

Debit   Corporation tax   } with any over-provision made in the
Credit Profit and loss   } previous year (reverse entries for an
                                   under-provision).

Prudence is applied in estimating corporation tax liabilities, consequently the provision may be greater than the liability that is eventually agreed with the Inspector.

Example 2

The 1960 Co. Ltd has balances on its corporation tax account at 1.1.19X7 of £8,000 with regard to 19X5 and £10,000 with regard to 19X6.

On 1.1.X7 the 19X5 liability of £8,000 is paid. At 31.12.X7 the 19X6 liability has finally been agreed in the sum of £9,500, payable on 1.1.X8. Provision is to be made for the estimated 19X7 liability of £15,000 payable on 1.1.X9.

The corporation tax account for 19X7 will appear as follows:

Note that this is a company that was trading prior to the introduction of corporation tax in 1965.

Corporation tax

	£		£
1.1.X7 Bank – CT 19X5	8,000	1.1.X7 Balance b/d	
31.12.X7 Profit and loss –		– CT 19X5	8,000
overprovision	500	– CT 19X6	10,000
Balance c/d		31.12.X7 Profit and loss	15,000
– CT 19X6	9,500		
– CT 19X7	15,000		
	£33,000		£33,000

Balance sheet extract at 31.12.X7

	£
Creditors: amounts falling due within one year:	
Other creditors	9,500
Creditors: amounts falling due after more than one year:	
Other creditors	15,000

Advanced Corporation Tax

Under the imputation system of corporation tax a company's net profit after tax is regarded as available for distribution without any further taxation charges arising except in exceptional circumstances. The amount of dividend declared is paid to the shareholders without any deduction of tax. In the hands of the shareholder the amount received is deemed to have already been taxed, and so it has a tax credit attaching to it. When the standard rate of income tax is 29%, the tax credit is $29/71 \times$ the amount received.

A company must pay to the Inland Revenue, within 14 days of the end of the quarter in which a dividend is paid, an amount equal to the tax credit attaching to the dividend. This is advanced corporation tax (ACT). The ACT is recoverable by deduction from the corporation tax payable on the profits of the accounting period during which the dividend was *paid*. The balance of corporation tax payable after deduction of ACT is known as 'mainstream' corporation tax. Note that ACT is not an additional liability, but merely earlier payment.

The tax credit represents income tax at the basic rate on the dividend if it had been declared grossed up by income tax, e.g. if a dividend of £7,100 is paid the tax credit will be $(29/71 \times £7,100)$ £2,900 giving a gross equivalent of (£7,100 + £2,900) £10,000. Tax at 29% on £10,000 = £2,900, the amount of the tax credit.

When the income tax rate was 30% the tax credit was $30/70$ of the net amount paid.

A company is not liable to corporation tax on the dividends it receives.

The tax credit attaching to any dividends received may be deducted in calculating the ACT payable on dividends paid.

If the recovery of ACT against the corporation tax liability is restricted, any unrelieved ACT may be recovered against the corporation tax on the last two years' profits, or may be carried forward to be recovered in the future. If it does not appear likely to be recovered, the irrecoverable ACT should be written off in the same profit and loss account as the dividend to which it relates.

The accounting entries are:

Debit	ACT recoverable	}	with ACT payable on dividends
Credit	ACT payable		declared.
Debit	ACT payable	}	with ACT paid.
Credit	Bank		
Debit	Corporation tax	}	with ACT recoverable against
Credit	ACT recoverable		corporation tax.
Debit	Profit and loss	}	with any irrecoverable ACT.
Credit	ACT recoverable		

At the balance sheet date any balance on the ACT payable account will be included on the balance sheet as a creditor. Any balance on the ACT recoverable account will be deducted from deferred tax if there is any, otherwise it will be included in the balance sheet as a debtor.

Dividends received by a company will be shown in the profit and loss account at the gross amount, the attaching tax credit being included separately under the heading of taxation.

Example 3

The 1980 Co. Ltd has an issued share capital of 100,000 £1 ordinary shares. At 1.1.X7 it had a credit balance on its corporation tax account of £9,500, being the provision for the corporation tax liability on the profits of the year ended 31.12.X6. This liability was agreed in the sum of £9,300 and was paid on 1.10.X7.

An interim dividend of 3.5% was paid on 1.8.X7, the related ACT being paid on 14.10.X7. Provision is to be made for a final dividend of 7% (payable in 19X8).

A dividend of £710 was received on 1.11.X7.

Corporation tax for 19X7 is estimated to be £14,000.

The basic rate of income tax is 29%.

The ledger accounts will appear as follows:

Investment income – dividends received

	£		£
		1.11.X7 Bank – net	710
31.12.X7 Profit and loss – gross	1,000	31.12.X7 Profit and loss –	
		tax credit	290
	£1,000		£1,000

Dividends payable

	£		£
1.8.X7 Bank	3,500	31.12.X7 Profit and loss:	
31.12.X7 Balance c/d	7,000	– interim	3,500
		– final	7,000
	£10,500		£10,500

ACT payable

	£			£
14.10.X7 Bank	1,430	1.8.X7 ACT recoverable		
		(29/71 × £3,500)		1,430
31.12.X7 Balance c/d	2,570	31.12.X7 ACT recoverable		
		(29/71 × £7,000 = £2,860		
		Less tax credit of £290)		2,570
	£4,000			£4,000

The balance of ACT payable of £2,570 will be payable to the Inland Revenue 14 days after the end of the quarter in which the dividend is paid.

ACT recoverable

	£		£
1.8.X7 ACT payable	1,430	14.10.X7 Corporation tax	1,430
31.12.X7 ACT payable	2,570	31.12.X7 Balance c/d	2,570
	£4,000		£4,000

The balance of ACT recoverable of £2,570 relates to a dividend that will be paid in 19X8 and it will be recoverable against the 19X8 corporation tax liability.

Corporation tax

	£		£
14.10.X7 ACT recoverable	1,430	1.1.X7 Balance b/d	
1.10.X7 Bank – CT 19X6	9,300	– CT 19X6	9,500
31.12.X7 Profit and loss –			
overprovision	200		
31.12.X7 Balance c/d – CT 19X7		31.12.X7 Profit and loss	14,000
(£14,000 – £1,430)	12,570		
	£23,500		£23,500

The balance of mainstream corporation tax for 19X7, £12,570, will be payable on 1.10.X8. In this illustration the ACT recovered against the 19X7 corporation tax liability relates only to the interim dividend paid on 1.8.X7. If any other dividend had been paid during 19X7, for example if a 19X6 proposed final dividend had been paid during the earlier part of 19X7, the ACT relating to that dividend would also have been recoverable against the 19X7 corporation tax.

Deferred Tax

Deferred tax is not an additional liability, it is merely a device for charging corporation tax to the profit and loss account in an earlier year than when the tax becomes a legal liability.

Debit	Profit and loss	}	with the deferred tax provision for the year (entry reversed for a reduction in deferred tax).
Credit	Deferred tax		

Unfortunately the reasons for making this simple entry are quite complicated!

Corporation tax is chargeable on the assessable profits determined by a tax computation in accordance with the tax law. The differences between the accounting profits and the assessable profits are classified by SSAP 15 Accounting for Deferred Tax into:

1 *Permanent differences* which are items added back or deducted in the tax computation which will not affect the tax liabilities of future years, e.g.
  a profits not taxable,
  b expenses disallowed, and
  c depreciation of assets that do not attract capital allowances;
2 *Timing differences* which are items added back or deducted in the tax computation which will reverse out in future years' tax computations, e.g.
  a accelerated capital allowances (capital allowances in excess of the depreciation charged in the profit and loss account for the year), and
  b short-term timing differences that will reverse out in the following year, e.g. interest accrued due which will be assessed only when received.

A timing difference may also arise in respect of a surplus on revaluation of fixed assets. Corporation tax will not be payable on the capital gain until the asset is sold, and even then may not be payable at that stage in certain circumstances.

Over a period of years the sum of the timing differences will be nil, because any originating difference will be reversed out in due course. For example, the total capital allowances in respect of a machine over its life will equal the total depreciation over the same period. If in the first year of the machine's life there is an originating difference, because capital allowances exceed the depreciation, then in later years this will be reversed out by depreciation exceeding capital allowances.

Deferred tax is becoming of less importance in the accounts of companies following changes in the tax legislation of recent years. These include the abolition of stock relief, the phased elimination of first year allowances and reduction in corporation tax rates.

Example 4

The equalizing effect of deferred tax transfers can be demonstrated using the following data:

1   Profit before depreciation £10,000 per annum.
2   Asset acquired at a cost of £9,000; the life of the asset is three years.
3   100% first year allowance can be claimed. The corporation tax rate is 50%. (These rates have been chosen for simplicity.)

The profit and loss account position will be as follows:

Year	1	2	3
	£	£	£
Profit	10,000	10,000	10,000
Depreciation	3,000	3,000	3,000
Net profit before tax	7,000	7,000	7,000
Corporation tax	(500)	(5,000)	(5,000)
	6,500	2,000	2,000
Deferred tax	(3,000)	1,500	1,500
Net profit after tax	£3,500	£3,500	£3,500

The transfer to and from deferred tax is calculated as follows:

Originating difference (allowance £9,000 *less* depreciation £3,000)	6,000		
Reversing differences (allowance £Nil *less* depreciation £3,000)		(3,000)	(3,000)
Corporation tax at 50%	3,000	(1,500)	(1,500)

It will be noted that unless the transfers to and from deferred tax had been made, the profit after tax would have ranged from £2,000 to £6,500 in years when the company was achieving the same profit performance.

The deferred tax account would be:

Deferred tax

	£		£
31.12.X2 Profit and loss	1,500	31.12.X1 Profit and loss	3,000
Balance c/d	1,500		
	£3,000		£3,000
31.12.X3 Profit and loss	1,500	1.1.X3 Balance b/d	1,500

An argument against deferred tax is that the liability may never arise due to fresh timing differences originating every year so that the reversal never occurs. In past years many companies have been in the situation of transferring amounts year after year to an ever increasing balance on the deferred tax account.

Deferred tax has been a controversial topic in recent years with arguments being made for three different approaches to its provision:

1   *Nil provision* where deferred tax is not set up, based on the argument that a legal tax liability does not exist at the balance sheet date;
2   *Full provision* where deferred tax is provided for all timing differences, based on the argument that this matches the future tax liability to the period in which the transaction takes place;
3   *Partial provision* where deferred tax is only provided where it is *probable* that the timing difference will reverse and the tax become payable in the foreseeable future.

SSAP 15, which has been revised, now requires deferred tax to be provided to the extent that it is *probable a liability or asset will crystallize*, i.e. the partial provision method. SSAP 15 also requires the balance on the deferred tax account to be adjusted if there is a change in the corporation tax rate (*the liability method*). Earlier standards had not allowed an adjustment to be made if the tax rate changed (*the deferral method*) on the grounds that deferred tax was a deferral of a past benefit rather than a provision for a future liability.

Any balance on the ACT recoverable account is deducted from the deferred tax balance in arriving at the deferred tax appearing on the balance sheet. SSAP 15 requires deferred tax to be disclosed in the published accounts and a note to be given of its major components and of any deferred tax that has not been provided.

The format for the published balance sheet given by the Companies ACT 1985 requires deferred tax to be included under the heading of 'Provisions for liabilities and charges'.

Example 5

A company has the following timing differences over a two year period:

	Timing differences	Corporation tax rate	Deferred tax
	£	%	£
1.1.X1 Balance b/f	100,000	35	35,000
31.12.X1 Originating timing differences	20,000	35	7,000
31.12.X2 Originating timing differences	10,000	30	3,000

The deferred tax account will include the adjustment necessary on the change in the tax rate as follows:

Deferred tax

	£		£
		1.1.X1 Balance b/d	35,000
31.12.X1 Balance c/d	42,000	31.12.X1 Profit and loss	7,000
	£42,000		£42,000
31.12.X2 Profit and loss:		1.1.X2 Balance b/d	42,000
– reduction in			
corporation tax rate			
(£120,000 × 5%)	6,000		
31.12.X2 Balance c/d		31.12.X2 Profit and loss	3,000
(£130,000 × 30%)	39,000		
	£45,000		£45,000

SSAP 8

This standard, The Treatment of Taxation under the Imputation System in the Accounts of Companies, requires the following to be shown in the published accounts:

1 Profit and loss account:
  – corporation tax
  – tax attributable to franked investment income
  – deferred tax
  – irrecoverable ACT.
2 Balance sheet:
  – ACT payable should be included in current liabilities
  – ACT recoverable should be deducted from deferred tax or, if there is no deferred tax account, shown as a deferred asset.

The tax attributable to franked investment income is the tax credit attaching to dividends received.

SSAP8 also requires the total of any overseas tax and any relief given against UK tax to be shown.

If there is no deferred tax account, ACT recoverable is included under debtors in the published balance sheet. This is because the format for the balance sheet in the Companies Act 1985 does not include an item for 'deferred assets'.

Summary

1 Income tax deducted from receipts and payments will be recovered from or paid to the Inland Revenue. Income tax is not an expense of a company.

2 Only the net amount of dividends payable will be included in the profit and loss account. ACT payable will be recoverable against the corporation tax liability on the profits of the period in which the dividend is paid.

3 When preparing a profit and loss account dividends received should be grossed up by the attaching tax credit, the tax being included in the taxation section of the profit and loss account.

4 The provision for the corporation tax for the year will be charged to the profit and loss account.

5 SSAP 8 specifies the treatment of taxation in the profit and loss account and balance sheet.

6 SSAP 15 requires deferred tax to be set aside where it is probable that a liability will crystallize.

Examination Hints

Taxation normally arises in the context of making the necessary adjustments when preparing a profit and loss account and balance sheet. If the income tax rate is given in the question do not omit to include ACT both payable and recoverable on the proposed dividend.

Questions are sometimes set requiring the ledger accounts to be written up. If a question contains both interest and dividends, remember that their treatment differs.

Try to answer the following questions before reading on.

Self-Assessment Questions

See page 305 for answers.

In each question, choose the correct answer from the five alternatives given.

16.1 Interest of £750 net is received. If the income tax rate is 25%, the interest will appear in the profit and loss account as:
a interest received £750
b interest received £1,000
c interest received £1,000 less income tax £250
d interest received £750 plus attaching tax credit £250
e interest received £1,000 less attaching tax credit £250.

16.2 Corporation tax payable is included on the balance sheet under:
a trade creditors
b other creditors
c provisions
d deferred tax
e reserves.

16.3 A company has an authorized share capital of £100,000, divided into ordinary shares of 50 pence each, of which 75,000 have been issued. A dividend of 7% is declared, income tax rate 30%. The total amount paid to shareholders is:
a £2,625
b £3,750
c £5,250
d £7,000
e £7,500.

16.4 A company has a 31 March accounting date. A preference dividend for the six months to 31 March 19X7 is paid on 1 April 19X7. The ACT on this dividend is recoverable by deduction against the corporation tax liability for the year to:
a 31.3.X6
b 31.12.X6

 c 31.3.X7
 d 31.12.X7
 e 31.3.X8.

If you have answered the above questions correctly, and are sure you understand the key points in this chapter, then try to answer questions 21 and 22 on pages 203–4 before moving on to Chapter 17.

CHAPTER 17

COMPANY ACCOUNTS: PROFIT AND LOSS ACCOUNTS

Chapter contents

Introduction **110** The published profit and loss account **110** Notes to the accounts **115** Earnings per share **115** Extraordinary items **116** Related companies **116** Summary **119** Examination hints **119**

Learning objectives

After studying this chapter you should be able to:

☐ prepare the profit and loss account of companies for presentation to shareholders in a form complying with the Companies Act 1985;

☐ prepare the notes to the accounts, supplementing the profit and loss account, that are required by the Act;

☐ calculate the basic earnings per share in accordance with SSAP 3;

☐ classify items as being exceptional, prior year adjustments or extraordinary in accordance with SSAP 6;

☐ define a related company and an associated company.

Introduction

All companies, regardless of size, have to prepare accounts for their shareholders that meet the disclosure requirements of the Companies Act 1985. Small and medium size companies are granted some exemptions from disclosure in the accounts that are filed with the Registrar of Companies. Details of these exemptions are given in Chapter 18.

Every registered company is required to produce accounts for its shareholders. The minimum content and format is laid down by the Companies Act 1985. These accounts are referred to as the published accounts and will contain less information than the accounts produced for the directors and managers of the company. The content of the published accounts is a compromise between providing full information to interested parties and safeguarding the privacy of the company. Making confidential information available to competitors could harm a company's trading position.

In addition to shareholders, the accounts will be made available to debenture holders, the inspector of taxes and, possibly, the company's bank, creditors and prospective investors.

A copy of the published accounts has to be filed with the Registrar of Companies. The company's file containing these accounts is open to inspection by the public. The filed accounts would normally be inspected by credit agencies and competitors; employees and potential take-over bidders may also be interested.

The published profit and loss account

Fully detailed annual accounts will be prepared for the directors of the company, but the profit and loss account prepared for presentation to the shareholders will be restricted to the information that has to be disclosed.

The two main alternative formats are as follows:

Companies Act 1985

Profit and loss account formats

Format 1

1 Turnover
2 Cost of sales
3 Gross profit or loss
4 Distribution costs
5 Administrative expenses
6 Other operating income
7 Income from shares in group
   companies
8 Income from shares in related
   companies
9 Income from other fixed asset
   investments
10 Other interest receivable and similar
   income
11 Amounts written off investments
12 Interest payable and similar charges
13 Tax on profit or loss on ordinary
   activities
14 Profit or loss on ordinary activities
   after taxation
15 Extraordinary income
16 Extraordinary charges
17 Extraordinary profit or loss
18 Tax on extraordinary profit or loss
19 Other taxes not shown under the
   above items
20 Profit or loss for the financial year

Format 2

1 Turnover
2 Change in stocks of finished goods and
   in work in progress
3 Own work capitalized
4 Other operating income
5 a Raw materials and consumables
   b Other external charges
6 Staff costs:
   a wages and salaries
   b social security costs
   c other pension costs
7 a Depreciation and other amounts
      written off tangible and intangible
      fixed assets
   b Exceptional amounts written off
      current assets
8 Other operating charges
9 Income from shares in group
   companies
10 Income from shares in related
   companies
11 Income from other fixed asset
   investments
12 Other interest receivable and similar
   income
13 Amounts written off investments
14 Interest payable and similar charges
15 Tax on profit or loss on ordinary
   activities
16 Profit or loss on ordinary activities
   after taxation
17 Extraordinary income
18 Extraordinary charges
19 Extraordinary profit or loss
20 Tax on extraordinary profit or loss
21 Other taxes not shown under the
   above items
22 Profit or loss for the financial year

The Act allows the accounts to be in the format of all expenses grouped together, and turnover and all income also being totalled. These two-sided versions of Formats 1 and 2 are given in the Act as Formats 3 and 4, but this form of presentation is rarely used in this country.

There is no significance in the alternative use of the description 'costs' as opposed to 'expenses'.

The formats are based on an EEC directive aimed at standardization within the Common Market.

In addition the following information must be shown for both formats:

1 Amounts transfered to and from reserves;
2 Dividends paid and proposed.

Format 1 is most commonly used in examinations, but you should also be prepared to use format 2 if required. The numbers identifying each item do not have to be shown. Any non-existent item is omitted. Note that *turnover* is the net sales of goods and services after deduction of trade discounts but not cash discounts. VAT should not be included.

Format 1 follows the normal accounting practice of allocating and apportioning expenses over the three functions of:

1 Production (cost of sales);
2 Sales, marketing and distribution (distribution costs);
3 Administration (administrative expenses).

Except for depreciation, the Act does not specify the expenses to be included under each of the above three functions.

Examination questions invariably do not contain all the items which are required to be disclosed by the Companies Act.

The allocation and apportionment of overheads is covered in most introductory costing textbooks.

The consolidation of parent and subsidiary company accounts is covered in Chapters 23 to 25.

Other operating income will include items not within the turnover definition, for example rents receivable.

Income from shares in group companies will be dividends received from group companies. *Income from shares in related companies* will include dividends received from associated companies (as defined by SSAP 1). *Extraordinary income and extraordinary charges* will be items to be treated as such in accordance with SSAP 6. *Other taxes* is an item that does not normally appear in the accounts of a UK company.

Example 1

The detailed profit and loss account prepared by a company for internal use is as follows:

Manufacturing, trading and profit and loss account
For the year ended 31 March 19X5

	£	£
Raw materials:		
Opening stock	19,200	
Purchases	123,125	
	142,325	
Less Closing stock	22,000	
		120,325
Direct wages		95,964
Prime cost		216,289
Overheads:		
Electricity	12,000	
Other expenses	20,300	
Salaries and wages	15,200	
Rent	4,320	
Rates	2,460	
Depreciation of plant and machinery	6,300	
		60,580
Manufacturing cost		276,869
Opening work in progress	8,100	
Less Closing work in progress	8,500	
		(400)
		276,469
Sales		424,550
Less Cost of sales:		
Finished goods:		
Opening stock	48,220	
Production cost	276,469	
	324,689	
Less Closing stock	51,500	
		273,189
Gross profit		151,361
Add Rents receivable		10,000
		161,361
Less:		
Administration expenses:		
General expenses	38,000	
Salaries and wages	32,365	
Interest payable	5,000	
Rent	1,440	

	£	£
Rates	820	
Depreciation of motor vehicles	360	
Electricity	1,832	
	79,817	
Selling and distribution expenses:		
Salaries and wages	14,000	
Advertising	12,500	
Motor running expenses	13,300	
Rent	1,440	
Rates	820	
Depreciation of motor vehicles	840	
Electricity	3,664	
	46,564	
		126,381
Profit before tax		34,980
Less Taxation		12,000
Profit after tax		22,980
Less Dividend		10,000
Retained profit		£12,980

Required:
Profit and loss account for publication to the shareholders.

Solution

Profit and loss account for the year ended 31 March 19X5 (Format 1)

	£	£
Turnover		424,550
Less Cost of sales		273,189
Gross profit		151,361
Less:		
Distribution costs	46,564	
Administrative expenses (W1)	74,817	
		121,381
		29,980
Add Other operating income		10,000
		39,980
Less Interest payable		5,000
		34,980
Less Corporation tax		12,000
Profit on ordinary activities after taxation		22,980
Less Dividend		10,000
Retained profit		£12,980

This description is not actually required by the format given in the Act. In practice companies do not always adhere strictly to the precise wordings given in the Act.

In answering examination questions it is helpful to cross reference your answer to your workings, for example:

Workings
1 Administrative expenses:

	£
Total per accounts	79,817
Less Interest payable shown separately	5,000
	£74,817

Interest payable is one of the items that is required to be disclosed separately.

Often examination questions require preparation of the published accounts from a trial balance. You will invariably need to open workings for:

1 Cost of sales
2 Distribution costs
3 Administrative expenses.

If format 2 was adopted the content of the profit and loss account would be:

Profit and loss account for the year ended 31 March 19X5
(Format 2)

	£	£
Turnover		424,550
Increase in stocks of finished goods and		
work in progress (W1)		3,680
Other operating income		10,000
		438,230
Less:		
Raw materials and consumables	120,325	
Staff costs – wages and salaries (W2)	157,529	
Depreciation (W3)	7,500	
Other operating charges (W4)	112,896	
		398,250
		39,980
Less Interest payable		5,000
		34,980
Less Corporation tax		12,000
Profit on ordinary activities after taxation		22,980
Less Dividend		10,000
Retained profit		£12,980

Workings

	£
1 Increase in stocks:	
Finished goods (£51,500 – £48,220)	3,280
Work in progress	400
	£3,680
2 Wages and salaries:	
Direct wages	95,964
Manufacturing overhead	15,200
Administrative expenses	32,365
Selling and distribution	14,000
	£157,529
3 Depreciation:	
Plant and machinery	6,300
Motor vehicles (£360 + £840)	1,200
	£7,500
4 Other operating charges:	
Electricity (£12,000 + £1,832 + £3,664)	17,496
Rent (£4,320 + £1,440 + £1,440)	7,200
Rates (£2,460 + £820 + £820)	4,100
Other expenses	20,300
General expenses	38,000
Advertising	12,500
Motor running expenses	13,300
	£112,896

Notes to the Accounts

The Act requires additional notes to the accounts to be given. The main notes supplementing the profit and loss account are:

1 Auditors' remuneration (including expenses);
2 Hire of plant and machinery (including finance charges);
3 Depreciation;
4 Directors' emoluments:
  a fees,
  b other emoluments,
  c emoluments waived,
  d pensions to present and past directors,
  e compensation for loss of office;
  and if the total emoluments ((a) + (b) but excluding the employer's pension contributions) *exceeds* £60,000, further notes are required of:
  f emoluments of the chairman.
  g emoluments of the highest paid director,
  h the numbers of all the directors analysed into bands of £5,000 starting at the band of £1 to £5,000.
5 Rents from land;
6 Income from listed investments;
7 Interest on loans redeemable after 5 years;
8 Employees (including directors):
  a average number of employees during the year,
  b total wages and salaries for the year,
  c total social security costs (including employer's national insurance contributions),
  d total pension costs (including employer's pension scheme contributions);
  e and for higher paid employees (other than directors) the numbers receiving emoluments in bands of £5,000 starting at £30,001 to £35,000;
9 Taxation – The basis on which tax is computed and the rate of tax;
10 Turnover – where a company carries on two or more classes of business the notes must contain a description of each class, its turnover and the profit before tax attributable to it; the turnover should be analysed between markets that are substantially different geographically;
11 Exceptional items;
12 Details of extraordinary items;
13 Transactions with directors.

Although not required by the Act:

  – SSAP 3 requires disclosure of the Earnings per share;
  – SSAP 6 requires disclosure of prior year items as well as exceptional and extraordinary items.

These SSAPs are considered in the next two sections of this chapter.

Earnings per share

SSAP 3 requires the basic earnings per share for the year to be disclosed and the basis of the calculation to be noted.
  It is calculated:

$$\frac{\text{Earnings for the year}}{\text{Number of shares}} = \text{pence per share}$$

The *earnings* are the profit (or loss) on ordinary activities after tax reduced by any preference dividends. In the case of consolidated accounts the earnings are further reduced by any minority shareholders' interest in the profits for the year of the subsidiary companies. (Consolidated accounts will be covered in Chapters 23 and 24.) The *number of shares* to be used in the calculation is the number of ordinary shares in issue and ranking for dividend at the end of the year.

The detailed disclosure provisions relating to published accounts are complex. This text covers the requirements that are likely to be met in examinations. An excellent and comprehensive reference text for use in practice is *Accounting Provisions of the Companies Act 1985* by B. Johnson and M. Patient (Farrington Publishers Ltd 1985). This covers the requirements of the Act and SSAPs, but it is, however, 900 pages long.

Directors' emoluments include gross pay, employers' pension contributions, taxable expense allowances and taxable benefits in kind. It does not include the employer's national insurance contributions.

The requirement is to show the total income from listed investments, which may be included in items 7 to 10 of Format 1. A listed investment is one that is quoted on the Stock Exchange list.

Additional requirements for notes, supplementing the balance sheet, are given in Chapter 18.

SSAP3 outlines the method for calculating earnings per share where there have been changes in the share capital during the year. It also allows the disclosure of earnings per share calculated on a nil distribution basis. Fully diluted earnings per share is also required to be disclosed in certain circumstances.

The requirement to disclose the earnings per share only applies to listed companies, i.e. those whose shares are quoted on a recognized stock exchange.

Extraordinary items

The objective of SSAP6 is to arrive at a profit on ordinary activities that is comparable from one year to the next. SSAP6 also requires all profits and losses to be taken to the profit and loss account. This rules out, for example, debiting an exceptional loss directly to a reserve account leaving the profit for the year unaffected. Items may only be taken to reserves if:

1 in accordance with SSAPs, e.g. goodwill written off per SSAP22;
2 required by law, e.g. share premium on issue of shares; or
3 permitted by law, e.g. preliminary expenses written off to the share premium account in accordance with the Companies Act 1985.

Redundancy costs arising from a reduction in the level of activities due to reorganization will normally be treated as exceptional, if they are material.

The *ordinary* activities of a company are those which are usually, frequently or regularly undertaken. They include any related activities in furtherance of, incidental to or arising from the ordinary activites.

SSAP 6 defines an *extraordinary item* as one which meets all three of the following criteria:

1 it derives from events or transactions outside the ordinary activities of the business;
2 it is material; and
3 it is not expected to recur either frequently or regularly.

Examples of extraordinary items are profits or losses arising from:

1 redundancy payments on closure of a segment of a business;
2 sale of a fixed asset investment in an associated company;
3 the expropriation of assets by a foreign government.

Exceptional items should be noted. These are items that do not meet the extraordinary item criteria but because of their size or incidence need to be disclosed in order to show a true and fair view. Examples of exceptional items are profits or losses arising from:

1 abnormal bad debts;
2 abnormal write-down of stock values;
3 insurance claim for loss of profits.

Prior year adjustments, if material, should be added to or deducted from the profit and loss account balance brought forward from the previous year. They only arise in respect of:

1 adjustments arising on the change of an accounting policy, or
2 the correction of fundamental errors in the accounts of previous years.

Prior year adjustments are rare. Amounts that are merely under- or overprovided in previous years are regarded as routine adjustments to accounting estimates and not as prior year adjustments. They should only be disclosed, as exceptional items, if they are material.

Related companies

The Act defines a related company as: 'Any body corporate (other than another group company) in which the investing company holds, on a *long-term* basis, a *qualifying capital interest* for the purpose of securing a contribution to the investing company's own activities by exercising any *control or influence* that arises from that interest.'

A 'qualifying capital interest' is one that carries rights to vote in all circumstances. If the qualifying capital interest is 20% or more of another company then it is presumed to be a related company.

Many companies use the description 'associated companies' in their accounts. SSAP 1 defines an associated company as: 'A company not being a subsidiary of the investing group or company in which:

1 the interest of the investing group or company is effectively that of a partner in a joint venture or consortium and the investing group or company is in a position to exercise a significant influence over the company in which the investment has been made; or
2 the interest of the investing group or company is for the long term and is substantial and, having regard to the disposition of the other shareholdings, the investing group or company is in a position to exercise a significant influence over the company in which the investment is made.'

An associated company is normally also a related company.

The significance of an investment being treated as being in a related company is that the income is disclosed separately in the published profit and loss account. If the related company is, as usual, also an associated company then SSAP 1 requires the equity method of treatment of the investment to be used in the consolidated accounts of a group. The equity method of accounting for associated companies is outlined in Chapter 23.

Example 2

Northbanks PLC are wholesalers. The following is their trial balance at 31 May 19X3.

	Debit	Credit
	£000	£000
Ordinary share capital, £1 shares		300
Share premium		200
Capital redemption reserve		90
Profit and loss account balance at 31.5.X2		217
Stock at 31.5.X2	318	
Sales		4,475
Purchases	3,624	
Discounts allowed	3	
Salaries and wages:		
– Warehouse	114	
– Salesmen	156	
– Administrative	83	
Vehicle running costs:		
– Distribution	140	
– Administrative	21	
General expenses:		
– Distribution	80	
– Administrative	16	
Director's remuneration	29	
Commissions received		5
Long-term investment	40	
Dividends received – gross		10
Tax credit attaching to dividends received	3	
Debtors	350	
Provision for doubtful debts		11
Trade creditors		280
Cash	21	
Premises – at valuation	500	
Equipment, cost and accumulated depreciation:		
– Warehouse	84	34
– Office	23	13
Interim dividend paid	21	
ACT paid	9	
	£5,635	£5,635

Notes:
1 Stock at 31 May 19X3 £362,000.
2 Depreciate equipment 20% reducing balance method.
3 Expense owing with regard to auditors' remuneration £12,000.
4 Provision for doubtful debts to be maintained at 4% of debtors.
5 Provide for corporation tax liability for the year £140,000.
6 A final dividend of 14p per share is proposed.

Required:
A profit and loss account for the year ended 31 May 19X3 prepared in accordance with the requirements of the Companies Act 1985 for submission to shareholders.

Note that a balance sheet is *not* required.

Solution

Northbanks PLC
Profit and loss account for the year ended 31 May 19X3

	£000	£000	Notes
Turnover		4,475	
Less Cost of sales (W1)		3,580	
Gross profit		895	
Less Distribution costs (W2)	503		
Administrative expenses (W3)	166		
		669	
		226	1
Add Other operating income	5		
Income from fixed asset investment	10		
		15	
		241	
Less Corporation tax	140		
Tax attributable to franked investment income	3		
		143	
Profit on ordinary activities after tax for the year		98	
Less Ordinary dividends:			
Interim – paid	21		
Final – proposed	42		
		63	
Retained profit		£35	2
Earnings per share		32.7 pence	3

Notes to the Accounts

1   Profit before tax is arrived at after charging:

	£000
Depreciation	12
Directors' remuneration	29
Auditors' remuneration	12
Wages and salaries (W4)	382

2   Movement on reserves:

	£000
Profit and loss account:	
At 1.6.X2	217
Retained profit	35
At 31.5.X3	£252

3   Earnings per share – calculated on profit on ordinary activities after tax of £98,000 divided by 300,000 ordinary shares of £1 each.

Workings

1   Cost of sales:

	£000
Stock at 1.6.X2	318
Purchases	3,624
	3,942
Less Stock at 31.5.X3	362
	£3,580

2 Distribution costs:

Salaries and wages:	
– Warehouse	114
– Salesmen	156
Vehicle costs	140
General expenses	80
Depreciation of equipment (20% × (£84 – £34))	10
Increase in provision for doubtful debts ((4% × £350) – £11)	3
	£503

3 Administrative expenses:

Discounts allowed	3
Salaries and wages	83
Vehicle costs	21
General expenses	16
Directors' remuneration	29
Depreciation of equipment (20% × (£23 – £13))	2
Auditors' remuneration	12
	£166

4 Wages and salaries – note to the accounts:

Warehouse	114
Salesmen	156
Administrative	83
Directors	29
	£382

Summary

1 The Companies Act 1985 specifies the information that has to be disclosed in the published accounts of a company.
2 The profit and loss account may be presented in either of the two main formats.
3 Additional notes to the accounts are required.
4 SSAP 3 requires listed companies to disclose the earnings per share.
5 SSAP 6 defines extraordinary items, exceptional items and prior year adjustments.
6 SSAP 1 defines an associated company. These companies meet the Companies Act definition of related companies.

Examination Hints

Examination questions frequently require both a published profit and loss account and balance sheet. Please refer to the examination hints at the end of the next chapter.

Try to answer the following questions before reading on.

Self-Assessment Questions

In each question, choose the correct answer from the five alternatives given. See page 305 for answers.

17.1 Which item will not be included in cost of sales:
   a royalty payable on goods manufactured

b   royalty payable on goods sold
c   power
d   production director's remuneration
e   insurance of factory buildings.

17.2   Which item will not be included in distribution costs:
a   carriage inwards
b   depreciation of lorries
c   maintenance of fork lift trucks
d   sales director's remuneration
e   insurance of sales representatives' cars.

17.3   Which item will not be included in administrative expenses:
a   auditors' fees
b   cash discounts allowed
c   bank overdraft interest
d   managing director's remuneration
e   depreciation of computer.

17.4   Which item need not be disclosed by way of note:
a   number of employees receiving remuneration greater than £30,000
b   pensions paid to directors
c   extraordinary gain
d   employer's national insurance contributions
e   interest on bank deposit.

17.5   An extremely large bad debt arises that relates to the previous year's sales but which had not been provided for in the previous year. Is it:
a   not disclosed
b   disclosed as a deduction from turnover
c   noted as an exceptional item
d   treated as a prior year adjustment
e   treated as an extraordinary item.

If you have answered the above questions correctly, and are sure you understand the key points in this chapter, then move straight on to Chapter 18.

CHAPTER 18

COMPANY ACCOUNTS: BALANCE SHEETS

Chapter contents

Introduction **121** The published balance sheet **121** Notes to the accounts **124** Post balance sheet events **127** Contingent liabilities **127** Small and medium size companies **128** Summary **129** Examination hints **129**

Learning objectives

After studying this chapter you should be able to:

☐ prepare a balance sheet for presentation to shareholders in a form complying with the Companies Act 1985;

☐ prepare the notes to the accounts, supplementing the balance sheet, that are required by the Act;

☐ treat post balance sheet events in accordance with SSAP 17;

☐ treat contingencies in accordance with SSAP 18 and the Act;

☐ define small and medium size companies and prepare accounts for filing in accordance with the exemptions granted by the Act.

Introduction

The published balance sheet follows closely the normal content and layout of the traditional style of balance sheet that is used for internal management purposes by many companies. As such it should not present you with too many problems, but care has to be taken to ensure that the disclosure provisions relating to the notes to the accounts are complied with.

SSAP 17 and SSAP 18 are concerned with the extent to which events that may take place after the date of the balance sheet should be included in, or excluded from, the accounts or disclosed by way of a note.

Companies that qualify as small companies are given some exemptions from disclosure in the accounts that are filed with the Registrar of Companies, although they still have to prepare full accounts meeting the requirements of the Act for their shareholders. This also applies to medium size companies, but the exemptions given are very limited.

The published balance sheet

It is necessary to learn format 1 (format 2 is also given below for comparison):

Companies Act 1985

Balance sheet formats

Format 1	*Format 2*
	ASSETS
A Called up share capital not paid	**A** Called up share capital not paid
B Fixed assets	**B** Fixed assets

I   Intangible assets
    1 Development costs
    2 Concessions, patents, licences, trade marks and similar rights and assets
    3 Goodwill
    4 Payments on account
	I Intangible assets
	    1 Development costs
	    2 Concessions, patents, licences, trade marks and similar rights and assets
	    3 Goodwill
	    4 Payments on account

II   Tangible assets
    1 Land and buildings
    2 Plant and machinery
    3 Fixtures, fittings, tools and equipment
    4 Payments on account and assets in course of construction
	II Tangible assets
	    1 Land and buildings
	    2 Plant and machinery
	    3 Fixtures, fittings, tools and equipment
	    4 Payments on account and assets in course of construction

III   Investments
    1 Shares in group companies
    2 Loans to group companies
    3 Shares in related companies
    4 Loans to related companies
    5 Other investments other than loans
    6 Other loans
    7 Own shares
	III Investments
	    1 Shares in group companies
	    2 Loans to group companies
	    3 Shares in related companies
	    4 Loans to related companies
	    5 Other investments other than loans
	    6 Other loans
	    7 Own shares

C Current assets	**C** Current assets

I   Stocks
    1 Raw materials and consumables
    2 Work in progress
    3 Finished goods and goods for resale
    4 Payments on account
	I Stocks
	    1 Raw materials and consumables
	    2 Work in progress
	    3 Finished goods and goods for resale
	    4 Payments on account

II   Debtors
    1 Trade debtors
    2 Amounts owed by group companies
    3 Amounts owed by related companies
    4 Other debtors
    5 Called-up share capital not paid
    6 Prepayments and accrued income
	II Debtors
	    1 Trade debtors
	    2 Amounts owed by group companies
	    3 Amounts owed by related companies
	    4 Other debtors
	    5 Called-up share capital not paid
	    6 Prepayments and accrued income

III   Investments
    1 Shares in group companies
    2 Own shares
    3 Other investments
	III Investments
	    1 Shares in group companies
	    2 Own shares
	    3 Other investments

IV Cash at bank and in hand	**IV** Cash at bank and in hand
D Prepayments and accrued income	**D** Prepayments and accrued income

E   Creditors: amounts falling due
within one year
1 Debenture loans
2 Bank loans and overdrafts
3 Payments received on account
4 Trade creditors
5 Bills of exchange payable
6 Amounts owed to group
   companies
7 Amounts owed to related
   companies
8 Other creditors including taxation
   and social security
9 Accruals and deferred income

F   Net current assets (liabilities)

G   Total assets less current liabilities

H   Creditors: amounts falling due after
more than one year
1 Debenture loans
2 Bank loans and overdrafts
3 Payments received on account
4 Trade creditors
5 Bills of exchange payable
6 Amounts owed to group
   companies
7 Amounts owed to related
   companies
8 Other creditors including taxation
   and social security
9 Accruals and deferred income

I   Provisions for liabilities and charges
1 Pensions and similar obligations
2 Taxation, including deferred
   taxation
3 Other provisions

J   Accruals and deferred income

K   Capital and reserves
  I Called up share capital
 II Share premium account
III Revaluation reserve
IV Other reserves
    1 Capital redemption reserve
    2 Reserve for own shares
    3 Reserves provided for by the
      articles of association
    4 Other reserves
  V Profit and loss account

LIABILITIES

A   Capital and reserves

  I Called-up share capital
 II Share premium account
III Revaluation reserve
IV Other reserves

    1 Capital redemption reserve
    2 Reserve for own shares
    3 Reserves provided for by the
      articles of association
    4 Other reserves

  V Profit and loss account

B   Provision for liabilities and charges

    1 Pensions and similar obligations
    2 Taxation including deferred
      taxation
    3 Other provisions

C   Creditors*
    1 Debenture loans
    2 Bank loans and overdrafts
    3 Payments received on account
    4 Trade creditors
    5 Bills of exchange payable
    6 Amounts owed to group
      companies
    7 Amounts owed to related
      companies
    8 Other creditors including taxation
      and social security
    9 Accruals and deferred income

D   Accruals and deferred income

*A note is required analysing the
amounts between those falling due
within one year and after more
than one year.

Comments

1 Format 1 is normally used by companies. Format 2 is very similar except that all the assets are grouped together with the result that net current assets (the working capital) is not shown.
2 Each item is designated by a letter, roman numeral or arabic numeral. These designations are not shown in the published balance sheet.
3 Any items in the format for which balances do not exist may be omitted, there is no need to show nil balances.
4 There are alternative positions for prepayments (C II 6 and D) and for accruals (E 9 and J); the first positions are normally used.

5   Items designated by arabic numerals (1,2, etc.) may be disclosed in notes rather than on the face of the balance sheet.

6   Fixed assets are analysed into intangible, tangible and investments. Investments that are not long term are included under current assets.

7   The totals F and G are specifically required to be shown.

8   The same descriptions are included under both E and H, being the analysis of creditors between short-term and long-term amounts.

Notes to the Accounts

The main notes required (in addition to those supplementing the profit and loss account) are:

For full disclosure requirements refer to *Accounting Provisions of the Companies Act 1985* by B. Johnson and M. Patient (Farrington Publishers Ltd 1985). Notes that relate primarily to the profit and loss account are given in Chapter 17.

1   *Accounting policies.* These will invariably include at least the depreciation bases used and the method used for valuing stock. The method used to translate any foreign currency items into sterling must be noted. (Disclosure of accounting policies is also required by SSAP 2 – see Chapter 1.)

2   *Fixed assets:*
   – Total cost or valuation at the beginning of the year
   – Additions during the year
   – Transfers
   – Disposals
   – Total cost or valuation at the end of the year

Land and buildings should be analysed between freehold, long leasehold and short leasehold. A short leasehold is one that has less than fifty years left to run.

   – Accumulated depreciation at the beginning of the year
   – Provisions made during the year
   – Transfers
   – Disposals
   – Accumulated depreciation at the end of the year

   (The above information for tangible fixed assets can best be given in a schedule, and noted, where necessary, for intangible fixed assets and fixed asset investments.)

   – The year and amount of any valuations included, and for valuations during the year, the name and qualifications of the valuer and the basis of valuation used.

3   *Listed investments.* The amount and market value.

4   *Debtors.* Any amounts included in debtors that do not fall due to be received within one year.

If an investment in another company amounts to more than 10% of that company's equity, a note is required of the name of the company, its country of incorporation and details of the shares held, including the proportion of the shares held.

5   *Creditors:*
   – Amounts that are secured and nature of security
   – Amounts repayable after five years including amounts repayable by instalments that will not be wholly repaid within five years
   – Reasons for any issue of debentures or loan stock.

6   *Pension commitments.* Details of provisions and also details of any commitments for which no provision has been made.

7   *Share capital:*
   – Number and nominal value of shares authorized and issued
   – Amount and period of any cumulative preference dividends in arrear
   – Redemption dates and terms of redemption.

8   *Reserves.* Movements for the year.

9   *Contingent liabilities.*

Contingent liabilities are considered in a following section of this chapter.

10   *Capital expenditure:*
   – Contracts that have not been provided for in the accounts
   – Expenditure authorized by the directors that has not yet been contracted.

Example 1

Chairs PLC, a manufacturing company, has an authorized share capital of £100,000 divided into 150,000 ordinary shares of 50p each and 25,000 8% preference shares of £1 each.

The draft balance sheet at 30 April 19X4 is as follows:

Assets:	£000
Land and buildings	140
Plant and machinery	83
Fixtures and fittings	34
Stock at lower of cost and net realizable value	64
Debtors	48
Bank	32
ACT recoverable	12
	£413

Liabilities:	
Ordinary shares	60
Preference shares	25
Share premium	30
Profit and loss account	132
10% loan stock	30
Corporation tax for year to 30.4.X4	53
Creditors	43
Dividends payable – preference	1
– ordinary	27
ACT payable	12
	£413

The following information is available:

1 Additions to fixed assets during the year were:

> Plant and machinery   £8,000
> Fixtures and fittings   £5,000

Plant and machinery that had cost £3,000 was sold at its book value of £1,000

2 The cost of fixed assets held at 30 April 19X4 is:

> Land and buildings   £170,000
> Plant and machinery   £120,000
> Fixtures and fittings   £50,000

Land and buildings are held on a lease that has 28 years left to run.

3 The depreciation charged to the profit and loss account for the year to 30 April 19X4 was:

> Land and buildings   £5,000
> Plant and machinery   £18,000
> Fixtures and fittings   £7,000

Required:
Balance sheet at 30 April 19X4 in a form suitable for presentation to shareholders that complies with the Companies Act 1985.

Solution

Chairs PLC
Balance sheet at 30 April 19X4

	£000	£000	Notes
Fixed assets:			
Tangible assets		257	1
Current assets:			
Stock	64		2
Debtors	60		3
Cash at bank	32		
	156		

	£000	£000	Notes
Less Creditors – amounts falling due within one year:			
Trade creditors	43		
Other creditors	93		4
	136		
Net current assets		20	
Total assets less Current liabilities		277	
Less Creditors – amounts falling due after more than one year:			
10% loan stock		30	
		£247	
Capital and reserves:			
Called-up share capital		85	5
Share premium account		30	
Profit and loss account		132	
		£247	

Notes

1 *Fixed assets:*

	Land and buildings (short leasehold)	Plant and machinery	Fixtures and fittings	Total
	£000	£000	£000	£000
Cost:				
At 1.5.X3 (balancing figures)	170	115	45	330
Additions		8	5	13
Disposal		(3)		(3)
At 30.4.X4	£170	£120	£50	£340
Depreciation:				
At 1.5.X3 (balancing figures)	25	21	9	55
Profit and loss account	5	18	7	30
Disposals		(2)		(2)
At 30.4.X4	£30	£37	£16	£83
Net book value:				
At 30.4.X4	£140	£83	£34	£257

2 *Stock* is valued at the lower of cost and net realizable value.

3 *Debtors:*

	£000
Trade debtors	48
ACT recoverable after more than one year	12
	£60

4 *Other creditors:*

	£000
Corporation tax	53
ACT payable	12
Dividends:	
– Preference	1
– Ordinary	27
	£93

5   *Share capital:*

	£000
Authorized:	
150,000 ordinary shares of 50p each	75
25,000 8% preference shares of £1 each	25
	£100
Issued:	
120,000 ordinary shares of 50p each	60
25,000 8% preference shares of £1 each	25
	£85

Post Balance Sheet Events

SSAP 17 Accounting for Post Balance Sheet Events defines post balance sheet events as both favourable and unfavourable events that occur between the date of the balance sheet and the date of the board meeting at which the accounts are approved. This date should be noted.

The events are classified between:

1   *Adjusting events* which provide new or additional evidence of conditions existing at the balance sheet date; and
2   *Non-adjusting events* which relate to conditions arising after the balance sheet date.

The accounts are adjusted (i.e. provisions are made) for:

1   Adjusting events, and
2   Events which indicate that the application of the going concern concept in preparing the accounts is not appropriate.

A *note* must be made to the accounts concerning the nature and amount of any non-adjusting events that are material to the proper understanding of the accounts or if they reverse 'window dressing'.

Examples of adjusting events are:

1   The sale of stock that was held at the balance sheet date at a selling value lower than cost. (Stock should be included on the balance sheet at the lower net realizable value.)
2   The insolvency of a customer included in debtors at the balance sheet date. (If the customer has not paid the amount owing at the balance sheet date it should be included in the provision for doubtful debts.)
3   The directors decide on the amount of dividends they recommend to be paid. (Provision should be made for the dividends.)

The balance sheet, of course, discloses the position at the balance sheet date and adjusting events are those that have to be taken account of in determining this position. This enables profits and losses to be reported in the year to which they relate.

Examples of non-adjusting events are:

1   Fixed assets lost in a fire.
2   A change in a foreign currency exchange rate creating a loss.
3   Closure of a factory.

Profits and losses arising from non-adjusting events are included in the accounts of the following year (the year in which they are earned or incurred).

Contingent liabilities

A contingent liability is one that may or may not arise in the future, but if it does it will be because of an event that has already taken place. Examples are:

1   A guarantee that has been given by the balance sheet date to reimburse a customer's bank should the customer default on repayment of an overdraft.

The accounts should be signed by two of the directors. This can be done at the foot of the balance sheet as follows:

The notes on pages (n) to (nn) from an integral part of these accounts.
Approved by the Board of Directors on   (date)   ....

.... } Directors
....

'Window dressing' transactions are undertaken primarily to alter the appearance of the balance sheet. Transactions which reverse window dressing have to be noted. For example, a note would be required if a company repaid loans on the last day of the accounting year and borrowed them back the next day.

SSAP 18 Accounting for Contingencies defines a contingency as a condition which exists at the balance sheet date where the outcome will be confirmed only on the occurrence or non-occurence of one or more future events.

2 A bill receivable that has been discounted before the balance sheet date but has not yet matured and is held by a third party who has the right to reclaim its value should the bill be dishonoured.

In both these cases a liability may arise in the future. The problem is should the liability be provided for, and if not, should it be noted, bearing in mind that some liabilities may be very unlikely to arise.

The practice recommended by SSAP 18 Accounting for Contingencies is to:

> Contingent losses need not be provided for if they are not probable or if it is not possible to estimate them.

1 *Provide* for probable losses that can be estimated with reasonable accuracy by the date the accounts are approved by the directors;
2 *Note* any material contingent losses that are not provided;
3 *Note* any probable contingent gain.

Not taking credit for probable gains but providing for probable losses is in accordance with the prudence concept.

The Companies Act 1985 requires any contingent liability that has not been provided to be noted. The note should contain:

1 The amount;
2 Its legal nature;
3 Details of any security given.

Small and medium size companies

> The concession to file modified accounts is not available, regardless of size, to a public company or a subsidiary of a public company.

Companies that qualify as small or medium in size may file *modified* accounts with the Registrar of Companies, but accounts complying with the full requirements of the Act still have to be prepared for shareholders.

The size limits are:

	Small company	Medium size company
Turnover did not exceed	£1,400,000	£5,750,000
Total assets did not exceed	£700,000	£2,800,000
The average number of employees did not exceed	50	250

> Total assets are the total of fixed and current assets (plus any called-up share capital that has not been paid).

Only two of the three conditions have to be met.

> The conditions only have to be met in the first year in the case of a newly formed company's first accounts.

To qualify a company has to meet the conditions for both the year and the preceeding year. It ceases to qualify if the conditions are not met for two consecutive years.

Exemptions given to small companies

A profit and loss account and a directors' report are not required to be filed. A *modified balance sheet* (which omits items identified in the format by arabic numerals) and some notes are required:

The modified balance sheet for a small company would look as follows:

	£	£
Fixed assets:		
Intangible assets	x	
Tangible assets	x	
Investments	x	
		x
Current assets:		
Stocks	x	
Debtors	x	
Investments	x	

	£	£
Cash	x	
	x	
Less Creditors – amounts falling due within one year	x	
Net current assets		x
Total assets *less* current liabilities		x
Less:		
Creditors – amounts falling due after more than one year	x	
Provisions for liabilities and charges	x	
		x
Net assets		x
Capital and reserves:		
Called-up share capital		x
Share premium account		x
Revaluation reserve		x
Other reserves		x
Profit and loss account		x
		x

Notes are only required for the following items:

1 Accounting policies
2 Share capital
3 Creditors payable after more than five years
4 Method used to translate foreign currency

Exemptions given to medium size companies

Very few exemptions are given. Turnover, cost of sales and other operating income need not be disclosed. The filed profit and loss account will commence with the amount of gross profit. Otherwise the normal full published accounts are filed.

Summary

1 The Companies Act 1985 specifies the information that has to be disclosed in the published accounts of a company.
2 There are two main formats for the balance sheet.
3 Additional notes are required.
4 SSAP 17 classifies post balance sheet events between adjusting and non-adjusting events.
5 SSAP 18 requires probable contingent liabilities to be provided for.
6 Companies that meet the Companies Act definition of 'small' may file modified accounts. Some exemption from full disclosure in the filed accounts is also given to 'medium size' companies.

Examination Hints

Questions requiring the preparation of accounts in accordance with the Companies Act 1985 can be analysed into preparing:

1 the profit and loss account
2 the balance sheet
3 notes to the accounts
4 workings.

It is helpful to head up four separate pages for these and to build up all four as you work through the question.

Deal with each piece of additional information given in the question in turn. If it is merely additional information required to be noted it can be entered straight into the notes. If adjustments are required they can be entered straight into an appropriate space on the pages for the profit and loss account and balance sheet or in your workings. If you know the formats you should be able to do this. Workings can be headed up for:

1   cost of sales
2   distribution costs
3   administrative expenses
4   other creditors
5   accruals

as these are invariably required. Remember that some adjustments will also need to be disclosed in the notes, e.g. provision made for directors' fees.

If a note is given for the movements on tangible fixed assets only the total net book value arrived at need be included in the balance sheet.

Do not worry if your answer has vacant lines where space has been left to accommodate items that were not present in the question. If there is no space to enter an item, enter it where you can and arrow it to its correct location.

Cross reference the workings and notes.

As always, read the question requirements carefully. Some questions may require the preparation of a detailed profit and loss account for internal use within the company first, in which case workings for cost of sales, distribution costs and administrative expenses will not be required as they can be extracted from the totals shown in the detailed profit and loss account.

Remember that full published accounts have to be prepared by small companies for the shareholders; the exemptions only apply to the filed accounts.

Try to answer the following questions before reading on.

Self-Assessment Questions

See page 305 for answers.

In each question, choose the correct answer from the five alternatives given.

18.1   A total is not shown in a published balance sheet for:
    a   total assets
    b   share capital
    c   working capital
    d   share capital and reserves
    e   net assets.

18.2   Which of the following fixed assets is not intangible:
    a   development costs
    b   patents
    c   trademarks
    d   goodwill
    e   loans receivable.

18.3   Which of the following post balance sheet events is an adjusting event:
    a   dividend recommendation
    b   window dressing reversal
    c   addition to fixed assets
    d   issue of shares
    e   sale of factory.

18.4   Which of the following is not required to be noted:
    a   provision for pensions
    b   a possible contingent loss
    c   a probable contingent gain
    d   a possible contingent gain
    e   a fixed assets on order.

18.5   Which of the following is not required to be noted;
    a   year of revaluation of a fixed asset
    b   loans stock redemption dates
    c   authorized share capital
    d   additions to fixed assets
    e   proceeds of sale of fixed assets.

If you have answered the above questions correctly, and are sure you understand the key points in this chapter, then try to answer questions 23, 24 and 25 on pages 204–6 before moving on to Chapter 19.

CHAPTER 19

DIRECTORS' REPORT

Chapter contents

Introduction **132**   Contents of the report **132**   Summary **134**   Examination hints **134**

Learning objective

After studying this chapter you should be able to:

☐ prepare a directors' report from given information in accordance with the requirements of the Companies Act 1985.

Introduction

The Act requires published accounts to contain:

1 a profit and loss account,
2 a balance sheet, and
3 a directors' report.

SSAP 10 requires a statement of source and application of funds to be included (see Chapter 20).
   Additionally most companies include a non-statutory chairman's report.

The directors' report gives shareholders additional information about the company's activities and its future prospects.

The published accounts of a company will contain a report by the directors. Information that must be included in the directors' report is specified by the Companies Act 1985. The wording of the report is not specified, and additional material may be included. The report is normally drafted by the company secretary and or accountant in accordance with instructions given and has to be approved by the directors in a board meeting.

Contents of the report

The items that are required to be included in the report are indicated by the headings and content of the following example.

To the shareholders
XYZ Ltd

Report of the directors for the year ended 31 December 19X7

Principal activities
The company is engaged in the manufacture and distribution of non-ferrous metal products.

Results and dividends		£
The profit after tax amounted to		100,000

The directors recommend dividends of:

	£	
Preference	12,000	
Ordinary – paid	15,000	
– proposed	25,000	
		52,000
Leaving retained profits of		£48,000

Significant changes in fixed assets
During the year premises were sold for £150,000. The proceeds were invested in new plant and machinery.

Market value of land and buildings
In the directors' opinion the market value of land and buildings considerably exceeds the net book value of £240,000 at which it is included in the balance sheet.

Directors' interest in shares and debentures of the company
Number of ordinary shares held:

	At 1.1.X7	At 31.12.X7
A. Brown	1,000	1,000
B. Black	3,000	11,000
C. Green	500	300

Shares held at the beginning of the year or at date of appointment as a director during the year. Details only given for persons who were directors at the end of the year. The name of any person who was a director at any time during the year must be given.

Directors' service contracts
There are no directors' service contracts in existence.

Political and Charitable gifts
The following contributions were made during the year:

	£
To UK charitable organizations	10,000
To UK political organizations:	
Conservative party	1,000
Other	150
	£1,150

Names required for political contributions exceeding £200.

Important post balance sheet events
The company acquired a new distribution depot in Northern Ireland in February 19X8.

Likely future developments
The company's plans to extend the manufacturing activities to Northern Ireland are nearing completion.

Research and development activities
The company continues to seek to extend and improve its products by applied research and a wide range of development projects.

Acquisition of own shares
100 ordinary shares of £1 each, being 0.1% of the total ordinary shares, were acquired by the company during the year for £250 and cancelled.

Employment of disabled people
The company's policy is to give full and fair consideration to applications for employment by disabled persons, having regard to their particular aptitudes and abilities.
    Employees who have become disabled and can no longer fulfil their duties are transferred, whenever possible, to alternative posts within the company.
    Training is provided where necessary.

Only required if number of employees exceeds 250.

Employee involvement
No action has been taken during the year to introduce, maintain or develop arrangements aimed at employee involvement.

Only required if number of employees exceeds 250. This section of the report could have been worded more diplomatically, but the point is that the company does not have to take action.

Substantial shareholders
On 31.1.X8 no person has an interest in 5% or more of the ordinary shares.

At a date not earlier than 1 month before the notice of the shareholders' meeting. Name, number of shares and % held are required. Any significant contract with a substantial shareholder must be disclosed.

Taxation status
The company is not a close company within the provisions of the Income and Corporation Taxes Act 1970.

BY ORDER OF THE BOARD

John Smith   Company Secretary 15.2.X8

Summary

1   The Companies Act 1985 requires a directors' report to be included in the published accounts. The Act specifies the information that should be disclosed in the report.

Examination Hints

The content of a directors' report will be dictated by the information contained in the question. It will not be necessary to invent information unless specifically required by the question to do so.

    The heading and conclusion of the report is fairly standard and should always be included. The narrative may be kept brief and to the point.

Try to answer the following questions before reading on.

Self-Assessment Questions

See page 306 for answers.

In each question, choose the correct answer from the five alternatives given.

19.1   Which of the following will not appear in a directors' report:
    a   dividends
    b   directors' holdings of shares
    c   directors' holdings of loan stock
    d   exports
    e   development projects.

19.2   A directors' report is signed by the company's:
    a   chairman
    b   managing director
    c   official receiver
    d   auditor
    e   secretary.

If you have answered the above questions correctly, and are sure you understand the key points in this chapter, then try to answer question 26 on page 207 before moving on to Chapter 20.

CHAPTER 20

COMPANY ACCOUNTS: FUNDS STATEMENTS

Chapter contents

Introduction **135**   Preparation of funds statements **135**   Interpretation of funds statements **142**   Summary **142**   Examination hints **143**

Learning objectives

After studying this chapter you should be able to:

☐ prepare a funds statement complying with the recommendations of SSAP 10;

☐ interpret a funds statement to comment on funds flow.

Introduction

The funds statement is prepared for the same accounting period as the profit and loss account. It identifies the movements in assets, liabilities and capital that have taken place during the year and the resultant effect on net liquid funds. It seeks to demonstrate clearly the manner in which the operations of the company have been financed and how its financial resources have been used. It does this by showing the sources from which funds have flowed into the business and how they have been applied.

SSAP 10 Statements of Source and Application of Funds requires that the audited financial accounts of a company should include a statement of source and application of net liquid funds. This requirement applies to all enterprises with a turnover or gross income of £25,000 per annum or more.

Net liquid funds are defined as cash at bank and in hand and cash equivalents (e.g. investments held as current assets) less bank overdrafts and other borrowings repayable within one year.

Preparation of funds statements

A funds statement is basically prepared by comparing the balance sheets at the beginning and end of a year and classifying the increases or reductions in the items on the balance sheets as either a source or application of funds. Some adjustments are required where the changes in the balance sheet figures do not by themselves represent the movements of funds.

Example 1: Basic principles

The following is the balance sheet of a small drugs wholesaling company together with the comparative figures for the previous year:

Balance sheet at......

	Previous year			Current year		
	£	£	£	£	£	£
Fixed assets:						
Cost		10,000			15,500	
Less Accumulated depreciation		4,000			6,800	
			6,000			8,700
Current assets:						
Stock		5,000			7,000	
Debtors		6,000			5,500	
Cash at bank		2,000			3,000	
		13,000			15,500	
Creditors – amounts due within one year:						
Creditors	4,800			5,000		
Taxation	3,000			4,000		
Dividend	1,000			1,500		
		8,800			10,500	
Net current assets			4,200			5,000
			£10,200			£13,700
Share capital			5,000			6,000
Share premium			—			500
Profit and loss account			5,200			7,200
			£10,200			£13,700

These figures reveal that although retained profits have increased by £2,000 cash at bank has only increased by £1,000. A funds statement will explain how this situation arose.

The statement is prepared on the basis that profits before tax are a source of funds and shows the separate effect on funds of the movement in the other balance sheet items from the previous year to the current year. The funds statement will balance providing the differences between the previous and current balance sheet figures for all balance sheet items are taken either to workings or directly to the funds statement. To ensure this tick off each item on the balance sheet as it is dealt with.

As a profit and loss account has not been given in this example the first stage must be to calculate the profit before tax for the current year, as follows:

Alternatively the profit and loss account can be reconstructed as follows:

Profit and loss account
– Debits	£
Tax	4,000
Dividend	1,500
Balance c/f (per current balance sheet)	7,200
	12,700
	£12,700

	£
Profit and loss account balance at end of current year	7,200
Less Profit and loss account balance at beginning of current year	5,200
Increase in retained profits	2,000
Add Taxation charge for current year	4,000
Dividends for current year	1,500
Profit before tax	£7,500

– Credits	£
Balance b/f (per previous balance sheet)	5,200
	5,200
Balancing figure = Profit before tax	7,500
	£12,700

The funds statement can now be prepared by taking the other balance sheet items directly to the funds statement as follows:

Statement of source and application of net liquid funds for the year ended (current year's balance sheet date)

	£	£
Source of funds:		
Profit before tax		7,500

	£	£
Adjustments for items not involving movement of funds:		
Depreciation	2,800	
Total generated from operations	10,300	
Funds from other sources:		
Issue of shares	1,500	
	11,800	
Application of funds:		
Dividends *paid*	(1,000)	
Tax *paid*	(3,000)	
Purchase of fixed assets	(5,500)	
		(9,500)
Increase in working capital		2,300
Increase in stock	2,000	
Decrease in debtors	(500)	
Increase in creditors	(200)	
Movement in net liquid funds		
Increase in bank	1,000	
		2,300

Depreciation is the depreciation charge for the year appearing in the profit and loss account.

Note that applications are bracketed.

Decreases in current asset items and increases in current liability items are bracketed.

This total must agree with the increase in working capital total above.

In checking through the preparation of this statement note the following:

1 *Depreciation.* The depreciation charge for the year in the profit and loss account of £2,800 (as evidenced by the increase in the accumulated depreciation on the two balance sheets) is added back as an adjustment to profit before tax. This is because depreciation is merely an accounting entry and does not give rise to an application of funds as do other profit and loss account expenses. Any other 'non-cash' charges, such as goodwill written off, would also have to be added back.
2 *Issue of shares.* The cash received on the issue of shares is shown as a source of funds. The amount shown is the total amount received, including the premium received on the shares issued as well as their nominal value.
3 *Dividends paid.* It has been assumed that the proposed dividend shown on the previous year balance sheet has been paid during the current year. No adjustment is required for the current year's dividend as it is at this stage purely an accounting entry and has not yet been paid.
4 *Tax paid.* The same assumption made for dividends has been applied to taxation.
5 *Purchase of fixed assets.* Evidenced by the increase in cost on the two balance sheets. It is the cost of new fixed assets purchased.
6 *Increase in working capital.* Note that this cannot be reconciled to the increase in working capital shown by the two balance sheets. This is because taxation and dividends are excluded from working capital for funds statement purposes. Note that the increases in taxation and dividends are *not* shown on the funds statement.

Consideration of this statement discloses that the major source of funds of the company during the year came from its trading operations (£10,300). However, payments of tax and dividends together with purchases of fixed assets left only a small increase in working capital (£2,300) with which to run the business on a day-to-day basis. £2,000 of this was taken up to finance increased stocks leaving only £300 to increase cash balances, but this was augmented to £1,000 by collecting additional cash in from debtors and taking some extra credit from creditors.

Example 2: Treatment of dividends, tax and fixed assets

The following information relates to a company engaged in the wholesale distribution of non-ferrous metals:

Profit and loss accounts for the year ended 31 December

	19X4		19X5	
	£	£	£	£
Sales		1,200,000		1,848,360
Less Cost of sales		805,000		1,386,270
Gross profit		395,000		462,090
Less Distribution expenses	195,400		223,200	
Administration expenses	104,600		112,500	
		300,000		335,700
Profit on ordinary activities before taxation		95,000		126,390
Less Tax:				
Corporation tax for year	33,000		40,000	
Less Overprovision in previous year	850		700	
	32,150		39,300	
Deferred tax	2,000		5,500	
		34,150		44,800
Profit on ordinary activities after taxation		60,850		81,590
Extraordinary items:				
Gain on sale of warehouse			60,000	
Less Taxation			18,000	
				42,000
Profit for the year		60,850		123,590
Dividends:				
Interim paid	7,000		8,400	
Proposed final	14,000		21,000	
		21,000		29,400
Retained profit for year		39,850		94,190
Balance brought forward from previous year		202,250		242,100
Bonus issue of ordinary shares		—		(100,000)
Balance carried forward		£242,100		£236,290

Note: Profit on ordinary activities before tax is arrived at after charging:

	£
Discount on issue of loan stock	700
Depreciation:	
Freehold warehouse	3,000
Vehicles and equipment:	
– charge for year	100,000
– under provision on vehicles sold	2,000

Vehicles that had cost £50,000 were sold during the year for £18,000. The net book value of these vehicles at time of sale was £20,000.

Balance sheets at 31 December

	19X4		19X5	
	£	£	£	£
Fixed assets:				
Freehold warehouse:				
Cost	300,000		—	
Less Accumulated depreciation	160,000		—	
		140,000		—
Vehicles and equipment:				
Cost	580,000		660,000	

	19X4		19X5	
	£	£	£	£
Less Accumulated depreciation	200,000		270,000	
		380,000		390,000
		520,000		390,000
Current assets:				
Stocks	200,800		312,250	
Debtors	143,150		208,200	
Cash at bank	—		99,840	
	343,950		620,290	
Creditors – amounts falling due within one year				
Creditors	48,800		37,100	
Corporation tax	30,000		48,400	
ACT payable	6,000		9,000	
Dividend	14,000		21,000	
Bank overdraft	37,050		—	
	135,850		115,500	
Net current assets		208,100		504,790
Total assets *less* Current liabilities		728,100		894,790
Creditors – amounts falling due after one year:				
10% loan stock	150,000		220,000	
Provisions for liabilities and charges:				
Deferred taxation:	36,000		38,500	
		186,000		258,500
		£542,100		£636,290
Called-up share capital:				
Ordinary shares of £1		200,000		400,000
Share premium account		100,000		—
Profit and loss account		242,100		236,290
		£542,100		£636,290

Notes
1 Deferred tax is after deduction of ACT recoverable of 19X4 £6,000; 19X5 £9,000.
2 There was a 1-for-1 issue of fully paid bonus shares during 1985.

If you consider these accounts carefully you will note that during 1985 there has been a considerable increase in stocks, debtors and cash which has been mainly funded from profits and by selling the warehouse. It is this sort of information that a funds statement seeks to disclose.

It is not necessary in this example to calculate the profit before tax in workings as it is given in the profit and loss account.

The loan stock in the balance sheet has increased by £70,000; however, only £69,300 was received and it is this amount that is shown as a source of funds. It can be calculated as follows:

The notes to the profit and loss account identify the items not involved in the movement of funds, i.e. the non-cash items, as:

	£
Depreciation (£3,000 + £100,000 + £2,000)	105,000
Discount on issue of loan stock	700

10% loan stock

	£		£
31.12.X5 Balance c/d (per closing balance sheet)	220,000	1.1.X5 Balance b/d (per opening balance sheet)	150,000
		31.12.X5 P&L a/c (per 1985 P&L a/c note)	700
	220,000		150,700
		Balancing figure = Cash received	69,300
	£220,000		£220,000

Extraordinary items are shown in the funds statement immediately after the profit before tax on ordinary activities, but any extraordinary items not involving movement of funds also have to be deleted, as is the case in this example. Instead, the proceeds on the sale of the warehouse is shown as a source, calculated as follows:

Disposal of freehold warehouse

	£			£
1.1.X5 Cost (per opening balance sheet)	300,000		1.1.X5 Accumulated depreciation (per opening balance sheet)	160,000
31.12.X5 P&L a/c (per extraordinary items section of 1985 P&L a/c)	60,000		31.12.X5 P&L a/c (depreciation for year per note)	3,000
	360,000			163,000
			Balancing figure = Cash received	197,000
	£360,000			£360,000

The tax related to this gain will not appear as an application until such time as it is paid.

Dividends shown in the funds statement are the dividends actually paid during the year. This can be determined by reconstructing the account:

Dividends

	£			£
31.12.X5 Balance c/d (per closing balance sheet)	21,000		1.1.X5 Balance b/d (per opening balance sheet)	14,000
			31.12.X5 P&L a/c:	
			– Interim paid	8,400
			– Proposed final (per 1985 P&L a/c)	21,000
	21,000			43,400
Balancing figure = Cash paid	22,400			
	£43,400			£43,400

The cash paid of £22,400 represents the 19X4 proposed dividend and the 19X5 interim dividend, both of which were paid during 19X5.

The amount of taxation paid can also be arrived at by reconstructing just one account for all the taxation items appearing in the profit and loss account and balance sheets as follows:

Alternatively separate working accounts could be opened for corporation tax, ACT payable, ACT recoverable and deferred tax. Combining these accounts into one is a short-cut that should only be taken in answering a funds statement question.

Taxation

	£			£
31.12.X5 Balances c/d:			1.1.X5 Balances b/d:	
– Corporation tax	48,400		– Corporation tax	30,000
– ACT payable	9,000		– ACT payable	6,000
– Deferred tax	47,500		– Deferred tax	42,000
– ACT recoverable	(9,000)		– ACT recoverable	(6,000)
(per closing balance sheet)			(per opening balance sheet)	
			31.12.X5 P&L a/c:	
			– Corporation tax	
			– Ordinary profit	40,000
			– extraordinary gain	18,000
			– Overprovision	(700)

	£			£
		– Deferred tax		5,500
		(per 19X5 P&L a/c)		
	95,900			134,800
Balancing figure =				
Cash paid	38,900			
	£134,800			£134,800

In this example there is only one year's corporation tax liability carried forward as a balance. Remember that for companies formed prior to 1965 there will be two years' liabilities to be carried forward.

The cash paid of £38,900 represents the following payments made during 19X5:

	£
Mainstream corporation tax on 19X4 profits	
(balance b/d £30,000 *less* overprovision £700)	29,300
ACT on 19X4 proposed dividend paid 19X5	
($^{30}/_{70}$ × £14,000)	6,000
ACT on 19X5 interim dividend paid 19X5	
($^{30}/_{70}$ × £8,400)	3,600
	£38,900

However, only the total needs to be entered in the funds statement; there is no need to do the above analysis in answering a funds statement question. Remember that no payment is made in respect of deferred tax.

The cash paid on the purchase of vehicles and equipment can be calculated as follows:

Vehicles and equipment – at cost

		£			£
1.1.X5	Balance b/d	580,000	31.12.X5	Disposal	50,000
				Balance c/d	660,000
		580,000			710,000
	Balancing figure =				
	Cash paid	130,000			
		£710,000			£710,000

Note that in this example the share issue is not a source of funds. Because it is a bonus issue no cash is received. The increase in share capital of £200,000 is compensated by the decreases in the reserves that have been capitalized, i.e. share premium £100,000 and profit and loss £100,000.

The funds statement will appear as follows:

Statement of source and application of net liquid funds
for the year ended 31 December 19X5

	£	£	£
Source of funds:			
Profit on ordinary activities before tax			126,390
Extraordinary item			60,000
			186,390
Adjustments for items not involving the movement of funds:			
Depreciation		105,000	
Discount on issue of loan stock		700	
Gain on sale of freehold warehouse		(60,000)	
			45,700
Total generated from operations			232,090
Funds from other sources:			
Issue of loan stock		69,300	
Sale of freehold warehouse		197,000	

The total of £232,090 is the total of internally generated funds.

	£	£	£
Sale of vehicles	18,000		
			284,300
			516,390
Application of funds:			
Dividends paid		(22,400)	
Taxation paid		(38,900)	
Purchase of vehicles and equipment		(130,000)	
			(191,300)
			£325,090
Increase in working capital			
Increase in stocks		111,450	
Increase in debtors		65,050	
Decrease in creditors		11,700	
Movement in net liquid funds:			
Decrease in bank overdraft	37,050		
Increase in cash at bank	99,840		
		136,890	
			£325,090

The total of £284,300 is the total of funds from outside sources.

Total funds raised are £516,390.

The increase in funds available to run the business on a day-to-day basis is £325,090.

This shows how the increased working capital has been utilized.

Interpretation of funds statements

Interpretation of the above statement discloses that profits were a major source of funds flow, which together with cash raised from loan stock borrowings and the sale of the warehouse produced an amount in excess of £500,000. This was used, after relatively small payments of dividends and tax, to finance expansion in the form of additional vehicles and equipment and increased stocks and debtors to service the expanded turnover. Even so, sufficient funds were not used to enable a remarkable turnaround in the cash position. The large cash balance presumably indicates that further expansion is envisaged.

When required to comment briefly on the position disclosed by a funds statement, identify the major sources and applications of cash. Often it is possible to link two movements, e.g. a share issue financing major purchases of fixed assets or large increases in stock resulting in a fall in cash at bank. Sources of funds can be analysed between internally generated (e.g. profits) and external sources (e.g. borrowings). Any decrease in the amount of working capital would normally be a cause for concern.

Uses of funds statements are:

1 An aid to managers, accountants and financial analysts in understanding and analysing the funds management of a company.
2 They are particularly helpful to shareholders in enabling them to reconcile profits with the cash position.
3 They are more easily understood by non-accountants than most accounting statements.

Summary

1 SSAP 10 requires the audited accounts of a company to include a statement of source and application of net liquid funds.
2 The statement will be prepared for the same period as the profit and loss account. It should disclose the total funds generated from operations, funds from other sources, applications of funds and movements within working capital.
3 A funds statement assists in the understanding of the funds management of the company, particularly in reconciling profits with the cash position.

Examination Hints

In answering an examination question, first read the question and note the balance sheet items in respect of which workings will be required. These will normally be dividends, tax and fixed assets.

Lay out the major headings of the funds statement in your answer and then work through the balance sheets entering straight into the funds statement all increases/decreases in balance sheet items for which no workings are required. Next head up 'Workings' and open ledger accounts for the remaining balance sheet items. Enter opening and closing balances and any profit and loss account transfers. The balancing figure on your workings accounts will be the cash items which can be entered into the funds statement. If time permits the funds statement can then be added up.

To avoid common errors, remember the following items appear in the funds statement:

1 Profit *before* tax.
2 Depreciation *for the year* is added back, this should include any under (over) provision on the sale of a fixed asset.
3 On sale of fixed assets the source of funds is the *cash received*.
4 Tax *paid* during the year, not the profit and loss account charge.
5 Dividends *paid* during the year, not the profit and loss account charge.

Try to answer the following questions before reading on.

Self-Assessment Questions

In each question, choose the correct answer from the five alternatives given.   See page 306 for answers.

20.1   A funds statement is required for:
    a   all organizations
    b   all companies
    c   all public limited companies
    d   any organization other than a charity
    e   all companies that are not 'small companies'.

20.2   Total funds generated from operations may be the:
    a   profit before tax
    b   profit before tax plus accumulated depreciation
    c   profit before tax less accumulated depreciation
    d   profit before tax plus depreciation charged to the profit and loss account for the year
    e   profit before tax less depreciation charged to the profit and loss account for the year.

20.3   A source of funds is the:
    a   net book value of motor vehicle sold
    b   proceeds on sale of motor vehicle
    c   accumulated depreciation on motor vehicle sold
    d   depreciation overprovided on sale of motor vehicle
    e   cost of the motor vehicle sold.

20.4   An application of funds is the:
    a   premium on issue of shares
    b   corporation tax provision for the year
    c   depreciation charge for the year
    d   dividends paid during the year
    e   proceeds of a loan stock issue.

20.5   Working capital is:
    a   current assets less current liabilities
    b   current assets

    c   total assets
    d   share capital and reserves
    e   cash at bank and in hand.

If you have answered all of the above questions correctly, and are sure you understand the key points in this chapter, then try to answer questions 27, 28 and 29 on pages 207–9 before moving on to Chapter 21.

CHAPTER 21

ACCOUNTING RATIOS AND INTERPRETATION

Chapter contents

Introduction **145** Accounting ratios **145** Reports **150** The limitations of ratio analysis **151** Summary **151** Examination hints **151**

Learning objectives

After studying this chapteer you should be able to:

- [ ] calculate the basic ratios used in the interpretation of accounts and comment on the position disclosed by the ratios;

- [ ] write a report comparing two sets of accounts;

- [ ] discuss the limitations of ratio analysis.

Introduction

Accounting ratios are calculated by comparing two figures present in a set of accounts. They are of maximum use in comparing the performance of an organization from one period to the next in the situation where there has been no major changes in the activities of the organization. The changes in the ratios will highlight any differences in performance.

Ratios are only an *aid* in trying to understand the financial position of an organization and how it has performed. It can be misleading to attach importance to a ratio in isolation, but generally all the ratios taken together will give a useful insight.

Communication between the accountants and managers in an organization can be helped by using ratios. Ratios are used as a basis for interfirm comparisons within trade associations. Financial analysts operating in the investment world apply ratios to the published accounts of listed companies. Some academics try to use ratios to identify if a company is in a position similar to other companies that have subsequently failed.

Accounting Ratios

The following accounts will be used in the following text as an illustration:

Potts Kitchen Utensils Ltd
Trading and profit and loss account for the year ended 31 May

	19X5		19X6	
	£	£	£	£
Sales		330,000		430,000

	19X5		19X6	
	£	£	£	£
Less Cost of sales:				
Opening stock	25,300		30,100	
Purchases	251,300		369,100	
	276,600		399,200	
Less Closing stock	30,100		59,200	
		246,500		340,000
Gross profit		83,500		90,000
Less Expenses:				
Salaries and wages	25,200		22,200	
Other expenses	21,000		23,700	
Depreciation	14,800		17,400	
Loan stock interest	2,000		7,200	
		63,000		70,500
Net profit before taxation		20,500		19,500
Corporation tax		10,500		11,500
Net profit after taxation		10,000		8,000
Dividend		6,000		6,000
Profit retained		4,000		2,000
Balance brought forward from previous year		14,000		18,000
Retained profits carried forward		£18,000		£20,000

Balance sheet at 31 May

	19X5		19X6	
	£	£	£	£
Fixed assets:				
At cost	71,500		122,000	
Less Accumulated depreciation	43,000		60,400	
		28,500		61,600
Current assets:				
Stocks	30,100		59,200	
Debtors	29,400		28,700	
Cash at bank	13,100		10,400	
	72,600		98,300	
Less Current liabilities:				
Trade creditors	9,800		8,300	
Expenses owing	1,800		2,100	
Taxation	10,500		11,500	
Dividend	6,000		6,000	
	28,100		27,900	
Working capital		44,500		70,400
Long-term capital employed		£73,000		£132,000
Financed by:				
Share capital:				
£1 ordinary shares		35,000		38,000
Reserves:				
Share premium		—		2,000
Retained profits		18,000		20,000
			18,000	22,000
Shareholders' capital employed		53,000		60,000
Long-term liabilities:				
10% loan stock		20,000		72,000
Long-term capital employed		£73,000		£132,000

This balance sheet has been laid out in the traditional narrative form. It is fairly similar to the Companies Act format but includes long-term liabilities as part of the funds financing the fixed assets and working capital, rather than deducting the long-term liabilities to arrive at net assets. It is perhaps easier for a non-accountant to understand. It emphasizes how the long-term capital employed has been used within the business and how much of this capital belongs to shareholders as opposed to long-term debt.

The ratios can be grouped under a number of main headings.

Return on capital employed

This is the most important ratio of all. It is sometimes referred to as the *primary ratio*. It measures the profit as a return on the capital that has been invested to earn that profit.

Return on ordinary shareholders' capital employed =

$$\frac{\text{Profit after tax less preference dividends}}{\text{Ordinary shares + Reserves}} \times 100$$

[1985]   [19X6]

$$\frac{£10,000}{£53,000} \times 100 = 18.87\% \qquad \frac{£\ 8,000}{£60,000} \times 100 = 13.33\%$$

> The return on long term capital employed may be calculated: $\frac{a}{b} \times 100$
>
> where:
>
> a = Profit after tax + (Interest on long-term debt – Tax relief)
>
> and
>
> b = Ordinary shares + Preference shares + Reserves + Long-term debt

The return has deteriorated. The return required by a business will be the after-tax return that could be earned on a risk free investment plus an additional return to compensate for the risk inherent in the business. Even if the 19X6 return is regarded by the management as adequate in this respect, the fall in the return is seriously large.

Two main areas dictate the return earned:

1 *Profitability* – the more profit that is earned from each pound of sales, the higher the return;
2 *Utilization of capital* – the more sales that can be financed by the capital employed, the higher the return.

Profitability ratios

The most important of these ratios is the margin earned on sales. A small movement in the gross profit percentage may have a very large effect on net profits.

Gross profit % $= \dfrac{\text{Gross profit}}{\text{Sales}} \times 100$

19X5   19X6

$$\frac{£83,500}{£330,000} \times 100 = 25.30\% \qquad \frac{£90,000}{£430,000} \times 100 = 20.93\%$$

> The primary ratio, the return on capital employed, is dependent on profitability and utilization of assets. Ratios relating to these are sometimes called 'the secondary ratios'.
>
> An alternative to the gross profit % is the mark-up, which is calculated:
>
> $\dfrac{\text{Gross profit}}{\text{Cost of sales}} \times 100$

There is a large fall which would normally have a disastrous effect on gross profits. However, sales have increased by £100,000 with the net result that gross profit has increased by £6,500. An increase in sales and a reduction in the gross profit % may be connected, e.g. a reduction in selling price attracting more custom.

Each expense may be calculated as a percentage of sales. The profit and loss account could be recast in percentages as follows:

	19X5	19X6
	%	%
Cost of sales	74.70	79.07
Salaries and wages	7.64	5.16
Other expenses	6.36	5.51
Depreciation	4.48	4.05
Loan stock interest	0.61	1.67
Taxation	3.18	2.68
Profit after tax	3.03	1.86
Sales	100.00	100.00

> In answering examination questions it would not normally be necessary to calculate each expense as a percentage of sales. Bear in mind that Gross profit % – Net profit % = Total expenses as a percentage of sales.

It would appear that most of the expenses are fixed in nature and the resulting reduction in these items as a percentage of sales has reduced the effect of the fall in the gross profit % on the net profit %. The increase in the amount of loan stock interest paid has had an adverse affect. The main feature is the reduction in salaries and wages despite increased turnover.

> Fixed expenses as a percentage of sales should reduce if sales increase. Directly variable expenses as a percentage of sales should remain constant even though sales increase or decrease.

Overall, the good features of increased sales and control of costs have not been sufficient to avoid a reduction of £2,000 in net profits after tax, following the large reduction in the sales margin.

Utilization ratios

The greater the amount of sales that can be supported by the smaller the amount of capital tied up in assets, the better the return on capital employed will be.

Sales to fixed assets $= \dfrac{\text{Sales}}{\text{Fixed assets}}$

19X5	19X6
$\dfrac{£330,000}{£28,500} = 11.58 : 1$	$\dfrac{£430,000}{£61,600} = 6.98 : 1$

The ratio of sales to each class of fixed asset may be calculated. For example, sales to premises would be important for a supermarket, sales to plant and machinery for engineers.

The performance has deteriorated remarkably; each £ of fixed assets supported £11.58 of sales in 19X5, but this fell in 19X6 to £6.98. However, both sales and fixed assets increased; the ratio could be misleading if the additions to fixed assets were made, as is probable, part way through the year.

Stockturn $= \dfrac{\text{Cost of sales}}{\text{Average stocks}}$

The stock figure used for the calculation is typically the average of the opening and closing stocks. Closing stocks only may be used if opening stocks are not available for an earlier period. A monthly stock average would give a more meaningful ratio for the year.

19X5	19X6
$\dfrac{£246,500}{(£25,300 + £30,100)/2} = 8.90 \text{ times}$	$\dfrac{£340,000}{(£30,100 + £59,200)/2} = 7.61 \text{ times}$

Ratios will vary from industry to industry. For example, the stockturn of a supermarket will be very much quicker than that of a jewellers.

The significance of this ratio is that, on average, stocks held were sold and replaced this number of times during the year. An alternative expression is that, on average, the items held in stock were sold every (365/8.90) 41 days in 19X5 and (365/7.61) 48 days in 19X6. The capital being tied up in stock for a longer period is a deterioration in performance as far as the return on capital employed is concerned.

Debtor collection period $= \dfrac{\text{Debtors}}{\text{Credit sales for year}} \times 365$

The debtor collection period is typically calculated in this way. If the data is available it would be more meaningful to express it in terms of sales during the later period of the year. Ratios can be validly compared from one year to the next providing the same basis of calculation is used for both years.

19X5	19X6
$\dfrac{£29,400}{£330,000} \times 365 = 33 \text{ days}$	$\dfrac{£28,700}{£430,000} \times 365 = 25 \text{ days}$

There is an improvement as sales on average are being collected more quickly. The collection period appears to be short, but this would depend on the terms given, again on average, to the customers. If the sales were effected on terms of payment by the end of the month following delivery, the credit period could be expected to be 45 days at least. In this example the assumption has been made that all sales were on credit terms; if the sales total had included any cash sales they should have been eliminated from the calculation.

Trade creditor payment period $= \dfrac{\text{Trade creditors}}{\text{Purchases for year}} \times 365$

Taking a longer credit period than has been agreed may result in loss of supplier goodwill and difficulties in obtaining supplies and credit.

19X5	19X6
$\dfrac{£9,800}{£251,300} \times 365 = 15 \text{ days}$	$\dfrac{£8,300}{£369,100} \times 365 = 9 \text{ days}$

A national supermarket chain with considerable buying power it can use in obtaining credit, a quick stockturn and all sales being cash sales would need proportionately less working capital than a small manufacturer. This would particularly be so if the manufacturer has little buying power, a long manufacturing process and has to give a long credit period to attract sales.

Remarkably little credit appears to have been taken. Creditors are a source of no cost capital. Maximization of this source of free credit will improve the return on capital employed. The period of credit that can be negotiated with suppliers depends on the status and purchasing power of the buyer.

In considering the periods calculated above one is assessing the *working capital cycle*. In 19X5 goods purchased on day 1 would have been held in stock typically for 41 days before being sold. With 33 days credit being given, cash for their sale would be received on day 74. Payment to the supplier being made on day 15 means that the business had to provide the finance themselves for a period of (74 – 15) 59 days. In 19X6 this period was (48 + 25 – 9) 64 days, an overall deterioration.

The working capital requirements of a business will vary considerably between industries and between large and small organizations.

Solvency ratios

A major area in interpretation of accounts is the consideration of the organization's financial strength. A company that is making losses may survive, but a profitable company that does not have sufficient cash in the bank when it is needed is risking court action by its creditors that could result in liquidation.

> The larger the reserves of a company the more losses it can absorb.

A company needs to have sufficient *working capital* to be able to utilize its fixed assets at a normal level and to gain the confidence of its creditors that funds are available to meet payments when they become due.

> It would obviously be inefficient to invest a large sum in shop premises leaving insufficient working capital to enable the shelves to be fully stocked.

$$\text{Current ratio} = \frac{\text{Current assets}}{\text{Current liabilities}}$$

19X5	19X6
$\frac{£72,600}{£28,100} = 2.58 : 1$	$\frac{£98,300}{£27,900} = 3.52 : 1$

If the ratio is 2:1 there is £2 of current assets available to cover every £1 of current liabilities and creditors will have confidence they will eventually be repaid. The company has an exceptionally strong working capital position in 19X5, which even so improves in the following year. There should be no difficulty in obtaining credit from suppliers. The company's stocks have nearly doubled and these appear to have been financed by additional working capital rather than by credit given by suppliers.

A large amount of working capital is normally tied up in stock, the position of the remainder is considered by the next ratio.

> Many companies get by with a working capital ratio much smaller than the ideal 2:1. Companies that are 'overtrading', i.e. undertaking more sales than can be satisfactorily financed by their working capital, will have liquidity problems. A statement of source and application of funds (see Chapter 20) will disclose the increase or reduction in working capital for the year.

$$\text{Liquid ratio} = \frac{\text{Current assets less stocks}}{\text{Current liabilities}}$$

19X5	19X6
$\frac{£42,500}{£28,100} = 1.51 : 1$	$\frac{£39,100}{£27,900} = 1.40 : 1$

The ideal is 1:1, in this situation there will be sufficient liquid assets available to repay the creditors. The company has an exceptionally strong liquid position with £1.40 of reasonably quickly realizable assets to cover every £1 of current liabilities, and a healthy cash balance.

> The liquid ratio is sometimes referred to as the 'quick ratio'.

When considering this ratio bear in mind that some current liabilities may not be due for payment for some months, particularly taxation. Many companies survive with a ratio that is far less than the ideal 1:1.

If a company experiences solvency problems, one course of action they may consider is to raise additional long-term finance. The relative proportions in which the long-term capital employed belongs to the ordinary shareholders (the equity interest) and has been provided by others is called the *gearing*. A company that has a lot of borrowings is *high geared* and is in a risky position if it cannot make further borrowings. A company with small borrowings is *low geared* and should be better placed to borrow their way out of trouble should it arise.

$$\text{Gearing} = \frac{\text{Fixed return capital}}{\text{Equity}}$$

$$= \frac{\text{Preference shares} + \text{Debentures} + \text{Loan stocks}}{\text{Ordinary shares} + \text{Reserves}}$$

19X5	19X6
$\frac{£20,000}{£53,000} = 0.38 : 1$	$\frac{£72,000}{£60,000} = 1.2 : 1$

> There are alternative methods of calculating gearing, for example:
>
> $$\frac{\text{Long-term debt}}{\text{Ordinary shares} + \text{Reserves} + \text{Preference shares}}$$
>
> Bear in mind when considering gearing that current liabilities may include a bank overdraft, making the borrowing position worse.

It is difficult in the UK to borrow more than £1 for every £1 of equity. A gearing ratio of 0.9:1 is high, a ratio of 0.1:1 is low.

A company has to make sufficient profits to cover fixed interest before profits become available for distribution to the ordinary shareholders. A small fall in the profitability of a high geared company may mean a large fall in the profits after interest available for the ordinary shareholders.

The calculation assumes that the additional shares were issued on 1.6.X5. The calculation of earnings per share and the requirements of SSAP 3 are covered in more detail in Chapter 17.

The company has moved from a reasonably low geared position to one where it is very highly geared. It would find it difficult to raise further long-term debt, particularly as borrowings exceed the book value of fixed assets. The extent to which the loan stock is secured is unknown. However, fixed assets are stated at cost and may include premises which, if they were to be revalued, may give rise to a revaluation reserve which would increase the equity. The change in gearing has arisen due to a further issue of 10% loan stock which it would appear has been used, together with funds generated from operations, to finance additions to fixed assets and to increase stocks.

Investors' ratios

Shareholders and their advisors would find the following ratios of interest.

Earnings per share:

$$\begin{array}{cc} 19X5 & 19X6 \\ \dfrac{£10,000}{35,000} = 28.6 \text{ pence} & \dfrac{£8,000}{38,000} = 21.1 \text{ pence} \end{array}$$

This deterioration has been caused by the fall in return on capital employed.

Dividends per share:

$$\begin{array}{cc} 19X5 & 19X6 \\ \dfrac{£6,000}{35,000} = 17.1 \text{ pence} & \dfrac{£6,000}{38,000} = 15.8 \text{ pence} \end{array}$$

The same total dividend was paid even though profits had fallen. The share capital had been increased by a small issue during the year resulting in a reduction in the dividend per share.

$$Dividend\ cover\ = \dfrac{\text{Profit after tax less preference dividends}}{\text{Ordinary dividends}}$$

Companies try at least to maintain the same dividend from year to year. A company with good dividend cover is in a better position to do this should profits fall.

Inconsistencies can sometimes be spotted in accounts, for example goodwill included in the balance sheet of a company making losses.

This ratio expresses the relationship between the amount of profit for the year which was available to be distributed as ordinary dividends and the actual amount of dividend declared.

$$\begin{array}{cc} 19X5 & 19X6 \\ \dfrac{£10,000}{£6,000} = 1.67 \text{ times} & \dfrac{£8,000}{£6,000} = 1.33 \text{ times} \end{array}$$

A greater proportion of profits have been distributed.

Interpretation of accounts involves more than the calculation and consideration of ratios. The accounts themselves need to be critically reviewed to ascertain situations not disclosed by the ratios and to form an opinion of the overall picture they disclose.

Reports

The following is an example of the form a report on the position shown by a set of accounts may take. The content of this report has been restricted to a brief overview of the position, although normally it would include the ratios and comments thereon given above.

To: The directors   Date:
          Potts Kitchen Utensils Ltd
From: A student

Report: A comparison of the position disclosed by the 19X6 accounts
          compared to the previous year.

The return on capital employed has fallen badly compared to the previous year. This was due to a reduction in profitability and to less efficient use of the capital employed.

The company's working capital and liquidity position has further improved from what was already a very strong position. However, the gearing of the company has increased to a high level.

It would appear that the company has embarked on a course of expansion, as evidenced by the material increases in stocks and fixed assets. Although turnover increased considerably over the previous year, it may be that the full effect of this policy will not be experienced until next year.

The limitations of ratio analysis

Ratios are a useful tool in trying to understand the position disclosed by a set of accounts. In assessing a company's performance and position it must be remembered that ratios are only as reliable as the accounting information. In particular:

1 The market value of fixed assets, particularly premises, may be higher than their book value. Capital employed would in this situation be understated and the return on capital employed overstated.
2 Profit is arived at by the exercise of judgement in selecting accounting policies. Comparison of profits between companies is not valid if different accounting policies are used, for example one company may write goodwill off against reserves when it is purchased, another may amortize it as a charge against profits over a number of years. Comparison of profits within one company over a number of years will be similarly affected if there have been changes in accounting policies.
3 Accounts are normally prepared under the historic cost convention. Typically this will disclose a higher profit and lower capital employed than current cost accounting.

> Accounting in a period of inflation is the subject of Chapter 22.

4 The accounts are often prepared for seasonal businesses at a date after the end of the peak period when stocks and debtors are low.
5 The accounts may have been subject to window dressing.

> Window dressing could include delaying the purchase of stock until after the end of the year so that stocks and creditors in the accounts are as low as possible.

Even the main use of ratios (comparison from one period to the next) may be affected by changes in activity during the periods, for example the closure of a factory.

Using ratios to compare one company with another is a difficult exercise. Comparison would only be truly valid for two identical companies – differences in size, location, industry, products and activities could make comparison of individual ratios meaningless. The comparison of the return earned on capital employed by different companies is valid, providing allowance is made for the different amounts of risk involved.

> For example, the return on capital employed for a large company operating in a stable area such as basic foods would reasonably be lower than that required for a small fashion clothes company.

Summary

1 The return earned on capital employed is the primary accounting ratio.
2 Other ratios relate to profitability, utilization of capital, solvency and the investors' position.
3 Ratios are a useful aid in interpreting accounts but have some limitations.

Examination Hints

Accounting seeks to portray a situation in terms of figures on a piece of paper; interpretation is making those figures come alive to deduce what the situation is. It is nowhere near as difficult as it may seem. What is required is the simple intention to understand what the figures represent, rather than treating them as a meaningless end product of the accounting process.

The calculation of ratios is a fairly mechanical exericse and should not present any problems once they have been learnt. If a question requires a comment on the position disclosed by the ratios, the comment should be on the situation itself, not merely on the change in two ratios. For example, 'The company is taking longer to collect its debts' is more meaningful than 'This year's debtor collection period is bigger'. If a question is wide ranging on a full set of accounts remember to comment on each of the main areas of:

1 return on capital employed;

2 profitability;
3 utilization of capital;
4 solvency;
5 gearing.

Look critically at the accounts. Remember that ratios are only an aid, they would not disclose, for example, that there is a debit balance on the profit and loss account!

Try to answer the following questions before reading on.

Self-Assessment Questions

See page 306 for answers.

In each question, choose the correct answer from the five alternatives given.

21.1   The primary ratio is the:
    a   gross profit %
    b   net profit %
    c   return on capital employed
    d   stockturn
    e   current ratio.

21.2   The shareholders' capital employed is the:
    a   ordinary shares
    b   ordinary shares + preference shares
    c   ordinary shares + preference shares + Reserves
    d   ordinary shares + reserves
    e   ordinary shares + preference shares + reserves + long-term debt.

21.3   Sales for the year were £150,000. Goods are sold at cost + 50%. Opening stocks were £10,000. Stockturn for the year was 8. Closing stocks were:
    a   £8,750
    b   £12,500
    c   £15,000
    d   £20,000
    e   £22,500.

21.4   The liquid ratio is the ratio of the following to current liabilities:
    a   cash in hand
    b   cash in hand and at bank
    c   cash, debtors and prepayments
    d   stock
    e   current assets.

If you have answered the above questions correctly, and are sure you understand the key points in this chapter, then try to answer questions 30 and 31 on pages 211–2 before moving on to Chapter 22.

CHAPTER 22

HISTORIC COST CONVENTION AND PRICE LEVEL CHANGES

Chapter contents

Introduction **153**   Weaknesses of historic cost accounts   **153**   Current cost accounting **154**   Current purchasing power **157**   Summary **158**   Examination hints **158**

Learning objectives

After studying this chapter you should be able to:

☐ outline the weaknesses of historic cost accounts in a period of inflation and discuss the need for adjustments to maintain the operating capacity of a business intact during a period of inflation;

☐ outline the adjustments that may be made to the historic cost profit by current cost accounting;

☐ explain the concept of current purchasing power.

Introduction

Accounting in a period of inflation is a very contentious area. It is generally recognized that historic cost accounts are inadequate, but there is disagreement on the alternatives.

Current purchasing power (CPP) is a method that was introduced by SSAP 7 but was subsequently withdrawn. Eventually this was replaced by SSAP 16, which adopted the current cost accounting (CCA) method. SSAP 16 had a turbulent history due to resistance by members of the accounting profession, and has now been withdrawn.

The urgency to introduce a new standard has lessened with the fall in the rate of inflation from the peaks that were being experienced at the height of the debate. It is likely that eventually a new standard that is acceptable to both industry and the profession will be introduced.

The CPP method was developed by the Accounting Standards Committee (ASC) in the early 1970s. Replacement cost accounting had been in use in a few companies since the 1940s and was the basis for CCA as recommended by the Sandilands Report (issued by a government committee chaired by Lord Sandilands).

Weaknesses of historic cost accounts

Accounts have always been prepared using the historic cost convention. Fundamentally assets are recorded at their cost at the date of the transaction. An advantage of this is that it is objective because no judgement has to be exercised to determine the gross cost of the fixed assets. Because transactions are recorded at factual values the accounts are very reliable. However, in periods of inflation the historic costs can be out of date and the profit and loss account and balance sheet can show a misleading picture. The main reasons for this are as follows:

1 *Cost of sales* is stated at the historic cost of the products sold. It is argued that the cost should be the replacement price of the products, otherwise profits will be overstated.

Judgement will, of course, have to be exercised in determining the accounting policies appropriate for the business and in applying them. Examples of this are estimating asset lives for depreciation purposes and writing down current assets to any lower net realizable values.

For example, if goods are purchased for £1,000 and sold for £1,500 the historic cost gross profit is £500. If the replacement price of the goods sold was £1,300, the current cost gross profit would be £200. The increase in purchase price of the goods of £300 is a *holding gain*. Holding gains arise from holding stocks and fixed assets during a period of inflation. In current cost accounting the holding gain would be placed to a revaluation reserve and not be treated as a distributable profit.

The historic gross profit therefore includes holding gains on stocks that need to be retained by the company if they wish to keep their operating capacity (the ability to finance their manufacturing and trading operations) intact. If holding gains on stocks are distributed the company will not retain sufficient funds to finance the replacement purchase of the stocks, and will not be able to operate at the same level of activity due to shortage of funds.

2 *The depreciation charge for the year* is stated at a proportion of the original cost. This historic depreciation is normally less than the depreciation which would be charged if the fixed asset was valued at current cost.

For example, if an asset was purchased for £9,000 with a three year life and no residual value, the historic cost depreciation charge would be £3,000 per annum. If at the end of the first year the replacement price of the asset had risen to £12,000, the value consumed in earning profits for the year is £4,000. If depreciation of only £3,000 is charged, and the company distributes all of its profits, insufficient funds will be retained to meet the replacement cost of the asset.

Historic cost depreciation is not sufficient to enable the company to maintain its operating capacity. It is argued that the increase in replacement price is a holding gain that should be placed to revaluation reserve, and the depreciation should be based on current cost.

Fixed assets are non-monetary items, the holding gains on which will be the increase, due to inflation, in the written-down net book value brought forward from the previous year.

3 *Monetary items* will reduce in purchasing power during a period of inflation. A monetary item is one for which there is a contract to receive or pay a fixed number of pounds. Because the number of pounds is fixed the market value cannot be changed to allow for inflation, as is the case for non-monetary items.

For example, a company that has £10,000 in the bank throughout a year when inflation of 20% takes place will suffer a loss in the general purchasing power of the £10,000 of £2,000 at year-end prices. Conversely the company will make gains on monetary liabilities; the purchasing power of a loan received, for example, will be greater than the purchasing power of the same number of pounds repaid at a later date after a period of inflation.

Monetary assets include debtors, bank and cash balances. Monetary liabilities include creditors, debentures and loan stocks payable. Note that during a period of inflation holding gains arise only on non-monetary assets.

Most companies will be in the position of having more monetary liabilities than monetary assets. The loss on the monetary assets needs to be retained in the company to maintain the company's ability to continue trading at the same level of activity. The gain on monetary liabilities could be recognized as a profit, particularly to offset any interest charges on loans. Current cost accounting recognizes the effect of monetary items in a 'gearing' adjustment.

Under CPP accounting the gain on net monetary liabilities was credited to the CPP profit and loss account.

4 *The fixed assets* in the company will be understated if they are included at written down historic cost which is less than the written down current replacement price. Undervalued assets have attracted unwanted takeover bids in the past. They can also have an adverse effect on the company's borrowing power as the gearing shown by historic cost accounts may be higher than is really the case. This problem has been overcome by many companies by revaluing their land and buildings within their historic cost accounts.

5 *The capital employed* in the company will be understated if assets are included at written-down historic cost. An underlying problem with historic cost accounts during a period of inflation is that if conventionally determined profits are all distributed the capital employed will be insufficient to finance the same level of activity at increased prices.

Current cost accounting

Current cost accounting is a valuation method where fixed assets are included, in most cases, at their written-down replacement cost. The replacement cost is determined ideally by actual market replacement prices. Where these cannot be determined, indices published by the government's statistical office are used.

Profits are determined after charging the current cost of fixed assets consumed in earning the profits and the replacement cost of goods sold. The excess of sales value over replacement cost is the operating gain. The holding gains on stocks and fixed assets are not taken to the profit and loss account, but credited to a revaluation reserve entitled 'Current cost reserve'.

SSAP 16 required four adjustments to be made to the historic profit.

Cost of sales adjustment (COSA)

This is the holding gain on stock. It is normally calculated in total for the year by indexing the opening and closing stocks to mid-year prices and comparing the movement with the movement in the historic stocks.

Example 1

Trading account for the year ended 31.12.X8

	£000		£000
Opening stocks	4,000	Sales	30,000
Purchases	24,000		
	28,000		
Less Closing stocks	9,000		
	19,000		
Gross profit	11,000		
	£30,000		£30,000

Stock buying prices index:

  – for opening stock   150
  – for closing stock   200
  – for year   175

The COSA will be calculated:

	Historic		Current cost
	£000		£000
Stock at 31.12.X8	9,000	× 175/200 =	7,875
Less Stock at 1.1.X8	4,000	× 175/150 =	4,667
Increase	5,000	*Less*	3,208 = £1,792,000

Profits should be reduced by the holding gain on stocks during the year of £1,792,000, which should be credited to the current cost reserve.

Additional depreciation

This is the additional amount required for depreciation to be charged on current cost rather than historic cost.

Example 2

	£000	£000
Fixed Assets		
Cost at 1.1.X8		6,000
Less Cumulative depreciation:		
To 1.1.X8	2,250	
To 31.12.X8	750	
		3,000
Net book value		£3,000

The COSA is an approximation. In a non-seasonal business the sales and purchases can be assumed to be already stated, in total, at mid-year prices. If opening and closing stocks are restated at mid-year prices the trading account will reflect the position as if all goods had been bought and sold half way through the year. This has the effect of charging the replacement price at point of sale against sales.

Fixed assets have been depreciated at 20% per annum using the reducing balance method. The replacement cost of fixed assets at 31.12.X7 is £8,000,000 and at 31.12.X8 £10,000,000.

The fixed assets may be restated at current cost as follows:

	Cost	Depreciation
	£000	£000
Historic cost to 1.1.X8	6,000	2,250
Revaluation surplus to 1.1.X8	2,000	
Backlog depreciation to 1.1.X8		
(£2,000 × £2,250/£6,000)		750
Brought forward	8,000	3,000
Revaluation surplus for year	2,000	
Backlog depreciation for 19X8		
(£2,000 × £3,000/£8,000)		750
	10,000	3,750
Profit and loss:		
Historic depreciation (20/100 × £6,000		
– £2,250)		750
Additional depreciation ((20/100 ×		
£10,000 – £3,750) – £750)		500
At 31.12.X8	£10,000	£5,000

SSAP 16 allows the additional depreciation for the year to be alternatively calculated on the mid-year replacement price. In this case a transfer to current cost reserve is required for the depreciation relating to the increase in replacement price from the middle of the year to the year-end. This is called 'current year backlog depreciation'.

The revaluation surplus will be credited to the current cost reserve and backlog depreciation debited to the same account. The additional depreciation will be debited to the profit and loss account.

Monetary working capital adjustments (MWCA)

Under SSAP 16, monetary items are analysed between working capital items and items taken to the gearing adjustment. MWCA items are debtors less creditors.

Example 3

Cash at bank and in hand is normally included in the gearing adjustment.

	At 31.12.X7	At 31.12.X8
	£000	£000
Debtors	4,200	5,000
Creditors	4,000	4,500

The relevant index at 31.12.X7 stood at 120 and at 31.12.X8 140, the average for the year being 130.

The MWCA will be calculated:

	Historic		Indexed
	£000		£000
Debtors *Less* Creditors:			
31.12.X8	500	× 130/140	464
Less at 1.1.X8	200	× 130/120	217
Increase	300	Less	247 = £53,000

Profits should be reduced by the loss on net monetary working capital items during the year of £53,000, which should be credited to the current cost reserve.

Gearing adjustment

SSAP 16 envisaged a rather complicated 'gearing' adjustment. Rather than recognizing gains on net monetary liabilities it adopted a different approach.

The argument is that the current cost adjustments of COSA, additional depreciation and MWCA are required to keep the operating capacity of the business intact by avoiding overstating (and thus overdistributing) profits. However, to the extent that the operating capacity has been provided by third parties rather than the shareholders these adjustments are not required, and a proportion may be added back to profits.

The proportion is calculated by analysing the balance sheet items (other than fixed assets, stock, debtors and creditors) between the shareholders' interest and net borrowings as follows:

The gearing adjustment is an adjustment to the COSA, additional depreciation, and MWCA.

	At 1.1.X8	At 31.12.X8	Average	%
	£000	£000	£000	
Ordinary shares	2,500	2,500		
Profit and loss	1,000	6,393		
Current cost reserve	2,000	4,607		
	£5,500	£13,500	9,500	79.2
Debentures	2,000	2,000		
Bank overdraft	2,000			
Cash at bank		(1,000)		
	£4,000	£1,000	2,500	20.8
			£12,000	100.0

The gearing adjustment will be calculated:

	£000
COSA	1,792
Additional depreciation	500
MWCA	53
	£2,345 × 20.8% = £488,000

The gearing adjustment of £488,000 will be deducted from interest charges in the profit and loss account and debited to the current cost reserve.

Note that debtors and creditors are not included in the gearing adjustment even though they are monetary items. This is because they are included in the MWCA.

Current purchasing power

The CPP method was adopted by the now withdrawn SSAP 7. It was based on restating non-monetary items in pounds of current purchasing power at the balance sheet date. CPP amounts were arrived at by indexing the amounts in the historic cost accounts to their equivalent amounts, in terms of the equivalent number of present day pounds, using the Retail Price Index.

Example 4
At 1.1.X1 a company purchased a machine at a cost of £10,000 when the retail price index stood at 200. The asset was depreciated 25% straight line and appeared in the historic cost balance sheet at 31.12.X2 as:

One area of contention has been how to measure the inflation experienced. The CPP method restated all items in the accounts by indexing them to their equivalent purchasing power at the end of the year using the Retail Price Index (the RPI). The RPI is not a reliable indicator of the rate of inflation experienced by any particular company. However, the method was seeking to ascertain the amount of profits that needed to be retained in order to maintain the general purchasing power of the equity shareholders' capital employed.

	£	£
Machinery:		
At cost	10,000	
Less Accumulated depreciation	5,000	
		5,000

At 31.12.X2 the Retail Price Index stood at 250. The machine may be restated in pounds of purchasing power at 31.12.X2 as:

	£CPP	£CPP
Machinery:		
At cost (£10,000 × 250/200)	12,500	
Less Accumulated depreciation (£5,000 × 250/200)	6,250	
		6,250

Compare this with the CCA approach of showing fixed assets at their written-down replacement cost.

CPP is a true inflation adjusted method as it takes account of subsequent inflation on amounts expended in the past. All figures in CPP accounts (except the balance sheet monetary items) are restated in pounds of current purchasing power at the balance sheet date. All items are therefore stated using the same unit of value. In a balance sheet prepared using historic costs the non-monetary assets are stated at balances that represent pounds that had been spent at different times. This is not very helpful when you consider that pounds spent in earlier periods would have had greater purchasing power than pounds spent in later periods.

Compare this with the CCA approach of keeping the operating capacity of the business intact.

The approach of CPP is to keep the purchasing power of the shareholders' interest intact by, typically, reducing historic cost profits to a level that can be distributed and still leave the shareholders' interest at the equivalent level in terms of purchasing power as it was at the beginning of the year.

A major use of CPP is to compare profits, and other items, over a period of time.

Example 5

	19X1	19X2	19X3
Historic profits	£10,000	£12,000	£14,000
Retail Price Index (say)	200	250	300
Profits restated in £CPP 19X3:			
(£10,000 × 300/200)	15,000		
(£12,000 × 300/250)		14,400	
(£14,000 × 300/300)			14,000

As can be seen, what appears in the historic accounts to be a smooth trend in profit increases is in fact a trend of profit reduction after allowance is made for inflation.

Summary

1 The underlying problem of historic cost accounts during a period of inflation is that the distribution of historic cost profits may result in insufficient profits being retained to enable the company to continue trading at the same level of activity.
2 Current cost accounting counters this problem by reducing historic cost profits by adjustments to the cost of sales, for additional depreciation and monetary working capital. The effect of these adjustments is reduced by a gearing adjustment. Non-monetary assets are disclosed on the balance sheet at current cost values.
3 Current purchasing power accounting restates non-monetary assets in the balance sheet at the equivalent purchasing power at the balance sheet date of the historic cost amounts.
4 A major use of CPP is to compare profits over a period of years.
5 CCA is concerned with the operating capacity financed by the shareholders, CPP with the purchasing power of the shareholders' funds.

Examination Hints

Questions requiring the preparation of inflation adjusted accounts are unlikely until a new SSAP is published to replace SSAP 16.

Questions may be set requiring a written rather than numerical answer. In answering such a question plan your answer by jotting down, in workings, headings for points you wish to make, and rearranging these into a logical order prior to writing your answer. As you are writing, any further points that occur to you can be added to your list to avoid them being overlooked later.

In answering a 25 mark (45 minutes) question, it would be reasonable to spend 5 to 10 minutes on the planning stage. Your answer should cover all relevant areas. The scope of your answer is very important; a first class answer on only 5 of the 10 areas an examiner is looking for can only hope to score half marks at best. However, do not spoil your answer by including points outside the scope of the question, and do not waste time by making the same point twice.

Try to answer the following questions before reading on.

Self-Assessment Questions

In each question, choose the correct answer from the five alternatives given.

See page 306 for answers.

22.1   A non-monetary item is:
    a   creditors
    b   taxation payable
    c   loan stocks
    d   debtors
    e   stocks.

22.2   Goods purchased for £100 were sold for £160 at a time when their replacement cost was £120. The holding gain and operating profit are:
    a   £20 + £20
    b   £20 + £40
    c   £20 + £60
    d   £40 + £20
    e   £60 + £20.

22.3   A fixed asset was purchased for £10,000 when the relevant index was 250. Depreciation is provided at 10% on cost. At 1.1.X7 the index was 300 and at 31.12.X7 330.

The current cost depreciation for the year 19X7 will be:
    a   £1,000
    b   £1,200
    c   £1,320
    d   £2,500
    e   £3,300.

22.4   In a period of inflation a CCA loss is suffered on holding:
    a   monetary liabilities
    b   net monetary liabilities
    c   net monetary assets
    d   plant and machinery
    e   stocks.

If you have answered the above questions correctly, and are sure you understand the key points in this chapter, then try to answer questions 32 and 33 on page 212 before moving on to Chapter 23.

CHAPTER 23

CONSOLIDATED ACCOUNTS: BALANCE SHEETS

Chapter contents

Introduction **160** SSAP14 Group Accounts **161** SSAP1 Associated Companies **161** Consolidated balance sheets **161** Adjustments **166** SSAP22 Accounting for Goodwill **167** SSAP23 Mergers **167** Summary **169** Examination hints **169**

Learning objectives

After studying this chapter you should be able to:

☐ define a subsidiary company and state the circumstances in which consolidated accounts should be prepared in accordance with SSAP 14;

☐ explain the term 'equity method of accounting' as used in SSAP 1;

☐ prepare a simple consolidated balance sheet for two or more companies using the acquisition method;

☐ make any necessary adjustments for intra-group balances and stocks;

☐ state the accounting treatment of goodwill required by SSAP 22;

☐ prepare a simple consolidated balance sheet using the merger method in accordance with SSAP 23 and state the circumstances in which the use of the method is appropriate.

Introduction

Each company within the group will keep its own accounting records and prepare its own accounts. Consolidated accounts are prepared by summarizing into one the accounts of all the companies. It is a memorandum exercise in the sense that the consolidated accounts will not appear in the books of any of the companies. The adjustments will be made in the consolidation working papers only.

A company that holds, as an investment, more than 50% of the voting shares of another company is in the position of being able to exercise considerable control over that company.

The company holding the shares will be the parent, the other company will be its subsidiary.

The Companies Act 1985 requires the parent company to prepare group accounts for presentation to its shareholders, in addition to its own balance sheet. A parent company may well undertake many of its activities through subsidiary companies. The parent's shareholders will only be given a complete picture of the assets and liabilities under their control and the total profits being earned by the group accounts.

Some knowledge of SSAPs 1, 14, 22 and 23 is required, but by far the most important learning objective is the mechanics of preparing a consolidated balance sheet using the acquisition method.

SSAP 14 Group Accounts

A company is the subsidiary of another if the other company:

1 is a member and controls the composition of the board, or
2 holds over half the equity share capital.

If the parent company is in turn the subsidiary of another company, then its own subsidiary is also a subsidiary of that company.

The parent company must prepare group accounts unless it is itself a wholly owned subsidiary of another company. Consolidated accounts are a form of group accounts which present the information as if the companies were a single entity. Only rarely will group accounts be presented that do not consolidate the accounts of all the companies.

The parent company must ensure that where practicable the subsidiaries use the same accounting policies and prepare their accounts to the same date.

The accounts of a subsidiary may be excluded from consolidation if:

1 its activities are dissimilar, or
2 the parent does not have effective control, or
3 it is subject to severe long-term restrictions (e.g. exchange control regulations), or
4 the control is only temporary.

> Only rarely will a holder of less than half of the ordinary shares be able to control the composition of the board of directors. Directors are normally appointed by shareholders' vote.

> If a subsidiary is not consolidated, it will normally be accounted for in the parent's accounts using the equity method. (This is the method that is also used for associated companies.)

SSAP 1 Associated Companies

If there are any associated companies they must be accounted for in the consolidated accounts using the equity method in accordance with SSAP 1. Under this method the dividends receivable from associated companies are omitted from the profit and loss account and instead the following are included:

1 share of associated companies' profit before tax;
2 share of associated companies' tax.

The share of profit after tax that has not actually been received as a dividend will be shown as a reserve on the balance sheet, the amount shown as the investment in the associated company being increased by the same amount.

> Refer to Chapter 17 for the definition of an associated company.

Consolidated balance sheets

The acquisition method of consolidation combines the balance sheets of the parent and subsidiary companies as if they were one entity owned by the shareholders of the parent company. If a subsidiary is not wholly owned, the interest of the holders of the other shares in the subsidiary (the minority interest) is shown as a separate item on the balance sheet. Thus all the assets under the control of the parent company's directors are shown, and the extent to which they belong to the outside minority shareholders is disclosed.

When a parent acquires shares in a subsidiary the double entry in the parent's books is:

Debit	Investment in subsidiary	– with purchase price of shares acquired.
Credit	Share capital	– with nominal value of any shares issued by the parent in satisfaction of the purchase price.
Credit	Share premium	– with any premium on the shares issued.
Credit	Bank	– with any cash paid.

Example 1

The balance sheets of two companies at 31 December 19X3 were:

	West Ltd	Wood Ltd
	£000	£000
Fixed assets	612	153
Current assets		
Stock	94	42
Debtors	163	16
Cash	20	4
	889	215
Less Creditors	72	25
	£817	£190
Financed by:		
£1 ordinary shares	500	80
Unappropriated profits	317	110
	£817	£190

On 1 January 19X4 West Ltd acquired 56,000 ordinary shares in Wood Ltd by issuing, to the holders of the shares, 90,000 shares in West Ltd valued at £1.50 per share in exchange.

The entries in West's books will be:

Debit	Investment in Wood Ltd	– £135,000
Credit	£1 ordinary shares	– £90,000
Credit	Share premium	– £45,000

After this entry the balance sheets of the two companies at 1 January 19X4 will be:

Acquisitions are sometimes made purely by cash payment. If this had been the case the double entry would have been;

Debit   Investment in Wood Ltd   —   £135,000
Credit   Cash at bank   —   £135,000

	West Ltd	Wood Ltd
	£000	£000
Fixed assets	612	153
Investment – 56,000 ordinary shares in Wood Ltd	135	
Current assets:		
Stock	94	42
Debtors	163	16
Cash	20	4
	1,024	215
Less Creditors	72	25
	£952	£190
Financed by:		
£1 ordinary shares (500 + 90)	590	80
Share premium	45	
Unappropriated profits	317	110
	£952	£190

The minority shareholders' interest is (24,000/80,000 × 100) 30%.

West Ltd owns (56,000/80,000) 70% of the ordinary shares of Wood Ltd which becomes its subsidiary. When West Ltd next presents its published accounts to its shareholders they will include consolidated accounts.

The consolidated balance sheet is prepared from the balance sheets of the two companies (and workings) as follows:

1 *Assets* of both companies are added together.
2 *Investment in subsidiary* is omitted.
3 *Liabilities* of both companies are added together.
4 *Share capital* is that of the parent company only.
5 *Reserves* are the parent company's reserves plus the parent's share of any movement in the subsidiary's reserves after the date it became a subsidiary (i.e. post-acquisition).
6 *Minority interest* is the outside shareholders' proportion of the share capital and reserves of the subsidiary.
7 *Goodwill* is the difference between the cost of the investment and the fair value of the

share of net assets, at the date of acquisition, belonging to the shares acquired. It is written off against the consolidated reserves.

In calculating goodwill the share of net assets is more easily obtained by calculating the parent's share of the share capital and reserves of the subsidiary at the date of acquisition. The reserves should include any surplus on revaluation arising from a revaluation of the fixed assets. This approach makes the workings simpler. Remember that the share capital and reserves will equal the net assets.

The best treatment is to revalue assets to their fair values in the books of the subsidiary at the date of acquisition. If this is not done the revaluation may be made as a consolidation adjustment.

Workings are normally required to calculate the minority interest, goodwill and the consolidated reserves.

The double entry in the consolidation workings to calculate the minority interest is:

| Debit | Subsidiary's share capital | } | with shares held by the minority |
| Credit | Minority interest | | shareholders. |

| Debit | Subsidiary's reserves | } | with amount belonging to the |
| Credit | Minority interest | | minority shareholders. |

The double entry required to set off the cost of the investment against the shares and reserves acquired is:

| Debit | Cost of control | } | with the cost of the investment. |
| Credit | Investment in subsidiary | | |

| Debit | Subsidiary's share capital | } | with the nominal value of the |
| Credit | Cost of control | | shares acquired. |

| Debit | Subsidiary's reserves | } | with the parent's share of the |
| Credit | Cost of control | | reserves at the date of acquisition. |

If the cost of the investment exceeds the share capital acquired and the reserves attaching to the share capital, the surplus is goodwill arising on acquisition. This goodwill will be the balancing figure on the cost of control account and is written off to reserves by:

| Debit | Consolidated reserves | } | with the goodwill arising. |
| Credit | Cost of control | | |

If negative goodwill arises the entry is reversed. Negative goodwill is the capital reserve that arises when the cost of the investment is less than the share of capital and reserves acquired.

Example 2

Continuing with West Ltd and Wood Ltd the following working accounts will be needed to produce a consolidated balance sheet immediately after the acquisition.

Working 1

Minority interest

	£000		£000
		£1 ordinary shares	24
		30% unappropriated profits	
Balance	57	(£110)	33
	£57		£57

Working 2

Cost of control

	£000		£000
Investment	135	£1 ordinary shares	56
		70% unappropriated profits	
		(£110)	77
		Goodwill (balancing figure)	
		(W3)	2
	£135		£135

Working 3

Consolidated unappropriated profits

	£000		£000
Goodwill written off (W2)	2	West	317
Balance	315	Wood – (all pre-acquisition)	—
	£317		£317

The consolidated balance sheet can now be prepared from the balance sheets of the two companies.

West Ltd and subsidiary company
Consolidated balance sheet at 1 January 19X4

	£000
Fixed assets (£612 + £153)	765
Current assets:	
Stock (£94 + £42)	136
Debtors (£163 + £16)	179
Cash at bank (£20 + £4)	24
	1,104
Less Creditors (£72 + £25)	97
	£1,007
Financed by:	
£1 ordinary shares	590
Share premium	45
Unappropriated profits (W3)	315
	950
Minority shareholders' interest in subsidiary company (W1)	57
	£1,007

Remember that a consolidated balance sheet is prepared from the balance sheets of the parent and subsidiary companies. No entries are made in the books of the companies for the consolidation adjustments; the working accounts will only appear in the consolidation working papers.

In the above balance sheet the reserves are those of the parent company only; all the reserves of the subsidiary are pre-acquisition. In subsequent years the consolidated reserves will include the parent's share of post-acquisition increases in the reserves of the subsidiary.

The different treatment of pre- and post-acquisition profits prevents purchased reserves being distributed to the shareholders of the parent company as a dividend.

Example 3

The balance sheets of the two companies one year after the date of acquisition are:

Balance sheets at 31 December 19X4

	West Ltd		Wood Ltd	
	£000	£000	£000	£000
Fixed assets		641		180
Investment in subsidiary company		135		
Current assets:				
Stock		98		65
Debtors		171		42
Cash at bank		22		10
		1,067		297
Less Creditors		108		87
		£959		£210

	West Ltd		Wood Ltd	
	£000	£000	£000	£000
Financed by:				
£1 ordinary shares		590		80
Share premium		45		
Unappropriated profits:				
At 1.1.X4	317		110	
Retained profit for 19X4	7		20	
		324		130
		£959		£210

The workings to consolidate the balance sheets will be:

Working 1

Minority interest

	£000			£000
			£1 ordinary shares	24
			30% unappropriated profits	
			(£130)	39
Balance	63			
	£63			£63

Working 2

Cost of control

	£000			£000
Investment	135		£1 ordinary shares	56
			70% *pre-acquisition*	
			unappropriated profits	77
			Goodwill (balancing figure)	
			(W3)	2
	£135			£135

Working 3

Consolidated unappropriated profits

	£000			£000
Goodwill written off (W2)	2		Wood Ltd	324
			West Ltd – 70% *post-acquisition*	
			unappropriated profits	
			(70/100 × £130 – £110)	14
Balance	336			
	£338			£338

West Ltd and subsidiary company
Consolidated balance sheet at 31 December 19X4

	£000	£000
Fixed assets		821
Current assets:		
Stock	163	
Debtors	213	
Cash at bank	32	
	408	
Less Creditors	195	
		213
		£1,034

Note that Wood's unappropriated profits have been dealt with as follows:

	£000
30% — Minority interest	39
70% — Pre-acquisition (to cost of control)	77
— Post-acquisition (to consolidated reserves)	14
	£130

Every reserve on a subsidiary's balance sheet would be apportioned in the same way.

The balance of unappropriated profits of £336,000 agrees with the workings. This can be analysed as:

	£000
Balance b/f	
Wood	317
West (all pre-acquisition)	—
Goodwill written off	(2)
	315

Retained profit for the year:		
Wood	7	
West (70% × £20)	14	
	£336	

	£000	£000
Financed by:		
£1 ordinary shares		590
Share premium		45
Unappropriated profits (W3):		
At 31.12.X3	317	
Retained profit for the year	21	
Goodwill written off	388	
	2	336
		971
Minority shareholders' interest in subsidiary company (W1)		63
		£1,034

Adjustments

Amounts owing by one group company to another are *not* included in the consolidated balance sheet, the debtor appearing in one balance sheet being contra'd against the creditor appearing in the other company's balance sheet. Any differences between the two balances should be identifiable to goods in transit or cash in transit which should be included in the consolidated balance sheet. The treatment is similar to that for inter-branch accounts outlined in Chapter 14.

The adjustment required is:

Debit	Creditors	– with the credit balance.
Debit	Goods in transit	– if any.
Debit	Cash in transit	– if any.
Credit	Debtors	– with the debit balance.

A *stock provision* should be made for any unrealized profits included in stocks held by one group company that have been purchased from another group company at cost plus. The adjustment is:

> Consolidated profits should not include any profits made on sales within the group if the goods are still held as stocks by one of the group companies. Charging the increase in the provision to the profit and loss account eliminates any such unrealized profit.

Debit	Consolidated profit and loss	} with the increase needed in the
Credit	Stock provision	} provision. (Reverse if decrease).

In the first year of making such a provision the whole provision is charged to the consolidated profit and loss account. In later years it is only necessary to charge any additional amounts required. This treatment is very similar to that for increases required in a doubtful debt provision.

The stock provision is deducted from stocks in preparing the consolidated balance sheet. This has the effect of eliminating the unrealized profit so that the stocks are included at their cost to the group as a whole.

In addition to the above adjustments some miscellaneous points that may arise in a consolidation are as follows:

1 *Preference shares:*
  a of the parent company – these should be included as part of the share capital in the consolidated balance sheet;
  b of the subsidiary company – if these are held as an investment by the parent company they should be credited to the cost of control account. If they are not held by the parent company they should be credited to the minority interest.
2 *Debentures and loan stocks* of both the parent and the subsidiary are liabilities and should be included as such in the consolidated balance sheet. If the parent company holds some debentures or loan stocks of the subsidiary company as an investment the nominal value of these should be credited to the cost of control account. Only the amount held by outsiders should be included as a liability in the consolidated balance sheet.
3 *Proposed dividends payable by the subsidiary company* must be included as receivable in the accounts of the parent company. In preparing the consolidated balance sheet the debtor for the dividend receivable in the parent's balance sheet is set off against the dividend payable in the subsidiary's balance sheet. Any difference between the two

> The entry in the parent's accounts to raise a debtor for dividends receivable will be:
>
> Debit Dividend receivable (a debtor in the balance sheet)
> Credit Profit and loss

amounts will be the dividend payable to the minority shareholders which should be included in the consolidated balance sheet as a current liability.

SSAP 22 Accounting for Goodwill

The main recommendations of this standard are as follows:

1 Goodwill should only be included in the accounts of companies if it has been purchased; this would include goodwill arising on the acquisition of a subsidiary. Once included goodwill should not be revalued.
2 Goodwill that is purchased should be written off against reserves. If it is not practicable to do this, it should be written off to the profit and loss account over its useful life.
3 Negative goodwill (the capital reserve arising on acquisition if the fair value of the net assets acquired exceeds the consideration given) should be credited to reserves.
4 The accounting policy followed for goodwill should be disclosed as a note to the accounts.

> SSAP 22 is a fairly long standard that fully discusses goodwill and its possible accounting treatments. Goodwill is defined as the difference between the value of a business as a whole and the value of its separable net assets.

SSAP 23 Mergers

SSAP 23 Accounting for Acquisitions and Mergers allows the merger method of consolidation to be used if *all* of the following conditions are met:

1 An offer to acquire their shares was made to all the holders of the ordinary and any other voting shares of the subsidiary; and
2 As a result of the offer the parent company owns at least 90% of the subsidiary's shares; and
3 The parent did not hold more than 20% of the subsidiary's shares before it made the offer; and
4 At least 90% of the purchase consideration is in the form of ordinary shares in the parent.

> SSAP 23 was issued in 1985. Prior to the Companies Act 1981 the use of the merger method did not comply with the requirements of the Companies Acts.

> Refer to SSAP 23 for full details of the conditions.

The merger method is used in the situation where shares in a subsidiary are purchased by issuing shares in the parent in exchange. The subsidiary must be at least 90% owned, and at least 90% of the consideration must have been in the form of shares, not cash.

In these circumstances the approach is that the two companies have merged, rather than that the parent has acquired the subsidiary. In the parent's books the investment is not recorded at cost but at the nominal value of the shares issued by the parent, plus any cash given. (Under the acquisition method any shares issued by the parent are recorded at their market value, the excess of this over the nominal value being credited to the share premium account.)

When consolidating, the investment in the parent's balance sheet is set off against the nominal value of the shares in the subsidiary's balance sheet, any difference being treated as an adjustment to the consolidated reserves and not as if it was goodwill. The most important point to note is that all the reserves of the subsidiary are consolidated, no apportionment between pre-acquisition and post-acquisition reserves is made.

> The traditional method of consolidation in the UK has been the acquisition method. The merger method is most appropriate when two equal size companies merge purely by a share exchange. SSAP 23 now allows the merger method to be used in situations where the conditions are met.

Example 4

The balance sheets of two companies at 31 December 19X6 were:

	Enery Ltd	Couper Ltd
	£000	£000
Fixed assets	400	300
Net current assets	200	150
	£600	£450
£1 ordinary shares	250	300
Share premium	100	—
Profit and loss account	250	150
	£600	£450

Enery Ltd acquired 270,000 ordinary shares in Couper Ltd on 1 January 19X7 by issuing 200,000 ordinary shares valued at £2.50 each and paying £27,000 in cash. The offer had been made to all the shareholders of Couper Ltd.

In these circumstances the merger method of consolidation may be used. The conditions laid down by SSAP 23 are met because:

1   The offer was made to all the shareholders of Couper Ltd; and
2   Enery Ltd hold (270,000/300,000 × 100) 90% of the shares of Couper Ltd; and
3   Enery Ltd did not hold any shares in Couper Ltd before the offer; and
4   The shares issued were at a fair value of (200,000 × £2.50) £500,000. This represents 94.9% of the total consideration of (shares £500,000 + cash £27,000) £527,000.

The balance sheets of the two companies after the merger will be:

The investment in Couper Ltd consists of:

	£000
200,000 Shares of £1 issued at nominal value	200
Cash paid	27
	£227

Note that the shares are recorded at their nominal value. No share premium entry is required.

	Enery Ltd	Couper Ltd
	£000	£000
Fixed assets	400	300
Investment in Couper Ltd:		
270,000 ordinary shares	227	
Net current assets		
(£200 – £27)	173	150
	£800	£450
£1 ordinary shares		
(£250 + £200)	450	300
Share premium	100	—
Profit and loss	250	150
	£800	£450

Working 1

The adjustment to the reserves on consolidation will be:

Consolidation reserve adjustment

	£000		£000
Investment	227	Nominal value of shares	
Reserve arising on merger		acquired	270
(balancing figure)	43		
	£270		£270

Working 2

The minority interest is:

Minority interest

	£000		£000
		Ordinary shares	30
Balance	45	10% of profit and loss account	15
	£45		£45

The consolidated balance sheet at 1 January 19X7 using the merger method will be:

	£000
Fixed assets	700
Current assets	323
	£1,023
£1 ordinary shares	450
Share premium	100
Consolidation reserve (W1)	43
Profit and loss account (£250 + 90% × £150)	385
	978
Minority interest (W2)	45
	£1,023

Summary

1   SSAP 14 defines a subsidiary company. It requires a parent company to prepare group accounts.
2   SSAP 1 requires investments in associated companies to be accounted for using the equity method of accounting.
3   Consolidated balance sheets will include the assets and liabilities of the parent and subsidiary companies. Any minority shareholders' interest in a subsidiary company is disclosed.
4   SSAP 22 recommends that goodwill is written off against reserves. If this is not practicable it should be amortized over its useful life.
5   SSAP 23 allows the merger method of consolidation to be used if certain conditions are met.

Examination Hints

Consolidated accounts can be a very complex area but at the level of the Association's examinations the questions should be simple and straightforward. You should obtain a good mark for an acquisition method consolidated balance sheet by applying the basic rules:

1   Share capital is that of the parent company only.
2   Reserves are all the reserves of the parent plus its proportion of the post-acquisiton increases in the reserves of the subsidiary.
3   Goodwill is arrived at by offsetting the cost of the investment against the proportion of the share capital and reserves of the subsidiary at the date of acquisition that belongs to the parent company.
4   Minority interest is the outside shareholders' proportion of the subsidiary's share capital and reserves at the date of the balance sheet that is being prepared.
5   All the assets and liabilities of the parent company and the subsidiary are included except any inter-company items which should be offset.

The basic rules for a merger method consolidated balance sheet differ for the following items:

1   All the reserves are consolidated; no distinction is made between pre- and post-acquisition reserves.
2   'Goodwill' is the difference between the nominal value of the shares issued (plus any cash paid) by the parent and the nominal value of the shares in the subsidiary that are acquired in exchange. It does not represent the real value of goodwill and is an adjustment to the consolidated reserves.

SSAPs 1, 14, 22 and 23 are advanced areas and are not as important, within the context of the syllabus, as the basic consolidation process. You should, however, be familiar with the conditions laid down by SSAP 23 which should be met before the merger method may be used.

As always you should read the question carefully to determine precisely what it is that the examiner requires. To avoid making errors take special note of the date of acquisition and the date of the balance sheet you are required to prepare. Double check your calculation of the percentage owned by the parent company and by any minority interest.

Try to answer the following questions before reading on.

Self-Assessment Questions

In each question, choose the correct answer from the five alternatives given.

See page 307 for answers.

23.1   A parent company invested £30,500 in 80,000 ordinary shares of 10 pence each in a subsidiary. The subsidiary's issued share capital and reserves of at the date of acquisition were £10,000 and £20,000. The goodwill arising on the acquisition will be:

a   £500
b   £2,500
c   £6,500
d   £16,000
e   £22,000.

23.2   The issued share capital of a subsidiary is 100,000 ordinary shares of 50 pence each. The reserves are currently: share premium £20,000, general reserve £30,000 and profit and loss account £10,000. The parent company owns 75,000 of the ordinary shares. The minority interest is:

a   £12,500
b   £17,500
c   £27,500
d   £40,000
e   £82,500.

23.3   Using the data given in question 23.2, the reserves at the date of acquisition were: share premium £20,000, general reserve £20,000 and profit and loss account £1,000. The total of the consolidated reserves will currently include the following amount in respect of the subsidiary.

a   £2,250
b   £4,750
c   £6,750
d   £14,250
e   £19,000.

23.4   The balance sheet of a parent company includes debtors of £30,000 and that of its subsidiary includes debtors of £20,000. The balance sheets also show creditors of £15,000 and £5,000 respectively. Included in these amounts are inter-company balances of £1,000 owed by the subsidiary to the parent company. The consolidated debtors and creditors will be:

a   £45,000 and £25,000
b   £48,000 and £18,000
c   £49,000 and £19,000
d   £50,000 and £20,000
e   £51,000 and £21,000.

If you have answered the above questions correctly, and are sure you understand the key points in this chapter, then try questions 34, 35 and 36 on pages 212–14 before moving on to Chapter 24.

CHAPTER 24

CONSOLIDATED ACCOUNTS: PROFIT AND LOSS ACCOUNTS

Chapter contents

Introduction **171** Consolidated profit and loss accounts **171** Summary **175** Examination hints **175**

Learning objective

After studying this chapter you should be able to:

☐ prepare a simple consolidated profit and loss account.

Introduction

A consolidated profit and loss account is prepared by combining the profit and loss accounts of the parent company and its subsidiaries. It will show the profit for the year made by the whole group of companies. It is necessary to show this total profit so that the shareholders of the parent company know how much profit has been made on their behalf.

If a subsidiary is only partly owned, the amount of the subsidiary's profit after tax that belongs to the minority shareholders is shown as a deduction in the consolidated profit and loss account.

The payment of a dividend by a subsidiary company to its parent will not affect the group profit. When the accounts are consolidated the dividend received will be offset by the dividend paid. Such dividends will merely shuffle profits from the subsidiary's own profit and loss account to the profit and loss account of the parent company.

A parent company that publishes a consolidated profit and loss account will not also publish its own profit and loss account, but a note will analyse the consolidated profit and loss account balance between the balance on the parent's profit and loss account and on the subsidiaries.

If the minority interest includes holders of preference shares in a subsidiary, the preference dividend is included in the minority interest's share of profits for the year. The minority interest share of profits in respect of ordinary shares will be their proportion of profits after tax less preference dividends.

Consolidated profit and loss accounts

These will follow the normal format for the profit and loss account. Each item included will be the total of the parent's item plus all of the subsidiary's item, even though it may only be partly owned. The minority shareholders' share of the profit after tax is disclosed as an additional item that is deducted on the face of the profit and loss account.

Miscellaneous points are as follows:

1 *Inter-company sales* are excluded, the sale by one company being set off against the purchase by the other company.
2 *Other inter-company* transactions are excluded by being set off.

Dividends payable by a subsidiary to its minority shareholders will not appear on the consolidated profit and loss account. The *whole* of the minority interest's share of profits after tax is deducted; this will include any dividends payable to them.

3 *The increase in any stock provision* is included in cost of sales as an additional item.

4 *Dividends* will be the dividends of the parent company only. Inter-company dividends are excluded by being set off.

Example 1

The profit and loss accounts of two companies for the year ended 30 June 19X7 are:

	Winter Ltd		Green Ltd	
	£000	£000	£000	£000
Sales		1,000		300
Less Cost of sales		600		180
Gross profit		400		120
Less:				
Distribution costs	100		30	
Administration expenses	150	250	50	80
		150		40
Income from shares in group company		16		
Profit before tax		166		40
Taxation		50		10
Profit after tax		116		30
Proposed dividend		80		20
Retained profit		36		10
Balance b/f		200		150
Carried forward		£236		£160

The dividend receivable by Winter Ltd of £16,000 is 80% of the dividend payable by the subsidiary.

Green Ltd is an 80% owned subsidiary of Winter Ltd which was acquired when the balance on its profit and loss account was £100,000.

The consolidation will be:

Winter Ltd and subsidiary company
Consolidated profit and loss account for the year ended
30 June 19X7

	£000	£000
Sales (£1,000 + £300)		1,300
Less cost of sales (£600 + £180)		780
Gross profit		520
Less:		
Distribution costs (£100 + £30)	130	
Administration expenses (£150 + £50)	200	330
Profit before tax		190
Less Taxation (£50 + £10)		60
Profit after tax		130
Less Minority interest (£20% × £30)		6
		124
Less Proposed dividend (parent company only)		80
Retained profit		44
Balance b/f		240
Carried forward (Note 1)		£284

No entry is required for minority interest if the subsidiary is wholly owned.

The retained profit can be proved:

	£
Winter Ltd	36,000
Green Ltd (80% × £10,000)	8,000
	£44,000

The profit and loss balance brought forward is:

	£
Winter Ltd	200,000
Green Ltd: 80% of post-acquisition (£150,000 – £100,000)	40,000
	£240,000

Note to the accounts
1 Profit and loss account:

	Parent company	Subsidiary company	Total
	£000	£000	£000
At 1.7.X6	200	40	240
Retained profit for the year	36	8	44
At 30.6.X7	£236	£48	£284

In considering this answer note that the balance carried forward on the consolidated profit and loss account consists of all of the parent's balance plus 80% of the post-acquisition increase in the profit and loss balance of the subsidiary:

	£000
Winter Ltd	236
Green Ltd (80/100 × (£160,000 – £100,000))	48
	£284

The consolidated balance sheet would be prepared in the normal way.

Example 2

The trial balances of two companies at 31 December 19X6 are as follows:

	Spring Ltd		Cabbage Ltd	
	£	£	£	£
Sales		386,000		81,000
Cost of sales	284,000		41,000	
Expenses	46,000		9,000	
Taxation for year	20,000		2,000	
Fixed assets	46,350		40,000	
Stock at 31.12.X6	30,000		9,000	
Debtors	20,000		10,000	
Bank	11,650		12,500	
Investment in Cabbage Ltd	30,000			
Creditors		28,500		6,000
£1 ordinary shares		50,000		30,000
Profit and loss balance at 31.12.X5		23,500		6,500
	£488,000	£488,000	£123,500	£123,500

Included in the sales of Spring Ltd are sales to Cabbage Ltd of £10,000; the cost to Spring Ltd of these goods was 25% below the prices at which they were sold to the subsidiary. Of these goods $\frac{1}{5}$ remain unsold and are included in the stocks of Cabbage Ltd at £2,000.

Spring Ltd holds 22,500 £1 ordinary shares of Cabbage Ltd, the investment having been made when the reserves of Cabbage Ltd were £3,000.

Spring Ltd proposes to pay a dividend of £10,000.

Required:
Consolidated profit and loss account for the year ended 31 December 19X6 and a consolidated balance sheet at that date.

Solution
To produce the consolidated accounts that are required, the profit and loss accounts for the two companies will have to be prepared first as follows:

Profit and loss accounts for the year ended
31 December 19X6

	Spring Ltd	Cabbage Ltd
	£	£
Sales	386,000	81,000
Less Cost of sales	284,000	41,000
Gross profit	102,000	40,000
Less Expenses	46,000	9,000
Profit before tax	56,000	31,000
Less Taxation	20,000	2,000
Profit after tax	36,000	29,000
Proposed dividend	10,000	
Retained profits	26,000	29,000
Balance brought forward	23,500	6,500
Carried forward	£49,500	£35,500

The inter-company sales of £10,000 will need to be eliminated and a stock provision of (25/100 × £2,000) £500 made. There appears to be no inter-company balances.

Spring owns (22,500/30,000) 75% of the shares in Cabbage Ltd. The minority interest is therefore 25%.

The profit and loss accounts may now be consolidated:

Spring Ltd and subsidiary company
Consolidated profit and loss account for the year ended
31 December 19X6

	£
Sales (£386,000 + £81,000 – £10,000)	457,000
Less Cost of sales (£284,000 + 41,000 – £10,000 + £500)	315,500
Gross profit	141,500
Less Expenses (£46,000 + £9,000)	55,000
Profit before tax	86,500
Taxation (£20,000 + £2,000)	22,000
Profit after tax	64,500
Less Minority interest (25/100 × £29,000)	7,250
	57,250
Proposed dividend	10,000
Retained profit	47,250
Balance brought forward (£23,500 – Goodwill £5,250)	
+ 75% (£6,500 – £3,000))	20,875
Carried forward (Note 1)	£68,125

The retained profit can be proved:

	£
Spring Ltd	26,000
Less Stock provision	500
	25,500
Cabbage Ltd (75% × £29,000)	21,750
	£47,250

The profit and loss balance *carried* forward is:

	£	£
Spring Ltd		49,500
Less Stock provision	500	
Goodwill written off	5,250	5,750
		43,750
Cabbage Ltd (75% of post-acquisition £35,500 – £3,000)		24,375
		£68,125

Note to the accounts
1 Profit and loss account:

	Parent company	Subsidiary company	Total
	£	£	£
At 1.1.X6 (£23,500 – Goodwill £5,250)	18,250		
+ 75% × (£6,500 – £3,000)		2,625	20,875
Retained profit for the year	25,500	21,750	47,250
At 31.12.X6	£43,750	£24,375	£68,125

Workings
The workings for the consolidated balance sheet will need to be prepared before arriving at the profit and loss balance brought forward, as goodwill should be written off against reserves. The workings are:

Minority interest

	£		£
		£1 ordinary shares	7,500
		Profit and loss balance	
Balance	16,375	(25% × £35,500)	8,875
	£16,375		£16,375

Cost of control

	£		£
Investment	30,000	£1 ordinary shares	22,500
		75% pre-acquisition profit and	
		loss balance (75% × £3,000)	2,250
		Goodwill (balancing figure)	5,250
	£30,000		£30,000

Consolidated stocks

	£		£
Spring	30,000	Stock provision	500
Cabbage	9,000	Balance	38,500
	£39,000		£39,000

The balance sheet will be:

Consolidated balance sheet at 31 December 19X6

	£	£	£
Fixed assets			86,350
Current assets:			
Stocks		38,500	
Debtors		30,000	
Bank		24,150	
		92,650	
Less:			
Creditors	34,500		
Dividend	10,000	44,500	48,150
			£134,500
Financed by:			
£1 ordinary shares			50,000
Profit and loss account			68,125
			118,125
Minority shareholders' interest in			
subsidiary company			16,375
			£134,500

Summary

1 A consolidated profit and loss account combines the profit and loss accounts of the parent and subsidiary companies.
2 Any minority shareholders' interest in the profits after tax of a subsidiary will be deducted.
3 Inter-company transactions are eliminated from the consolidation.

Examination Hints

If the profit and loss accounts of the companies are given in the question it will be possible to proceed straight to your answer. If the question merely contains trial balance items it will be necessary first to prepare working profit and loss accounts for each company to determine its profit after tax for the year.

To avoid common errors in the preparation of consolidated profit and loss accounts remember to:

1 deduct inter-company sales from both sales and cost of sales;
2 show the minority interest (in the profit after tax of the subsidiary) as a deduction;
3 include as dividends payable the dividends of the parent company only.

Try to answer the following questions before reading on.

Self-Assessment Questions

See page 307 for answer.

In each question, choose the correct answer from the five alternatives given.

24.1 A subsidiary is 60% owned. Sales for the year are Parent £100,000, Subsidiary £100,000. The parent's sales include goods sold to the subsidiary for £10,000. The consolidated sales will be:
a £150,000
b £160,000
c £170,000
d £190,000
e £200,000.

24.2 A subsidiary is 80% owned. Its profits for the year before tax are £100,000, taxation for the year is £30,000 and it provides for a dividend of £45,000. The minority interest for the year deducted in the consolidated profit and loss account is:
a £5,000
b £9,000
c £14,000
d £20,000
e £56,000.

24.3 The issued share capital of a subsidiary is 100,000 £1 ordinary shares and 20,000 10% £1 preference shares. The parent company holds 70,000 of the ordinary shares, but none of the preference shares. The subsidiary's profit after tax for the year is £50,000. The minority interest for the year deducted in the consolidated profit and loss account is:
a £9,000
b £10,500
c £16,400
d £17,000
e £29,167.

If you have answered the above questions correctly, and are sure you understand the key points in this chapter, then try to answer question 37 on page 215 before moving on to Chapter 25.

CHAPTER 25

STOCKS AND WORK IN PROGRESS

Chapter contents

Introduction **177**   Valuation of stocks **177**   Long-term contract work in progress **178**   Contract accounts **178**   Disclosure requirements **180**   Summary **180**   Examination hints **180**

Learning objectives

After studying this chapter you should be able to:

☐ describe and apply the principles for valuation of stock in accordance with SSAP 9 Stocks and Work in Progress;

☐ describe and apply the recommendations of SSAP 9 in determining the amount of profit to be included in the valuation of long-term contract work in progress;

☐ write up a contract account;

☐ state the disclosure requirements of SSAP 9.

Introduction

The valuation placed upon stocks and work in progress (WIP) is of fundamental importance to most organizations. SSAP 9 gives guidance in two main areas: the valuation of purchased and manufactured stocks and the valuation of the long-term work in progress of contractors, with particular emphasis on the extent to which profit may be included in the long-term WIP valuation.

Valuation of stocks

A trader will normally have a stock of purchased products. A manufacturer on the other hand may have stocks of purchased raw materials and components, WIP (partly manufactured goods) and finished goods. In addition most organizations will have stocks of consumable stores such as heating oil, petrol and maintenance materials. The valuation principle that is applied to these stocks is that they should be valued at the *lower of cost* and *net realizable value*.

Cost is the cost of purchase plus any other expenditure incurred in the normal course of business in bringing the product to its present location and condition, including any costs of conversion. Unit cost, average cost and FIFO are acceptable methods. *Cost of conversion* includes:

1 direct labour, direct expenses and sub-contracted work, and
2 production overheads allocated on the basis of the normal level of activity.

Net realizable value is the estimated selling price before any cash discount *less*:

Cost of purchase is the purchase price and any import duties, transport and handling costs, and any other directly attributable costs.

The base stock and LIFO methods are not acceptable.

Note that production overheads may be included in the valuation of work in progress and finished goods. Both variable and fixed production overheads are included. Selling and administration overheads are excluded.

1 All further costs to completion, and
2 All costs to be incurred on marketing, selling and distributing.

Net realizable value may be lower than cost if:

1 Selling prices are reduced, or
2 Stocks are damaged, deteriorated or obsolete.

The fundamental rule of the lower of cost and net realizable value is applied to separate items, or groups of similar items, of stocks rather than to all stock in total.

Example 1

The following items are in stock:

	Cost £	Net realizable value £	Stock valuation £
Product A	10,000	15,000	10,000
Product B	5,000	4,000	4,000
			£14,000

Long-term contract work in progress

The rule for valuation is at cost plus any attributable profit less any foreseeable losses. Progress payments received and receivable should be deducted. Details are as follows:

Long-term contracts arise in the accounts of shipbuilders, civil engineers, building contractors, etc.

1 A *long-term contract* is a separate contract for the manufacture or building of a single entity where a substantial proportion of the work will extend for more than one year.
2 *Attributable profit* is the part of the total profit on the contract earned on the work done by the accounting date. The profit must be reasonably foreseeable. A prudent approach should be taken in estimating the further costs to be incurred to complete the contract.
3 *Foreseeable losses* are the total losses, both incurred and to be incurred, estimated for the particular contract.
4 *Progress payments* are payments receivable from the customer on account during the course of the contract.

This method of valuation enables profits to be recognized each year as they are earned. The alternative would be not to take profit until the contract is completed, but this would result in unacceptable fluctuations in the reported profits of companies that undertake only a few contracts at a time.

Example 2

A contract is undertaken for a contract price of £10,000,000. Costs to date on the contract are £4,000,000. Total costs of the contract are estimated to be £8,000,000. Progress payments receivable to date are £3,600,000.

Profit has been taken on the basis of:

$$\frac{\text{Costs to date}}{\text{Total contract costs}}$$

× Total contract profit

This method is not mandatory, and other methods of calculating the profit earned to date may be acceptable. Prudence must be exercised in estimating the total contract costs to completion.

The valuation of the long-term contract work in progress may include profit of (£4,000,000/£8,000,000 × Total profit £2,000,000) £1,000,000.

The balance sheet extract will be:

	£
Long-term contract work in progress:	
At cost plus attributable profit	5,000,000
Less Progress payments receivable	3,600,000
	£1,400,000

Contract accounts

A contractor will maintain a separate account for each contract to which will be debited:

1 Materials sent to site
2 Direct wages
3 Subcontractor fees
4 Direct expenses
5 Plant and equipment sent to site.

At the balance sheet date balances will be carried down for the assets of stocks of materials not used and plant and equipment at valuation. Balances will also be carried down for any expenses prepaid and owing.

Profit earned for the year will be debited to the contract account and credited to the profit and loss account. The remaining balance on the contract account is carried down as WIP. It represents the costs of work done to date plus attributable profit.

Example 3

The data given below refers to a contract for the construction of a small theatre, the work being undertaken by Green and Nephew Ltd for a contract sum of £500,000.

Details of the contract during the first year are as follows:

	£
Direct materials	129,500
Direct wages	74,000
Direct expenses	20,400
Administrative expenses charged to the contract	6,100
Costs to date	£230,000

At the accounting date the position is that 80% of the work done above has been certified by the architect at a valuation of £220,000. Certificates for progress payments amounting to £198,000 have been issued for this work. Cash of £160,000 had been received by Green and Nephew Ltd in respect of this work certified.

It is estimated that the contract will taken another 12 months to complete and that the total profit earned on the contract will be £85,000.

Required:
The ledger accounts recording the above.

Solution
In considering this contract note that the contract is for a period of more than one year and therefore credit may be taken for attributable profit. The contract price is £500,000 and total profit is estimated to be £85,000, therefore total costs are estimated at (£500,000 – £85,000) £415,000. The contract is at least (£220,000/£500,000) 44% completed and the outcome may be assumed to be foreseeable.

Profit earned may be calculated:

$$\text{Total profit} \times \frac{\text{Costs to date}}{\text{total costs}} = £85,000 \times \frac{£230,000}{£415,000} = £47,108$$

The contract account will appear as follows:

Theatre contract

	£		£
Direct materials	129,500		
Direct wages	74,000		
Direct expenses	20,400		
Administrative exps.	6,100		
	230,000		
Profit and loss	47,108	Balance c/d – WIP	277,108
	277,108		277,108

An alternative method of calculating profit to be taken could be:

Total contract profit ×

$$\frac{\text{Value of work certified}}{\text{Contract price}}$$

Other methods will be used. Sometimes a very prudent approach of reducing profit taken by

$$\frac{\text{Cash received}}{\text{Value of work certified}}$$

is adopted.

Progress payment certificates will be issued as the work done is valued. These are debited to the customer and credited to a progress payments account. Cash received from the customer is credited to his account. These accounts will be as follows:

A retention of 10% has been deducted from the value of work done in calculating progress payments due. A final progress payment certificate for these retention monies will be issued on the satisfactory completion of the contract.

Customer

	£		£
Progress payments due	198,000	Cash	160,000
		Balance c/d	38,000
	£198,000		£198,000

Progress payments

	£		£
		Customer	198,000

On the balance sheet the balance on the customer's account will be included in debtors and the progress payments deducted from the WIP as follows:

Green and Nephew Ltd
Balance sheet extract

	£	£
Current assets:		
Long-term work in progress	277,108	
Less Progress payments received and receivable	198,000	79,108
Debtor		38,000

At the end of the contract the progress payments account is closed by transfer to the contract account. Any final balance on the contract account will then represent profit earned that has not been taken in earlier periods, and is transferred to the profit and loss account.

Disclosure requirements

SSAP 9 requirements are:

The categories are: purchased goods, consumable stores, raw materials and components, WIP and finished goods.

1 Stocks and WIP should be analysed into each of the main categories.
2 The accounting policies used in calculating cost, net realizable value, attributable profit and foreseeable losses should be given by way of a note.
3 Long-term contract WIP should be stated at:
   a cost plus attributable profit less foreseeable losses, *less*
   b progress payments received and receivable.

Summary

1 SSAP 9 requires stocks and work in progress to be valued at the lower of cost and net realizable value.
2 Cost will include any production overheads; these should be allocated on the basis of the normal level of activity.
3 Unit cost, average cost and FIFO are acceptable methods.
4 Long-term contract work in progress is valued at cost plus any attributable profits less any foreseeable losses. Progress payments received and receivable should be deducted.
5 A contractor will maintain a separate account for each contract.

Examination Hints

Questions may be set requiring a written answer on the principles of stock valuation and/or the application of the principles to numerical data. A short time spent on planning a written answer will normally improve its relevance and scope.

Try to answer the following questions before reading on.

Self-Assessment Questions

In each question, choose the correct answer from the five alternatives given.

See page 307 for answers.

25.1 Which of the following stocks are not consumable stores in the accounts of a refrigerator manufacturer;
 a stationery
 b canteen supplies
 c cleaning materials
 d lubricating oils
 e components.

25.2 Goods purchased to be resold, cost £10,000, have been damaged. At the balance sheet date their replacement buying price is £9,000. They can be sold in the normal course of business for £14,000, providing £4,500 is spent on rectifying the damage. Their stock value is:
 a £8,500
 b £9,000
 c £9,500
 d £10,000
 e £14,000.

25.3 Which of the following overheads may not be included in the overhead element of the valuation of finished goods:
 a depreciation of plant and machinery
 b advertising
 c insurance of factory contents
 d factory cleaner's wages
 e rent of factory.

25.4 Costs to date on a long-term contract are £40,000. Estimated future costs to completion are £430,000. The contract sum is £460,000. The WIP will be included on the balance sheet at:
 a (£30,000)
 b (£10,000)
 c nil
 d £30,000
 e £40,000.

If you have answered the above questions correctly, and are sure you understand the key points in this chapter, then try to answer questions 38 and 39 on page 216 before moving on to Chapter 26.

CHAPTER 26

OTHER SSAPs

Chapter contents

Introduction **182**   Government grants **182**   Depreciation **182**   Research and development **183**   Investment properties **184**   Summary **184**   Examination hints **184**

Learning objective

After studying this chapter you should be able to:

☐ appreciate the rules and recommendations contained in:
- SSAP 4 The Accounting Treatment of Government Grants,
- SSAP 12 Accounting for Depreciation,
- SSAP 13 Accounting for Research and Development,
- SSAP 19 Accounting for Investment Properties.

Introduction

This chapter outlines the recommendations of the SSAPs that are not included elsewhere in this book.

Government Grants

Grants receivable by companies may be classified into two types: revenue grants which are contributions towards expenses, and capital grants which are contributions towards the cost of acquiring fixed assets.

SSAP 4 is one of the shortest standards. It outlines the following accounting treatment for these grants.

1 *Revenue-based grants* should be credited to the profit and loss account in the same period as the expenditure to which they relate is charged.

2 *Capital-based grants* should be credited to a 'deferred credit' account from which it should be transferred to the credit of the profit and loss account over the life of the asset. This treatment has a similar effect on profits as the alternative treatment allowed in SSAP 4 of crediting the grant to the fixed asset cost account and only depreciating the net amount.

The alternative treatment has the disadvantage that not all fixed assets are shown at cost. Capital expenditure in certain parts of the country may attract grants and there may be different book values for identical assets depending merely on where they are located.

Depreciation

SSAP 12 defines depreciation as the wearing out, consumption or other loss of value of a fixed asset whether arising from use, effluxion of time or obsolescence through technology and market changes. The accounting treatment required by SSAP 12 is as follows:

1 Provision for depreciation of fixed assets having a finite useful life should be made by allocating the cost (or revalued amount) less estimated residual values of the assets as fairly as possible to the periods expected to benefit from their use.
2 Where there is a revision of the estimated useful life of an asset, the unamortized cost should be charged over the revised remaining useful life.
3 However, if at any time the unamortized cost of an asset is seen to be irrecoverable in full, it should be written down immediately to the estimated recoverable amount which should be charged over the remaining useful life.
4 Where there is a change from one method of depreciation to another, the unamortized cost of the asset should be written off over the remaining useful life on the new basis commencing with the period in which the change is made. The effect should be disclosed in the year of change, if material.
5 Where assets are revalued in the financial statements, the provision for depreciation should be based on the revalued amount and current estimate of remaining useful life, with disclosure in the year of change of the effect of the revaluation, if material.
6 The following should be disclosed in the financial statements for each major class of depreciable asset:
   a the depreciation methods used;
   b the useful lives or the depreciation rates used;
   c total depreciation allocated for the period;
   d the gross amount of depreciable assets and the related accumulated depreciation.

Freehold land will normally have an infinite life and need not be depreciated. An exception to this is freehold land used for mineral extraction, e.g. a gravel pit. Buildings on the other hand do have a finite life and should be depreciated, freehold buildings over their useful life, leasehold buildings over their useful life or the length of the lease if that is shorter.

The fundamental principle is that costs may be carried forward to be matched against future income arising from the asset.

SSAP 12 does not specify the depreciation methods which may be used. Explanations of the common depreciation methods are to be found in most basic accounting text books.

Research and development

Some companies are faced with a considerable problem in deciding on the accounting treatment of expenditure on research and development. The most prudent approach is to write it off in the year in which it is incurred. This may not be practical for some companies, particularly if they have spent very large amounts on developing a product that has not yet reached the manufacturing stage. Application of the accruals concept would require development expenditure to be carried forward to be charged against the income arising from selling the product. However, it is difficult to estimate whether the product will be successful and how many will be made over what period of time.

The accounting treatment required by SSAP 13 is as follows:

1 Expenditure on pure and applied research should be written off in the year of expenditure.
2 Development expenditure should be written off in the year of expenditure except in the following circumstances, when it may be deferred to future periods:
   a there is a clearly defined project, and
   b the related expenditure is separately identifiable, and
   c the outcome of such a project has been assessed with reasonable certainty as to:
      – its technical feasibility, and
      – its ultimate commercial viability considered in the light of factors such as likely market conditions (including competing products), public opinion, consumer and environmental legislation, and
   d if further development costs are to be incurred on the same project the aggregate of such costs together with related production, selling and administration costs are reasonably expected to be more than covered by related future revenues, and
   e adequate resources exist, or are reasonably expected to be available, to enable the project to be completed and to provide any consequential increases in working capital.
3 Development costs that are to be deferred should be charged to future periods on a systematic basis by reference to the numbers sold each year or the period over which the product is expected to be sold.
4 The following should be disclosed in the financial statements:
   a movements on the deferred development expenditure account;
   b the accounting policy followed;
   c deferred development expenditure should be shown separately on the balance sheet and should not be included in current assets.

Pure research is work directed primarily towards the advancement of knowledge. Applied research seeks practical uses of knowledge that has arisen from pure research. Development work is on the introduction or improvement of specific products.

SSAP 13 applies both prudence and the matching concept. It allows expenditure to be carried forward only if there is a reasonable certainty that it will be recovered.

The Companies Act 1985 requires development costs that are carried forward to be included as an intangible asset in the balance sheet.

Investment properties

An investment property is land and/or buildings owned by a company as an investment. They must not be occupied by the company or another company within the group. Normally the investment properties will be let to third parties.

Valuation at open market value would take account of the age and condition of the buildings.

SSAP 19 is a rather specialized standard that requires investment properties to be included in the balance sheet at their open market value, the surplus on revaluation each year being credited to an 'investment revaluation reserve'.

Investment properties, being revalued each year, should not be depreciated in accordance with SSAP 12 unless they are held on a lease, when they should be depreciated at least over the last 20 years of the lease.

Summary

1 SSAP 4 deals with the accounting treatment of revenue-based and capital-based grants.
2 SSAP 12 requires fixed assets that have a finite life to be depreciated and specifies the additional notes required for each major class of fixed assets.
3 SSAP 13 requires expenditure on research to be written off. It allows development expenditure to be carried forward to be charged to future periods only if certain conditions are met.
4 SSAP 19 is a specialized standard that requires investment properties to be included at open market value.

Examination Hints

Questions may be set requiring knowledge of the basic rules laid down by SSAPs. Read the question requirements carefully and consider the number of marks allocated in deciding on the scope and depth of your answer.

Try to answer the following questions before reading on.

Self-Assessment Questions

See page 307 for answers.

In each question, choose the correct answer from the five alternatives given.

26.1   Which of the following would not normally be depreciated:
    a   freehold land
    b   freehold buildings
    c   long leasehold land
    d   long leasehold buildings
    e   short leasehold land and buildings.

26.2   A fixed asset costs £10,000 and was to be depreciated on the straight line basis over an estimated life of 5 years. The asset would have no residual value. During the second year the estimated life was revised to a total of 4 years only. The depreciation charge for the second year will be:
    a   £2,000
    b   £2,500
    c   £2,667
    d   £3,000
    e   £4,667.

26.3   Which of the following is not a condition that has to be met before development costs may be carried forward:
    a   it is a clearly defined project
    b   it develops an existing product
    c   it is technically feasible

    d it is commercially viable
    e adequate resources exist.

26.4   Which of the following may be an investment property:
    a premises occupied by owner
    b premises let to a subsidiary
    c premises let to a parent
    d premises let to a fellow subsidiary
    e premises let to an associated company.

If you have answered the above questions correctly, and are sure you understand the key points in this chapter, then try to answer questions 40 and 41 on page 217 before moving on to the sample examination paper on page 219.

PART TWO
QUESTIONS AND ANSWERS

In this part of the book there are four groups of questions and answers:

☐ **Examination questions** (which start on page 189). Each question is linked to a particular chapter in Part One. You should not attempt to answer these questions until you are sure you fully understand the chapter to which it relates, and in most cases all preceding chapters too. The suggested answers (which start on page 241) have been separated from the questions so that you are encouraged to try to answer them yourself *before* checking through the given answers.

☐ **Sample examination paper** (which starts on page 219). This should be attempted under simulated examination conditions. Do not look at the answers (which start on page 296) until afterwards.

☐ **Further examination questions** (which start on page 225). You may be exhausted with questions by this stage, but these have been provided so that you can get some additional practice if you wish. Your tutor or lecturer may wish to set some of these questions as a formal exercise, so check with him or her before attempting any. Answers have *not* been provided.

☐ **Answers to the Self-Assessment Questions** in Part One (which start on page 302).

EXAMINATION QUESTIONS

Question 1

The accounts of a medium sized public company have been prepared, but before they can be published certain notes must be drafted to explain the calculations of some of the figures in the accounts, and to show that the accounts conform to best accounting practice. As an accounting technician you are a member of the team engaged in writing these notes, with special responsibility for the note on accounting policies.

See page 241 for answer.

Required

a   Name the four fundamental accounting concepts which under SSAP 2 are presumed to be observed when accounts are prepared, and indicate briefly what is meant by the terms 'accounting bases' and 'accounting policies'. Explain how the fundamental concepts are related to accounting bases and accounting policies.

(13 marks)

b   Give FOUR examples of matters for which different accounting bases may be recognized, including a brief explanation of how each one may have a material effect on the reported results and financial position of the business.

(12 marks)
(Total 25 marks)
(AAT June 1983)

Question 2

At the 1 July 19X7 the balance due from I. E. Jack Ltd to the Customs and Excise in respect of VAT was £15,000. The following transactions were undertaken in the quarter to 30 September 19X7:

See page 241 for answer.

	£
Sales	230,000 (including VAT)
Purchases	172,500 (including VAT)
Payments for expenses	30,000 (including VAT of £2,000)
Payment to Customs and Excise	15,000

The standard rate of VAT is 15%.

Required

a   The VAT account for the period to 30 September 19X7.
b   State how any balance on the VAT account will be included in the balance sheet.
c   Explain the circumstances in which VAT may be included in items appearing in a profit and loss account.

(10 marks)

Question 3

Alan, Bob and Charles are in partnership sharing profits and losses in the ratio 3:2:1 respectively.

See page 242 for answer.

The balance sheet for the partnership as at 30 June 1982 is as follows:

	£	£		£	£
Capital			Fixed assets:		
Alan		85,000	Premises		90,000
Bob		65,000	Plant		37,000
Charles		35,000	Vehicles		15,000
		185,000	Fixtures		2,000
					144,000
Current account:			Current assets:		
Alan	3,714		Stock	62,379	
Bob	(2,509)		Debtors	34,980	
Charles	4,678	5,883	Cash	760	98,119
Loan—Charles		28,000			
Current liabilities:					
Creditors:		19,036			
Bank overdraft		4,200			
		£242,119			£242,119

Charles decides to retire from the business on 30 June 1982, and Don is admitted as a partner on that date. The following matters are agreed:

1 Certain assets were revalued— Premises £120,000
                               — Plant   £35,000
                               —Stock   £54,179
2 Provision is to be made for doubtful debts in the sum of £3,000.
3 Goodwill is to be recorded in the books on the day Charles retires in the sum of £42,000. The partners in the new firm do not wish to maintain a goodwill account so that amount is to be written back against the new partners' capital accounts.
4 Alan and Bob are to share profits in the same ratio as before, and Don is to have the same share of profits as Bob.
5 Charles is to take his car at its book value of £3,900 in part payment, and the balance of all he is owed by the firm in cash except £20,000 which he is willing to leave as a loan account.
6 The partners in the new firm are to start on an equal footing so far as capital and current accounts are concerned. Don is to contribute cash to bring his capital and current accounts to the same amount as the original partner from the old firm who has the lower investment in the business. The original partner in the old firm who has the higher investment will draw out cash so that his capital and current account balances equal those of his new partners.

Required:
a Account for the above transactions, including goodwill and retiring partner's accounts.
                                                                (20 marks)
b Draft a balance sheet for the partnership of Alan, Bob and Don as at 30 June 1982.
                                                                (5 marks)
                                                                (Total 25 marks)
                                                                (AAT June 1982)

Question 4

See page 244 for answer.

Michael and Peter are partners in a wholesale business supplying electrical goods to the retail trade. Their profit sharing ratio is Michael 4/7 and Peter 3/7.

George is the general manager of the business, employed at a salary of £12,000 per annum. In recognition of his efforts on behalf of the firm, Michael and Peter decide to take George into partnership as from 1 October 1983. The original partners take little active interest in the business, but since they have provided most of the capital employed they decide to pay interest on partners' fixed capital sums at 10% per annum from 1 October 1983. George is to receive a partnership salary of £8,000 per annum, and a one fifth share of the profits. The remaining profits are to be shared equally by Michael and Peter.

George recently received a legacy from an aunt, and he has consented to bring in £25,000 to the firm from the date of his partnership. It was mutually agreed by the partners that from 1 October 1983 the premises would be revalued at £90,000 and the lease was renegotiated to run for 20 years from that date; equipment and vehicles would be valued at £32,250 with a 4 year life from that date; obsolete stock which cost £1,700 was to be written off. Goodwill was to be valued on the same date as £35,000. Partners' capital accounts were to be adjusted to reflect this goodwill valuation, but no goodwill account was to be raised in the books. No entries to reflect these transactions had been made in the books of the business except to record the receipt of £25,000 from George, and to stop payment of his salary as general manager.

A trial balance as at 31 December 1983, the normal year end of the business, shows:

	£	£
Gross profit (earned evenly over the year)		136,840
Leasehold premises (net book value		
1 January	70,000	
Equipment and vehicles (net book value		
1 January 1983)		
Stock at end of year	120,000	
Administrative expenses	60,000	
Bank	4,526	
Capital accounts: Michael		100,000
Peter		50,000
George		25,000
Drawings: Michael	18,750	
Peter	14,235	
George	4,625	
Debtors and creditors	13,827	44,123
	£355,963	£355,963

Notes:
1 Depreciation is normally provided by the straight line method using a 21 year life for premises, and for equipment and vehicles a 5 year life. Book value at 1 January 1983 is analysed as:
   Premises cost £84,000 less cumulative depreciation £14,000 = book value £70,000. Equipment and vehicles cost £65,000 less cumulative depreciation £15,000 = book value £50,000.
2 Administration expenses include George's salary as general manager up to 30 September 1983.
3 The obsolete stock has not yet been scrapped.

Required:
Draft a profit and loss account for the year ending 31 December 1983; capital and current accounts for the partners; and a balance sheet as at 31 December 1983.

(23 marks)
(AAT June 1984)

Question 5

Mike, Jim and Martin are in partnership and have traded together successfully for many years, making and selling identification equipment for the export packaging trade. Early in 1982 Jim perceived a new business opportunity which he intended to develop on his own,

See page 246 for answer.

and advised his partners that he would leave the partnership on 31 December 1982. Mike and Martin considered the situation and agreed to convert the business to a limited company on that date. The new company was to be incorporated as Matchless Markers Ltd.

The balance sheet of the partnership as at 31 December 1982 is as follows:

	£	£		£	£
Partners capital:			Fixed assets:		
Mike	200,000		Freehold property		
Jim	200,000			400,000	
Martin	100,000		Plant	170,181	
		500,000	Vehicles	28,409	
			Fixtures & fittings		
				21,670	620,260
Current accounts:			Current assets:		
Mike	27,412		Stock	218,948	
Jim	62,840		Debtors	121,250	
Martin	24,139		Cash	10,416	
		114,391			350,614
Loan account:					
Mike		140,000			
Current liabilities:					
Trade creditors		216,483			
		£970,874			£970,874

During December 1982 the partners met to agree the terms of the changes outlined above. They agreed that:

1   Part of the premises were not required by the new company, and were to be sold for £75,000. Jim was to be allowed to retain his car at a valuation of £4,000, and he would also take out of the business some stock valued for balance sheet purposes at £20,000.
2   The remaining assets and current liabilities of the partnership, except cash, were to be purchased by Matchless Markers Ltd for consideration of £700,000. Legal and valuation expenses related to these changes were £500, and were to be borne by the partnership, and paid immediately.
3   The consideration was to be paid partly by the issue of 14% debentures to Mike in lieu of his loan account with the partnership, and to Jim to cover his remaining investment in the partnership after he has been paid all the cash in the partnership bank account. The balance of the consideration will be settled by the issue of ordinary shares of £1 each to Mike and Martin.

Required:
Draft closing entries for the partnership books.

(25 marks)
(AAT December 1982)

Question 6

See page 247 for answer.

John Graham, Bill Murphy and Bob Wilkins are trading in partnership together, sharing profits and losses equally. The balance sheet of the business as at 31 December 1983 is shown below.

	£	£
Capital		
—Graham		70,000
—Murphy		35,000
—Wilkins		21,000
		126,000

	£	£
Current accounts		
—Graham	5,000	
—Murphy	8,000	
—Wilkins	(3,000)	
		10,000
Loan account		
—Mrs Wilkins		100,000
Net capital employed		£236,000
Represented by:		
Fixed assets, at book value		
—Land and building		450,820
—Plant		77,115
—Vehicles		18,065
		546,000
Current assets		
—Stock	37,000	
—Debtors	51,000	
	88,000	
Less: Current liabilities		
—Trade creditors	(91,400)	
—Hire purchase on car	(3,000)	
—Overdraft	(303,600)	
Working capital		(310,000)
Net assets		£236,000

The partnership business has made losses in recent years, and the bank and trade creditors are pressing for repayment of funds advanced to the business. Graham and Murphy consider the suggestion that they should inject more capital into the business, but decide against this plan. Wilkins is now bankrupt so cannot advance more funds. The partners decide to sell the business as at 31 December 1983 to Exodus PLC, a company in the same trade.

The terms of the sale are as follows:

1 Exodus PLC agree to purchase the land and buildings, plant, two of the vehicles, and the stock, all for £501,000.
2 The third vehicle, a car, which has a book value of £6,000, is to be taken by Murphy as part of his capital repayment. The price agreed for the car is £4,000, but Murphy also agrees to settle personally the hire purchase debt owing on the car.
3 The partners collect the debts of their business, but because of their haste, £4,000 of bad debts are incurred, and £2,000 of cash discounts are allowed.
4 The consideration is to be partly settled by Exodus PLC by the payment of £368,600 in cash, and the assumption of the trade creditors (all except a personal contact of Graham who is owed £10,000 and is paid separately by the partnership). The balance of the consideration is to be settled by the issue of £1 ordinary shares in Exodus PLC at par to the partners.

Required:
Draft ledger accounts to close the books of the partnership.

(25 marks)
(AAT December 1983)

Question 7

See page 249 for answer.

Peter and Paul entered into a joint venture to purchase a job lot of stock from the liquidator of a company for £102,000. The stock was paid for on 1 April, Peter drawing a cheque for £60,000 and Paul £42,000. Each party was to receive 10% interest per annum on these sums, the balance of any profits or losses to be shared equally. The following transactions relating to the join venture took place:

		£
April 2	Purchase of a lorry by Peter	5,000
5	Advertising costs paid by Paul	1,000
8	Warehouse rent paid by Paul	3,000
30	Cash sales collected by Peter	20,000
30	Cash sales collected by Paul	80,000
May 31	Cash sales collected by Paul	30,000
31	Motor running expenses incurred by Peter were agreed at	1,000

The joint venture ceased on 31 May.

It was agreed that Peter should take over the remaining unsold stock valued at £3,000 and that Paul would buy the lorry at a valuation of £4,500. Final settlement between the parties was effected on 30 June.

Required:
a The joint venture account in the books of:
  i Peter, and
  ii Paul.
b The memorandum joint venture account.

(20 marks)

Question 8

See page 250 for answer.

On 20 November 19X8 Silver sent 100 typewriters, that had cost £30 each, to Bleu on consignment. Silver incurred freight charges of £400.

On 31 December 19X8, the date at which Silver prepared his accounts, the following account sales was received from Bleu:

	£	£
Sales – 40 typewriters at £60		2,400
Less:		
Handling charges	100	
Commission on sales (10%)	240	
		340
Balance due		£2,060

Required:
Write up the ledger accounts in the books of Silver to record the above transactions for the year ended 31 December 19X8.

(15 marks)

Question 9

See page 251 for answer.

a The Carreau Co. Ltd are manufacturers of decorative tiles. Their products are transported to wholesalers throughout the UK in stout wooden containers which are returnable by the customers.

These activities give rise to accounting entries of a specialist nature, and you have been called in to advise and write up the appropriate accounts for the company's container transactions.

Required:
List the significant items which a system for accounting for containers should disclose.

(5 marks)

b The company charges its customers a deposit for each container, part of the deposit being refunded if the container is returned within 2 months of the date of dispatch. Each container is charged to the customer at £10, and £8 is refunded on its return.

On 1 January 1985 there were 150 containers in the warehouse and 420 containers in customers' hands, but still returnable. All containers are valued at £6 each at the beginning and end of the quarter.

During the quarter to 31 March 1985 a further 240 containers were purchased at £8 each. 1,870 containers were charged to customers. 1,750 were returned for a refund and 220 were retained by customers. Repairs to containers cost £560 and 75 containers were scrapped during the period.

Required:
Post and balance the containers stock account and the containers suspense account.

(18 marks)
(Total 23 marks)
(AAT June 1985)

Question 10

Gunthorpe Grit PLC have entered into an agreement to extract gravel from land owned by the Trent River Conservancy Board (TRCB), a public authority. The agreement specifies a royalty of £5 per tonne extracted, with a minimum payment of £25,000 per annum. Any shortfall from this amount can be reclaimed by the extractor only in the year following the shortfall, after which it is irrecoverable. Royalty payments are made by the extractor on the last day of each year.

See page 251 for answer.

Production figures for the first three years of the agreement were:

1980—2,000 tonnes
1981—7,000 tonnes
1982—8,000 tonnes

Required:

a Post and balance the appropriate accounts in the ledger of Gunthorpe Grit PLC, for the years 1980/82 inclusive

(10 marks)

b Post and balance the appropriate accounts in the ledger of Trent River Conservancy Board, for the years 1980/82 inclusive.

(10 marks)

c Explain briefly why an owner will insert a shortworkings clause into a royalty agreement.

(5 marks)
(Total 25 marks)
(AAT June 1983)

Question 11

Bulwell Aggregates Ltd wish to expand their transport fleet and have purchased three heavy lorries with a list price of £18,000 each. Robert Bulwell has negotiated hire-purchase finance to fund this expansion, and the company has entered into a hire-purchase agreement with Granby Garages PLC on 1 January 1981. The agreement states that Bulwell Aggregates will pay a deposit of £9,000 on 1 January 1981, and two annual instalments of £24,000 on 31 December 1981 and 1982, and a final instalment of £20,391 on 31 December 1983.

See page 252 for answer.

Interest is to be calculated at 25% on the balance outstanding on 1 January each year and paid on 31 December each year.

The depreciation policy of Bulwell Aggregates Ltd is to write off the vehicles over a four year period using the straight line method and assuming a scrap value of £1,333 for each vehicle at the end of its useful life.

Required:
Account for the above transactions in the books of Bulwell Aggregates Ltd showing the

entries in the profit and loss account and balance sheet for the years 1981, 1982, 1983 and 1984.
Calculations to the nearest £.

(15 marks)
(AAT June 1982)

Question 12

See page 255 for answer.

Bulwell Aggregates Ltd wish to expand their transport fleet and have purchased three heavy lorries with a list price of £18,000 each. Robert Bulwell has negotiated hire-purchase finance to fund this expansion, and the company has entered into a hire-purchase agreement with Granby Garages PLC on 1 January 1981. The agreement states that Bulwell Aggregates will pay a deposit of £9,000 on 1 January 1981, and two annual instalments of £24,000 on 31 December 1981 and 1982, and a final instalment of £20,391 on 31 December 1983.

Interest is to be calculated at 25% on the balance outstanding on 1 January each year and paid on 31 December each year.

The depreciation policy of Bulwell Aggregates Ltd is to write off the vehicles over a four year period using the straight line method and assuming a scrap value of £1,333 for each vehicle at the end of its useful life.

The cost of the vehicles to Granby Garages is £14,400 each.

Required:
Account for the above transactions in the books of Granby Garages PLC, showing the entries in the hire purchase trading account for the years 1981, 1982, 1983. This is the only hire-purchase transaction undertaken by this company.
Calculations to the nearest £.

(10 marks)
(AAT June 1982)

Question 13

See page 256 for answer.

Ambridge Archery Traders Limited have been established as suppliers of archery equipment to club archers for a number of years. The management have decided to extend the range of services they offer to clients. So from 1 January 1983, which is the start of their accounting year, they have introduced a hire- purchase scheme available to customers who purchase certain expensive bows. Their hire-purchase terms require a deposit of 25% of the selling price of the bow, followed by twelve equal monthly instalments.

A summary of hire-purchase transactions undertaken during the year has been carefully maintained and is as follows:

	£
Goods sold on hire-purchase—cost	65,000
Goods sold on hire-purchase—selling price	90,000
Deposits received	22,500
Instalments received	49,600
Instalments due but not received	400

During the year bows sold for £2,800 were repossessed. These bows originally cost £2,000. Deposits of £700 and instalments of £300 had been received on these bows. The expenses of repossessing the items amounted to £30. The management estimate that they will be able to sell all the repossesed bows for £1,500 in their forthcoming sale, but point out that repairs costing £400 will be required before the repossessed bows can be sold.

Required:
a Draft appropriate ledger accounts to record the transactions set out above; and

(17 marks)

b show entries in the balance sheet as at 31 December 1983 which would be derived from these transactions, and write a short explanation of the items concerned.

(6 marks)
(Total 23 marks)
(AAT June 1984)

Question 14

Rock commenced business on 1 September 1983 selling televisions and videos on cash and hire–purchase terms. The following summarized trial balance was extracted from his books of account as at 31 August 1984.

See page 257 for answer.

	£ Dr	£ Cr
Bank overdraft		8,475
Capital (cash introduced on 1 September 1983)		50,000
Cash sales: televisions (600 at £300 each)		180,000
Creditors		121,000
Debtors	1,000	
Drawings	16,000	
Fixed assets at cost	45,000	
Hire purchase debtors: televisions	105,000	
videos	342,000	
Hire purchase sales: televisions (350 at £400 each)		140,000
Hire purchase sales: videos (380 at £1,260 each)		478,800
Purchases:		
televisions (1,000 at £150 each)	150,000	
videos (400 at £350 each)	140,000	
Retailing expenses	179,275	
	£978,275	£978,275

Additional information:

1 During the year, Rock purchased 1,000 televisions at a cost of £150 each. He sold them either on cash terms for £300 each or on hire–purchase. The hire–purchase terms were an initial deposit of £100, followed by two annual instalments of £150 each, payable by the customer on the first and second anniversary respectively of the date of purchase of the television.
2 Rock had also purchased 400 videos for £350 each. Although he was prepared to sell them on cash terms (for £1,000 each), all the video sales had been on hire–purchase. An initial deposit of £360 was required, followed by two annual instalments of £450 each, payable by the customer on the first and second anniversary respectively of the date of purchase of the video.
3 In the annual accounts. Rock decided to take credit for gross profit on hire–purchase sales in accordance with the following policy:
  a televisions: to allow for both the ordinary gross profit and hire–purchase interest in proportion to the total cash collected from customers sold televisions on hire–purchase terms; and
  b videos: to take the ordinary gross profit on videos sold on hire–purchase in the year of sale, and to apportion the interest on hire–purchase equally over the two years of the agreement.
4 Depreciation is to be provided on fixed assets at 20% per annum on cost.

Required:
a Prepare columnar trading, profit and loss accounts for the year to 31 August 1984 for:
  i televisions,
  ii videos, and

iii the business as a whole, and a combined profit and loss account for the year to 31 August 1984.

(17 marks)

b Prepare a balance sheet as at 31 August 1984.

(8 marks)
(Total 25 marks)
(AAT Pilot Paper)

Question 15

See page 259 for answer.

a Your client, Jean Fitter operates a succesful shop in the High Street, with ample storage space attached, and now intends to open a branch establishment in another town some distance away. The key to Jean's success to date has been her flair for buying the right things at the right time for resale, and she now wishes to increase the outlets for her buying skill. She intends to supply the branch from her existing premises, and to allow no credit to customers.

Required:
Outline the accounting system which you would recommend to record the transactions of the new branch. Your answer should include the system to be operated at the branch, and comment as to the advantages which accrue from the system.

(13 marks)

b During the first months trading at the new branch the following transactions took place:

	£
Goods sent to branch at cost totalled	42,000
Goods returned from branch to head office, at cost	2,000
Cash banked by branch	44,000
Expenses paid for the branch were:	
Rent	580
Rates	250
Wages	1,860
General expenses	1,426

The branch reports that closing stock at selling price is £4,800. Goods are invoiced to the branch at selling price which is cost plus a mark up of 25% on cost.

Required:
Write up the appropriate branch accounts in the head office books.

(12 marks)
(Total 25 marks)
(AAT December 1982)

Question 16

See page 260 for answer.

Sunil Patel is the proprietor of a thriving business in Leicester. He owns a shop which sells handbags, cases and various leather goods. The business is organized from offices above the shop, with ample storage space in the warehouse at the rear of the premises. Mr. Patel seeks to expand his business and has opened a branch shop in Nottingham.

Sales are on cash or credit terms. Credit customers settle their account through the office at Leicester. This office maintains all the accounting records for the business. Mr Patel undertakes the buying of goods, which are then charged out from the stores to the branch at selling price, i.e. cost plus 25% mark up.

The Branch Manager is responsible for banking cash takings on daily basis and is permitted to use cash received from sales to meet local expenses and pay the shop wages each week.

The branch account is balanced monthly.

The following figures relate to the Nottingham branch for November 1984, and are shown at selling prices.

	£
Balances at 1 November:	
Branch stock	21,620
Branch debtors	14,270
Transactions during November:	
Goods transferred to branch from store	119,330
Goods returned to store from branch	1,245
Cash banked in Nottingham	54,837
Credit sales in Nottingham	65,241
Damaged stock written off at Nottingham	315
Credit sales returned by customer to Nottingham	916
Receipts from Nottingham credit customers banked in Leicester	58,793
Branch expenses paid in Nottingham	3,432
Branch wages paid in Nottingham	1,920
Stock taken on 30 November at Nottingham (at selling price)	13,500
Branch expenses paid by Leicester office	14,861
Bad debts written off Nottingham branch debtors	1,815

Provision is to be made for a commision of 1% of branch gross profit to the branch manager.

Required:

a Write up the appropriate ledger accounts for the above transactions of the Nottingham branch in the head office ledger.

(17 marks)

b Advise Mr Patel of four possible reasons for any stock loss that has been shown up by the accounts.

(6 marks)
(Total 23 marks)
(AAT December 1984)

Question 17

The Oxford Trading Company has a branch at Croydon. The branch keeps its own books and the relevant trial balances as at 31 March 1972 were as follows:

See page 262 for answer.

	Oxford	Croydon
	£	£
Debits		
Freehold premises (at cost)	20,005	—
Cash at bank	4,652	595
Debtors	3,093	3,572
Remittances to head office	—	50,800
Stock 1 April 1971 at cost	17,300	9,020
Furniture and fittings	3,530	870
Rent and rates	2,636	3,315
Goods from head office (at cost)	—	37,028
Purchases	90,844	—
General expenses	5,678	3,250
Wages and salaries	12,585	8,393
Croydon branch current account	52,578	—
Drawings—Mr Brown	10,000	—
	£222,901	£116,843

	Oxford	Croydon
	£	£
Credits		
Remittances from branch	50,325	—
Sales	94,637	61,348
Creditors	8,238	468
Capital 1 April 1971	32,122	—
Head office current account	—	52,027
Goods to branch (at cost)	37,579	—
Bank overdraft	—	3,000
	222,901	£116,843

Additional information is provided as follows:

1 Stock valuations at cost at 31 March 1972 were Oxford £15,790, Croydon £4,215.
2 The original cost of the furniture and fittings were £4,500 (head office) and £1,000 (branch). Provision for depreciation is to be made at 10% on the present balances for the year ended 31 March 1972.
3 Bonuses to the staff at head office and at the branch are to be provided at the rate of 10% of the profits before charging the bonuses.
4 Goods sent by head office to the branch on 24 March 1972 costing £551 were stolen in transit. The insurance company had admitted in full the claim for the cost of the goods. No entry had been made for this in the books.

Mr Brown, the owner of the organization, has requested you to:

Prepare the trading and profit and loss account for the head office and the branch for the year ended 31 March 1972, and a balance sheet at the same date.

(12 marks)
(CACA June 1972)

Question 18

See page 263 for answer.

Allied Athletic Traders is a sportswear retailing business. The main shop is situated in London, but there is a branch shop in Cambridge. The branch maintains its own ledgers, and is autonomous under the direction of its manager. Goods are supplied to the Cambridge branch by the London head office, which charges them out at cost, whilst Cambridge remits cash to the head office from time to time.

The trial balances of London and Cambridge as at 31 December 1983 are as follows:

	London	Cambridge
	£	£
Freehold premises (includes land at £20,000)	47,000	—
Cash at bank	—	750
Remittances to head office	—	55,900
Stock at 1 January 1982	22,500	9,620
Debtors	1,741	4,650
Fixtures and fittings, at cost	11,000	6,751
Vehicles, at cost	9,000	4,900
Rent and rates	2,418	4,210
Goods from head office, at cost	—	36,489
Purchases	96,471	—
General expenses	7,850	1,211
Wages and salaries	13,490	3,208
Cambridge branch current account	69,486	—
Drawings by Proprietor	15,802	—
	£296,758	£127,689

	London	Cambridge
	£	£
Retained earnings, 1 January 1983	35,180	—
Remittances from branch	55,450	—
Sales	84,740	53,453
Creditors	17,456	895
Proprietors capital	45,000	
Head office current account		67,541
Goods to Branch, at cost	38,434	—
Bank overdraft	6,498	—
Cumulative depreciation to date:		
Premises	2,000	—
Fixtures and fittings	5,600	3,000
Vehicles	6,400	2,800
	£296,758	£127,689

The following information is relevant:
1 Depreciation is to be provided on cost as follows:
Buildings—2% straight line
Fixtures and fittings—10% straight line
Vehicles—20% straight line
2 Stocks at 31 December 1983 were:
London £28,500
Cambridge £2,600
3 Goods costing £1,095 were sent from London to Cambridge on 28 December 1983, but had not arrived by 31 December 1983.
   Goods costing £850 were dispatched from London to Cambridge on 1 June 1983. These goods have been lost and a claim is pending against Stock Insurance Ltd.
4 Provision is to be made for a bonus to be paid to the managers of the London and Cambridge branches in the sum of 10% of the branch profit after charging the bonus.
5 Cambridge rent is prepaid £500 and London rates are in arrears of £200 as at 31 December 1983.

You are required to:
a Prepare a trading and profit and loss account for the London shop, and for the Cambridge branch, for the year ended 31 December 1983, and a balance sheet for Allied Athletic Traders as at that date.

(23 marks)

b Suggest the most significant factor in the accounts prepared above which should be brought to the attention of the proprietor of the business.

(2 marks)
(25 marks)
(AAT December 1983)

Question 19

The balance sheet of Aye plc as at 31 December 1981 is as follows:

See page 265 for answer.

Share capital:	Authorized	Issued
	£	£
10% redeemable preference shares at £1 each	150,000	150,000
Ordinary shares of 10 pence each, fully paid	1,000,000	200,000
	£1,150,000	350,000

Reserves:		
Share premium account		20,000
Fixed asset replacement reserve		40,000

Share capital:	Authorized	Issued
	£	£
General reserve		350,000
Long-term liabilities:		
20% debentures (1980–1983)		100,000
		£860,000
Represented by:		
Net assets		£860,000

During 1982 the following transactions took place:

1   The debentures were repaid at a premium of 5% on 1 January.
2   £100,000 of 12% convertible loan stock was issued at a discount of 3% on 1 January.
3   The preference shares were redeemed at par on 30 June.
4   500,000 ordinary shares were issued at a premium of 50% on 30 June.
5   A three for five bonus (or capitalization) issue was made to ordinary shareholders on 1 December
6   Holders of 20% of the loan stock exercised their conversion rights on 31 December at a rate of 800 ordinary shares for every £100 of loan stock held.

Required:
a   Draft journal entries including those relating to cash to record the transactions detailed above.
(20 marks)

b   Explain why a capital redemption reserve fund was opened during the year.
(5 marks)
(Total 25 marks)
(AAT December 1982)

Question 20

See page 266 for answer.

An extract from the balance sheet of a public company as at 31 December 1984 is as follows:

	Authorized	Issued
	£	£
Share Capital:		
14% redeemable preference shares		
of £1 each	500,000	300,000
Ordinary shares of 25 pence each	2,000,000	1,400,000
	£2,500,000	1,700,000
Reserves:		
Share premium account		100,000
Premises revaluation reserve		290,000
General reserve		670,000
		2,760,000
Long-term liabilities:		
18% debentures (1983–1986)		400,000
Total assets less current liabilities		£3,160,000

During 1985 the following transactions took place:

1   On 1 January the preference shares were redeemed at par and 400,000 ordinary shares were issued at a price of 35p.
2   On 30 June the debentures were repaid at a premium of 1% and £300,000 of 14% convertible loan stock was issued at a discount of 2%.

3   On 30 December holders of £50,000 of loan stock exercised their conversion rights at a rate of 320 ordinary shares for every £100 of loan stock they held.

Required:

a   Draft journal entries including those relating to cash to record the transactions detailed above.

(17 marks)

b   Calculate the capital gearing ratio for the beginning and end of the year and comment on the change in gearing experienced over the year.

(6 marks)
(Total 23 marks)
(AAT December 1985)

NB   Part (b) of this question is an interpretation of accounts topic. You may wish to refer to the section of Chapter 21 that deals with gearing before attempting your answer.

Question 21

Incorporated Developments PLC maintains separate accounts for the provision for corporation tax, current and future.

See page 268 for answer.

Balances extracted from its books at the year ended 31 December 1981 were as follows:

	Debit	Credit
	£	£
Deferred taxation reserve		178,000
Provision for corporation tax—current (year ended 31 December 1980)		94,208
Provision for corporation tax—future (year ended 31 December 1981		140,000
Advanced corporation tax payable		36,000
Advanced corporation tax recoverable	36,000	
Proposed dividend		84,000

During the year to 31 December 1982 the following transactions took place:

1   Mainstream corporation tax on the profit for 1980 was paid on 1 January 1982.
2   The proposed dividend was approved at the AGM and paid on 1 May 1982. ACT on that dividend was paid on 15 June 1982.
3   An interim dividend of £42,000 was paid on 1 September 1982, and ACT on that dividend was paid on 5 November 1982.
4   The assessment for corporation tax for 1981 was agreed with the Inland Revenue on 10 October in the sum of £127,431.
5   On 31 December 1982 a trading profit before tax of £520,000 was computed; estimated corporation tax on this profit was provided in the sum of £170,000 and a dividend of £105,000 was proposed.
6   There is no movement on the reserve for deferred taxation during the year.

Required:

a   Write up the appropriate accounts to record the transactions detailed above.

(19 marks)

b   Draft an extract from the balance sheet as at 31 December 1982 to disclose the balances, remaining on the accounts drafted in (a) above.

NB   Assume an income tax rate of 30%.

(6 marks)
(Total 25 marks)
(AAT December 1982)

Question 22

See page 269 for answer.

a Explain what you understand by the 'imputation system' of taxation.

(3 marks)

b Set out, with an example, the rules for the payment and recovery of advanced corporation tax (ACT).

(10 marks)

c How would you treat the following transactions in the profit and loss account and/or the balance sheet of a public company according to the requirements of best accounting practice? The year end of the company is 31 December 19..

   i The company receives a dividend of £24,500 on its investment in the shares of another company, on 30 September.

   ii The company provides for a final dividend of £91,000 at the year end.

   iii The company pays a half year's interest on £100,000 of 12% debentures on 31 December.

NB Assume an income tax rate of 30%.

(12 marks)
(Total 25 marks)
(AAT December 1983)

Question 23

See page 270 for answer.

The following list of balances was extracted from the books of Greenware Ltd on 31 December 1984.

	£
Sales	2,640,300
Administration expenses	220,180
Selling and distribution costs	216,320
Interest paid on loan stock	10,000
Dividends received	2,100
Profit on sale of premises	40,000
Purchases	2,089,600
Stocks at 1.1.84	318,500
Cash at bank	20,640
Trade debtors	415,800
Provsion for doubtful debts at 1.1.84	10,074
Bad debts	8,900
Creditors	428,250
10% loan stock	200,000
Long-term investments in listed companies	20,000
Office equipment	110,060
Vehicles	235,000
£1 ordinary shares	200,000
Profit and loss account at 1.1.84	144,276

Notes:
1 Provide for £10,000 loan stock interest payable 1.1.85.
2 Provide for administration expenses paid in advance at 31.12.84 £12,200, and distribution costs owing at 31.12.84 £21,300.
3 Provision for doubtful debts is to be maintained at 3% of debtors.
4 Stocks at 31.12.84 £340,600.
5 Provide for corporation tax payable 1.10.85 £45,000.
6 The directors recommend a dividend of 28 pence per share.
7 ACT is to be calculated assuming a standard income tax rate of 30%.

Required:

Prepare for presentation to the shareholders a profit and loss account for the year ended 31 December 1984 and a balance sheet as at that date, which comply, in so far as the information given allows, with the requirements of the Companies Act.

(20 marks)

Question 24

Redwood PLC is a retailing company. The following trial balance has been extracted from the books of account as at 30 June 1984:

See page 272 for answer.

	£000	£000
	Dr	Cr
Accrued expenses		26
Acumulated depreciation on furniture and fittings (at 1 July 1983)		100
Administration expenses	150	
Advanced corporation tax (paid on interim dividend)	3	
Autitors' remuneration	20	
Cash at bank and in hand	56	
Debenture interest (gross)	5	
Debenture loan stock (10%)		50
Deferred taxation		40
Distribution costs	100	
Dividends received (on 1 June 1984)		14
Fixed assets: listed investments	70	
Furniture and fittings at cost	200	
Hire charges (distribution plant, machinery, equipment and vehicles)	340	
Interim dividend (paid on 1 January 1984)	7	
Issued share capital		280
Purchases	500	
Prepaid expenses	29	
Profit and loss account (balance at 1 July 1983)		90
Sales (exclusive of VAT)		1,200
Share premium account		70
Stock (at 1 July 1983)	200	
Trade creditors		60
Trade debtors	250	
	£1,930	£1,930

Additional Information:

After compiling the trial balance, it was realized that some transactions had not been entered in the books of account, and the following additional information should be allowed for in the preparation of the published accounts:

1 Stock at 30 June 1984 was valued at £300,000.
2 Depreciation of £40,000 (classed as an administration expense) is to be charged on the furniture and fittings for the year to 30 June 1984. There were no purchases or sales of furniture during the year.
3 Administration expenses include directors' emoluments of £55,000.
4 The corporation tax payable (based on the profits for the year to 30 June 1984 at a rate of 50%) is estimated to amount to £50,000. The current standard rate of income tax is 30%.
5 Redundancy costs of £30,000 (not expected to recur) had accrued on 30 June 1984, but upon which there will be corporation tax relief of £15,000.
6 The company proposes to pay a final ordinary dividend of 10%.

7 The market value of the fixed assets listed investments at 30 June 1984 was £85,000.
8 The authorized share capital of the company was 350,000 ordinary shares of £1 each.

Required:
Prepare the company's profit and loss account for the year to 30 June 1984 and a balance sheet as at that date in accordance with the Companies Acts and with best practice (in so far as the information permits).
RELEVANT notes to the accounts along with your workings should be submitted with your answer.

(25 marks)
(AAT Pilot paper)

Question 25

See page 275 for answer.

Alpine Athletic Training PLC is a manufacturer of sports equipment. Set out below is a Trial Balance extracted from the books of the company as at 31 December 1983.

	£	£
Sales		2,925,900
Cost of sales	1,785,897	
Selling expenses	120,000	
Administrative expenses	649,296	
Debtors/creditors	469,332	371,022
Provision for doubtful debts		22,500
Directors' remuneration	181,500	
Audit fee	3,000	
Debenture interest	7,500	
Half year preference dividend paid on 30.6.83	2,100	
ACT paid on 14.7.83	900	
Premises at cost	600,000	
Plant and machinery at cost	135,000	
Provision for depreciation on plant and Machinery at 1.1.83		60,000
Motor vehicles at cost (salesmens' cars)	54,000	
Provision for depreciation on motor vehicles at 1.1.83		24,000
Stock in trade and work in progress at 31.12.83	282,528	
Trade investment at cost	72,000	
Bank overdraft		354,528
Profit and loss account balance at 1.1.83		65,103
General reserve		30,000
Ordinary share capital		300,000
7% preference share capital		60,000
10% debentures (1990/93) secured on premises		150,000
	£4,363,053	£4,363,053

The following information is also related to the accounts for the year to 31 December 1983.

1 The bad debt provision is to be increased to an amount which is equal to 1% of the turnover for the year.
2 The directors' remuneration is divided amongst the four directors of the company as follows:

	£
Chairman	24,000
Managing director	60,000
Finance director	49,500
Sales director	48,000
	£181,500

In addition provision much be made for directors' fees of £3,000 to each of the above directors.

3 Depreciation is to be provided for the year as follows:
Buildings 2% on cost
Plant and machinery 10% on cost
Motor Vehicles 25% on written down value
The only changes in fixed assets during the year were an addition to plant and machinery in early January 1983 costing £30,000, and the purchase of premises for £600,000, comprising £150,000 for buildings and £450,000 for land.

4 A provision of £60,000 is to be made for corporation tax at 52% based upon the profits for the year. This will be payable on 30 September 1984.

5 The half year preference dividend to 31 December 1983 and a final dividend of 6·5 pence a share on the ordinary share capital, are to be provided in the accounts.

6 The sum of £15,000 is to be transferred to general reserve.

7 The authorized preference share capital is £60,000 in £1 shares.

8 The authorized ordinary share capital is £600,000 in 50p shares. All shares in issue are fully paid.

9 Assume the standard rate of income tax to be 30%.

10 Administrative expenses include £5,244 interest on the overdraft.

11 The directors consider the value of the trade investment to be £15,000. It consists of 10,000 20p ordinary shares in Crampon Limited, a company with an issued share capital of 200,000 ordinary shares.

Required:
Within the limits of the above information, prepare the final accounts of Alpine Athletic Training PLC for the year ended 31 December 1983 in a form suitable for presentation to the members and which complies with the requirements of the Companies Acts.

The required information should be shown as part of the accounting statements or by way of note, whichever is considered most appropriate.

(31 marks)
(AAT June 1984)

Question 26

You have joined the accounting team of a company which has recently acquired status as a public limited company. The accounts for issue to the members have been drafted and the auditiors have reminded the chief accountant that a directors' report will be required, to be attached to the published accounts.

See page 280 for answer.

Required:
Write a memo to the chief accountant setting out the matters which should be covered in the directors' report, in accordance with the Companies Acts.

(23 marks)
(AAT December 1984)

Question 27

Kitchen Utensils Wholesalers Ltd
Balance sheet at 31 May 1982

See page 280 for answer.

	£		£
£1 ordinary shares	35,000	Fixed assets—at cost	71,500
Retained profits	15,000	*Less* Accumulated depreciation	43,000

	£		£
10% loan stock	£20,000		28,500
Creditors	15,900	Stocks	30,100
Taxation	10,200	Debtors	29,400
Dividend	5,000	Cash	13,100
	£101,000		£101,100

Balance Sheet at 31 May 1983

	£		£
£1 ordinary shares	40,000	Fixed assets—at cost	122,000
Retained profits	20,000	*Less* Accumulated depreciation	60,400
10% loan stock—repayable 1995	72,000		61,600
Creditors	10,400		
Taxation	11,500	Stocks	59,200
Dividend	6,000	Debtors	28,700
		Cash	10,400
	£159,000		£159,900

Trading and profit and loss account for year ended 31 May 1983

	£		£
Opening stock	30,100	Sales	430,000
Purchases	367,800		
Carriage inwards	1,300		
	399,200		
Less Closing stock	59,200		
	340,000		
Gross profit c/d	90,000		
	430,000		430,000
Salaries and wages	22,200	Gross profit b/d	90,000
Expenses	23,700	Commission received	3,000
Depreciation	17,400		
Loan stock interest	7,200		
Taxation	11,500		
Dividend	6,000		
Net profit retained	5,000		
	£93,000		£93,000

Required:
A statement of sources and applications of funds for the year ended 31 May 1983.

(15 marks)

Question 28

See page 281 for answer.

The following summarized information relates to Candle PLC for the year to 30 September 1984:

Profit and loss account for the year 30 September 1984

	£000	£000
Net profit		312
Taxation		(104)
Net profit after taxation		208
Dividends:		
interim (paid on 1 April 1984)	(14)	
final (proposed)	(35)	
		(49)
Retained profit for the year		£159

Balance sheet at 30 September 1984

	1984		1983	
	£000	£000	£000	£000
Fixed assets:				
Land and buildings at cost	380		380	
Less: Accumulated depreciation	120		100	
		260		280
Machinery and fittings at cost	500		225	
Less: Accumulated depreciation	156		85	
		344		140
		604		420
Current assets:				
Stocks	190		185	
Debtors	170		100	
Cash at bank	30		15	
		390		300
		£994		£720
Financed by:				
Capital and reserves:				
Called up share capital		300		250
Revenue reserves		10		10
Profit and loss account		274		115
		584		375
Debenture stock:				
10% debenture stock		60		50
Deferred taxation		85		70
Current liabilities:				
Creditors	147		25	
Taxation	68		100	
Proposed dividend	35		70	
ACT on proposed dividend	15		30	
		265		255
		£994		£720

Additional information:

1 During the year some machinery was sold for £6,000. Its original cost was £25,000 and its net book value at 30 September 1983 was £10,000.
2 The standard rate of income tax is 30%.

Required:

a Prepare a statement of source and application of funds for the year to 30 September 1984 in a format that accords with best practice.

(20 marks)

b Summarize briefly the use of such a statement by financial analysts.

(5 marks)
(Total 25 marks)
(AAT Pilot Paper)

Question 29

The Light Engineering Company Ltd has balance sheets for the last two years as follows: See page 283 for answer.

Balance sheets as at 31 December

	1980	1981
	£	£
Fixed assets:		
Goodwill	25,000	20,000
Land and buildings	199,000	296,000
Plant	83,500	71,500
Vehicles	9,300	16,683
Fixtures and fittings	16,880	17,841
	333,680	422,024
ACT recoverable	10,286	8,572
Current assets:		
Stock	31,219	21,304
Debtors	41,406	46,360
Bank	18,612	—
	£435,203	£498,260
Capital:		
Share capital	100,000	200,000
Share premium	—	27,250
Unappropriated profit	149,617	21,315
14% redeemable preference shares	100,000	—
Capital redemption reserve fund	—	100,000
Deferred taxation	—	10,000
Long–term loans:		
16% loan stock	—	70,000
Current libilities:		
Creditors	33,840	15,317
Overdraft	—	516
Proposed dividend on ordinary shares	10,000	20,000
Tax payable	31,460	25,290
ACT payable	10,286	8,572
	£435,203	£498,260

Notes to the accounts:
1   100,000 ordinary shares of £1 each were issued at a premium of 30p a share.
    £70,000 of 16% loan stock was issued at a discount of 2½%.
    The preference shares were redeemed at a premium of 1%.
    The premium and the discount have been written off to the share premium account.
2   A provision of £20,000 was made for future corporation tax of which £10,000 was transferred to deferred taxation account.
3   £5,000 was written off goodwill to the profit and loss account.
4   Analysis of fixed assets:

	Building	Plant	Vehicles	Fittings
	£	£	£	£
Opening balance	220,000	147,000	28,512	36,240
Purchases	100,000	23,000	16,418	4,602
Disposals	—	31,000	18,460	—
Closing Balance	320,000	139,000	26,470	40,842
Depreciation:				
Opening balance	21,000	63,500	19,212	19,360
Profit and loss A/c	3,000	28,000	4,890	3,641
Disposals	–	24,000	14,315	–
Closing balance	24,000	67,500	9,787	23,001
Net book value	296,000	71,500	16,683	17,841

During the year plant was sold for £11,000 and vehicles were sold for £2,800.

Required:

a Compute the trading profit, and taxation paid during the year by reconstructing the profit and loss appropriation account and the taxation account.

(8 marks)

b Draft a funds flow statement for the year to 31 December 1981, in accordance with SSAP 10.

(12 marks)

c Comment briefly on what the statement reveals.

(5 marks)
(Total 25 marks)
(AAT June 1982)

Question 30

Cee Ltd and Dee Ltd are subsidiaries of Eff PLC. They are in the same trade but operate in different areas. Their accounts for the year ending 30 September 1982 are as follows:

See page 285 for answer.

£000s	Cee Ltd		Dee Ltd	
	£	£	£	£
Profit and Loss Account				
Sales		720		860
Less: Cost of sales		560		671
Gross profit		160		189
Less: Overheads		110		150
Net profit before tax		50		39
Corporation tax	20		15	
Dividend	10	30	12	27
Retained profit for the year		£20		£12
Balance Sheet				
Share capital		300		100
Reserves		120		52
		420		152
8% debentures		—		60
		£420		£212
Represented by:				
Fixed assets:				
Cost		330		260
Less: Depreciation		100		80
		230		180
Current Assets:				
Stock	140		86	
Debtors	155		150	
Cash	15		16	
	310		252	
Less: current liabilities:				
Taxation	20		15	
Creditors	90		172	
Bank overdraft	—		21	
Dividend	10		12	
	120		220	
Net current assets		190		32
		£420		£212

All sales are on credit terms.

Required:

a Compare the profitability and the financial position of the two companies, using suitable ratios.

(15 marks)

b Comment briefly on your findings.

(10 marks)
(Total 25 marks)
(AAT December 1982)

Question 31

See page 285 for answer.

A managing director returns from a frustrating interview with the manager of a bank where the business has its account. He turns to your for advice stating:

'The bank manager told me that the working capital ratio is too low, and the gearing ratio too high. As far as I am concerned this is just meaning-less jargon.'

Required:
Briefly explain the bank manager's statement in words which the managing director will understand.

(23 marks)
(AAT June 1984)

Question 32

See page 286 for answer.

'One can imagine a science fiction society in which money's purchasing power and the relative worth of assets never vary. In such a sleepy setting, historical accounts would be admirable. In the world as we know it they invite criticism. When prices are rising briskly traditional accounts are beset by several ailments...'

You are required to:
Identify and discuss the weaknesses suffered by historical cost accounts during a period of rising prices.

(25 marks)
(AAT December 1983)

Question 33

See page 286 for answer.

'One area of agreement is that historical cost accounts alone are not sufficient in times of changing prices for a true appreciation of a company's financial position and especially dividend policy.'

Peter Godfrey
Chairman–Accounting Standards Committee

Required:
Discuss the impact of inflation on the profit and loss account and the balance sheet of a company prepared under historic cost convention, with special reference to the company's financial position and dividend policy.

(23 marks)
(AAT December 1985)

Question 34

See page 286 for answer.

The following summarized balance sheets relate to the Fog group of companies as at 30 September 1984:

	Fog plc	Mist Ltd	Rain Ltd
	£000	£000	£000
Fixed assets:			
Plant at net book value	200	40	30
Investments:			
100,000 ordinary shares of £1 each in Mist Ltd	150	—	—
40,000 ordinary shares of £1 each in Rain Ltd	70	—	—
	220	—	—
Current assets:			
Stocks	150	90	80
Debtors	250	40	20
Cash at bank and in hand	50	20	10
	450	150	110
	£870	£190	£140
Financed by:			
Share capital:			
Authorized, issued and fully paid ordinary shares of £1 each	500	100	50
Revenue reserves	90	40	70
	590	140	120
Current liabilities:			
Creditors	280	50	20
	£870	£190	£140

Additional information:

1 Fog acquired its shares in Mist on 1 October 1982. At that time Mist's revenue reserves amounted to £30,000.
2 Fog acquired its shares in Rain on 30 September 1983. Rain Ltd's profit for the year to 30 September 1984 was £30,000.
3 Included in Mist's stock at 30 September 1984 was £15,000 of goods received from Fog during the year. Fog had invoiced them to Mist at cost plus 50%.
4 During the year to 30 September 1984, Mist had sold goods costing £50,000 to Rain for £70,000. Rain still had half of these goods in stock at 30 September 1984.
5 The respective company's debtors and creditors at 30 September 1984 include the following inter-company debts:
   a Fog owed Mist £20,000;
   b Fog owed Rain £10,000;
   and
   c Rain owed Mist £5,000.
6 In its consolidation accounting policies, Fog eliminates unrealized profits without charge to minorities.

Required:
Prepare Fog's consolidated balance sheet as at 30 September 1984. The balance sheet is not for publication.

(25 marks)
(AAT Pilot Paper)

Question 35

Holdings PLC is a manufacturing company with a small factory in the London area. The balance sheet of the company at 30 June 1985 is as follows:

See page 288 for answer.

	£	£
Fixed assets: Buildings	195,000	
Plant	80,000	
Vehicles	25,000	

	£	£
		300,000
Investment in Subsid Ltd at cost		134,680
70,000 10% debentures in Subsid Ltd		70,000
Current assets: Stock	145,731	
Debtors	163,419	
Cash	68,870	
	378,020	
Less: Current liabilities—trade creditors	(156,800)	
Net current assets		221,220
Total assets less current liabilities		£725,900
Share capital		595,000
Reserves		120,900
Unappropriated profits		10,000
		£725,900

Holdings PLC bought 504,000 ordinary shares in Subsid Ltd on 1 July 1981 when the credit balance on that company's profit and loss account stood at £2,400, and the general reserve stood at £20,000. The debentures were acquired at par.

During June 1985 Holdings PLC sold goods which had cost £30,800 to Subsid Ltd, at its usual mark-up price of 25 per cent on cost. At 30 June 1985 Subsid Ltd had neither sold any of these goods nor paid Holdings PLC for them. The liabilities of Subsid Ltd also include a full year's interest on the debentures, set against profit but not yet paid.

Holdings PLC has not yet taken credit for any debenture interest receivable.

The balance sheet of Subsid Ltd as at 30 June 1985 is as follows:

	£	£	£
Fixed assets: Premises			140,000
Vehicles			23,858
			163,858
Current assets: Stock		151,701	
Debtors		53,941	
		205,642	
Current liabilities—trade creditors	64,054		
Overdraft	10,046		
		(74,100)	
Net current assets			131,542
Total assets less current liabilities			295,400
Long-term liabilities—10% debentures			(105,000)
			£190,400
Share capital: 840,000 ordinary shares of 25p			210,000
General reserve			25,000
Profit and loss account			(44,600)
			£190,400

Required:
Draft a consolidated balance sheet for Holdings PLC and Subsid Ltd as at 30 June 1985. (Show your workings.)

(23 marks)
(AAT December 1985

Question 36

See page 290 for answer.

The following is the summary of the balance sheets of Oswald Ltd and Tudor Ltd at 31 March 1985

	Oswald Ltd	Tudor Ltd
	£	£
Issued share capital in ordinary shares of £1 each	100,000	50,000
Reserves	112,000	32,000
Net assets	£212,000	£82,000

Oswald Ltd purchased 30,000 shares in Tudor Ltd on 31 March 1983 at a cost of £50,000. The following is the summary of the balance sheet of Tudor Ltd at 31 March 1983:

	£
Issued share capital in ordinary shares of £1 each	50,000
Reserves	24,000
Net assets	£74,000

Required:

a Prepare a summary of the consolidated balance sheet of the group at 31 March 1985.

(15 marks)

b Explain what the items of goodwill and minority interest represent.

(5 marks)

(Total 20 marks)

Question 37

Balance sheets at 31 December 1984

See page 291 for answer.

	A Ltd	B Ltd
	£	£
Investment in B Ltd	71,500	—
Other net assets	226,500	118,000
	£298,000	£118,000
£1 ordinary shares	100,000	40,000
General reserve	50,000	10,000
Profit and loss account balance	128,000	56,000
Proposed dividends	20,000	12,000
	£298,000	£118,000

Profit and loss accounts for year ended 31 December 1984

		A Ltd		B Ltd
	£	£	£	£
Net profit after tax		100,000		40,000
Dividends received		3,000		
Dividends payable:		103,000		
Interim	5,000		4,000	
Proposed final	20,000	25,000	12,000	16,000
		78,000		24,000
Balance b/f		50,000		32,000
Balance c/f		£128,000		£56,000

A Ltd acquired 30,000 ordinary shares in B Ltd on 1.1.84.

Required:

Consolidated profit and loss account for the year ended 31 December 1984, and the consolidated balance sheet at 31 December 1984.

(20 marks)

Question 38

See page 292 for answer.

a Name five groups into which business stocks can be categorized. State the general rule for the accounting treatment of stock and relate that rule to the concepts or conventions on which accounting is based.

(9 marks)

b Explain how best accounting practice, embodied in Statement of Standard Accounting Practice 9, follows the general rule.

(12 marks)

c Baggaley Leather Goods operate a shop selling ladies shoes and handbags. Until recently they had always purchased goods for resale, but have decided to make all the handbags they sell, from 1981.

The trading account for the year to 31 December 1981 shows the following figures for handbag sales through the shop:

	£
Opening stock at cost (500 × £3)	1,500
Received from workship at transfer price (10,000 × £4)	40,000
	41,500
Less: Closing stock (1,000 × £4)	4,000
Cost of sales	37,500
Gross profit	22,500
Sales	£60,000

Mr Baggaley comments that buying the bags from his own workship at £4 each was a mistake, since he could have bought them through the trade at £3.80. However, he says the workshop did well to produce them at £3.50 each and show a profit of 50p on each one.

Show how the stock of handbags would appear in the balance sheet as at 31 December 1981.

(4 marks)
(Total 25 marks)
(AAT June 1982)

Question 39

See page 293 for answer.

a Outline the special problems which are experienced when accounting for long-term contracts, and explain the rules adopted by best accounting practice to overcome these problems.

(12 marks)

b Bradmore Builders Ltd are a firm of building contractors. In the present conditions of slack trade they have only one current contract. Operating data for the contract for the year ended 30 June 1984 is as follows:

Contract	A
	£
Contract price	620,000
Value of work certified	570,000
Cash received from contractee	480,000
Work in progress at 1 July 1983	447,850
Costs incurred during the year:	
Materials	46,412
Labour	31,283
Overhead excluding depreciation	12,513
Plant—valuation at 1 July 1983	83,465
Plant—valuation at 30 June 1984	87,220
Plant—purchased during year 1983/4	21,478
Cost of work not yet certified	3,458

The contract is nearing completion and the quantity surveyors estimate that a further £25,000 will be incurred to complete the job, and that any plant remaining on the site will be sold for £70,000 at completion. No further plant purchases are planned for this contract.

The work in progress figure for the contract as at 1 July 1983 included an estimated profit of £26,480.

Required:
Draft the appropriate ledger accounts to record the transactions disclosed above in the books of Bradmore Builders Ltd; and show how they would appear in the balance sheet as at 30 June 1984.

(11 marks)
(Total 23 marks)
(AAT June 1984)

Question 40

In preparing the annual accounts of Penn PLC for the year to 30 June 1984 you come across a number of problems which you think may require special treatment in the published accounts of the company. A brief summary of each problem is listed below:

See page 294 for answer.

1 A major and fundamental error is discovered which will require an adjustment to last year's profit, that is, that of the year to 30 June 1983.
2 There has been a substantial increase in the amount of expenditure incurred on applied research.
3 The financial director has suggested that an additional amount should be transferred to the deferred taxation account to cover for new originating timing differences arising in the year.
4 The directors' aggregate emoluments have increased from £55,000 in the previous year to £85,000 in the current year.
5 The company paid £250 to a major political party.
6 During the year the company closed one of its largest factories in France.
7 As from 1 July 1983, the company's method of pricing the issue of goods to production was changed from a LIFO (last-in, first-out basis) to a FIFO (first-in, first-out) basis.
8 An interim dividend was paid on 10 January 1984 on which ACT was paid on 14 April 1984.
9 It is now believed that considerable expenditure incurred on developing an existing product during the year is likely to prove highly beneficial to the company.
10 You have estimated that 30% of the current year's gross profit has been earned as a result of a special and quite unique order.

Required:
State how and where you would treat each of the above problems in the published accounts of Penn PLC, being careful to explain clearly the reasons for your decision.

(25 marks)
(AAT Pilot Paper)

Question 41

Exe PLC is a company in the building industry, which also operates several factories which make preformed and prestressed concrete products.

See page 295 for answer.

How would you deal with any FIVE of the following transactions in the accounts of Exe PLC as at 31 December 1982, according to best accounting practice:

a Shortly before the end of the financial year Exe PLC bought 5% of the voting shares in Wye PLC which, when added to its previous holding, amounts to a 20·8% share stake in Wye PLC.

(5 marks)

b During the year Exe PLC revalued its headquarters building, of which it owns the freehold. The only entry in the books concerning this property records the cost when built as £500,000, but the valuer now suggests a value of £1,250,000, with the land contributing £400,000 of that amount.

(5 marks)

c Exe PLC has opened a research department to develop new techniques which the company intends to exploit in the future. The department has cost £47,000 to operate in the year, and the board suggest that this expenditure should be carried forward to set off against revenue at a future date under the matching convention.

(5 marks)

d On 5 February 1983 the net realizable value of raw material stock as at 31 December 1982 was found to be £40,000 lower than their historic cost. On 25 January 1983, the board decided to close a factory situated at Exeter.

(5 marks)

e During the year an abnormal provision of £50,000 was made for losses on a long–term contract. On another contract a mistake was discovered in the calculation of stocks of work in progress as at 31 December 1980. The amount had been overstated by £36,000.

(5 marks)

f During the year Exe PLC received a capital grant from a Government agency, in the sum of £30,000, against the purchase by the company of plant in the sum of £120,000.

(5 marks)

(Total 25 marks)

(AAT December 1982)

SAMPLE EXAMINATION PAPER

AAT Financial Accounting (Paper 9) June 1986

Time allowed — 3 hours

Number of questions set — 5

Answer FOUR questions only

Question 1 and 2 (compulsory) from section A, and TWO from section B

All questions carry equal marks.

SECTION A (COMPULSORY)

1   Paper Products has a head office in London and a branch in Bristol. The following information has been extracted from the head office books of account as at 31 March 1986:

See page 296 for answer.

1   Information relating to the branch:

Balances	Opening £000	Closing £000
Bank book account (positive balance)	3	12
Branch debtors	66	81
Branch stock (at transfer price)	75	90

Transactions during the year:	£000
Bad debts written off	15
Branch general expenses (paid from bank branch account)	42
Cash received from credit customers and banked	390
Cash sales banked	120
Cash transferred from branch to head office bank account	459
Credit sales	437
Discounts allowed to credit customers	9
Goods returned by credit customers	8
Goods returned from branch (at transfer price from head office)	30
Goods sent to branch (at transfer price from head office)	600

2   Information relating to head office:
    Balances:

	Opening £000	Closing £000
Stock	180	220

Transactions during the year:	£000
Bad debts written off	24
Cash sales	1,500
Credit sales	2,000
Discounts allowed to credit customers	29
General expenses	410
Goods returned by credit customers	40
Purchases	2,780

Additional information:

1   Most of the accounting records relating to the branch are kept by the head office in its own books of account.
2   All purchases are made by the head office, and goods are invoiced to the branch at selling price, that is, at cost price plus 50%.

Required:
a   Write up the following ledger accounts for the year to 31 March 1986, being careful to bring down any balances as at that date:
    i   branch stock account;
    ii goods sent to branch account;
    iii branch stock adjustment account;
    iv branch debtors account; and
    v   branch bank account.

(15 marks)

b   Compile Paper Products trading, and profit and loss account for the year to 31 March 1986.

(6 marks)

c   Examine briefly the merits and demerits of Paper Products' method of branch book-keeping including comment on the significance of the 'balancing figure' in the branch stock account.

(4 marks)
(Total 25 marks)

See page 297 for answer.

2   The following information has been extracted from the accounts of Witton Way Ltd:

Profit and loss account for the year to 30 April 1986

	1985 £000	1986 £000
Turnover (all credit sales)	7,650	11,500
Less: Cost of sales	(5,800)	(9,430)
Gross Profit	1,850	2,070
Other expenses	(150)	(170)
Loan interest	(50)	(350)
Profit before taxation	1,650	1,550
Taxation	(600)	(550)
Profit after taxation	1,050	1,000
Dividends (all ordinary shares)	(300)	(300)
Retained Profits	£750	£700

Balance sheet at 30 April 1986

	1985	1986
	£000	£000
Fixed assets:		
Tangible assets	10,050	11,350
Current assets:		
Stocks	1,500	2,450
Trade debtors	1,200	3,800
Cash	900	50
	3,600	6,300
Creditors: Amounts falling due within one year	2,400	2,700
Net current assets	1,200	3,600
Total assets less current liabilities	11,250	14,950
Creditors:		
Amouts falling due after more than one year		
Loans and other borrowings	350	3,350
	£10,900	£11,600
Capital and reserves:		
Called–up share capital	5,900	5,900
Profit and loss acccount	5,000	5,700
	£10,900	£11,600

Additional information:
During the year to 30 April 1986, the company tried to stimulate sales by reducing the selling price of its products and by offering more generous credit terms to its customers.

Required:
a Calculate SIX accounting ratio specifying the basis of your calculations for each of the two years to 30 April 1985 and 1986 respectively which will enable you to examine the company's progress during 1986.

(9 marks)

b From the information available to you, including the ratios calculated in part (a) of the question, comment upon the company's results for the year to 30 April 1986 under the heads of 'liquidity', 'profitability', 'efficiency' and 'shareholders' interests'.

(11 marks)

c State what additional information you would require in order to assess the company's attempts to stimulate sales during the year to 30 April 1986.

(5 marks)
(Total 25 marks)

SECTION B (Answer TWO questions from this Section)

3 The following information has been extracted from the books of account of Rufford PLC for the year to 31 March 1986:

See page 298 for answer.

	Dr	Cr
	£000	£000
ACT (paid on 14 October 1985)	3	
Administration expenses	97	
Deferred taxation		24
Depreciation on office machinery (for the year to 31 March 1986)	8	
Depreciation on delivery vans (for the year to 31 March 1986)	19	
Distribution costs	33	
Dividends received (from a UK listed company on 31 July 1985)		14

	Dr	Cr
	£000	£000
Factory closure expenses (net of tax)	12	
Interest payable on bank overdraft (repayable within five years)	6	
Interim dividend (paid on 30 September 1985)	21	
Interest receivable		25
Purchases	401	
Retained profit at 31 March 1985		160
Sales (net of VAT)		642
Stock at 1 April 1985	60	

Additional Information:

1 Administrative expenses include the following items:

	£000
Auditors' remuneration	20
Directors' emoluments	45
Travelling expenses	1
Research expenditure	11
Hire of plant and machinery	12

2 It is assumed that the following tax rates are applicable for the year to 31 March 1986:

	%
Corporation tax	50
Income tax	30

3 There was an overprovision for corporation tax of £3,000 relating to the year to 31 March 1985.

4 Corporation tax payable for the year to 31 March 1986 (based on the profits for that year) is estimated to be £38,000. The company, in addition, intends to transfer a further £9,000 to its deferred taxation account.

5 A final dividend of £42,000 for the year to 31 March 1986 is expected to be paid on 2 June 1986.

6 Stock at 31 March 1986 was valued at £71,000.

7 As a result of a change in accounting policy, a prior year charge of £15,000 (net of tax) is to be made.

8 The company's share capital consists of 420,000 ordinary shares of £1 each. There are no preference shares, and no change had been made to the company's issued share capital for some years.

Required:

a In so far as the information permits, prepare the company's published profit and loss account for the year to 31 March 1986 in the vertical format in accordance with the Companies Act 1985 and with related statements of standard accounting practice.
(NB: A statement of the company's accounting policies is NOT required.)

(20 marks)

b Prepare balance sheet extracts in order to illustrate the balances still remaining in the following accounts at 31 March 1986:
 i corporation tax;
 ii advanced corporation tax;
 iii proposed dividend; and
 iv deferred taxation.
(NB: a detailed balance sheet is NOT required.)

(5 marks)
(Total 25 marks)

See page 300 for answer.   4 Proudie, Slope and Thorne were in partnership sharing profits and losses in the ratio

3:1:1. The draft balance sheet of the partnership as at 31 May 1986 is shown below:

	£000	£000	£000
Fixed assets:	Cost	Depreci- ation	Net book value
Land and buildings	200	40	160
Furniture	30	18	12
Motor vehicles	60	40	20
	£290	£98	192
Current Assets:			
Stocks		23	
Trade debtors	42		
Less: Provision for doubtful debts	1		
		41	
Prepayments		2	
Cash		10	
		76	
Less: Current liabilities			
Trade creditors	15		
Accruals	3		
		18	
			58
			£250
Financed by:			
Capital accounts:			
Proudie		100	
Slope		60	
Thorne		40	
			200
Current accounts:			
Proudie		24	
Slope		10	
Thorne		8	
			42
			242
Loan:			
Proudie			8
			£250

Additional information:
1 Proudie decided to retire on 31 May 1986. However, Slope and Thorne agreed to form a new partnership out of the old one, as from 1 June 1986. They agreed to share profits and losses in the same ratio as in the old partnership.
2 Upon the dissolution of the old partnership, it was agreed that that the following adjustments were to be made to the partnership balance sheet as at 31 May 1986:
   a Land and buildings were to be revalued at £200,000.
   b Furniture was to be revalued at £5,000.
   c Proudie agreed to take over one of the motor vehicles at a value of £4,000, the remaining motor vehicles being revalued at £10,000.
   d Stocks were to be written down by £5,000.
   e A bad debt of £2,000 was to be written off, and the provision for doubtful debts was then to be adjusted so that it represented 5% of the then outstanding trade debtors as at 31 May 1986.
   f A further accrual of £3,000 for office expenses was to be made.
   g Professional charges relating to the dissolution were estimated to be £1,000.
3 It had not been the practice of the partners to carry goodwill in the books of the

partnership, but on the retirement of a partner it has been agreed that goodwill should be taken into account. Goodwill was to be valued at an amount equal to the average annual profits of the three years expiring on the retirement. For the purpose of including goodwill in the dissolution arrangement when Proudie retired, the net profits for the last three years were as follows:

	£000
Year to 31 May 1984	130
Year to 31 May 1985	150
Year to 31 May 1986	181

The net profit for the year to 31 May 1986 had been calculated before any of the items listed in 2 above were taken into account. The net profit was only to be adjusted for items listed in 2 (d), 2 (e), and 2 (f) above.

4   Goodwill is not to be carried in the books of the new partnership.
5   It was agreed that Proudie's old loan of £8,000 should be repaid to him on 31 May 1986, but any further amount owing to him as a result of the dissolution of the partnership should be left as a long-term loan in the books of the new partnership.
6   The partners' current accounts were to be closed and any balances on them as at 31 May 1986 were to be transferred to their respective capital accounts.

Required:

a   Prepare the revaluation account as at 31 May 1986.

(12 marks)

b   Prepare the partners' capital accounts as at the date of dissolution of the partnership, and bring down any balances on them in the books of the new partnership.

(9 marks)

c   Prepare Slope and Thorne's balance sheet as at 1 June 1986.

(4 marks)
(Total 25 marks)

See page 301 for answer.

5   In preparing the published accounts of a company, *briefly* state the *significant* accounting/disclosure requirements you would have in mind in ensuring that the accounts comply with best accounting practice as embodied in the statements of standard accounting practice:

a   Value added tax.

(3 marks)

b   Earnings per share.

(3 marks)

c   The disclosure requirements for each major class of depreciable assets.

(4 marks)

d   Research expenditure.

(2 marks)

e   Capital-based grants relating to fixed assets.

(3 marks)

f   Goodwill arising on consolidation

(4 marks)

g   The disclosure requirements relating to generally accepted fundamental accounting concepts.

(3 marks)

h   The accounts of a subsidiary company having similar activities to that of the holding company.

(3 marks)
(Total 25 marks)

FURTHER EXAMINATION QUESTIONS

Question 1

Explain the fundamental accounting concepts of prudence, accurals, consistency and going concern.

(10 marks)

Question 2

Explain how the fundamental accounting concepts are applied in the accounting treatment of debtors.

(10 marks)

Question 3

A company buys and sells goods some of which are:

a subject to VAT at the standard rate of 15%;
b zero rated (those where no VAT is chargeable on sales but any VAT charged on purchases is recoverable);
c exempt (those where no VAT is chargeable on sales and where any VAT charged is not recoverable).

You are given the following information:

1 The balance on the VAT account at the end of July was £4,700. This amount was paid on 30 August.
2 Purchases, including VAT at 15%, during the quarter were:
   £69,000 for standard rated goods;
   £ 6,900 for zero rated goods;
   £ 2,300 for exempt goods.
3 Sales, not including VAT, during the quarter were:
   £100,000 for standard rated goods;
   £ 10,000 for zero rated goods;
   £ 5,000 for exempt goods.
4 All items purchased are for resale.

You are required:
To write up a company's value added tax account, sales account and purchases account in its ledger for the months of August, September and October, and to show the balance outstanding on the VAT account at the end of the quarter.

(10 marks)
(CIMA November 1985)

Question 4

Smith and Jones are in partnership sharing profits and losses in the ratio 3:2. The following trial balance has been extracted from the books of account as at 31 December 1984:

	Debit	Credit
	£	£
Capital accounts:		
Smith		25,000
Jones		20,000
Current accounts:		
Smith		1,400
Jones	300	
Net profit for the year		
to 31 December 1984		30,000
Fixed assets (net book value)	50,000	
Stock	16,000	
Debtors	9,000	
Creditors		2,000
Bank	3,100	
	£78,400	£78,400

Notes:
1   No appropriations of profit for the year have yet been made.
2   Jones is entitled to a salary of £5,000 per annum.
3   Interest on capital is to be allowed at 10% per annum.
4   Smith decides to retire on 31 December 1984 and Robinson will join Jones in partnership as from 1 January 1985; profits and losses will be shared equally between Jones and Robinson.
5   The goodwill of the old partnership is estimated to be worth £5,000 and adjustment should be made between the old and new partners in respect of this amount, but no goodwill account is to be opened.
6   Robinson is to introduce £10,000 as his capital into the new partnership.
7   The amount owing to Smith on his retirement is to be retained as a loan to the new partnership, except for £12,500 which will be repaid on 1 January 1985.

Required:
a   Smith and Jones' profit and loss appropriation account for the year ended 31 December 1984.

(5 marks)

b   Partners' capital and current accounts, in columnar form.

(10 marks)

c   The balance sheet of Jones and Robinson as at 1 January 1985.

(5 marks)
(Total 20 marks)

Question 5

John, Keith and Len are in partnership sharing profits in the ratio of 3:2:1 respectively.
   A balance sheet for the partnership as at 31 March 1983 is shown below:

	£		£
Capital accounts:		Fixed assets:	
John	100,000	Premises	100,000
Keith	80,000	Plant	52,000
Len	40,000	Office furniture	27,000
	220,000		179,000

		£			£
Current accounts:	£		Current assets:		
John	6,450		Stock	29,500	
Keith	14,978		Debtors	51,500	
Len	(2,636)		Cash	10,412	
		18,792			
Trade creditors		31,620			
		£270,412			£270,412

Len retired on 31 March 1983, and John and Keith formed a company, Jake Ltd, to take over the business on that date.

Details of the changes agreed were as follows:

1 The assets of the business, other than cash, were to be taken over by the company at a valuation of £284,000, but were to be recorded in the book of Jake Ltd at the same book value as in the partnership books. Trade creditors were to be paid by the partnership.

2 The authorized capital of Jake Ltd was:
135,000 ordinary shares of £1 each
65,000 12% preference shares of £1 each

3 The company raised a 16% debenture loan of £70,000 from a merchant bank.

4 Jake Ltd paid for its acquisition as follows:
  i 135,000 ordinary shares issued to John and Keith to satisfy their capital accounts;
  ii 16% debentures issued to John, Keith and Len to repay their current accounts;
  iii the balance in cash.

Required:

a Calculate the current account balances of the partners to be satisfied by the issue of debentures.

(5 marks)

b Draft journal entries to record these transactions in the books of Jake Ltd.

(14 marks)

c Prepare a balance sheet for Jake Ltd as at 1 April 1983.

(6 marks)
(Total 25 marks)
(AAT June 1983)

Question 6

Arnold and Bennett engaged in a joint venture to purchase £25,000 work of stock from a bankrupt. The stock was paid for by two cheques on 1 January 1972, Arnold contributing £15,000 and Bennett £10,000. The following arrangements were agreed:

  i Each party was to receive interest of 10% actual on his original contribition.
  ii Each party was to receive commission of 10% on all cash collected by him from sales of stock.
  iii All profits or losses after deduction of agreed expenses, interest and commission were to be divided equally.
  iv A separate set of books would not be kept for the venture.

The following transactions took place:

1972			£
Jan.	3	Arnold purchased a lorry for	1,000
		Bennet purchased a van for	500
	5	Advertising costs met by Arnold were	25
	6	Arnold hired a warehouse for the period of the joint venture and paid rent of	250
	21	Cash sales collected by Arnold	5,000
		Cash sales collected by Bennett	5,000

1972			£
Feb.	5	Cash sales collected by Arnold	7,500
		Cash sales collected by Bennett	8,000
	10	Advertising costs met by Bennett	75
	28	Cash sales collected by Arnold	3,000
		Cash collected by Bennett (including £750 from sale of the lorry)	7,750

Expenses incurred by the parties were agreed as follows:

Motor expenses—Arnold		220
—Bennett		180
Incidentals—Arnold		20
—Bennett		10

It was agreed that Bennett should buy the van at a valuation of £250. Settlement between the parties was effected in cash on 5 March 1972.

You are required to show:
a a memorandum account for the venture as a whole, and
b a joint venture account in the books of each party.

(18 marks)
(CACA June 1973)

Question 7

Snap Ltd prepares its accounts at 31 May each year.

On 8 January Snap Ltd consign to M. Crackle 1,000 sacks of cornflour that had cost £10,000 and pay freight £500 and insurance £200. 300 sacks are contaminated in transit and an insurance settlement of £2,700 is received by Snap Ltd on 3 March.

M. Crackle sells 350 sacks for £8,000 and on 31 May remits the balance due after charging his selling expenses of £350 and commision of £400.

Required:
Write up the consigment to Crackle account as it would appear in the books of Snap Ltd at 31 May.

(10 marks)

Question 8

On preparing the accounts of a company you discover that some products had been sent to a customer for trial purposes on a sale or return basis. These items had, however, been passed through the books as sales at the time of delivery. At the time of preparing the accounts the trial period had not yet expired.

Required:
Discuss the above treatment and explain, giving reasons, any alternative accounting treatment that you would prefer.

(10 marks)

Question 9

PB Limited supplies goods in returnable containers. The containers are bought at £8 each, charged to customers at £10 each and, if returned within three months, credited at £6 each. At the year-end all containers whether in the company's warehouse or in the hands of customers (return period unexpired) are valued at £4 each.

On 1 October 1980 there were 1,000 containers in the company's warehouse and 10,000 in the hands of customers, still within the return period.

During the year ended 30 September 1981, the following transactions occurred:

— 6,000 containers were purchased

— 23,000 containers were despatched to customers
— 22,000 containers were returned by customers
— 2,000 containers were retained by customers after expiry of the return period
— 500 containers in the company's warehouse were sold as scrap for a total sum of £50.

A physical stock-taking at the year-end revealed that 1,500 containers were missing from the company's warehouse.

You are required:
To record the above transactions in the containers stock account and containers suspense account of PB Limited.

(15 marks)
(CIMA November 1981)

Question 10

A company has leased a machine for the production of vacuum bellows. The lease provides that a royalty of £10 for every 100 bellows produced should be paid and that such payment was not to be less than £20,000 per annum. Any shortworkings in the first year of leasing the machine could be recouped out of royalties payable in the second year.
    The lease of the machine commenced on 1 April 1986. The following are the numbers of bellows produced:

	Quantity
Year ended 31 March 1987	150,000
Year ended 31 March 1988	230,000
Year ended 31 March 1989	250,000

The companies books are closed on 31 March each year.

You are required:
To write up the royalties account, shortworkings account and the account of the lessor, as they would appear in the books of the company, from 1 April 1986 to 31 March 1989.

(10 marks)

Question 11

A company acquired a motor car under a hire-purchase agreement dated 1 July 1985. The details of the transaction were as follows:

	£
Cash price	11,600
Deposit	2,000
Total interest	2,400

The agreement provides for 24 equal monthly instalments to be paid commencing on 31 July 19X1.
    The company's accounts are prepared annually to 31 December. Depreciation of motor vehicles is provided on a straight line basis at the rate of 30% per annum.

From the information given you are required to prepare the following accounts for the years ended 31 December 1985, 1986 and 1987:

a   Motor vehicle
b   Provision for depreciation of motor vehicle
c   Hire-purchase company re motor vehicle
d   Hire-purchase interest suspense.

(15 marks)

Question 12

Tom Potter set up in business on 1 January 1977 to sell snooker tables of a standard size and quality designed for home use. He leased a store-room and needed no fixed assets. His opening capital was £8,000, represented initially by the bank balance. The tables were purchased for £72 each and sold for cash or monthly credit terms for £100 each. Towards the end of the first year Tom decided to try hire–purchase trading, financing it himself. He required a deposit of £30 followed by 18 monthly instalments of £5 each, the first one payable one month after purchase.

During the year he bought a total of 300 tables and sold 210 of them for cash or on monthly credit terms. His hire–purchases sales were 12 in October, 20 in November and 30 in December, but two of those sold in October had to be repossessed in December—the deposit and one instalment had been paid in each case. One of the repossessed tables was badly damaged and would need repairs estimated at £24 after which it would probably be offered for sale at half the normal cash price. The other one had hardly been used and could be treated as new stock.

It can be assumed that all the hire purchase sales were made on the first day of the month and that the instalments were paid promptly on the last day of each month (e.g. for the October sales, three instalments would have been received by 31 December.) Not being too sure about the accounting implications of hire–purchase trading, Tom Potter credited all sales to the sales account, including the total HP price for hire–purchase sales, and debited either debtors or bank. At the end of the year he had the following balances:

Trial balance 31 December 1977

	Dr	Cr
	£	£
Capital		8,000
Purchases	21,600	
Sales		28,400
Debtors	6,270	
Creditors		576
Expenses	1,800	
Drawings	6,400	
Bank balance	946	
	£37,016	£37,016

Required:
Calculate the net profit for the year and prepare the balance sheet at 31 December 1977.

(20 marks)

(CACA June 1978)

Question 13

D. Ltd, a retail organization, has a branch at Norwich. All purchases are made by the head office in London, goods for the branch being delivered to it direct and charged out at selling price, which is normally cost plus 33⅓%. The branch keeps a sales ledger and certain subsidiary books, but other transactions are recorded only in the books of the London office.

On 1 January 1973 stock at the branch was valued at £9,600 (selling price) and debtors amounted to £1,257. At the end of 1973 the following information became available regarding branch activities in 1973:

	£
Cash sales	12,800
Credit sales	6,350
Goods sent to the branch at selling price	22,800
Goods returned to London at selling price	160
Goods returned to branch by credit customers	320
Bad debts	185

	£
Cash discounts relating to debtors	210
Authorized reductions in selling price	855
Expenses paid by branch	1,000
Expenses allocated to branch by head office	1,200
Cash received from debtors	6,200

On 31st December, 1973, stock at the branch at selling price was valued at £10,800.

You are required to:
Prepare the stock, debtors, and profit and loss accounts in respect of the Norwich branch.

(12 marks)

(CACA June 1974)

Question 14

Scott and Gray are in partnership carrying on a business as retailers sharing profits and losses: Scott two-thirds, Gray one third. The partners are entitled to interest on their fixed capitals at the rate of 8% per annum. No interest is to be charged on drawings.

There is a head office with a shop attached, and a branch shop.

All goods are purchased by head office, and goods sent to the branch are charged out at cost.

Scott acts as buyer for the business, whilst Gray manages the head office shop. Byron is employed to managed the branch shop. Gray and Byron are entitled to a commission based on the profits of the shop under their control. The commission is to be 10% of the profits after charging such commission.

The trial balance as on 31 March 1972 was as follows:

	Head office books		Branch books	
	Dr	Cr	Dr	Cr
	£	£	£	£
Furniture, fixtures and fittings at cost	1,900		1,400	
Bank balances	930			1,920
Stock, 31 March 1971	16,000		5,600	
Sundry debtors	8,500		3,700	
Sundry creditors		7,100		500
Purchases	45,000			
Sales		46,900		31,520
Goods sent to branches		21,860	21,560	
Trade expenses	4,000		2,200	
Wages and salaries	5,500		3,980	
Postage, carriage and travelling expenses	2,700		1,210	
Drawings and fixed capital accounts:				
Scott	3,300	15,000		
Gray	2,000	6,000		
Branch and head office current accounts	8,400			5,000
Provision for depreciation of furniture, fixtures and fittings		640		460
Provision for doubtful debts		730		250
	£98,230	£98,230	£39,650	£39,650

The following additional information is given to you:
  1 Stocks valued at cost on 31 March 1972 were: head office £18,163, branch £7,840.
  2 Depreciation on furniture, fixtures and fittings is to be provided at 10% of cost.
  3 Goods charged out at £300 on 31 March 1972 had been recorded in the head office books but were not received at the branch until after that date. These goods did not

appear in the books at the branch, and had not been included in the stock-take. On the same date the branch had sent cash of £3,100 to head office. This payment had been entered in the branch books, but had not been recorded in the head office books.

4 The provision for doubtful debts as regards head office debtors is to be decreased to £700, and increased to £300 as regards those of the branch.

Any adjustments required are to be made in the head office books.

You are required to:

a prepare trading and profit and loss accounts showing the net profit of the head office and branch respectively, also the appropriation account for the year ended 31 March 1972,

b draw up the balance sheet as on that date, and

c show the closing entries in the branch current account and an analysis of the closing balance on that account.

(25 marks)
(CACA December 1972)

Question 15

JHP Limited is a company with an authorized share capital of £10,000,000 in ordinary shares of £1 each, of which 6,000,000 shares had been issued and fully paid on 30 June 1981.

The company proposed to make a further issue of 1,000,000 of these £1 shares at a price of £1.40 each, the arrangements for payment being:

a £0.20 per share payable on application, to be received by 1 July 1981;

b allotment to be made on 10 July 1981 and a further £0.50 per share (including the premium) to be payable;

c the final call for the balance to be made, and the money received, by 30 April 1982.

Applications were received for 3,550,000 shares and were dealt with as follows:

i applicants for 50,000 shares received an allotment in full,

ii applicants for 300,000 shares received an allotment of one share for every two applied for; no money was returned to these applicants, the surplus on application being used to reduce the amount due on allotments,

iii applicants for 3,200,000 shares received an allotment of one share for every four applied for; the money due on allotment was retained by the company, the excess being returned to the applicants.

iv the money due on final call was received on the due date.

You are required:

To record these transactions (including cash items) in the journal of JHP Limited.

(10 marks)
(CIMA May 1982)

Question 16

Manufacturers PLC is an old established company. The members of the accounts department are drafting the final accounts for the year to 30 June 1985 for publication. Certain items are not as yet completed and you are required to finalize them.

Taxation:
The published accounts for the year to 30 June 1984 contain the following figures:

	£
Proposed dividend	560,000
Provision for corporation tax payable:	
1 January 1985	970,000

	£	£
1 January 1986		890,000
ACT payable on proposed dividend		240,000
Deferred taxation reserve:	£	
Timing differences	1,890,000	
less ACT recoverable	240,000	
		1,650,000

No dividends were paid during the year to 30 June 1984. During the year to 30 June 1985 the company paid the dividend proposed in 1984 and its related ACT, the corporation tax due on 1 January 1985 and an interim dividend of £175,000 together with ACT on this dividend. After some negotiation the corporation tax due on 1 January 1986 has been agreed with the Inland Revenue as £840,000. A sum of £780,000 is to be provided for taxation on profits in the year to 30 June 1985, and £150,000 is to be transferred from the deferred taxation reserve. The directors intend to propose a final dividend of £420,000 for the year to 30 June 1985.

Required:
Compute the figure for taxation to be shown in the published profit and loss account for the year to 30 June 1985, and prepare the related balance sheet items.

(12 marks)
(AAT June 1985)

Question 17

Able and Active Traders PLC is a company in the import wholesale trade. The company has an authorized share capital of 1,000,000 8% redeemable preference shares £1 each and 6,000,000 ordinary shares of 25p each.

The trial balance of the company as at 31 December 1985 is as follows:

	£	£
Profit and loss a/c balance at 1.1.85		316,436
General reserve		54,000
Ordinary share capital		1,200,000
8% preference share capital		800,000
12% debentures repayable 1995/97		
secured on the premises		400,000
Sales		11,400,650
Cost of sales	8,235,634	
Directors' remuneration	190,000	
Distribution costs	843,696	
Administration expenses	1,073,650	
Debtors/creditors	775,438	696,792
Goodwill	40,000	
Provision for doubtful debts		51,600
Debenture Interest paid	24,000	
Half year preference dividend paid		
on 30.6.85	32,000	
ACT paid on 14.7.85	13,714	
Trade investment at cost	166,000	
Bank overdraft		99,216
Land and buildings at cost	3,000,000	
Plant and machinery at cost	310,000	
Provision for depreciation on		
buildings at 1.1.85		220,000
Provision for depreciation on plant		
and machinery at 1.1.85		44,000

	£	£
Motor vehicles at cost (salesmen's cars)	170,000	
Provision for depreciation on motor		
vehicles at 1.1.85		70,000
Stocks at 31.12.85	478,562	
	£15,352,694	£15,352,694

The following information is also related to the accounts for the year to 31 December 1985.

1 The directors' remuneration is divided amongst the five directors of the company as follows:

Salaries	£
Chairman	30,000
Managing director	58,000
Purchasing director	34,500
Sales director	32,000
Finance director	35,500
	£190,000

In addition, provision must be made for Directors' Fees of £5,000 to each of the above directors.

2 The directors have reviewed the debtors ledger balances and have decided to increase substantially the doubtful debts provision to £130,680.

3 Depreciation is to be provided for the year as follows:

Buildings   2% on cost
Plant and machinery   10% on cost
Motor vehicles   25% on written down value

Land at cost amounted to £1,000,000. There were no disposals of fixed assets during the year. The only purchases were plant and machinery costing £60,000 in August 1985.

Goodwill is to be amortized over a five year life commencing this year.

4 Administration expenses include £10,340 interest on the bank overdraft, and £30,000 of directors' pension costs.

5 Due to an oversight, the audit fee paid of £12,000 has been added to the cost of sales figure. A further £10,000 is to be provided for this expense.

6 A provision of £220,000 is to be made for corporation tax at 40% based upon the profits for the year. This will be payable on 30 September 1986.

7 The half year preference dividend to 31 December 1985 and a dividend of 2 pence a share on the ordinary share capital, are to be provided in the accounts.

8 The sum of £200,000 is to be transferred to general reserve.

9 Assume the basic income tax rate to be 30%.

10 The current market value of the trade investment is £51,000. The investment consists of 72,000 50p ordinary shares in Oriental Marketing PLC, a company with an issued ordinary share capital of £900,000.

Required:

Draft in a form suitable for publication and in accordance with the Companies Act 1985, so far as the information above will permit:

a A profit and loss account for the year ended 31 December 1985,

(10 marks)

b A balance sheet as at that date, and

(10 marks)

c Relevant notes to the accounts.

(11 marks)
(Total 31 marks)
(AAT December 1985)

Question 18

In its published accounts a limited company is required by the Companies Act 1985 to disclose various information in relation to its directors. You are required to state the information that should be disclosed, differentiating between that which will appear in the notes to the accounts and that which will appear in the directors report.

(10 marks)

Question 19

Brickwood PLC are timber merchants and distributors of building materials. The accounts for the year ended 31 December 1984 are now in draft, but a funds flow statement is needed for publication with the other accounting statements, which contain the following information:

Balance sheet as at 31 December

	£	£	£	£
		1984		1983
Tangible fixed assets—note 1		2,648,615		2,657,759
Fixed asset investments		124,835		104,750
		2,773,450		2,762,509
Current assets:				
Stocks	3,175,403		2,056,817	
Debtors	3,069,481		2,147,623	
Cash and Bank Balances	3,814		3,496	
	6,248,698		4,207,936	
Deduct creditors:				
Payable within				
one year:				
Trade creditors	2,643,434		2,069,471	
Bank borrowings	1,296,817		890,206	
Taxation	487,564		560,738	
Proposed dividends	178,000		115,200	
	4,605,815		3,635,615	
Net current assets		1,642,883		572,321
Total assets less				
current liabilities		4,416,333		3,334,830
Less: Creditors falling due after				
more than one year:				
Loan capital:				
10% mortgage (1990)	300,000		300,000	
11% unsecured loan				
stock (1997/1999)	180,000		—	
Deferred taxation	240,620		80,204	
		720,620		380,204
		£3,695,713		£2,954,626
Financed by:				
Share capital		800,000		600,000
Reserves:				
Share premium		50,000		—
General reserve		2,135,650		1,935,650
Unappropriate profit		710,063		418,976
		£3,695,713		£2,954,626

Profit and loss account for the year ending 31 December

	£	£	£	£
		1984		1983
Turnover		6,394,014		5,466,456
Cost of sales		4,186,755		3,774,337
Gross profit		2,207,259		1,692,119
Selling and				
distribution costs	638,241		530,260	
Administration expenses	479,636		390,184	
Interest;				
Long term	39,900		30,000	
Short term	120,000		90,000	
		1,277,777		1,040,444
Profit before taxation and				
extraordinary items		929,482		651,675
Deduct taxation		301,875		303,647
Profit after taxation				
and before				
extraordinary items		627,607		348,028
Extraordinary items—surplus				
on sale of properties		41,480		20,652
Profit after extraordinary				
items		669,087		368,680
Dividends for year	178,000		115,200	
Appropriation to				
general reserve	200,000		100,000	
		378,000		215,200
Unappropriated profit				
for the year		£291,087		£153,480

Note 1:

Fixed assets:	Freehold properties	Leasehold properties	Plant and equipment	Total
	£	£	£	£
Cost or valuation at 1.1.1984	1,896,423	458,561	1,178,260	3,533,244
Additions	61,211	25,406	237,409	324,026
	1,957,634	483,967	1,415,669	3,857,270
Disposals	148,263	—	75,216	223,479
At 31.12.1984	1,809,371	483,967	1,340,453	3,633,791
Depreciation:				
At 1.1.1984	17,372	156,478	701,635	875,485
Disposals	2,164	—	61,423	63,587
	15,208	156,478	640,212	811,898
Depreciation for the year	16,187	23,046	134,045	173,278
At 31.12.1984	31,395	179,524	774,257	985,176
Book value:				
At 31.12.1983	1,879,051	302,083	476,625	2,657,759
At 31.12.1984	1,777,976	304,443	566,196	2,648,615

Plant disposal concerns machinery sold at its book value.

Required:
A funds flow statement for the year to 31 December 1984 in good form for publication.

(23 marks)

(AAT December 1984)

Question 20

The proprietor of the St Denys Press Ltd, a small printing firm, has read about a scheme whereby significant accounting ratios are prepared on an average basis for the industry as a whole, and published as a yardstick against which individual firms can gauge their own performance and efficiency. He has acquired a set of ratios for firms in the class appropriate to his own, and now seeks to make a comparison, with your assistance. He provides you with the following information:

Significant accounting ratios for a printing business
with a turnover in the range appropriate

Return on net capital employed	14 per cent
Gearing ratio	20 per cent
Turnover ratio	2 times
Current ratio	1:6:1
Quick asset ratio	1:1:1
Gross profit ratio	14 per cent
Net profit ratio	7 per cent
Stock turnover period	30 days
Debtors collection period	30 days
Creditors payment period	60 days

St Denys Press Ltd profit and loss account for year to 31 December 1984

	£	£
Sales (80 per cent on credit terms)		2,880,416
Opening stock	168,271	
Plus purchases	1,804,630	
	1,972,901	
Less Closing stock	220,412	
Material cost	1,752,489	
Labour	502,641	
Factory overheads	371,240	
Cost of sales		2,626,370
Gross profit		254,046
Expenses		180,731
Net profit before loan interest		73,315
Long-term loan interest		30,000
Profit available for distribution		£43,315

St Denys Press Ltd balance sheet as at 31 December 1984

	£	£	£
Share capital			250,000
General reserve			296,000
Unappropriated profit			4,692
Equity interest			550,692
Long-term loan			300,000
Net capital employed			£850,692
Represented by:			
Fixed assets			468,207
Current assets:			
Stock		220,412	
Debtors		357,620	
Cash		4,838	
		582,870	
Current liabilities:			
Trade creditors	150,385		

	£	£	£
Taxation	50,000		
		200,385	
			382,485
Net assets			£850,692

Required:
a Compute the appropriate ratios; and

(10 marks)

b Comment to the proprietor on your findings

(13 marks)

(**NB** Work to one decimal place)

(Total 23 marks)
(AAT June 1985)

Question 21

Discuss why the main current cost adjustments that may be made to the profits disclosed by accounts prepared under the historic cost convention are necessary.

(20 marks)

Question 22

On 1 January 1983 Anglian Air Transformers Limited (Anglian) purchased all the ordinary shares of Industrial Air Supplies Limited (Industrial). On that date the balance sheet of Industrial disclosed unappropriated profit of £2,000. The balance sheet of the two companies as at 31 December 1983 were as follows:

	Anglian		Industrial	
	£	£	£	£
£1 ordinary shares		720,000		250,000
Reserves		154,000		24,000
Unappropriated profit		11,420		4,850
Equity interest		885,420		278,850
Long–term liabilities		150,000		80,000
Net capital employed		£1,035,420		£358,850
Represented by:		£		£
Fixed assets		580,000		217,000
Shares in Industrial		300,000		—
Current assets	290,415		239,565	
Current account with				
Industrial	27,861		—	
Current liabilities	(162,856)		(84,629)	
Current account with				
Anglian	—		(13,086)	
Working capital		155,420		141,850
Net assets		£1,035,420		£358,850

Notes:
1 Industrial has paid a dividend of 10 pence a share on its ordinary capital during the year out of a net profit after tax of £31,850 for the year to 31 December 1983.
2 £4,000 was appropriated from profits to reserve by Industrial at 31 December 1983.
3 Anglian sells goods to Industrial at a price of cost plus 15%. The current assets of Industrial at 31 December 1983 include stock in the sum of £56,994 which had been purchased from Anglian.
4 A cheque for £5,000 was sent from Industrial to Anglian on 28 December 1983 but it did not reach its destination until 5 January 1984.

5   Goods were despatched from Anglian to Industrial on 20 December 1983, together
with an invoice for £9,775, but they had not arrived at Industrial by 1 January 1984.

Required:
Draft a consolidated balance sheet for the group formed by Anglian and Industrial as at 31
December 1983, together with your calculations for goodwill, intergroup stock
adjustment and current account reconciliation.

(23 marks)
(AAT June 1984)

Question 23

Colley Ltd acquired 80,000 £1 ordinary shares in Flower Ltd on 1 January 1987. The trial
balances of the two companies at 31 December 19X8 are as follows:

	Colley Ltd		Flower Ltd	
	£	£	£	£
Sales		800,340		200,100
Cost of sales	562,780		142,000	
Expenses	123,330		32,900	
Taxation	27,000		3,000	
Stock at 31.12.87	112,820		46,270	
Fixed assets	213,000		88,000	
Debtors	140,300		62,050	
Bank	48,790		17,300	
Creditors		62,680		31,020
£1 ordinary shares		200,000		100,000
Profit and loss balance at 1.1.87		315,000		60,400
Investment in Flower Ltd	150,000			
	£1,378,020	£1,378,020	£391,520	£391,520

Included in the debtors and creditors of the respective companies are intercompany
balances of £4,500.
   The directors of Colley Ltd propose to pay a dividend of 20 pence per share.

Required:
Consolidated profit and loss account for the year ended 31 December 1987 and a
consolidated balance sheet at that date.

(20 marks)

Question 24

You have recently been appointed to the post of accountant to a medium sized
engineering company. The managing director has just returned from a one day
conference on accounting principles which was addressed by an eminent academic.
   The managing director is puzzled by the following statement made at the conference:
   'The convention of conservatism must always override the accruals principle whenever
   they are in conflict, especially with reference to the accounting treatment of stocks of
   raw material and finished goods.'

Required:
Explain the statement in a way which will help the managing director to understand best
accounting practice applied to stocks.

(23 marks)
(AAT June 1985)

Question 25

To what extent does SSAP 13 allow research and development expenditure to be carried forward to be written off in later periods? Explain how the fundamental accounting concepts, as defined by SSAP 2, are complied with in such treatment.

(10 marks)

ANSWERS TO EXAMINATION QUESTIONS

Answer to question 1

a The four fundamental accounting concepts are:
— going concern
— accruals
— consistency and
— prudence

    Accounting bases are methods which will apply the fundamental concepts in accounting. Because of the variety of businesses and transactions there may be more than one acceptable method for particular items.

    Accounting policies are the specific accounting bases used by companies as being most appropriate to their circumstances.

b Different accounting bases may be used for the following items that may have a material effect on the accounts:

Depreciation— The depreciation method selected will determine the year-by-year charge to the profit and loss account, which in turn determines the net book value included on the balance sheet.

Stocks— The valuation method used will affect the measurement of the profit for the year and the valuation placed upon the asset on the balance sheet.

Hire-purchase sales— The method used to recognize when profit and interest is earned will affect the amount of income taken to the profit and loss account each year and the amount at which hire-purchase debtors are included on the balance sheet.

Development costs— The method used to determine the amount of costs to be charged each year to the profit and loss account will affect profits and the amount included in the balance sheet for development costs carried forward to future years.

Answer to question 2

a

VAT

	£		£
30.9.X7 Purchases (15/115 × £172,000)	22,500	1.7.X7 Balance b/d	15,000
Cash	2,000	30.9.X7 Sales (15/115 × £230,000)	30,000
Cash	15,000		
Balance c/d	5,500		
	£45,000		£45,000

b The balance in the VAT account will be included in the figure for creditors appearing under current liabilities in the balance sheet.

c The items appearing in the profit and loss account of a non-registered trader will include any related VAT on purchases and expenses. The items appearing in the profit, and loss account of the registered trader will normally not include any VAT. The exceptions to this are any items that include non-recoverable VAT, i.e. entertaining expenses and depreciation of motor cars.

Answer to question 3

a
ALAN, BOB AND CHARLES
Capital accounts

	Alan	Bob	Charles	Don		Alan	Bob	Charles	Don
	£	£	£	£		£	£	£	£
Goodwill	18,000	12,000	—	12,000	Bal. b/d	85,000	65,000	35,000	—
Motor car			3,900		Goodwill	21,000	14,000	7,000	
Bank			48,900		Loan			8,000	
Balance c/d	96,400	72,600	—	(12,000)	Revaluation	8,400	5,600	2,800	
	£114,400	£84,600	£52,800	—		£114,400	£84,600	£52,800	—
Bank (W1)	30,023				Bal. b/d	96,400	72,600		(12,000)
Bal. c/d	66,377	72,600			Bank (W1)				82,091
				70,091					
	£96,400	£72,600		£70,091		£96,400	£72,600		£70,091

Goodwill

	£		£
Capital accounts		Capital accounts	
Alan (3/8)	21,000	Alan (3/8)	18,000
Bob (2/3)	14,000	Bob (2/7)	12,000
Charles (1/4)	7,000	Don (2/3)	12,000
	£42,000		£42,000

Note that an account for goodwill has been opened as this is specifically required by the question. Normally the contra entries on the partners' accounts will be sufficient.

Current accounts

	Alan	Bob	Charles	Don		Alan	Bob	Charles	Don
	£	£	£	£		£	£	£	£
					Bal. b/d	3,714	(2,509)	4,678	
Bank			4,678						
Bal. c/d	3,714	(2,509)	—						
	£3,714	£(2,509)	£4,678	—		£3,714	(2,509)	4,678	—
					Bal. c/d	3,714	(2,509)		

Revaluation

	£		£
Plant (£35,000 – £37,000)	2,000	Premises (120,000 – £90,000)	£30,000
Stock (£54,179 – £62,379)	8,200		
Doubtful debts	3,000		
Surplus on revaluation:			
Alan (3/6)	8,400		
Bob (2/6)	5,600		
Charles (1/6)	2,800	16,800	
	£30,000		£30,000

b

ALAN, BOB AND DON
Balance sheet at 30 June 1982

	£	£
Fixed assets:		
Premises	120,000	
Plant	35,000	
Vehicles (£15,000 –£3,900)	11,100	
Fixtures	2,000	168,100
Current assets:		
Stock	54,179	
Debtors (£34,980 – £3,000)	31,980	
Cash	760	
	86,919	
Less Current liabilities:		
Creditors	19,036	
Bank overdraft (W2)	5,710 24,746	62,173
		£230,273

Financed by:

Partners' accounts:

	Alan	Bob	Don	Total
	£	£	£	£
Capital accounts	66,377	72,600	70,091	209,068
Current accounts	3,714	(2,509)	—	1,205
	£70,091	£70,091 £70,091		210,273
Loan				20,000
				£230,273

Workings:

1 The balances on the partners' accounts after the retirement of Charles but before the cash adjustments required by Note 6 are:

	Alan	Bob	Don
	£	£	£
Capital accounts	96,400	72,600	(12,000)
Current accounts	3,714	(2,509)	–
	£100,114	£70,091	£(12,000)

Of Alan and Bob, the lowest investment is that of Bob, £70,091. The cash payable to Alan to reduce his investment to that of Bob is (£100,114 – £70,091) £30,023. Don will introduce cash of (£12,000 + £70,091) £82,091.

In this solution the end result is that the total of each partners' capital and current accounts is the same. This appears to be the end position required by the question, although it would be more realistic if the partners were to be left with the same balances on their capital accounts and nil balances on their current accounts.

b 2

Bank

	£		£
		Balance b/d	4,200
Don — capital	82,091	Charles — capital	48,900
		— current	4,678
Balance c/d	5,710	Alan — capital	30,023
	£87,801		£87,801

Answer to question 4

In this question a partnership change is effected part-way through the year. It is necessary to analyse the profit and loss account to determine the profit made in the first nine months, to be divided as per the old partnership agreement, and the profit for the last three months of the period to be divided in accordance with the new partnership agreement.

Profit and loss account for year ended 31 December 1983

	1.1.83 to 30.9.83		1.10.83 to 31.12.83	
	£	£	£	£
Gross profit ($9/12 \times$ £136,840)		102,630		
($3/12 \times$ £136,840)				34,210
Less:				
Administrative expenses:				
— George's salary	9,000		—	
— Other	38,250		12,750	
Depreciation:				
— Premises (W1)	3,000		1,125	
— Equipment and vehicles (W2)	9,750		2,016	
		60,000		15,891
		£42,630		£18,319
Division:				
Salary — George ($3/12 \times$ £8,000)			2,000	
Interest on capital:				
— Michael ($10/100 \times 3/12 \times$ £113,600)			2,840	
— Peter ($10/100 \times 3/12 \times$ £56,700)			1,418	
— George ($10/100 \times 3/12 \times$ £18,000)			450	
Residue of profit:				
— Michael ($4/7$)	24,360		($2/5$) 4,645	
— Peter ($3/7$)	18,270		($2/5$) 4,644	
— George			($1/5$) 2,322	
		£42,630		£18,319

Note that only nine months of George's salary, £9,000 ($9/12 \times$ £12,000), had been paid. Other administrative expenses of £51,000 (£60,000 less George's salary of £9,000) are apportioned $9/12$ and $3/12$ to the two periods.

Capital accounts

	Michael	Peter	George		Michael	Peter	George
	£	£	£		£	£	£
Goodwill—contra (W4)	14,000	14,000	7,000	Bal. b/d	100,000	50,000	
Bal.c/d	113,600	56,700	18,000	Revaluation (W3)	7,600	5,700	
				Goodwill—contra (W4)	20,000	15,000	
				Bank			25,000
	£127,600	£70,700	£25,000		£127,600	£70,700	£25,000

Current accounts

	Michael	Peter	George		Michael	Peter	George
	£	£	£		£	£	£
Drawings	18,750	14,235	4,625	Salary			2,000
				Interest			
				on capital	2,840	1,418	450
Bal. c/d	13,095	10,097	147	Residue of profit:			
				To 30.9.83	24,360	18,270	

	Michael	Peter	George		Michael	Peter	George
	£	£	£		£	£	£
				To 31.12.83	4,645	4,644	2,322
	£31,845	£24,332	£4,772		£31,845	£24,332	£4,772

Note that normally there would be opening balances on Michael and Peter's current accounts. These have been omitted by the question.

Balance sheet at 31 December 1983

	£	£
Fixed assets:		
Premises at valuation	90,000	
Less Accumulated depreciation	1,125	88,875
Equipment and vehicles at valuation	32,250	
Less Accumulated depreciation	2,016	30,234
		119,109
Current assets:		
Stock (£120,000 – £1,700)	118,300	
Debtors	13,827	
Bank	4,526	
	136,653	
Less Current liabilities:		
Creditors	44,123	92,530
		£211,639

Financed by:
Partners' accounts:

	Michael	Peter	George	Total
	£	£	£	£
Capital accounts	113,600	56,700	18,000	188,300
Current accounts	13,095	10,097	147	23,339
	£126,695	£66,797	£18,147	£211,639

Workings

1 Premises

		£			£
1.1.83	Bal. b/d—net book value	70,000	30.9.83	Profit and loss	
				($\frac{1}{21}$ × £84,000 × $\frac{9}{12}$)	3,000
30.9.83	Revaluation	23,000		Bal. c/d—at valuation	90,000
		£93,000			£93,000
1.10.83	Bal. b/d	90,000	31.12.83	Profit and loss	
				($\frac{1}{20}$ × £90,000 × $\frac{3}{12}$)	1,125
				Bal. c/d	88,875
		£90,000			£90,000

2. Equipment and vehicles

1.1.83	Bal. b/d—net book value	50,000	30.9.83	Profit and loss	
				($\frac{1}{5}$ × £65,000 × $\frac{9}{12}$)	£0,750
				Bal. c/d—at valuation	32,250
				Revaluation	8,000
		£50,000			£50,000
1.10.X3	Bal. b/d	32,250	31.12.83	Profit and loss	
				($\frac{1}{4}$ × £32,250 × $\frac{3}{12}$)	2,016
				Bal. c/d	30,234
		£32,250			£32,250

3

Revaluation

	£		£
30.9.83 Equipment & vehicles	8,000	30.9.83 Premises	23,000
Stock	1,700		
Capital a/cs—surplus:			
Michael (4/7) 7,600			
Peter (3/7) 5,700	13,300		
	£23,000		£23,000

4 Goodwill contra:

	Old partnership		New partnership
	£		£
Michael (4/7)	20,000	(2/5)	14,000
Peter (3/7)	15,000	(2/5)	14,000
George	—	(1/5)	7,000
	£35,000		£35,000

This is a large question which is probably worth more than the 23 marks allocated.

Answer to question 5

MIKE, JIM AND MARTIN

Realization

	£		£
Freehold property	400,000	Creditors	216,483
Plant	170,181	Bank—premises	75,000
Vehicles	28,409	Jim—motor car	4,000
Fixtures and fittings	21,670	—stock	20,000
Stock	218,948	Matchless Markers	700,000
Debtors	121,250		1,015,483
Bank—expenses	500		
	960,958		
Profit and realization:			
Mike	18,175		
Jim	18,175		
Martin	18,175		
	£1,015,483		£1,015,483

The question does not state the partners' profit sharing ratio. In the absence of this information it has been assumed that they shared profits and losses equally, as would be the case if there was no agreement.

Bank

	£		£
Balance b/d	10,416	Realization-expenses	500
Realization—premises	75,000	Jim	84,916
	£85,416		£85,416

Partners' accounts

	Mike	Jim	Martin		Mike	Jim	Martin
	£	£	£		£	£	£
Realization:							
—motor car		4,000		Capital accounts	200,000	200,000	100,000
—stock		20,000		Current accounts	27,412	62,840	24,139
Bank		84,916		Realization:			
				—profit	18,175	18,175	18,175
		108,916			245,587	281,015	142,314
Matchless Markers Ltd:							
—14% debentures							
(bal. fig.)		172,099					
—£1 shares (bal. fig.)	245,587		142,314				
	£245,587	£281,015	£142,314		£245,587	£281,015	£142,314

Loan — Mike

	£		£
Matchless Markets Ltd:			
— 14% debentures	140,000	Balance	140,000

Matchless Markers Ltd

	£		£
Realization:		Loan—14% debentures	140,000
—purchase price	700,000	Jim—14% debentures	172,099
		Mike—£1 ordinary shares	245,587
		Martin—£1 ordinary shares	142,314
	£700,000		£700,000

Answer to question 6

GRAHAM, MURPHY AND WILKINS

Realization

	£		£
Land and buildings	450,820	Exodus PLC	501,000
Plant	77,115	Murphy—motor car	
Vehicles	18,065	(£4,000+£3,000)	7,000
Stock	37,000	Bank—Debtors	
Debtors	51,000	(£51,000 – £4,000 – £2,000)	45,000
			553,000
		Loss on realization:	
		Graham (¼)	27,000
		Murphy (¼)	27,000
		Wilkins (¼)	27,000
	£634,000		£634,000

Creditors

	£		£
Exodus PLC	81,400	Balance b/d	91,400
Bank	10,000		
	£91,400		£91,400

Bank

	£		£
Realization—debtors	45,000	Balance b/d	303,600
Exodus PLC	368,600	Creditors	10,000
		Loan—Mrs Wilkins	100,000
	£413,600		£413,600

The question does not mention that the loan from Mrs Wilkins was repaid, but it must be assumed that it was.

Exodus PLC

	£		£
Realization—purchase price	501,000	Bank	368,600
		Creditors taken over	81,400
		Shares in Exodus PLC	
		(balancing figures — refer to	
		explanation at end of solution)	51,000
	£501,000		£501,000

If the creditors taken over had been credited to the realization account, the transfer from the realization account to the account of Exodus PLC would then have been for the net purchase price only, i.e. (£501,000 for the assets less £81,400 creditors) £419,600.

Partners' Accounts

	Graham £	Murphy £	Wilkins £		Graham £	Murphy £	Wilkins £
Realization—				Capital accounts	70,000	35,000	21,000
motor car		7,000		Current accounts	5,000	8,000	(3,000)
Loss on realization	27,000	27,000	27,000	HP loan		3,000	
Shares in Exodus				Deficiency—contra	(6,000)	(3,000)	9,000
PLC (bal. Fig.)	42,000	9,000					
	£69,000	£43,000	£27,000		£69,000	£43,00	£27,000

Note that Wilkins had a deficiency of £9,000. Because he is bankrupt and cannot introduce cash to settle this, it has to be borne by the other partners. *Garner* v. *Murray* applies; the deficiency is apportioned in proportion to the last agreed capitals of £70,000 and £35,000. The contra is therefore to Graham (£70,000/£105,000 × £9,000) £6,000 and Murphy (£35,000/£105,000 × £9,000) £3,000.

Loan — Mrs Wilkins

	£		£
Bank	100,000	Balance b/d	100,000

Hire-purchase loan re motor car

	£		£
Murphy—loan taken over	3,000	Balance b/d	3,000

The partners would normally agree between themselves who will take how many of the shares in Exodus PLC. The question gives no information on this point. Normally the shares would be taken in the same proportions as their profit sharing ratio, the balances left on the capital accounts being settled by cash payments to, and possibly from, the partners. Because there is no mention of a cash settlement in the question (and there is no balance left on the bank account) it has been assumed that the partners agreed to take the shares in settlement of the balances due on their capital accounts.

The balance of the purchase price due from Exodus PLC was £51,000.

The balances due to the partners were:

	£
Graham	42,000
Murphy	9,000
	£51,000

Exodus PLC therefore issued 42,000 £1 ordinary shares at par to Graham and 9,000 to Murphy.

Answer to question 7

a

i

PETER AND PAUL
Peter's books
Joint venture with Paul

	£		£
Apr. 1 Bank—purchase	60,000	Apr. 30 Bank—cash sales	20,000
2 Bank—lorry	5,000	May 31 Purchases—stock	
May 31 Motor running expenses	1,000	taken over	3,000
Interest receivable	1,000		
Profit and loss	11,900		
	78,900		23,000
		Jun. 30 Bank—Paul	55,900
	£78,900		£78,900

ii

Paul's Books
Joint venture with Peter

	£		£
Apr. 1 Bank—purchases	42,000	Apr. 30 Bank—cash sales	80,000
5 Bank—advertising	1,000	May 31 Bank—cash sales	30,000
8 Bank—rent	3,000	Motor vehicles—lorry	
		taken over	4,500
May 31 Interest receivable	700		
31 Profit and loss	11,900		
	58,600		114,500
Jun. 30 Bank—Peter	55,900		
	£114,500		£114,500

b

Peter and Paul
Memorandum joint venture account for the period April and May

	£	£
Sales (£20,000 + £110,000)		130,000
Less Purchases (£60,000 + £42,000	102,000	
Less Stock taken over	3,000	
		99,000
Gross profit		31,000
Less:		
Depreciation of motor lorry (£5,000 –£4,500)	500	
Motor running expenses	1,000	
Advertising	1,000	
Rent	3,000	
		5,500
Net profit		25,500

	£	£
Divided:		
Interest on contributions:		
Peter (10% × £60,000 × $^2/_{12}$)	1,000	
Paul (10% × £42,000 × $^2/_{12}$)	700	
Residue of profit:		
Peter ($^1/_2$)	11,900	
Paul ($^1/_2$)	11,900	
		25,500

Answer to question 8

Books of Silver
Consignment of typewriters to Bleu

		£			£
20.11.X8	Goods (100 × £30)	3,000	31.12.X8	Bleu—sales (40 × £60)	2,400
	Bank—freight	400		Balance c/d:	
31.12.X8	Bleu:			—stock (W1)	2,100
	—handling charges	100			
	—commission	240			
	Profits on consignments	760			
		£4,500			£4,500
1.1.X9	Balance b/d	2,100			

Bleu re consignment of typewriters

		£			£
31.12.X8	Consignment—sales	2,400	31.12.X8	Consignment	
				—handling charges	100
				—commission	240
				Balance c/d	2,060
		£2,400			£2,400
1.1.X9	Balance b/d	2,060			

Goods sent on consignment

		£			£
31.12.X8	Trading account	3,000	20.11.X8	Consignment to Bleu	3,000

Profits and losses on consignments

		£			£
31.12.X8	Profit and loss account	760	31.12.X8	Consignment to Bleu	760

Workings
1   The stock valuation is calculated as follows:

Quantity of typewriters sent	100
Less number sold	40
Number in stock at 31 December	60

Total of costs to present location and condition re 100 items:

	£
Cost of goods sent	3,000
Freight	400
Handling charges	100
	£3,500

Stock valuation:

(60/100 × £3,500)	£2,100

Answer to question 9

a The significant items that a system for accounting for containers should disclose are:

— the stocks of containers owned;
— the returnable value of containers out with customers;
— the profit or loss on containers for the period.

  Note that the balances on the customers' accounts in respect of containers will be included in the balances on the customers' accounts in the sales ledger.

b

Containers stock

	Quantity	Price	£		Quantity	Price	£
1.1.X5 Balance b/d:				31.3.X5 Hire charges	—		3,740
Stock:				Retentions	220	£8	1,760
—warehouse	150	£6	900	Scrapped	75	—	—
—customers	420	£6	2,520	Balance c/d:			
31.3.X5 Purchases	240	£8	1,920	Stock:			
Repairs	—		560	—customers	320	£6	1,920
Profit and loss (bal. fig.)			2,690	—Stock (bal. fig.)	195	£6	1,170
	810		£8,590		810		£8,590

Containers suspense

	Quantity	Price	£		Quantity	Price	£
31.3.X5 Hire charges—				1.3.X5 Balance b/d	420	£8	3,360
(1,870 × £2)			3,740	31.3.X5 Debtors	1,870	£10	18,700
Debtors-returns	1,750	£8	14,000				
Retentions	220	£8	1,760				
Balance c/d (bal. fig.)	320	£8	2,560				
	2,290		£22,060		2,290		£22,060

Answer to question 10

a

Ledger of Gunthorpe Grit PLC

Royalties payable

		£			£
19X0	TRCB (2,000 × £5)	10,000	19X0	Operating account	10,000
19X1	TRCB (7,000 × £5)	35,000	19X1	Operating account	35,000
19X2	TRCB (8,000 × £5)	40,000	19X2	Operating account	40,000

(Note that a gravel extraction company would prepare an 'operating account' rather than a 'manufacturing account').

TRCB

		£			£
19X0	Bank	25,000	19X0	Royalties payable	10,000
				Shortworkings	
				recoverable	15,000
		£25,000			£25,000
19X1	Bank	25,000	19X1	Royalties payable	35,000
	Shortworkings				
	recoverable	10,000			
		£35,000			£35,000
19X2	Bank	£40,000	19X2	Royalties payable	£40,000

Shortworkings recoverable

	£		£
19X0 TRCB	15,000	19X0 Balance c/d	15,000
19X1 Balance b/d	15,000	19X1 TRCB	10,000
		Profit and loss—	
		irrecoverable	5,000
	£15,000		£15,000

b *Ledger of Trent River Conservancy Board*

Royalties receivable

	£		£
19X0 Revenue account	10,000	19X0 Gunthorpe Grit PLC	10,000
19X1 Revenue account	35,000	19X1 Gunthorpe Grit PLC	35,000
19X2 Revenue account	40,000	19X2 Gunthorpe Grit PLC	40,000

(Note that a conservancy board would prepare a 'revenue account' rather than a 'profit and loss account'. This is a point that requires specialist knowledge and you should not lose any marks for being unaware of it).

Gunthorpe Grit PLC

	£		£
19X0 Royalties receivable	10,000	19X0 Bank	25,000
Shortworkings			
allowable	15,000		
	£25,000		£25,000
19X1 Royalties receivable	35,000	19X1 Bank	25,000
		Shortworkings	
		allowable	10,000
	£35,000		£35,000
19X2 Royalties receivable	£40,000	19X2 Bank	£40,000

Shortworkings allowable

	£		£
19X0 Balance c/d	15,000	19X0 Gunthorpe Grit PLC	15,000
19X1 Gunthorpe Grit PLC	10,000	19X1 Balance b/d	15,000
Revenue account—			
irrecoverable	5,000		
	£15,000		£15,000

(The entries in the books of the TRCB mirror the entries in the books of Gunthorpe Grit PLC.)

c An owner may insert a shortworkings clause to ensure that he will *receive* a minimum amount of income every year. This particularly applies if output is likely to be low in the initial years. The right to recovery of the shortworkings in the future may be restricted to a limited period in order to ensure that extraction is not delayed, but takes place over a reasonably short period of years.

Answer to question 11

Motor lorries

	£		£
1.1.81 Granby Garages—cash price	54,000		

Provision for depreciation
of motor lorries

	£			£
31.12.82 Balance c/d	25,002	31.12.81 P&L		12,501
		31.12.82 P&L		12,501
	£25,002			£25,002
31.12.83 balance c/d	37,503	1.1.83 Balance b/d		25,002
		31.12.83 P&L		12,501
	£37,503			£37,503
31.12.84 Balance c/d	50,004	1.1.84 Balance b/d		37,503
		31.12.84 P&L		12,501
	£50,004			£50,004

Granby Garages PLC

	£		£
1.1.81 Bank—deposit	9,000	1.1.81 Motor lorries—HP price	77,391
31.12.81 Bank—1st instal.	24,000		
31.12.81 Balance c/d	44,391		
	£77,391		£77,391
31.12.82 Bank—2nd instal.	24,000	1.1.82 Balance b/d	44,391
31.12.82 Balance c/d	20,391		
	£44,391		£44,391
31.12.83 Bank—final instal.	20,391	1.1.83 Balance b/d	20,391

HP interest suspense

	£		£
1.1.81 Granby Garages		31.12.81 P&L (W2)	11,250
— total interest (W1)	23,391	31.12.81 Balance c/d	12,141
	£23,391		£23,391
1.1.82 Balance b/d	12,141	31.1.82 P&L (W2)	8,063
		31.12.82 Balance c/d	4,078
	£12,141		£12,141
1.1.83 Balance b/d	4,078	31.12.83 P&L (W2)	4,078

Profit and loss account extracts
Year ended 31 December

	1981	1982	1983	1984
	£	£	£	£
Expenses:				
Depreciation	12,501	12,501	12,501	12,501
Hire–purchase interest	11,250	8,063	4,078	—

Balance sheet extracts
At 31 December

	1981	1982	1983	1984
	£	£	£	£
Fixed assets:				
Motor lorries at cost	54,000	54,000	54,000	54,000
Less Accumulated depreciation	12,501	25,002	37,503	50,004
	£41,499	£28,998	£16,497	£3,996

	1981	1982	1983	1984
	£	£	£	£
Long–term liabilities:				
Obligations under hire-purchase contracts (W3)	16,313			
Current liabilities:				
Obligations under hire-purchase contracts (W3)	15,937	16,313		
Note to balance sheet:				
Net book value of fixed assets held under hire–purchase				
contracts	41,499	28,998	16,497	—

Workings

1 Calculation of total interest:

	£
Deposit	9,000
2 instalments × £24,000	48,000
Final instalment	20,391
Hire–purchase price	77,391
Less cash price—3 × £18,000	54,000
Total interest	23,391

2 Interest apportionment:

	£
Cash price	54,000
Less Deposit	9,000
Balance of cash price	45,000
31.12.81 Interest 25%	11,250
	56,250
31.12.81 1st instalment	24,000
	32,250
31.12.82 Interest 25%	8,063
	40,313
31.12.82 2nd instalment	24,000
	16,313
31.12.83 Interest 25%	4,078
	20,391
31.12.83 Final instalment	20,391
	—

Calculation of depreciaiton charge:

	£
Cash price per vehicle	18,000
Less Scrap value	1,333
Total depreciation over	
useful life	£16,667

÷ 4 years = £4,167 per vehicle per annum × 3 vehicles = £12,501 per annum.

3

The hire–purchase loans shown on the balance sheet are the balance of the cash price outstanding, arrived at by netting the balance on the hire–purchase interest suspense account against the balance of the hire–purchase price shown on the hire–purchase company's account, namely:

	1981	1982
	£	£
Granby Garages PLC	44,391	20,391
Less Hire-purchase interest suspense	12,141	4,078
	£32,250	£16,313

These balances have to be further analysed for 1981:

	£
Payable within one year (instalment of £24,000 less future interest of £8,063 included)	15,937
Payable after one year (instalment of £20,391 less future interest of £4,078 included)	16,313
	£32,250

(The accounting entries in the books of the seller for this question are given in the answer to question 12.)

Answer to question 12

Hire purchase sales

	£		£
31.12.81 Hire-purchase trading		1.1.81 Bulwell Aggregates—	
	54,000	cash price	54,000

Hire-purchase interest suspense

	£		£
31.12.81 Hire purchase trading	11,250	1.1.81 Bulwell Aggregates	23,391
31.12.81 Balance c/d	12,141		
	£23,391		£23,391
31.12.82 Hire-purchase trading	8,063	1.1.82 Balance b/d	12,141
31.12.82 Balance c/d	4,078		
	£12,141		£12,141
31.12.83 Hire-purchase trading	4,078	1.1.83 Balance b/d	4,078

Bulwell Aggregates Ltd

	£		£
1.1.81 Hire-purchase sales		1.1.81 Bank—deposit	9,000
HP price		31.12.81 Bank—1st inst.	24,000
		31.12.81 Balance c/d	44,391
	£77,391		£77,391
1.1.82 Balance b/d	44,391	31.12.82 Bank—2nd inst.	24,000
		31.12.82 Balance c/d	20,391
	£44,391		£44,391
1.1.83 Balance b/d	20,391	31.12.83 Bank—final inst.	20,391

Hire–purchase trading account extracts

	1981	1982	1983
	£	£	£
Sales	54,000		
Less Cost of sales (3 × £14,400)	43,200		
Selling profit	10,800		
Interest	11,250	8,063	4,078
Hire-purchase profit	£22,050	£8,063	£4,078

This is the same data as that given in question 11 dealing with the books of the buyer. Refer to the answer to that question for workings calculating the hire-purchase interest.

Answer to question 13

a

Cost of goods sold

	£		£
31.12.83 Purchases	65,000	31.12.83 HP trading	65,000

HP sales

	£		£
31.12.83 HP trading	90,000	31.12.83 Customers	90,000

Customers

	£		£
31.12.83 HP sales	90,000	31.12.83 Bank—deposits rec'd	22,500
		—inst. rec'd	49,600
		Repossessed goods	1,800
		Balance c/d:	
		—due	400
		—not due	15,700
	£90,000		£90,000

Repossessed goods

	£		£
31.12.83 Customers	1,800	31.12.83 HP trading unrealized profit	514
31.12.83 Bank—expenses	30	31.12.83 Balance c/d:	
		stock	1,100
		HP trading loss	216
	£1,830		£1,830

HP trading account

	£		£
31.12.83 Cost of goods sold	65,000	31.12.83 Sales	90,000
31.12.83 Gross earnings c/d 25,000			
	£90,000		£90,000
31.12.83 Repossessed goods:		31.12.83 Gross earnings b/d	25,000
—unrealized profit	514		
—loss	216		
	730		
Provision for unrealized profit	4,357		
HP profit	19,913		
	£25,000		£25,000

Provision for unrealized profit on HP sales

	£		£
31.12.83 Balance c/d	4,357	31.12.83 HP trading	4,357

In this question the normal selling price of the goods on cash sales is not given. It is not possible to calculate the selling profit and interest as separate items. The gross earnings (hire–purchase price less cost) will be apportioned in total over the life of the agreement.

The gross earnings on the sale of the goods which were repossessed was (£2,800–£2,000) £800. The cash collected from customers was (£700 + £300) £1,000, leaving a balance of £1,800 due. The proportion of profit and interest not earned at the date of repossession will be:

$$\frac{\text{Balance outstanding}}{\text{HP sales}} \times \text{Gross earnings} = \frac{£1,800}{£2,800} \times £800 = £514$$

The repossessed goods remain unsold and are carried down as stock in hand on the repossessed goods account. They are valued at the lower of cost (£2,000) and net realizable value (£1,500 – £400) £1,100.

The provision for unrealized profit is the amount not yet earned on the instalments not yet due:

$$\frac{\text{Balance outstanding}}{\text{HP sales}} \times \text{Gross earnings} = \frac{£15,700}{£90,000 - £2,800} \times £25,000 - £800 = £4,357$$

Note that it has been necessary to delete from sales and earnings the amounts relating to the repossessed goods.

b Balance sheet entries at 31 December 1983:

Stocks   £1,100
HP debtors   £11,743

Stocks represent the repossessed goods held at the balance sheet date for resale. They are valued at net realizable value as it is lower than the original cost of these goods.

HP debtors represents the amounts receivable from the customers (£16,100) less the amount of gross earnings that will be recognized as profit in the future (£4,357).

Answer to question 14

a   Trading and profit and loss accounts for the year ended 31 August 1984

	Televisions		Videos		Whole Business	
	£	£	£	£	£	£
Sales—cash sales		180,000		—		180,000
—HP sales (W3)		140,000		380,000		520,000
		320,000		380,000		700,000
Less Cost of sales:						
Purchases	150,000		140,000		290,000	
Less Stock (W1)	7,500		7,000		14,500	
		142,500		133,000		275,500
Gross earnings/selling profit		177,500		247,000		424,500
Provision for unrealized profit (W2)		(65,625)				(65,625)
HP interest earned (W4)				49,400		49,400
Gross profit		£111,875		£296,400		408,275
Less:						
Retailing expenses					179,275	
Depreciation					9,000	
						188,275
Net profit						£220,000

b

Balance sheet as at 31 August 1984

	£	£	£
	Cost	Depreciation	
Fixed assets	45,000	9,000	36,000
Current assets:			
Stock		14,500	
Debtors		1,000	
HP debtors (W5)		331,975	
		347,475	
Less Current liabilities:			
Creditors	121,000		
Bank overdraft	8,475		
		129,475	
Working capital			218,000
			254,000
Financed by:			
Capital introduced			50,000
Net profit			220,000
			270,000
Less Drawings			16,000
			254,000

Workings

1 Stocks are calculated:

	Televisions	Videos
Number purchased	1,000	400
Less Cash sales	(600)	—
HP sales	(350)	(380)
Number in stock	50	20
Cost	£150	£350
Stock valuation	£7,500	£7,000

2 Provision for unrealized profit on HP sales of televisions:

$$\frac{£105,000}{£140,000} \times 350 \times (£400 - £150) = £65,625$$

3 HP sales of videos are analysed:

	£	£
Cash price	1,000 × 380	380,000
Interest	260 × 380	98,800
HP price	£1,260 × 380	£478,800

4 Interest earned on video sales is to be apportioned equally over the two years of the agreement (the straight line method).
It is not possible to calculate from the data given the number of months of interest earned on each contract during 1984. The interest can only be apportioned:

1984	£49,400	credit to profit and loss account
1985	£49,400	carried foward
	£98,800	

5 HP debtors are:

		£
Televisions	(£105,000 – £65,625)	30,375
Videos	(£342,000 – £49,400)	292,600
		£331,975

Answer to question 15

a The transactions of the branch should be recorded within the existing accounting system.

The branch manager should requisition supplies of goods from head office. Delivery notes should accompany the goods specifying the selling price of the items. The branch manager should sign for the goods delivered. Goods supplied to the branch should be charged to a branch stock account at selling price. All sales should be recorded on a cash till and the till rolls and accompanying copy bank paying-in slips should be returned to head office weekly. Cash sales banked by the branch should be credited to the branch stock account.

Periodically the stock at the branch should be counted and valued at selling price and a return made of this by the branch manager to head office. Any discrepancy between the balance on the branch stock account and the actual stocks should be investigated. Occasional stock counts by independant personnel will be necessary.

Any proposed reductions in selling price should be notified to head office by the branch manager for approval and recording on the branch stock account.

Detailed stock records should be maintained at the branch but these may be restricted to quantities only.

The branch manager should be given a petty cash float. A summary of expenditure, supported by vouchers, should be returned to head office for weekly re-imbursement.

Personnel records and the payroll should be maintained at head office. All expense invoices relating to the branch should pass through the head office accounting system after approval by the branch manager. Separate expense accounts for the branch should be opened in the head office books.

The advantages that will accrue from such a system include:

— no need to employ accounting staff at the branch;
— the accounting information is readily available to the proprietor at head office;
— the proprietor can dictate the selling prices at the branch;
— control is exercised over branch stocks and cash takings to identify any shortages.

b

Branch stock (at selling price)

	£		£
Goods sent	52,500	Goods returned	2,500
		Bank — cash sales	44,000
		Stock deficiency (bal. fig.)	1,200
		Balance c/d — stock	4,800
	£52,500		£52,500

Goods sent to branch

	£		£
Branch stock — returns	2,000	Branch stock	42,000
Head office trading	40,000		
	£42,000		£42,000

Branch stock adjustment

	£		£
Branch stock — returns	500	Branch stock (25/100×£42,000)	10,500
Branch stock (W1)	240		

	£		£
Branch profit and loss—gross profit	8,800		
Balance c/d (W2)	960		
	£10,500		£10,500

Branch profit and loss account

	£		£
Stock deficiency—at cost (W1)	960	Gross profit	8,800
Rent	580		
Rates	250		
Wages	1,860		
General expenses	1,426		
Net profit	3,724		
	£8,800		£8,800

Workings

1   Stock deficiency is analysed:

	£
At cost (100/125 × £1,200)	960
Profit not realized (25/125 × £1,200)	240
	£1,200

2   Provision for unrealized profit on closing stock:
25/125 × £4,800 = £960

Answer to question 16

a   Nottingham branch stock (at selling price)

		£			£
1.11.84	Balance b/d — stock	21,620	30.11.84	Goods returned to HO	1,245
30.11.84	Goods sent	119,330		Bank — cash sales	54,837
	Debtors — returns	916		Debtors — credit sales	65,241
				Damaged stock	315
				Expenses pd from cash sales	3,432
				Wages pd from cash sales	1,920
				Balance c/d — stock	13,500
				Stock deficiency	1,376
		£141,866			£141,866

Goods sent to Nottingham branch

		£			£
30.11.84	Goods returned		30.11.84	Branch stock	95,464
	(100/125 × £1,245)	996			
	HO trading	94,468			
		95,464			95,464

Nottingham branch stock adjustment

		£			£
30.11.84	Goods returned (25/125 × £1,245)	249	1.11.84	Balance b/d (25/125 × £21,260)	4,324
	Damaged stock (25/125 × £315)	63	30.11.84	Branch stock (25/125 × £119,330)	23,866
	Stock deficiency (25/125 × £1,376)	275			
	Balance c/d — stock provision				
	(25/125 × £13,500)	2,700			
	Branch p/l — gross profit	24,903			
		£28,190			£28,190

Nottingham branch debtors

	£		£
1.11.84 Balance b/d	14,270	30.11.84 Credit sales	
30.11.84 Credit sales	65,241	returns	916
		Bank	58,793
		Bad debts	1,815
		Balance c/d	17,987
	£79,511		£79,511

Nottingham branch bad debts

	£		£
30.11.84 Debtors	1,815	30.11.84 Profit and loss	1,815

Nottingham branch stock losses

	£		£
30.11.84 Branch stock—damaged stock			
(100/125 × 315)	252		
Branch stock—deficiency			
(100/125 × £1,376)	1,101	30.11.84 Profit and loss	1,353
	£1,353		£1,353

Nottingham branch expenses

	£		£
30.11.84 Branch stock	3,432		
Bank	14,861	30.11.84 Profit and loss	18,293
	£18,293		£18,293

Nottingham branch wages

	£		£
30.11.84 Branch stock	1,920		
Balance c/d—commission	249	30.11.84 Profit and loss	2,169
	£2,169		£2,169

Nottingham branch profit and loss account for the month of November 1984

	£		£
Stock losses	1,353	Gross profit	24,903
Expenses	18,293		
Wages	2,169		
Bad debts	1,815		
Net profit	1,273		
	£24,903		£24,903

b Possible reasons for the stock losses include:
— cash takings misappropriated;
— credit sales not recorded;
— goods sold at less than the standard selling price of cost plus 25%;
— error in stock count.

Answer to question 17

OXFORD TRADING COMPANY

Trading and profit and loss account
For the year ended 31 March 1982

	Head office		Branch	
	£	£	£	£
Sales		94,637		61,348
Less Cost of sales:				
Opening stocks	17,300		9,020	
Purchases	90,844		—	
Transfer	(37,579)		37,028	
	70,565		46,048	
Less Closing stocks	15,790		4,215	
		54,775		41,833
Gross profit		39,862		19,515
Less				
Depreciation of furniture and fittings	353		87	
Rent and rates	2,636		3,315	
General expenses	5,678		3,250	
Wages and salaries	12,585		8,393	
		21,252		15,045
Profit before bonuses		18,610		4,470
Less Staff bonuses (10%)		1,861		447
Net profit		£16,749		£4,023

Balance sheet at 31 March 1982

	£	£	£
Fixed assets:			
Freehold premises		20,005	
Furniture and fittings			
(£3,530 – £353 + £870 – £87)		3,960	
			23,965
Current assets:			
Stocks (£15,790 + £4,215)		20,005	
Debtors (W1)		7,216	
Cash at bank (W2)		5,722	
		32,943	
Less Current liabilities:			
Creditors (£8,238 + £468)	8,706		
Staff bonuses (£1,861 + £447)	2,308		
Bank overdraft	3,000		
		14,014	
Net current assets			18,929
			£42,894
Financed by:			
Capital:			
At 1.4.1981		32,122	
Net profit for year:			
— head office	16,749		
— branch	4,023		
		20,772	
		52,894	
Less Drawings		10,000	
			£42,894

Workings

1

	£
Debtors:	
Oxford	3,093
Croydon	3,572
Insurance claim re stock	551
	£7,216

2

	£
Cash at bank:	
Oxford	4,652
Croydon	595
Cash in transit (£50,800 – £50,325)	475
	£5,722

In considering the above note that the goods that were stolen in transit have not been included in stocks as goods in transit. Instead a debtor has been raised on the insurance company for the amount of the claim.

The interbranch accounts will be finalized as follows:

Head office books

Croydon branch

	£		£
Balance per trial balance	52,578	Remittances per trial balance	50,325
Net profit	4,023	Insurance company re stock claim	551
		Balance c/d — cash in transit	475
		Balance c/d	5,250
	£56,601		£56,601

Branch books

Head office

	£		£
Remittances per trial balance	50,800	Balance per trial balance	52,027
Balance c/d	5,250	Net profit	4,023
	£56,050		£56,050

Answer to question 18

ALLIED ATHLETIC TRADERS

Trading and profit and loss accounts for the year ended 31 December 19 3

	London		Cambridge	
	£	£	£	£
Sales		84,740		53,453
Less Cost of sales				
Opening stock	22,500		9,620	
Purchases	96,471			
Transfers	(38,434)		36,489	
	80,537		46,109	
Less Closing stock	28,500		2,600	
		52,037		43,509
Gross profit		32,703		9,944
Less Expenses:				

	London		Cambridge	
	£	£	£	£
Rent and rates				
(£2,418 + £200)	2,618			
(£4,210 − £500)			3,710	
General expenses	7,850		1,211	
Wages and salaries	13,490		3,208	
Depreciation				
— buildings	540			
— fixtures and fittings	1,100		675	
— vehicles	1,800		980	
		27,398		9,784
Net profit before bonuses		5,305		160
Less Manager's bonus				
(10/110 × £5,305)		482		
(10/110 × £160)				15
Net profit		£4,823		£145

Balance sheet at 31 December 1983

	£	£	£
Fixed assets:	Cost	Acc. Dep.	
Freehold premises	47,000	2,540	44,460
Fixtures and fittings	17,751	10,375	7,376
Vehicles	13,900	11,980	1,920
	£78,651	£24,895	53,756
Current assets:			
Stocks (W1)		32,195	
Debtors (£1,741 + £4,650 + £850) (W3)		7,241	
Prepayment		500	
Bank (£750 + £450) (W2)		1,200	
		41,136	
Less Current liabilities:			
Creditors	18,351		
Expenses owing (£200 + £482 + £15)	697		
Bank overdraft	6,498		
		25,546	
			15,590
			£69,346
Financed by:			
Capital			45,000
Retained earnings:			
At 1 January 19 3		35,180	
Net profit:			
— London	4,823		
— Cambridge	145		
		4,968	
		40,148	
Less Drawings		15,802	
			24,346
			£69,346

Workings

1

Stocks:	£
— London	28,500
— Cambridge	2,600

Stocks:	£
— Goods in transit (W3)	1,095
	£32,195

2

Remittances to head office	55,900
Remittances from branch	55,450
Cash in transit	£450

3

Goods sent to branch	38,434
Goods from head office	36,489
Goods not received	£1,945
of which:	
Stock — goods in transit	1,095
Debtors — insurance claim	850
	£1,945

a In considering this answer note that the accounts are for a sole trader. No profit and loss appropriation account is required, the net profits being credited straight to the capital account or the current account if one is kept. In this example the current account is called 'Retained earnings', but this description is more normally used for the balance left on the profit and loss account of a limited company.

The following accounts are not required to answer the question, but are given for information.

Head office books

Cambridge branch

	£		£
Balance per trial balance	69,486	Bank — remittances	55,450
Net profit	145	Insurance company	850
		Balance c/d — goods in transit	1,095
		Balance c/d — cash in transit	450
			57,845
		Balance c/d	11,786
	£69,631		£69,631

Branch books

London head office

	£		£
Bank — remittances	55,900	Balance per trial balance	67,541
Balance c/d	11,786	Net profit	145
	£67,686		£67,686

b The most significant factor in the accounts that needs to be brought to the attention of the proprietor is that the drawings far exceed the net profit for the year.

Answer to question 19

a

JOURNAL

		Debit	Credit
		£	£
1.1.82	20% debentures (1980/83)	100,000	
	Share premium — premium on redemption	5,000	
	Bank		105,000
	Repayment of debentures at £105.		

		Debit	Credit
		£	£
1.1.82	Bank	97,000	
	Share premium — discount on issue	3,000	
	12% convertible loan stock		100,000
	Issue of loan stock at £97.		
30.6.82	10% preference shares	150,000	
	Bank		150,000
	Redemption at par.		
30.6.82	Bank	75,000	
	Ordinary shares of 10 pence		50,000
	Share premium		25,000
	Issue of 500,000 shares at 15 pence.		
30.6.82	General reserve	75,000	
	Capital redemption reserve		75,000
	Transfer required by the Companies Act 1985.		
1.12.82	Capital redemption reserve	75,000	
	Share premium	37,000	
	General reserve	38,000	
	Ordinary shares of 10 pence		150,000
	3 for 5 bonus issue of 1,500,000 shares of 10 pence		
31.12.82	12% convertible loan stock	20,000	
	Ordinary shares of 10 pence		16,000
	Share premium		4,000
	Conversion of £20,000 loan stock to 160,000		
	ordinary shares on terms of 800 shares per £100		
	of stock.		

Workings

Share premium

	£		£
Premium on redemption of			
debentures	5,000	Balance b/d	20,000
Discount on issue of loan stock	3,000	Premium on share issue	25,000
Bonus issue	37,000		
	£45,000		£45,000

b The capital redemption reserve was created to meet the requirements of the Companies Act 1985. If share capital is redeemed other than out of the proceeds of a new issue the transfer is required to be made out of distributable profits. It is designed to keep the capital of the company intact and provides a degree of protection to creditors of the company.

Answer to question 20

a

JOURNAL

		Debit	Credit
		£	£
1.1.85	14% redeemable preference shares	300,000	
	Bank		300,000
	Redemption at par.		

		Debit	Credit
		£	£
1.1.85	Bank	140,000	
	Ordinary shares of 25 pence		100,000
	Share premium		40,000
	Issue of 400,000 shares at 35 pence.		
1.1.85	General reserve	160,000	
	Capital redemption reserve		160,000
	Transfer required by the Companies Act 1985.		
30.6.85	18% debentures 1983/86	400,000	
	Share premium — premium on redemption	4,000	
	Bank		404,000
	Redemption at £101.		
30.6.85	Bank	294,000	
	Share premium — discount on issue	6,000	
	14% convertible loan stock		300,000
	Issue at £98.		
30.12.85	14% convertible loan stock	50,000	
	Ordinary shares of 25 pence		40,000
	Share premium		10,000
	Conversion to 160,000 ordinary shares on terms of		
	320 shares for £100 stock.		

b

Equity:	31.12.84	31.12.85
	£000	£000
Ordinary share (W1)	1,400	1,540
Capital redemption reserve		160
Share premium (W2)	100	140
Premises revaluation reserve	290	290
General reserve (W3)	670	510
	£2,460	£2,640
Fixed return capital:		
14% preference shares	300	—
18% debentures	400	—
14% convertible loan stock (W4)	—	250
	£700	£250
Gearing		
(£700/£2,460)	0.3:1	
(£250/£2,640)		0.1:1

The company was low geared at the beginning of the year. The redemption of the preference shares and debentures during the year has further reduced the gearing. Only a small proportion of the company's long-term capital employed has been financed by debt.

Workings

1

	£000
Ordinary shares at 31.12.84	1,400
Issued	100
Loan stock conversion	40
	£1,540

2

Share premium at 31.12.84	100
Premium on issue of shares	40

	£000
Premium on redemption of debentures	(4)
Discount on issue of loan stock	(6)
Premium on conversion of loan stock	10
	£140

3

General reserve at 31.12.84	670
Capital redemption reserve	(160)
	£510

4

14% Convertible loan stock issued	300
Conversion to ordinary shares	(50)
	£250

Answer to question 21

a

Deferred tax

	£		£
31.12.82 Balance c/d	178,000	1.1.82 Balance b/d	178,000

Corporation tax

	£		£
1.1.82 Bank	94,208	1.1.82 Balance b/d	
15.6.82 ACT recoverable	36,000	— CT 1980	94,208
5.11.82 ACT recoverable	18,000	— CT 1981	140,000
31.12.82 Profit and loss — over-			
provision	12,569	— CT 1982	170,000
Balance c/d:			
— CT 1981	127,431		
— CT 1982 (£170,000 –			
(£36,000 + £18,000))	116,000		
	£404,208		£404,208

(See note at end of this answer.)

ACT payable

	£		£
15.6.82 Bank	36,000	1.1.82 Balance b/d	36,000
5.11.82 bank (30/70 + £42,000)	18,000	1.9.82 ACT recoverable —	
		interim div.	18,000
31.12.82 Balance c/d	45,000	31.12.82 ACT recoverable — final	
		div. (30/70 × £105,000)	45,000
	£99,000		£99,000

ACT recoverable

	£		£
1.1.82 Balance b/d	36,000	15.6.82 Corporation tax	36,000
1.9.82 ACT payable	18,000	5.11.82 Corporation tax	18,000
31.12.82 ACT payable	45,000	31.12.82 Balance c/d	45,000
	£99,000		£99,000

Dividends

	£		£
1.5.82 Bank	84,000	1.1.82 Balance b/d	84,000
1.9.82 Bank — interim	42,000	31.12.82 Profit and loss	147,000
21.12.82 Balance c/d — proposed	105,000		
	£231,000		£231,000

b   Balance sheet extract at 31 December 1982

£

Creditors: amounts falling due within one year:
Other creditors — taxation   127,431
           — ACT Payable   45,000
           — dividend   105,000
Creditors: amounts falling due after more than one year:
Other creditors — taxation   116,000
Provisions for liabilities and charges:
Deferred taxation (£178,000 – £45,000)   133,000

Note:
The question states that 'Incorporated Developments PLC maintains separate accounts for the provision for corporation tax, current and future.' To meet this requirement an account could be maintained for each year's corporation tax as follows:

Corporation tax 1980

		£			£
1.1.82	Bank	94,208	1.1.82	Balance b/d	94,208

Corporation tax 1981

		£			£
31.12.82	Profit and loss —				
	overprovision	12,569	1.1.82	Balance b/d	140,000
	Balance c/d	127,431			
		£140,000			£140,000

Corporation tax 1982

		£			£
15.6.82	ACT recoverable	36,000			
5.11.82	ACT recoverable	18,000	31.12.82	Profit and loss	170,000
31.12.82	Balance c/d	116,000			
		£170,000			£170,000

Answer to question 22

a Under the 'imputation system' of corporation tax dividends received from another company are imputed to have already been subject to tax and no further tax is payable by the receiving company on the dividend. A dividend received by an individual has a tax credit attaching to it.

    The company paying the dividend has to account to the Inland Revenue for advanced corporation tax, but may recover this by deduction from its corporation tax liability.

b Refer to Chapter 16.

£

c   **i** Profit and loss account:
      Dividends received (100/70 × £24,500)   35,000
      Tax attributable to franked investment income (30/70 × £24,500)   (10,500)

  ii Proft and loss account:
      Dividend — proposed   (91,000)
      Balance sheet:
      Creditors: amounts falling due within one year
      — Dividends   91,000
      — ACT payable   39,000
      ACT recoverable (deducted from deferred tax if any, otherwise
        included in debtors)   39,000

iii Profit and loss account:

	£
Debenture interest	(6,000)
Balance sheet:	
Creditors: amounts falling due within one year:	
— Income tax	1,800

Answer to question 23

GREENWARE LTD

Profit and loss account for the year ended 31 December 1984

	£	£	Note
Turnover		2,640,300	
Less Cost of sales (W1)		2,067,500	
Gross profit		572,800	
Less Distribution costs (W2)	248,920		
Administrative expenses (W3)	207,980		
		456,900	
		115,900	
Add Income from listed investments (W4)		3,000	
		118,900	
Less Interest payable (W5)		20,000	
Profit on ordinary activities before tax		98,900	
Less Corporation tax	45,000		
Tax attributable to franked investment income	900		
		45,900	
Profit on ordinary activities after tax		53,000	
Add Extraordinary gain — profit on sale of premises		40,000	
Profit after tax for the year		93,000	
Less Ordinary dividend — proposed		56,000	
Retained profit		£37,000	
Earning per share		26.5 pence	5

Balance sheet as at 31 December 1984

	£	£	Notes
Fixed assets:			
Tangible assets:			
Office equipment	110,060		
Vehicles	235,000		
		345,060	
Investments		20,000	
		365,060	
Current assets:			
Stocks	340,600		
Debtors	438,626		
Cash at bank	20,640		
	799,866		
Less Creditors: amounts falling due within one year			
Trade creditors	428,250		
Other creditors	124,100		2
Accruals (W8)	31,300		
	583,650		

	£	£	Notes
Net current assets		216,216	
Total assets less current liabilities		581,276	
Less Creditors: amounts falling due after more than			
one year			
10% loan stock		200,000	
		£381,276	
Capital and reserves			
Called–up share capital		200,000	3
Profit and loss account		181,276	4
		£381,276	

(Note that this question is unusual in that the information required by the Companies Act in relation to fixed assets has not been supplied. Information that is required to be disclosed is often omitted from examination questions merely to restrict the size of the questions.)

Notes to the accounts

1

	£
Debtors:	
Trade debtors (W6)	403,326
ACT recoverable after more than one year (W7)	23,100
Prepayment	12,200
	£438,626

2

	£
Other creditors:	
Proposed dividend	56,000
Corporation tax	45,000
ACT payable (W7)	23,100
	£124,100

3

Share capital:	Issued
	£
200,000 ordinary shares of £1	200,000

4 Movements on reserve — profit and loss account:

	£
At 1.1.84	144,276
Retained profit	37,000
At 31.12.84	£181,276

5 Earnings per share: calculated on profits on ordinary activities after tax of £53,000, divided by 200,000 ordinary shares = 26.5 pence.

Workings

1

Cost of sales	£
Stocks at 1.1.84	318,500
Purchases	2,089,600
	2,408,100
Less Stocks at 31.12.84	340,600
	£2,067,500

2	Distribution costs:		£
	Selling and distribution costs		216,320
	Accrual		21,300
	Bad debts		8,900
	Increase in bad debts provision ((3/100 × £415,800) − £10,074)		2,400
			£248,920

3	Administration expenses:		£
	Per trial balance		220,180
	Prepayments		(12,200)
			£207,980

4	Income from investments:		£
	Dividends received		2,100
	Attaching tax credit (30/70 × £2,100)		900
	Gross		£3,000

5	Interest payable:		£
	Per trial balance		10,000
	Accrual		10,000
			£20,000

6	Trade debtors:		£
	Per trial balance		415,000
	Less Provision for doubtful debts:		
	At 1.1.84	10,074	
	Increase	2,400	
			12,474
			£403,326

7	ACT payable:	
	((30/70 × (£56,000 − £2,100))	= £23,100
	or alternative calculation:	

		£
30/70 of dividend £56,000		24,000
Less Tax credit on dividends received		900
ACT Payable		23,100

(This amount is also included in debtors as ACT recoverable. If a deferred tax account existed it would have been deducted from the deferred tax balance.)

8	Accruals:	£
	Distribution costs	21,300
	Loan stock interest	10,000
		£31,300

Answer to question 24

REDWOOD PLC

Profit and loss account for the year ended 30 June 1984

	£000	£000	Notes
Turnover		1,200	1
Less Cost of sales (W1)		400	
Gross profit		800	
Less Distribution cost (W2)	440		
Administrative expenses (W3)	210		
		650	
		150	

	£000	£000	Notes
Add Income from fixed asset investment (W4)		20	2
		170	
Less Interest payable		5	
Profit on ordinary activities before tax		165	3
Less Corporation tax	50		
Tax attributable to franked investment income (W4)	6		
		56	4
Profit on ordinary activities after tax		109	
Less Extraordinary item:			
Redundancy costs	30		
Less Tax relief	15		
		15	
Profit after tax for the year		94	
Less Dividends:			
Interim — paid	7		
Final — proposed	28		
		35	
Retained profit		£59	11
Earnings per share 38.9 pence			12

Balance sheet at 30 June 1984

	£000	£000	Notes
Fixed assets:			
Tangible assets:			
Furniture and fittings		60	5
Investments		70	6
		130	
Current assets:			
Stock	300		7
Debtors	279		8
Cash at bank and in hand	56		
	635		
Less Creditors: amounts falling due within one year			
Trade creditors	60		
Other creditors (W5)	66		9
Accruals (W6)	56		
	182		
Net current assets		453	
Total assets less current liabilities		583	
Less Creditors: amounts falling due after more than one year			
10% debenture loan stock	50		
Provisions for liabilities and charges			
Deferred tax (W7)	34		
		84	
		£499	
Capital and reserves:			
Called-up share capital		280	10
Share premium account		70	
Profit and loss account		149	11
		£499	

Notes to the accounts

1 Turnover consists of sales excluding VAT.

	£000
2 Income from investments:	
Dividends from quoted company	20

	£000
3 Profit on ordinary activities before tax is after charging:	
Auditors remuneration	20
Hire charges	340
Depreciation	40
Directors' emoluments	55

4 Corporation tax is based on the profits for the year at a rate of 50%.

Fixed assets — furniture and fittings:

5	£000
Cost	200
Accumulated depreciation:	
At 1.7.83	100
Profit and loss account	40
At 30.6.84	£140
Net book value	60

	£000
6 Investments:	
Market value at 30 June 1984	85

	£000
7 Stocks:	
Goods for resale	300

	£000
8 Debtors:	
Trade debtors	250
Prepayments	29
	£279

	£000
9 Other creditors:	
Proposed dividends	28
Corporation tax	32
ACT payable	6
	£66

	£000
10 Share capital:	
Authorized:	
350,000 ordinary shares of £1 each	350
Issued:	
280,000 ordinary shares of £1 each	280

	£000
11 Movement on reserves:	
Profit and loss account:	
At 1.7.83	90
Retained profit for the year	59
At 30.6.84	£149

12 Earnings per share are calculated on profit on ordinary activities after tax of £109,000 divided by 280,000 ordinary shares of £1 each.

Workings

1 Cost of sales:	£000
Opening stock	200
Purchases	500
	700
Less Closing stock	300
	£400

2 Distribution costs:	£000
Per trial balance	100
Hire charges	340
	£440

3 Administrative expenses:	£000
Per trial balance	150
Auditors' remuneration	20
Depreciation of furniture and fittings	40
	£210

4 Dividends are shown gross:
100/70 × £14,000 = £20,000
Tax attributable to dividends:
30/70 × £14,000 = £6,000

5 Other creditors:	£000
Corporation tax:	
Provision on ordinary profits	50
Less Relief on extraordinary loss	(15)
	35
Less ACT paid on interim dividend	(3)
	32
Proposed dividend	28
ACT payable on proposed dividend:	
30/70 × (£28 – £14)	6
	£66

6 Accruals:	£000
Accrued expenses	26
Redundancy costs	30
	£56

7 Deferred tax:	£000
Per trial balance	40
Less ACT recoverable re proposed dividend	6
	£34

Answer to question 25

This is a complex question and it may be helpful to outline the action required on the additional information given in the question.

1 The increase in the doubtful debts provision is to be added to selling expenses.
The increased provision is deducted from debtors.
2 Administrative expenses should be increased by providing £12,000 for directors' fees.
This is to be included in the balance sheet as an accrual. The sales director's

remuneration and fees should be transferred to distribution costs. As the total directors' emoluments exceed £60,000 additional disclosure notes are required.

3 Depreciation is to be provided. The additions to fixed assets must be disclosed in a note.

4 Provision is to be made for corporation tax. The basis of calculating the provision must be disclosed in a note.

5 Provision is to be made for the final preference and ordinary dividends. Provision is to be made for ACT payable, the rate of income tax being given in note 9. The ACT recoverable is included in debtors as there is no deferred tax account from which it could be deducted.

6 Disclose as a movement on reserves.

7 Disclose as a note.

8 Disclose as a note.

9 See (5).

10 Transfer to interest payable.

11 The holding is less than 20% of the share capital of Crampon Ltd. It is not a related company. The holding in fact is less than 10% and therefore the additional disclosure notes (name of company etc.) are not required. The action required is to write down the cost of the investment on the assumption that the fall in value is permanent.

ALPINE ATHLETIC TRAINING PLC

Profit and loss account for the year ended 31 December 1983

	£	£	Notes
Turnover		2,925,900	1
Less Cost of sales (W1)		1,802,397	
Gross Profit		1,123,503	
Less Distribution costs (W2)	185,259		
Administrative expenses (W3)	789,552		
		974,811	
		148,692	2
Less Amount written off investment	57,000		
Interest payable (W4)	20,244		
		77,244	3
Profit on ordinary activities before tax		71,448	
Less Corporation tax		60,000	4
Profit on ordinary activities after tax		11,448	
Less Dividends			
Preference — paid	2,100		
— proposed	2,100		
	4,200		
Ordinary — proposed	39,000		
		43,200	
Reduction in retained profits		£31,752	
Earnings per share		1.2 pence	10

(It is unusual in an examination question for the dividends to exceed the profit for the year. It is probable that the examiner did not expect the trade investment, stated in the trial balance at a cost of £72,000, to be written down to the directors' estimate of its value of £15,000 (given in note 11 to the question). The Act requires a write-down if the reduction in value is expected to be permanent. This would seem to be a reasonable assumption to make from the information given.)

Balance sheet at 31 December 1983

	£	£	Notes
Fixed assets:			5
Tangible assets		681,000	
Investments		15,000	
		696,000	
Current assets:			
Stock	282,528		
Debtors	457,687		6
	740,215		
Less Creditors: amounts falling due within one year			
Bank overdraft	354,528		
Trade creditors	371,022		
Other creditors (W6)	117,814		7
Accruals (W7)	19,500		
	862,864		
Net current assets		(122,649)	
Total assets less current liabilities		573,351	
Less Creditors: amounts falling due after more than one year			
10% debentures 1990/93 (secured on premises)		150,000	
		£423,351	
Capital and reserves:			
Called-up share capital		360,000	8
Other reserves:			
General reserve		45,000	9
Profit and loss account		18,351	9
		£423,351	

Notes to the accounts

1 Turnover consists of sales.
2 Profit on ordinary activities before tax is arrived at after charging:

	£	£
Directors' fees	12,000	
Directors' remuneration	181,500	
		193,500
Audit fee		3,000
Depreciation		24,000

Directors' emoluments include:

	£
Chairman	27,000
Highest paid director	63,000

The directors' gross emoluments were within the following bands:

Number	
1	£25,001 – £30,000
2	£50,001 – £55,000
1	£60,001 – £65,000

3 Interest payable:

	£
On overdraft	5,244
On debentures repayable after 5 years	15,000
	£20,244

4   Corporation tax is based on profits for the year at a rate of 52%.

5   Fixed assets:

	Freehold land	Freehold buildings	Plant and machinery	Motor vehicles	Total
	£	£	£	£	£
Cost					
At 1.1.83	—	—	105,000	54,000	159,000
Additions	450,000	150,000	30,000	—	630,000
At 30.12.83	£450,000	£150,000	£135,000	£54,000	£789,000
Depreciation:					
At 1.1.83	—	—	60,000	24,000	84,000
Profit and loss account	—	3,000	13,500	7,500	24,000
At 31.12.83	—	£3,000	£73,500	£31,000	£108,000
Net book value	450,000	147,000	61,500	22,500	681,000

Accounting policy: depreciation is provided each year as follows:

Buildings	—2% of cost
Plant and machinery	— 10% of cost
Motor vehicles	— 25% of the written down value

No depreciation is provided in respect of freehold land (land has been assumed to be freehold).

Investments:	
	£
At cost	72,000
Less Amount written off	(57,000)
	£15,000

6 Debtors:

	£
Trade debtors (W5)	440,073
ACT recoverable after more than one year	17,614
	£457,687

7 Other creditors

	£
Dividends — preference	2,100
— ordinary	39,000
Corporation tax	59,100
ACT payable	17,614
	£117,814

8 Share capital:

	£
Authorized:	
1,200,000 ordinary shares of 50 pence each	600,000
60,000 7% preference shars of £1 each	60,000
	£660,000
Issued:	
600,000 ordinary shares of 50 pence each	300,000
60,000 7% preference shares of £1 each	60,000
	£360,000

9   Movement on reserves:

	Profit and loss account	General reserve
	£	£
At 1.1.83	65,103	30,000
Reduction in retained profits	(31,752)	
Transfer	(15,000)	15,000
At 31.12.83	£18,351	£45,000

10 Earnings per share are calculated on profit on ordinary activities after tax less preference dividend of £7,248, divided by 600,000 ordinary shares of 50 pence each.

Workings

1 Cost of sales:	£
Per trial balance	1,785,897
Depreciation of building (2/100 × £150,000) (assumed to be factory)	3,000
Depreciation of plant and machinery (10/100 × £135,000)	13,500
	£1,802,397

2 Distribution costs:	£
Selling expenses	120,000
Depreciation of salesmens' cars ((25/100 × (£54,000 – £24,000))	7,500
Increase in provision for doubtful debts ((1/100 × £2,925,900) – £22,500))	6,759
Sales director's emoluments transferred from administrative expenses	
(£48,000 + £3,000)	51,000
	£185,259

3 Administrative expenses:	£
Per trial balance	649,296
Directors' remuneration	181,500
Accrual for directors' fees (4 × £3,000)	12,000
Transfer of sales director's emoluments	(51,000)
Audit fee	3,000
Transfer of overdraft interest	(5,244)
	£789,552

4 Interest payable:	£
Debenture interest:	7,500
— per trial balance	
— accrual (assume debentures were in issue for the whole year)	7,500
Overdraft interest transferred from administrative expenses	5,244
	£20,244

5 Trade debtors:	£
Per trial balance	469,332
Provision for doubtful debts (£22,500 + £6,759)	(29,259)
	£440,073

6 Other creditors	
Corporation tax:	£
— provision	60,000
— ACT paid (re interim preference dividend)	(900)
	59,100
ACT payable re proposed dividends ((30/70 × (£2,100 + £39,000))	17,614

	£
Dividends:	
— preference	2,100
— ordinary	39,000
	£117,814

7 Accruals:	£
Directors' fees	12,000
Debenture interest	7,500
	£19,500

Answer to question 26

This is a straightforward question requiring a memo stating the items that should be included in a directors' report. Check your answer against the report given on page 000 of Chapter 19 of this book.

Note that the form of the memo should be:

Memorandum
To: Chief Accountant
From: Assistant
Date: December 1984
Topic: Contents of a Directors' Report

Answer to question 27

KITCHEN UTENSILS WHOLESALERS LTD

Statement of source and application of net liquid funds
for the year ended 31 May 1983

	£	£
Source of funds:		
Profit before tax (W1)		22,500
Adjustment for items not involving the movement of funds:		
Depreciation		17,400
Total generated from operations		39,900
Funds from other sources:		
Share issue	5,000	
Issue of 10% loan stock	52,000	
		57,000
		96,900
Application of funds:		
Dividends paid	(5,000)	
Tax paid	(10,200)	
Purchase of fixed assets	(50,500)	
		(65,700)
Increase in working capital:		31,200
Increase in stocks	29,100	
Decrease in debtors	(700)	
Decrease in creditors	5,500	
Movement in net liquid funds:		
Decrease in cash	(2,700)	
		31,200

This is a comparatively simple question that should not present any problems to a student who has mastered the basic principles.

Workings

1

	£
Net profit retained	5,000
Add back:	
Dividend	6,000
Taxation	11,500
Profit before tax	£22,500

Answer to question 28

CANDLE PLC

a Statement of source and application of net liquid funds for the year ended 30 September 1984

	£000	£000
Source of funds:		
Profit before tax		312
Adjustment for items not involving the movement of funds:		
Depreciation (W2)		110
Total generated from operations		422
Funds from other sources:		
Issue of shares	50	
Issue of 10% debenture stock	10	
Sale of machinery and fittings	6	
		66
		488
Application of funds:		
Dividends paid (W3)	(84)	
Tax paid (W4)	(136)	
Purchase of machinery and fittings (W1)	(300)	
		(520)
Decrease of working capital		(32)
Increase in stocks	5	
Increase in debtors	70	
Increase in creditors	(122)	
Movement in net liquid funds:		
Increase in cash at bank	15	
		(32)

a *Workings*

1 Machinery and fittings — cost

	£000		£000
1.10.83 Balance b/d	225	30.9.84 Disposal	25
Balancing figure = Cash paid	300	30.9.84 Balance c/d	500
	£525		£525

2 Machinery and fittings accumulated depreciation

	£000		£000
30.9.84 Disposal	15	1.10.83 Balance b/d	85
30.9.84 Balance c/d	156	Balancing	
		Figure = P&L a/c	86
	£171		£171

Machinery and fittings disposal

	£000		£000
30.9.84 Cost	25	30.9.84 Acc. Deprec.	15
		30.9.84 Proceeds	6
		Balancing	
		Figure = P&L a/c	4
	£25		£25

Depreciation P & L a/c charge for the year: £000	
Land and buildings (£120–£100)	20
Machinery and fittings	86
Machinery and fittings disposal	4
	£110

3

Dividends

	£000		£000
30.9.84 Balance c/d	35	1.10.83 Balance b/d	70
Balancing figure = Cash paid	84	30.9.84 P&L a/c	49
	£119		£119

4

Taxation

	£000		£000
30.9.84 Balances c/d:		1.10.83 Balances b/d:	
Tax	68	Tax	100
ACT payable	15	ACT payable	30
Deferred tax	100	Deferred tax	100
ACT recoverable	(15)	ACT recoverable	(30)
Balancing figure = cash paid	136	30.9.84 P&L a/c	104
	£304		£304

Although this account is all that is necessary for workings to answer the question it is of interest to note that ACT recoverable has been netted off against deferred tax on the two balance sheets as follows:

	30.9.83	30.9.84
	£000	£000
Deferred tax	100	100
Less ACT recoverable	30	15
Per balance sheet	£70	£85

There has been no deferred tax transfer to or from the profit and loss account during the year, the opening and closing balance remaining at £100,000.

An alternative calculation of tax paid which would use note 2 to the question is:

	£000
Corporation tax provision b/f	100
ACT on 30.9.83 proposed dividend paid in year to 30.9.84	30
ACT on interim dividend paid in year to 30.9.84 ($\frac{30}{70} \times$ £14,000)	6
	£136

Note that the corporation tax balance at 30.9.84 represents:

	£000
P & L a/c charge	104
Less ACT paid on dividends paid during year to 30.9.94 (£30+£6)	36
	£68

b Refer to Chapter 20, pp.000–00 and 000–00.

Answer to question 29

LIGHT ENGINEERING CO. LTD

a Profit and loss appropriation account for the year ended 31 December 1981

	£		£
Taxation	20,000	Trading profit (balancing figure)	11,698
Capital redemption reserve	100,000	Balance b/f previous year	149,617
Dividend	20,000		
Balance c/f	21,315		
	£161,315		£161,315

Taxation

	£		£
1.1.81 Balance b/d:		1.1.81 Balance b/d:	
ACT recoverable	10,286	Corporation tax	31,360
		ACT payable	10,286
Balancing figure = Tax paid	16,170	31.12.81 P&L a/c	20,000
31.12.81 Balances c/d:		31.12.81 Balance c/d:	
Corporation tax	25,290	ACT recoverable	8,572
ACT payable	8,572		
Deferred tax	10,000		
	£70,318		£70,318

b Statement of source and applications of net liquid funds
for the year ended 31 December 1981

	£	£	£
Source of funds:			
Profit before tax (a)			11,698
Adjustments for items not involving the movement of funds:			
Goodwill written off (W1)		5,000	
Depreciation (W2)		36,876	
			41,876
Total generated from operations			53,574
Funds from other sources:			
Issue of shares		130,000	
Issue of 16% loan stock		68,250	
Sale of fixed assets (W3)		13,800	
			212,050
			265,624
Application of funds:			
Redemption of preference shares		(101,000)	
Dividend paid		(10,000)	
Taxation paid (a)		(16,170)	
Purchase of fixed assets (W4)		(144,020)	
			(271,190)
Decrease in working capital			(5,566)
Decrease in stocks		(9,915)	
Increase in debtors		4,954	

	£	£	£
Decrease in creditors		18,523	
Movement in net liquid funds:			
Decrease in cash at bank	(18,612)		
Increase in bank overdraft	(516)	(19,128)	(5,566)

b *Workings*

1 Goodwill written off has been treated as a charge against operating profits as it is being written off over a period of years.

2 Depreciation charge for the year:

	£
Building	3,000
Plant	28,000
Vehicles	4,890
Fittings	3,641
Overprovision on plant disposal	(4,000)
Underprovision on vehicle disposal	1,345
	£36,876

Plant disposal

	£		£
31.12.81 Cost	31,000	31.12.81 Accumulated depreciation	24,000
Balancing figure = Profit			
loss account	4,000	Proceeds	11,000
	£35,000		£35,000

Vehicle Disposal

	£		£
31.12.81 Cost	18,460	31.12.81 Accumulated depreciation	14,315
		Proceeds	2,800
		Balancing figure = P/l a/c	1,345
	£18,460		£18,460

3 Proceeds of sale of fixed assets:

	£
Plant	11,000
Vehicles	2,800
	£13,800

4 Purchase of fixed assets:

	£
Buildings	100,000
Plant	23,000
Vehicles	16,418
Fittings	4,602
	£144,020

c The funds statement reveals major applications of funds in repayment of preference shares and the purchase of fixed assets. Internally generated funds were supplemented by isuing ordinary shares and loan stock to meet these applications.

The reduction in working capital combined particularly with the decrease in creditors has resulted in a bank overdraft.

Answer to question 30

CEE LTD AND DEE LTD

a

Ratio	Cee Ltd		Dee Ltd	
Return on capital employed	(30/420)	7.14%	(24/152)	15.79%
Profitability:				
Gross profit %	(160/720)	22.22%	(189/860)	21.98%
Overheads%	(110/720)	15.28%	(150/860)	17.44%
Utilization of assets:				
Sales to fixed assets	(720/230)	3.13:1	(860/180)	4.78:1
Stockturn — based on closing stocks	(560/140)	92 days	(671/86)	47 days
Debtor collection period	(720/155)	79 days	(860/150)	64 days
Solvency position:				
Current ratio	(310/120)	2.58:1	(252/220)	1.15:1
Liquid ratio	(170/120)	1.42:1	(166/220)	0.75:1
Gearing		0:1	(60/152)	0.39:1

b Dee Ltd has the best performance, earning a return that is more than double that of Cee Ltd. The return of Cee Ltd would appear to be low by normal standards.

Dee Ltd in fact earns less net profit per £ of sales than Cee Ltd, mainly due to proportionately higher overheads. This may possibly be due to its location, but more probably due to debenture and bank overdraft interest.

Dee Ltd appears to utilize its assets much more efficiently, servicing a higher turnover with less fixed assets and stock. It also collects its debtors more quickly.

Cee Ltd has a very strong solvency position; Dee Ltd has far less working capital but is in a reasonable position due to a short stockturn period and quick debtor collection. However, payment of creditors must present Dee Ltd with a problem. It also has a bank overdraft. There would appear to be room for Dee Ltd to borrow some additional working capital, if required, as it is reasonably low geared. Cee Ltd does not utilize its capacity to borrow.

Answer question 31

Working capital is current assets less current liabilities. It is the amount of capital employed left, after investment in fixed assets, to run the business. It has to be sufficient to service the day–to–day need of the business in terms of stocks and debtors to utilize the fixed assets at maximum efficiency. To a certain extent current assets may be financed by creditors, which are a free form of credit because they do not incur interest charges.

The working capital ratio, the current ratio, is the proportion of current assets to current liabilities. If it is too low it means that the majority of the current assets are being financed by creditors rather than by the company's own capital. If the working capital ratio is too low creditors may lose confidence in the company, which may experience difficulties in obtaining credit.

Gearing is the proportion of fixed return capital to equity. If the gearing ratio is high it means that too much of the capital employed in fixed assets and working capital has been provided by preference shareholders and, more importantly, by long–term borrowings such as debentures and loan stocks. High gearing indicates that the company has probably exhausted its capacity to make further borrowings and has to bear large interest charges in the profit and loss account.

The bank manager's view appears to be that the company has too many creditors and too much long–term debt in relation to its assets. In this situation difficulties may arise in paying creditors and it may not be possible to raise further borrowings. A solution would be the injection of further funds by an issue of additional ordinary shares.

Answer to question 32

In historic cost accounts assets, liabilities income and expenses are stated at the amounts payable or receivable when the transaction was entered into. These values are easily determined and historic cost accounts have the virtue of being factual. However, in time of rising prices such an approach is, by itself, inadequate because of the following problem areas:

1 The cost of sales will not reflect the increase in buying prices during the period that the stock has been held. It is argued that such gains arising from holding stocks during a period of inflation, should not be recognized as trading profits but placed to reserve. If these gains are retained in the company they will ensure sufficient funds are retained to meet the increased replacement prices of stock.
2 The depreciation charge will not reflect the amount of the current value of an asset consumed in earning profits. Unless an additional charge is made the company may find it has insufficient funds to enable it to replace its assets.
3 Losses due to holding monetary assets and gains arising from holding monetary liabilities are not recognized. If losses due to the effect of inflation on monetary working capital are charged to the profit and loss account and placed to reserve the operating capacity of the business will be maintained. Gains arising on long–term debt could also be recognized, or the previously mentioned losses reduced by a gearing adjustment.
4 Fixed assets will be stated on the balance sheet at out–of–date values. This may particularly be so in the case of land and buildings. Understatement of the book value of fixed assets may adversely affect a company's borrowing position.
5 The return on capital employed calculated on information given in historic cost accounts may be misleadingly high due to overstatement of profit and under-statement of asset values.

(Note that the quality of the answer is more important than length. Thinking time must be devoted to identifying all the major important areas that an examiner would expect to be included within an answer, and to the points that should be made within each area.)

Answer to question 33

An answer to this question should make the same points as are included in the answer to question 32.

The question places special emphasis on dividend policy. The significance of this is the need, in times of inflation, to retain sufficient profits to be able to maintain the operating capacity of the business. If historic cost profits were all distributed this would not be the case. Current cost profits are operating profits only and may be distributed without adversely affecting the operating capacity.

Answer to question 34

FOG PLC AND SUBSIDIARY COMPANIES

Consolidated balance sheet at 30 September 1984

	£000	£000
Fixed assets:		
Plant at net book value		270
Current assets:		
Stocks (W4)	305	
Debtors (W5)	275	
Cash at bank and in hand	80	
	660	
Less Creditors & amounts falling due within on year:		
Creditors (W6)	315	
		345
		£615

	£000	£000
Financed by:		
Share capital:		
Authorized, issued and fully paid ordinary shares of £1 each		500
Revenue reserves (W2)		91
		591
Minority shareholders' interest in subsidiary company (W3)		24
		£615

Workings

1 Fog holds (100,000/100,000) 100% of the shares of Mist and (40,000/50,000) 80% of the shares of Rain.

Cost of control re Mist

	£000		£000
Cost of investment	150	Ordinary shares	100
		Revenue reserves at 1.10.82	30
		Goodwill (W2)	20
	£150		£150

Cost of control re Rain

	£000		£000
Cost of investment	70	Ordinary shares	40
Negative goodwill (W2)	2	80% revenue reserves at 30.9.83	
		((80% × £70 – £30))	32
	£72		£72

2 Consolidated revenue reserves

	£000		£000
Stock provision:			
— Mist	5	Fog	90
— Rain	10	Mist — post-acquisition (£40 – £30)	10
Net goodwill written off (£20–£2)(W1)	18	Rain—80% post-acquisition (80% × £30)	24
Balance	91		
	£124		£124

3 Minority interest in Rain

	£000		£000
		20% ordinary shares	10
Balance	24	20% revenue reserves	14
	£24		£24

Consolidated stocks

	£000		£000
Fog	150	Stock provision:	
Mist	90	— Mist (50/150 × £15)	5
Rain	80	— Rain ((1/2 × (£70 – £50))	10
		Balance	305
	£320		£320

Consolidated debtors

	£000		£000
Fog	250	Inter-company contra	35
Mist	40		
Rain	20	Balance	275
	£310		£310

Consolidated creditors

	£000		£000
Inter-company contra (£20+£10+£5)	35	Fog	280
Balance	315	Mist	50
		Rain	20
	£350		£350

Answer to question 35

HOLDINGS PLC AND SUBSIDIARY COMPANY

Consolidated balance sheet at 30 June 1985

	£	£	£
Fixed assets:			
Land and buildings		335,000	
Plant		80,000	
Vehicles		48,858	
			463,858
Current assets:			
Stock (W5)		289,732	
Debtors (W6)		178,860	
Cash		68,870	
		537,462	
Less Creditors: amounts falling due within one year:			
Trade creditors (W7)	175,354		
Bank overdraft	10,046		
		185,400	
Net current assets			352,062
Total assets less current liabilities			815,920
Creditors: amounts falling due after more than one year:			
10% debentures (W8)			35,000
			£780,920
Financed by:			
Share capital			595,000
Reserves (W3)			128,660
Unappropriated profits (W4)			(18,900)
			704,760
Minority shareholders' interest in subsidiary company (W2)			76,160
			£780,920

Workings

1   Holdings own (504,000/840,000) 60% of Subsid.

Cost of control

	£		£
Cost of investment	134,680	Ordinary shares	
		(504,000×25 pence)	126,000
Cost of debentures	70,000	60% profit and loss at 1.7.81	1,440

	£		£
		60% general reserve at 1.7.81	12,000
Negative goodwill (W3)	4,760	Debentures acquired	70,000
	£209,440		£209,440

2   Minority interest

	£		£
		Ordinary shares	84,000
		40% general reserve	10,000
Balance	76,160	40% profit and loss	(17,840)
	£76,160		£76,160

3   Consolidated reserves

	£		£
		Holding	120,900
		60% Subsid — post-acquisition	
		((60% × (£25,000 – £20,000))	3,000
Balance	128,660	Negative goodwill (W1)	4,760
	£128,660		£128,660

4   Consolidated unappropriated profits

	£		£
Stock provision (25/100 × £30,800)	7,700	Holdings	10,000
		60% Subsid — post-acquisition	
		(60% × (£44,600) – £2,400))	(28,200)
Balance	(18,900)	Debenture interest receivable	7,000
	£(11,200)		£(11,200)

5   Consolidated stocks

	£		£
Holdings	145,731	Stock provision	7,700
Subsid	151,701	Balance	289,732
	£297,432		£297,432

6   Consolidated debtors

	£		£
Holdings	163,419	Inter-company contra re debtor for	
		stock (125/100 × £30,800)	38,500
Holdings — debenture interest	7,000	Inter-company contra re debtor for	
		debenture interest	7,000
Subsid	53,941	Balance	178,860
	£224,360		£224,360

7   Consolidated creditors

	£		£
Inter-company contra	38,500	Holdings	156,800
Inter-company contra	7,000	Subsid	64,054
Balance	175,354		
	£220,854		£220,854

8   Consolidated 10% debentures

	£		£
Holding — investment	70,000	Subsid	105,000
Balance	35,000		
	£105,000		£105,000

In considering this answer note that a debtor for debenture interest receivable has to be raised in the parent company's accounts. This is then set off against the debenture interest payable already included in the creditors of the subsidiary company. The debentures held by third parties are a liability of the group. The debentures held by the parent are set off against the cost of the investment.

Goods sold by the parent to the subsidiary were at a transfer value of (125/100 × £30,800) £38,500. As the subsidiary had not paid for these goods it must be assumed that this amount is included in both the parent's debtors and the subsidiary's creditors and has to be set off by contra.

Answer to question 36

a   OSWALD LTD AND SUBSIDIARY COMPANY

Summary of consolidated balance sheet at 31 March 1985

	£
Issued share capital:	
£1 ordinary shares	100,000
Reserves (W3)	111,200
	211,200
Minority interest (W2)	32,800
	£244,000
Net assets (W4)	£244,000

Workings

1   Cost of control

	£		£
Investment	50,000	£1 ordinary shares	30,000
		60% reserves — pre-acquisition	14,400
		Goodwill (W3)	5,600
	£50,000		£50,000

2   Minority interest

	£		£
		£1 ordinary shares	20,000
Balance	32,800	40% reserves	12,800
	£32,800		£32,800

3   Consolidated reserves

	£		£
Goodwill (W1)	5,600	Oswald	112,000
		Tudor:	
Balance	111,200	60% reserves — post-acquisition	
		(60% × £32,000 − £24,000)	4,800
	£116,800		£116,800

4   The consolidated net assets are:

	£
Oswald	212,000
Less Investment in Tudor Ltd	50,000
	162,000
Tudor	82,000
	£244,000

b   Goodwill is the excess of the cost of the investment in the subsidiary over the fair value of the share of net assets acquired. It represents the capitalized value of the super-profits that are expected in the future. The minority interest is the share capital and attaching reserves that are owned by outside shareholders in a subsidiary company. It represents the amount of net assets of the subsidiary that are financed by shareholders other than the parent company.

Answer to question 37

A LTD AND SUBSIDIARY COMPANY

Consolidated profit and loss account for the year ended 31 December 19X4

	£	£
Net Profit after tax		140,000
Less Minority interest (25% × £40,000)		10,000
		130,000
Less Dividends:		
Paid	5,000	
Proposed	20,000	25,000
		105,000
Balance brought forward		50,000
		155,000
Less Goodwill written off		10,000
Carried forward		£145,000

(Note that there were no post-acquisition profits brought forward at the beginning of the year re the subsidiary, as it was not acquired until the first day of the year.)

Consolidated balance sheet at 31 December 19X4

	£	£
Other net assets		344,500
Less Creditors: amounts falling due within one year:		
Proposed dividend	① 20,000	
Dividend payable to minority interest	② 3,000	23,000
		321,500
Financed by:		
£1 ordinary shares		100,000
General reserve		50,000
Profit and loss account balance		145,000
		295,000
Minority shareholders' interest in subsidiary company		26,500
		£321,500

Handwritten annotation:
① = A proposed
② = B = 12000 proposed
   9000 to A
   3000 to min.

Notes to the accounts
1 Profit and loss account:

	Parent company	Subsidiary company	Total
	£	£	£
At 1.1.X4	50,000	—	50,000
Retained profit for the year (£78,000 + £9,000)	87,000	18,000	105,000
Goodwill written off	(10,000)	—	(10,000)
At 31.12.X4	£127,000	£18,000	£145,000

Workings
A Ltd owns (30,000/40,000) 75% of B Ltd.

Minority interest

	£		£
		Ordinary shares	10,000
		25% general reserve (£10,000)	2,500
Balance	26,500	25% Profit & Loss a/c (£56,000)	14,000
	£26,500		£26,500

Cost of control

	£		£
Investment	71,500	Ordinary shares	30,000
		75% general reserve (£10,000)	7,500
		75% pre-acquisition	
		Profit & loss a/c (£32,000)	£24,000
		Goodwill	10,000
	£71,500		£71,500

Note that the general reserve of B Ltd must have existed at the date of acquisition as there is no transfer to it from the profit and loss account after acquisition. It is therefore entirely a pre-acquisition reserve.

The goodwill has been written off against the profit and loss account balance. It could equally well have been written off against the general reserve.

It is apparent from the profit and loss account of A Ltd that the proposed dividend receivable from B Ltd of (75% × £12,000) £9,000 has not been accrued as due. A debtor should be raised in A Ltd's accounts for this:

Debit   Dividend receivable   £9,000
Credit   Profit and loss   £9,000

The dividend receivable of £9,000 is then set off against B Ltd's dividend payable of £12,000 to show a net dividend payable to the minority interest of £3,000 on the consolidated balance sheet. The inter-company dividends do not appear in the consolidated profit and loss account.

Answer to question 38

a Categories of business stocks are goods purchased for resale, consumable stores, raw materials and components, work in progress and finished goods. The general rule is that stock should be valued at the lower of cost and net realizable value. This complies with the fundamental concepts of:

Prudence –   costs are not carried forward that will not be recovered in the future.

Consistency –   the same policy is applied from year to year.

Going concern –	the realizable value is that which will arise in the normal course of business in the future.
Accruals –	costs are only carried forward that can be matched to future income that will recover them.

b Refer to Chapter 25, pp.000–000.

c Balance sheet as at 31 December 19X1 extract:

Current assets:
Stocks of finished goods   £3,500

Note: Stocks are valued at the lower of cost and net realizable value.

(The situation appears to be that stocks are valued at transfer price. A stock provision of (1,000 × 50p) £500 will be required to reduce them to cost. The net realizable value is unknown, but is probably in the region of (Sales £60,000/9,500 handbags) £6.31 per handbag; higher than cost.)

Answer to question 39

a The special problems posed by long-term contracts are:
— profit is earned on the contract over a period of years;
— the profit earned each year has to be determined;
— a prudent approach has to be adopted to avoid taking profits if losses may arise on future work on the contract;
— if profits are not taken as earned, the reported profits will fluctuate unreasonably from year to year.

The rules adopted by SSAP 9 are:
— long-term contracts should be valued at cost plus attributable profit less any fore seeable losses;
— progress payments received and receivable should be deducted;
— the outcome of the contract should be reasonably foreseeable;
— profit taken should reflect the profit earned on the work done to date.
— provision should be made for all foreseeable losses.

b

Contract

		£			£
11.7.83	Balance b/d:				
	— WIP	447,850			
	— Plant	83,465			
To					
30.6.84	Materials	46,412			
	Labour	31,283			
	Overhead	12,513	30.6.84	Balance c/d:	
	Plant	21,478		— Plant	87,220
		643,001		— WIP (bal. fig.)	574,198
	Profit and loss (W1)	18,417			
		£661,418			£661,418

Customer

To		£	To		£
30.6.68	Progress payments	480,000	30.6.84	Cash	480,000

Progress payments receivable

		£	To		£
			30.6.84	Customer	480,000

(Note that in the absence of information it has been assumed that there are no progress payments outstanding.)

BRADMORE BUILDERS LTD

Balance Sheet extract at 30 June 19X4

	£	£
Fixed assets:		
Plant — at valuation		87,220
Current assets:		
Long-term contract work in progress	574,198	
Less Progress payments received	480,000	
		94,198

b *Workings*

1 Calculation of profits earned:

	£	£
Contract price		620,000
Less Costs to date per contact account	643,001	
Less Profit included	26,480	
	616,521	
Additional costs to completion	25,000	
	641,521	
Less Plant disposals	70,000	
		571,521
Estimated total profit		£48,479

Profit earned to date:

$$\text{Total profit} \times \frac{\text{Costs to date}}{\text{Total costs}} = £48,479 \times \frac{£616,521 - £87,220 \text{ (plant)}}{£571,521}$$

$$= £44,897$$

Profit for the year (£44,897 less profit taken in previous years £26,480) = £18,417.

The question does not specify the method to calculate profit earned. In these circumstances profit earned could alternatively have been calculated on the basis of:

$$\frac{\text{Value of work certified}}{\text{Total contract value}} \times \text{Total profit}$$

The contract is well advanced and the outcome may be assumed to be reasonably foreseeable.

Answer to question 40

The treatment required in the published account of Penn PLC is:

1. A major and fundamental error will be an adjustment, as a prior year item, to the balance brought forward on the profit and loss account, in accordance with SSAP 6.
2. Applied research costs will be charged to the profit and loss account in accordance with SSAP 13. If the increase is very substantial and has a material effect on profits for the year it should be disclosed as an exceptional item in accordance with SSAP 6.
3. The transfer to deferred tax account should be made, if it is probable that the timing differences will reverse, in accordance with SSAP 15. SSAP 8 requires the transfer to be shown separately in the taxation section of the profit and loss account.
4. As the directors' emoluments exceed £60,000 a note is required by the Companies Act 1985 of:
   — emoluments of the chairman;
   — emoluments of the highest paid director;
   — the number of the directors receiving emoluments in bands of £5,000.
5. The Companies Act 1985 requires the contribution and the name of the political party to be disclosed in the directors' report as it exceeds £200.

6   The costs arising from the closure of the factory, if material, should be disclosed as an extraordinary item in accordance with SSAP 6. The closure is not in the ordinary course of business and cannot be expected to recur frequently.

7   The adjustment to the opening stock should be treated as a prior year item in accordance with SSAP 6, and the profit and loss account balance brought forward adjusted. A note should be given on the change of accounting policy and its effect on profits for the year.

8   The interim dividend will appear in the profit and loss account. The ACT paid will be recorded against the corporation tax liability for the year, reducing the creditor on the balance sheet.

9   Development costs may be carried forward, as an intangible fixed asset, only if the criteria laid down by SSAP 13 are met. Otherwise it should be charged against profits.

10 The order would appear to be abnormal in size and to give rise to a material exceptional profit, and should be separately disclosed in accordance with SSAP 6.

Answer to question 41

a   The investment in Wye Ltd appears to be long term and should be treated as an investment in an associated company. SSAP 1 requires the share of profit before tax and share of tax to be included in the profit and loss account. On the balance sheet the share of post-acquisition profits not received by way of dividend is taken to a reserve and the amount at which the investment is shown is correspondingly increased.

b   The freehold property should be revalued to £1,250,000, the surplus on revaluation of £750,000 being credited to a revaluation reserve. The buildings element of £850,000 should be depreciated over its useful life in accordance with SSAP 12.

c   The research costs should be charged to the profit and loss account in accordance with SSAP 13. Only development costs that meet the criteria laid down by SSAP 13 may be carried forward.

d   Stocks should be valued at the lower of cost and net realizable value as per SSAP 9. If the stocks had been included in the stock valuation at cost this should be reduced by £40,000.

   The decision to close the factory is a non-adjusting event as defined by SSAP 17. It should be disclosed as a note to the accounts.

e   The abnormal provision of £50,000 for losses on a long-term contract should be disclosed as an exceptional item, in accordance with SSAP 6, if it is material in the context of the company's accounts. The mistake in the calculation of opening WIP would not appear to be a fundamental error and therefore not a prior year adjustment. It should be disclosed as an exceptional item as it is abnormal in incidence and is probably material.

f   The grant received of £30,000 is capital-based and in accordance with SSAP 4 should be credited to a deferred credit account from which it should be transferred to the credit of the profit and loss account over the asset's useful life.

ANSWERS TO QUESTIONS IN SAMPLE EXAMINATION PAPER

Answer to question 1

a i Branch stock

	£		£
Balance b/d — stock	75,000	Bank — cash sales	120,000
Debtors — returns	8,000	Debtors — credit sales	437,000
Goods sent to branch	600,000	Returns to head office	30,000
		Balance c/d — stock	90,000
		Deficit (bal. fig.)	6,000
	£683,000		£683,000
Balance b/d	90,000		

ii Goods sent to branch

	£		£
Returns	20,000	Goods sent — at cost	400,000
Trading account	380,000		
	£400,000		£400,000

iii Branch stock adjustment

	£		£
Returns	10,000	Balance b/d (50/150 × £75,000)	25,000
Stock losses	2,000	Goods sent	200,000
Balance c/d (50/150 × £90,000)	30,000		
Gross profit	183,000		
	£225,000		£225,000
		Balance b/d	30,000

iv Branch debtors

	£		£
Balance b/d	66,000	Bad debts	15,000
Credit sales	437,000	Bank	390,000
		Discounts allowed	9,000
		Returns	8,000
		Balance c/d	81,000
	£503,000		£503,000
Balance b/d	81,000		

v Branch bank

	£		£
Balance b/d	3,000	General expenses	42,000
Debtors	390,000	Head office bank	459,000
Cash sales	120,000	Balance c/d	12,000
	£513,000		£513,000
Balance b/d	12,000		

b   Trading and profit and loss account for the year ended 31 March 1986

	£000	£000
Head office:		
Sales — cash		1,500
— credit		1,960
		3,460
Less Cost of sales:		
Opening stocks	180	
Purchases	2,780	
Transfers	(380)	
	2,580	
Less Closing stocks	220	
		2,360
Gross profit		1,100
Branch — gross profit		183
Gross profit		1,283
Less:		
Bad debts (£24 + £15)	39	
General expenses (£410 + £42)	452	
Discounts allowed (£29 + £9)	38	
Stock deficit	4	
		533
Net profit		£750

c   The merit of the method used is that control is exercised over branch stocks and sales. Any stock shortages, failure to bank cash sales or to record credit sales will result in a deficiency on the branch stock account. In this answer a deficiency of £6,000 arises and would require investigation to determine the reasons for it arising.
     The demerit of the method is the administration costs involved.

Answer to question 2

a

1985		1985		1986
1 Liquidity ratio:				
Current assets – stock	2,100	0.9:1	3,850	1.4:1
Current liabilities	2,400		2,700	
2 Gross profit %:				
Gross profit × 100	1,850	24.2%	2,070	18.0%
Sales	7,650		11,500	
3 Loan interest %:				
Loan interest × 100	50	0.7%	350	3.0%
Sales	7,650		11,500	
4 Return on capital employed				
Profit after tax × 100	1,050	9.6%	1,000	8.6%
Share capital and reserves	10,900		11,600	
5 Debtor collection period:				
Debtors × 365	1,200	57 days	3,800	120 days
Sales	7,650		11,500	
6 Gearing:				
Long–term debt	350	0.03:1	3,350	0.29:1
Equity	10,900		11,600	

b *Liquidity*. The company does not appear to have any liquidity problems, liquidity having improved to a very satisfactory situation. At 30.4.86 there are sufficient debtors and cash to cover the payment of the current liabilities. This was not the case in the previous year.

Profitability. Net profit after tax has fallen slightly from £1,050,000 to £1,000,000 despite a large increase in sales. This fall is mainly due to the reduced margin (down from 24.2% to 18.0%), presumably because selling prices were reduced. The increase in loan interest payable consequent to the large increase in long-term borrowings also depressed profits.

Efficiency. Overall the company's performance was worse in 1986 with a fall in the return earned on capital employed, primarily due to the fall in profitability. The company has been less efficient in collecting debtors, although extended credit may have been given as a deliberate policy to expand sales.

Shareholders' interests. The shareholders' interest increased from £10,900,000 to £11,600,000 due to the retention of profits. Most of the capital employed has been provided from shareholders' funds. There was a significant increase in long-term debt; most of the funds needed to finance the increased turnover appear to have come from this source. Even so, the company is still reasonably low geared with ample scope for further borrowings if need be.

c Additional information needed:

— credit terms allowed to customers;
— selling prices in both years;
— analysis of sales and cost of sales between the major product lines.

Answer to question 3

a Profit and loss account for the year ended 31 March 1986

	£000	£000	Notes
Turnover		642	
Cost of sales (W1)		390	
Gross profit		252	
Distribution costs (W2)	52		
Adminstrative expenses (W3)	105		
		157	
		95	1
Income from fixed asset investment		20	2
Interest receivable		25	
		140	
Interest payable		6	3
		134	
Tax on ordinary activities		50	4
Profit on ordinary activities after tax		84	
Extraordinary loss, after tax:			
Factory closure		12	
Profit for the year		72	
Dividends:			
Interim paid	21		
Proposed final	42		
		63	
Retained profit		£9	5
Earning per share		20 pence	6

a *Notes*
  1 Profit is arrived at after charging:

	£000
Auditors' remuneration	20
Directors emoluments	45
Hire of plant and machinery	12
Depreciation (£8 + £19)	27

2 Dividends received re listed investments: £20,000

3 Interest on loan repayable within 5 years: £6,000

4 Taxation:

	£000
Corporation tax based on the profit on ordinary activities for the year at a rate of 50%	38
Less Overprovision in previous year	3
	35
Transfer to deferred tax	9
Tax attributable to franked investment income	6
	£50

5 Retained profits:

	£000
At 31 March 1985	160
Less Prior year adjustment on change of accounting policy	
For R & D costs	15
	145
Retained profit	9
At 31 March 1986	£154

6 Earnings per share are based on profit on ordinary activities after tax of £84,000 divided by 420,000 ordinary shares of £1.

Workings

1 Cost of sales:

	£000
Opening stock	60
Purchases	401
	461
Less Closing stock	71
	£390

2 Distribution costs:

	£000
Per trial balance	33
Depreciation of delivery vans	19
	£52

3 Administrative expenses:

	£000
Per trial balance	97
Depreciation of office machinery	8
	£105

b

Balance sheet extracts at 31 March 1986

	£000
Other creditors:	
Proposed dividend	42
Corporation tax (£38–ACT £3)	35
ACT payable (³⁄₇ × £42)	18
	95
Deferred taxation (£24 + £9 – ACT recoverable £18)	15

Answer to question 4

a

Revaluation

	£		£
Furniture	7,000	Land and buildings	40,000
Motor vehicles	6,000		
Stocks	5,000		
Bad debt	2,000		
Provision for doubtful			
debts	1,000		
Office expenses	3,000		
Professional charges	1,000		
Surplus on revaluation:			
Proudie (³⁄₅)	9,000		
Slope (¹⁄₅)	3,000		
Thorne (¹⁄₅)	3,000		
	£40,000		£40,000

b

Capital accounts

	Proudie	Slope	Thorne		Proudie	Slope	Thorne
	£	£	£		£	£	£
Motor vehicle	4,000			Capital accounts	100,000	60,000	40,000
Goodwill				Current accounts	24,000	10,000	8,000
contra 1:1		75,000	75,000	Goodwill			
Transfer-loan	219,000			contra 3:1:1	90,000	30,000	30,000
Balances c/d		28,000	6,000	Surplus on			
				revaluation	9,000	3,000	3,000
	£223,000	£103,000	£81,000		£223,000	£103,000	£81,000
				Balances b/d		28,000	6,000

Goodwill calculations:

	£
Profits: 1984	130,000
1985	150,000
1986	170,000
	£450,000÷3 =£150,000

c

SLOPE AND THORNE

Balance sheet at 1 June 1986

	£	£	£
Fixed assets:			
Land and buildings		200,000	
Furniture		5,000	
Motor vehicles		10,000	
			215,000
Current assets:			
Stock		18,000	
Debtors (£40,000 – £2,000)		38,000	
Prepayments		2,000	
Cash (£10,000 – £8,000)		2,000	
		60,000	
Less Current liabilities:			
Trade creditors	15,000		
Accruals (£3,000 + £3,000 + £1,000)	7,000		
		22,000	
			38,000
			253,000
Less Loan			219,000
			£34,000
Financed by:			
Partners' capitals:			
Slope		28,000	
Thorne		6,000	
			£34,000

Answer to question 5

a   VAT should not be included in sales. Only irrecoverable VAT should be included in purchases, expenses and fixed assets. VAT owing should be included as a creditor in the balance sheet.

b   All listed companies should publish their earnings per share figure. Earnings are after tax but before extraordinary items. The number of shares used is the number issued.

c   Depreciation methods used, the useful lives or the depreciation rates used, total depreciation for the period and the gross amount of depreciable assets and the related accumulated depreciation should be disclosed.

d   Expenditure on pure and applied research should be written off in the year of expenditure.

e   Capital-based grants relating to fixed assets should be credited to a deferred credit account and transferred from there to the credit of the profit and loss account over the life of the asset.

f   Goodwill arising on consolidation should be written off against reserves. If this is not practicable it should be written off over its useful life. Negative goodwill should be credited to reserves. A note should be given disclosing the accounting policy followed.

g   If accounts are prepared on the basis of assumptions that differ from any of the fundamental accounting concepts, the accounts should contain a clear statement to that effect and explain the facts.

h   The subsidiary company should use the same accounting policies and prepare accounts to the same date as its parent company. The parent company should prepare consolidated accounts and note the accounting policy used for consolidation.

ANSWERS TO SELF–ASSESSMENT QUESTIONS

Chapter 1

1.1 Conservatism is known as prudence. Accruals is sometimes known as the matching concept. The answer is (d); recording transactions at the historic cost at which they were effected is not identified in SSAP 2 as one of the four fundamental concepts.

1.2 The answer is (b). The net realizable value is not normally relevant to the book value of fixed assets if the company is a going concern. Current assets will be valued at the lower of cost and net realizable value.

1.3 The fact that expenses are accrued does not have to be noted, as all accounts are assumed to be prepared in accordance with this fundamental concept unless a clear statement to the contrary is made. The answer is (b).

Chapter 2

2.1 Answer (e) — VAT is never included in the sales taken to the profit and loss account. Remember that a non-registered trader will not be charging VAT to his customers. A registered trader, whether sole trader, partnership or company, merely acts as a collector of VAT for the Customs and Excise.

2.2 There is, of course, no VAT on wages. The input tax on the purchases, audit fee and purchase of motor lorries will be debited to the VAT account and recovered. The VAT on the purchase of a motor car fixed asset is included as part of the cost of the fixed asset, which is depreciated in the normal way–answer (d).

2.3 Answer (d) — the entry for purchases returns will be debit supplier with the credit note total, credit purchases (or purchases returns) with the goods value and credit VAT with the tax.

Chapter 4

4.1 Drawings are not an appropriation of profit but a withdrawal of that profit, so the answer is (c). The other items are all appropriations of profit. The double entry for cash drawings is debit current account and credit cash account.

4.2 The answer is (b). The surplus on revaluation is £60,000 (£150,000 − (£100,000 − £10,000)) of which B's share is $\frac{1}{4}$ = £15,000. His capital will rise to £35,000 (£20,000 + £15,000).

4.3 The answer is (c). The goodwill adjustment contra will be:
Debit: A £12,000 B £8,000 C £4,000 D £4,000 = £28,000
Credit: A £14,000 B £7,000 C 7,000   = £28,000

Note that this entry will also reduce B's capital account. This is because, due to the change in profit sharing ratio, he is gaining a greater share (from $\frac{1}{4}$ to $\frac{2}{7}$) of the unrecorded goodwill.

4.4 This is a difficult question. The appropriate answer is (a). Motor cars owned by a partnership are a partnership asset. Capital introduced by a partner is recorded in the partner's capital account (the cash received would have been recorded in the bank account, but may have been used for other purposes by the balance sheet date). A current account that is in debit is an asset, but it is normally included in the balance sheet as a deduction from the partner's capital account. Private expenses will be debited, when paid, to the current accounts, regardless of the period to which they relate. A loan from a partner would be shown as a long-term liability (or a current liability if it is repayable within 12 months).

Chapter 5

5.1 The answer is (a) — all profits, including gains and losses on fixed assets, are shared in the profit sharing ratio. The answer (e) would only apply if the partnership agreement was to share profits equally or if there was no agreement.

5.2 The answer is (b), the last agreed capitals, which will normally be those appearing on the last balance sheet.

5.3 The net assets have a book value of (£150,000 – £20,000) £130,000. The purchase price is (100,000 × £2) £200,000. The profit on realization is (£200,000 – £130,000) £70,000, so the answer is (e). The profit arises because the buyer places a higher value on the assets than is recorded in the books. Remember that a buyer may place a value on goodwill which is not normally recorded in the books.

5.4 The answer is (d), 20,000 shares. Although the number of shares each partner will receive is 20,000 the value placed upon them is (20,000 × £1.50) £30,000. Each partner will be debited with £30,000 and the purchaser's account credited with £90,000.

Chapter 6

6.1 Profits from a joint venture will be divided in accordance with the agreement between the parties; this may or may not be equally. The answer is therefore (e).

6.2 The answer is (d).

6.3 The answer is (e).

Chapter 7

7.1 The answer is (e). A loss on consignment will be a balancing figure on the credit side of the consignment account and is debited to the profits and losses on consignments account.

7.2 the answer is (a). Goods sent by the consignor will be debited to the consignment account and credited to the goods sent on consignment account.

7.3 The stock valuation will be ((30% × (£100,000 + £8,000 + £2,000)) £33,000, so the answer is (c).

Chapter 9

9.1 Stock is carried down from the credit side of the account, being brought down onto the debit side. The answer is therefore (a).

9.2 The answer is (c). If customers retain containers and do not return them within the time allowed they will not receive a credit note; the original delivery will stand as a sale.

9.3 The answer is (d). Containers on own premises (3,000) and returnable containers with customers (5,000) = 8,000. This represents the quantity purchased by the business (10,000) less those kept by the customers (2,000) = 8,000.

Chapter 10

10.1 The answer is (d). Royalties on 19X3 production will be (12,000 × £40) £480,000 less 19X2 shortworkings recoverable in 19X3 of £40,000 = £440,000.

10.2 Shortworkings recoverable would be included under current assets, so the answer is (c).

Chapter 11

11.1 Rentals payable under an operating lease are treated as expenses. Only assets acquired under finance leases are capitalized. The answer is (d).

11.2 The HP loan account is initially credited with the HP price. Any payments made are debited to the account. The balance represents (a). Note that the balance of the HP interest suspense account is deducted to arrive at the balance of the cash price outstanding at the balance sheet date.

11.3 Actuarial or sum of the digits methods are preferred but the straight line method may be acceptable. The most appropriate answer is (c).

11.4 An asset is not owned under either a finance or an operating lease. It is recorded as an asset under a finance lease but not under an operating lease. Rentals under an operating lease are treated as an expense; rentals under a finance lease are apportioned between finance charges and repayment of fair value. The answer is (d) — rentals under a finance lease represent at least 90% of the fair value of an asset, rentals under an operating lease may be substantially less.

Chapter 12

12.1 The selling profit may be taken at the time of the sale but interest is only taken as it is earned. The answer is therefore (b). Provision should be made for any HP debtor balance if recovery is considered to be doubtful. The answer (e) is also acceptable as some businesses adopt this conservative method.

12.2 $\dfrac{10 \times 11}{2}$ = 55, so the answer is (b).

12.3 The answer is (d). The important point to note is that future earnings of interest are eliminated from debtors.

12.4 Repossessed goods are valued using the normal method of SSAP 9, the lower of cost and net realizable value. The answer is therefore (d). Net realizable value is selling price less expenses to be incurred. Repossessed goods are second-hand and would normally have a much reduced selling price.

Chapter 13

13.1 If gross profit is 20% of sales, cost will be 80% of sales and gross profit as a percentage of cost will be (20/80 × 100) 25%. The answer is (c). This can be proved: if the mark–up on cost is 25%, the gross profit as a percentage of sales will be ((25/100 + 25) × 100)) 20%.

13.2 The selling price of ((100 + 50)/100 × £1,000)) £1,500 will be reduced by (10/100 × £1,500) £150 so the answer is (d).

13.3 The gross profit earned for the period is transferred from the branch stock adjustment account to the branch profit and loss account. An entry should be made for any known reason for the full mark–up not having been earned on sales, e.g. an authorized reduction in selling price. (c) is not strictly correct because the gross profit for the next period will be on sales of the opening stock (and not all of it may be sold in the next period), and of goods sent to the branch in the next period. The answer is (e) — the provision is for the mark–up included in stocks valued at selling price. This will be earned when the goods are sold in later periods.

13.4 (a), (b), (c) and (d) will give risk to stock surpluses. The answer is (e). If the cash has not been misappropriated but has been banked, the failure to record the cash sales should be discovered on carrying out a bank reconciliation.

Chapter 14

14.1 Cash in transit to head office is carried down as an asset, a debit balance, on the branch account in the head office books, so the answer is (a).

14.2 If there is only one account for the branch in the head office books (and not separate branch capital and current accounts), the answer is (a). The other four choices are reasons why net assets will build up in a branch.

14.3 Sales and purchases accounts will record transactions with third parties only. (a) is entry for goods received from head office, the entry for returns to head office is (e).

14.4 There will not be a branch profit and loss account in the books of the head office. The answer is (d). Entry (c) will be made in the books of the branch.

Chapter 15

15.1 The market value of shares is not disclosed in the accounts. The issue price includes any share premium — only the nominal value is taken to the share capital account, as and when it is receivable, so the answer is (d). However, for companies that are not in the process of issuing shares payable by instalments (c) and (d) will be the same, i.e. the whole nominal value of each share will have been called up. Any arrears of called-up share capital not received will be shown on the balance sheet as an asset.

15.2 Redeemable preferences shares are share capital, so the answer is (a).

15.3 Debentures are a liability to be repaid at a future date, so the answer is (d),

15.4 200,000 ordinary shares of 10 pence each = £20,000 will be issued by capitalizing the capital redemption reserve of £10,000 and retained earnings of £10,000, so the answer is (a).

Chapter 16

16.1 Interest is shown gross, the income tax deducted being reclaimed from the Inland Revenue. The answer is (b). Tax credits only attach to dividends, they do not apply to interest.

16.2 The Companies Act 1985 specifies that taxation should be included in other creditors, so the answer is (b).

16.3 A dividend of 7% × 75,000 × £0.50 = £2,625 will be paid, so the answer is (a).

16.4 Corporation tax is assessed on the profits of the accounting period, in this case the year to 31 March. The dividend is paid during the year to 31 March 19X8 and is recoverable by deduction from the corporation tax liability of that year, so the answer is (e).

Chapter 17

17.1 Royalities payable on sales will be a selling and distribution cost, so the answer is (b)

17.2 Carriage inwards will be included in the cost of sales, so the answer is (a).

17.3 Interest payable is disclosed as a separate item on the face of the profit and loss account, so the answer is (c).

17.4 A difficult question. (a), (b) and (d) have to be disclosed by way of a note. Extra-ordinary items are shown on the face of the profit and loss account and a note is required explaining their nature. The answer is (e) — interest on a bank deposit will be included in the profit and loss account in 'Other interest receivable', but there is no requirement for it to be disclosed separately in a note.

17.5 It would appear that disclosure is necessary on the grounds of materiality. Bad debts may not be deducted from turnover but may be included in distribution costs. Companies who regard bad debts as being incurred due to administrative failure, rather than a selling expense, may well include them in administrative expenses. It is not a prior year adjustment as it is not a fundamental error or a change of accounting policy. It derives from the normal course of business and is not therefore extraordinary in nature. If the bad debt had not been material in size it need not be disclosed as an expectional item even though it relates to the previous year. The answer is (c).

Chapter 18

18.1 Format 1 requires net current assets (working capital) to be shown. Because this requires the deduction of current liabilities from current assets it is not possible to show total assets (fixed assets plus current assets). The answer is (a). Net assets is the final total on the balance sheet; it equals share capital and reserves.

18.2 The answer is (e). Loans receivable will be included under investments.

18.3 Reversal of window dressing has merely to be noted, so the answer is (a). The other items do not relate to conditions existing at the balance sheet date and fall to be reported in the accounts for the following year. They should, however, be noted if they are material to the proper understanding of the accounts.

18.4 Details of provisions for pensions are required, as are notes on (b) and (c). The answer is (d). Fixed assets on order will be included in the note of capital expenditure contracted but not provided.

18.5   The answer is (e). Proceeds of sale of fixed assets are not shown; instead it is their cost and accumulated depreciation that appears in the fixed asset movements' note.

Chapter 19

19.1   Dividends are specifically required to be disclosed. The shareholdings of any persons who are directors at the end of the year have to be disclosed, as at the beginning and end of the year. Loan stocks fall within the definition of 'debentures' and so a director's holdings must also be shown. Development activities are disclosed. The answer is (d) — sales are analysed geographically in a note to the accounts.

19.2   The directors will approve the report and it will then be signed by the secretary, so the answer is (e).

Chapter 20

20.1   The most appropriate choice is (a), but note that funds statements are required by SSAP 10 for all organizations with a turnover or gross income of £25,000 per annum or more.

20.2   Funds are increased during the year by gross profit less expenses incurred. Taxation paid is shown separately in a fund statement, as are purchases of fixed assets. Funds generated from operations will therefore be profit before both depreciation charge for the year and tax. The answer is (d) — profit before tax shown in a profit and loss account is after charging depreciation for the year, consequently the depreciation charge has to be added back as an item not involving the movement of funds.

20.3   When a fixed asset is sold funds are increased by the sales proceeds receivable, so the answer is (b). The original purchase of the fixed asset would have been shown as an application of funds in the year of addition. The difference between the purchase price and the eventual sale proceeds will represent the cost to the organization of using the asset during its life and would have been taken to the profit and loss account as depreciation, as would the adjustment on the sale for depreciation under- or overprovided.

20.4   Dividends paid during the year, (d), is the answer. On a share issue the proceeds, nominal value and premium together are a source of funds. Only tax paid is an application of funds — the provision is merely a book-keeping entry. Depreciation charge for the year is treated as an item not involving the movement of funds.

20.5   Working capital is the amount of capital employed in an organization that is available for use in actually running the business. It could be defined as long-term capital employed less fixed assets. The more normal definition is the answer (a). Note, however, that some commentators refer to current assets as working capital, and current assets less current liabilities as *net* working capital. For funds statement purposes, working capital is regarded as being all current asset and current liability items other than tax and dividends payable.

Chapter 21

21.1   The answer is (c).

21.2   In the absence of any preference shares the shareholders' capital employed would be the equity (d). However, the better answer is (c).

21.3   The cost of sales will be (100/150 × £150,000) £100,000. Average stocks will be (£100,000/8) £12,500. As opening stocks were £10,000, closing stocks must be £15,000, so the answer is (c).

21.4   Liquid assets are normally taken to be all current assets other than stock, so the answer is (c).

Chapter 22

22.1   (a) to (d) are examples of monetary items — in each case a fixed number of pounds is payable or receivable. Stocks are non-monetary items, so the answer is (e).

22.2 The holding gain on the stocks, being the difference between their replacement price at the time of sale (£120) and their actual purchase price (£100), is £20. The operating profit is the difference between their sales value (£160) and replacement price at point of sale (£120), £40. The answer is (b).

22.3 The historic cost depreciation for the year will be £1,000 (10/100 × £10,000). The current cost depreciation will be the amount of the current cost consumed in earning profits for the year. The current cost will be (330/250 × £10,000) £13,200, 10% of which is £1,320. The answer is (c). Alternatively the historic cost depreciation for the year may be indexed to arrive at the current cost depreciation for the year, £1,000 × 330/250 = £1,320.

22.4 In a period of inflation a loss is suffered through holding monetary assets such as debtors and cash, so the answer is (c).

Chapter 23

23.1 The answer is (c). The cost of the investment of £30,500 is off set against (80% × (£10,000 + £20,000)) £24,000, giving goodwill arising of £6,500.

23.2 The answer is (c). Share capital and reserves are (£50,000 + £20,000 + £30,000 + £10,000) £110,000; the minority interest is 25% = £27,500.

23.3 The answer is (d). Post-acquisition increases in reserves are general reserve £10,000 and profit and loss account £9,000 = £19,000. The parent's share is 75% = £14,250.

23.4 The answer is (c). The debtors are parent (£30,000 – £1,000) £29,000 + subsidiary £20,000 – £49,000. Creditors are parent £15,000 + subsidiary (£5,000 – £1,000) £4,000 = £19,000.

Chapter 24

24.1 The answer is (d). Parent's sales (£100,000 – £10,000) £90,000 and subsidiary's sales £100,000 = £190,000.

24.2 The answer is (c). The minority interest is 20% of profits after tax of £70,000 = £14,000.

23.3 The answer is (c). The profits after tax are £50,000 less the preference dividend of £2,000, leaving £48,000 available to the ordinary shareholders. Of this £14,400 (30%) belongs to the minority interest in the ordinary shares. The total minority interest in profits after tax is preference £2,000 and ordinary £14,000 = £16,400.

Chapter 25

25.1 Components are purchased for incorporation into products for resale, so the answer is (e).

25.2 The lower of cost £10,000 and net realizable value (£14,000 – £4,500) £9,500 is the answer (c). The use of replacement price is not in accordance with SSAP 9. Stocks may be valued at costs that are going to be recovered, even if the replacement price is lower.

25.3 Only manufacturing overheads may be included. Advertising is a selling expense, so the answer is (b).

25.4 The total loss on the contract is estimated to be the contract sum of £460,000 less total costs (£40,000 + £430,000) £470,000 = £10,000. This amount is written off the WIP by debiting the profit and loss account and crediting the contract account. The WIP will then be valued at £30,000, so the answer is (d). No profit or loss should then arise in the future as the costs carried forward (£30,000) plus future costs (£430,000) will be covered by the contract price of £460,000.

Chapter 26

26.1 The answer is (a) — freehold land normally does not have a finite life.

26.2 Depreciation for year 1 was £2,000. The net book value of £8,000 is to be depreciated over the remaining 3 year life = £2,667 per annum. The answer is (c).

26.3 The development costs may relate to an entirely new product, so the answer is (b). An additional condition is that future revenues are likely to exceed cost.

26.4 Properties occupied by the owner company or companies that are members of the same group are not investment properties. The answer is (e).

Accounting bases 4
Accounting policies 4, 124
Accounting ratios 144–51
Accounting Standards Committee 3
Accruals concept 4
Acquisition method 161
Actuarial method 55
ACT payable 103–4
ACT recoverable 103–4
Adjusting events 127
Administrative expenses 111
Advanced corporation tax 103–4
Agent's accounts 40
Application and allotment account 91
Associated company 116, 161
Auditor's remuneration 115

Bonus issue 98–9
Branch account 78–9
Branch opening trial balance 86
Branch profit and loss account 80
Branch records 78–9
Branch stock account 72–5
Branch stock adjustment
    account 72–5

Call account 91
Capital accounts 12
Capital expenditure 124
Capital redemption reserve 94, 98,
    123
Cash in transit 79–80, 166
Chairman's report 132
Charitable gifts 133
Company Act formats 111, 122–3
Consignee's accounts 40
Consignment accounts 37
Consignor's accounts 37–8
Consistency concept 4
Container accounts 44–5
Contingent liabilities 124, 127–8
Contract account 178–9
Conversion to limited company 26
Corporation tax 102–3
Cost 176
Cost of sales 111, 153
Cost of sales adjustment 155
Creditor payment period 148
Current accounts 12–3, 85
Current cost accounting 154–7

Current cost reserve 155
Current purchasing power 157–8
Current ratio 148

Debenture redemption 96
Debenture redemption reserve 96
Debenture redemption sinking
    fund 97
Debentures 96, 166
Debtor collection period 148
Deferral method 107
Deferred development costs 183
Deferred tax 105–106
Depreciation 124, 154–5, 182–3
Development costs 122, 183
Directors' remuneration 115
Directors' report 132–3
Directors' service contracts 133
Directors' shares and debentures 133
Directors' transactions 115
Disabled employees 133
Disclosure of accounting policies 5
Discount on issue 96, 98
Distribution costs 111
Dividend cover 150
Dividend equalization reserve 96
Dividend per share 150
Dividends 111, 137, 140, 166, 172
Drawings 12

Earnings per share 115–6, 150
Employee involvement 133
Employees 115
Equity interest 90
Equity method 117
Exceptional items 116
Exemptions from Companies
    Act 128–9
Extraordinary items 111, 116, 140

Finance charges 63–4
Fixed assets 124
Fixed return capital 148
Forfeited shares account 93
Formation expenses 98
Formats 1 and 2 111, 122–3
Franked investment income 107
Fund statements 135–7
Fundamental concepts 4–5
Future developments 133

Garner v. Murray 28
Gearing 148–9
Gearing adjustment 156–7
General reserve 99
Going concern concept 4
Goods in transit 79–80, 166
Goods on sale or return 42
Goods sent to branch account 72
Goodwill 16–7, 122, 162–3, 167
Grants 182
Gross profit % 147
Group accounts 161

HP interest suspense account 56
Head office account 78–9
Head office records 70–3
Hire of plant and machinery 115
Hire purchase contract 53
Hire purchase interest 53
Historic cost 153–4

Income tax 101–2
Indexing 157–8
Inter company sales 171
Interest payable 111
Investment in subsidiary 162
Investment properties 184
Investments 122
Irrecoverable VAT 9
Issue of shares 137

Joint ventures 32–3

Liability method 107
Liquid ratio 148
Listed investments 124
Loan interest 115
Loan stocks 96
Long term contracts 178

Mark up 147
Medium size companies 128
Merger method 167
Minority interest 115, 162, 171–2
Modified accounts 128–9
Monetary items 154
Monetary working capital
    adjustment 156–7

Negative goodwill 163, 167

Net realizable value 177
Nominal value 90
Non-adjusting events 127
Notes to the accounts 115, 124

Ordinary shares 90

Parent company 161
Partnership appropriation account
  11–2, 17
Partnership Act 1890 11
Pension commitments 124
Political contributions 133
Post acquisition reserves 164, 167
Post balance sheet events 127, 133
Pre-acquisition reserves 164, 167
Preference shares 90, 166
Preliminary expenses 98
Premium on redemption 94, 96, 98
Primary ratio 147
Prior year adjustments 116
Progress payments 178
Provision for unrealized profit 87,
  166, 172
Provisions 99
Prudence concept 4
Published accounts 110
Purchase, own debentures 96–7

Quick ratio 148

Realization account 22–3
Redeemable shares 94
Related companies 116
Related companies – income 111
Related companies investments 122

Rents 116
Repossessed goods 68
Research and development 133, 183
Reserve transfers 111
Reserves 98
Return on capital employed 147
Revaluation account 14–5
Revaluation reserve 98, 123
Revaluations 124, 154
Revenue reserves 98
Rights issue 91
Royalties payable 48
Royalties receivable 50

Sales to fixed assets ratio 148
Share capital 91
Share capital called 123
Share issue 91
Share premium account 91, 94, 123
Share redemption 94, 98
Shortworkings 48
Sinking fund 97
Small companies 128
Solvency ratios 148
SSAP1 112, 161
SSAP2 5
SSAP3 115
SSAP4 182
SSAP5 9
SSAP6 112, 116
SSAP7 157
SSAP8 107
SSAP9 180
SSAP10 135
SSAP11 (withdrawn)
SSAP12 182–3

SSAP13 183
SSAP14 161
SSAP15 105
SSAP16 153, 155–6
SSAP17 127
SSAP18 107
SSAP19 184
SSAP20 (non-examinable)
SSAP21 60
SSAP22 167
SSAP23 167
Statements of Standard Accounting
  Practice 3–5
Statutory reserves 98
Stock losses account 73–5
Stock provision 87, 166, 172
Stock valuation 177–8
Stockturn 148
Straight line method 54
Subsidiary company 161
Substantial shareholders 133
Sum of the digits method 55

Tax credit 103–4
Tax paid 137, 140
Timing differences 105–6
Transfers at cost plus 86–7
Turnover analysis 115

Valuation of premises 133
VAT 7–10

Window dressing 127
Work in progress valuation 178
Working capital 137, 148